Yearbook of International Humanitarian Law

Volume 15

For further volumes:
http://www.springer.com/series/8912

Terry D. Gill
General Editor

Yearbook of International Humanitarian Law Volume 15, 2012

ASSER PRESS
CAMBRIDGE UNIVERSITY PRESS
Springer

General Editor
Terry D. Gill
Professor of Military Law
University of Amsterdam and Netherlands Defence Academy
Amsterdam/Breda
The Netherlands

Cover Photo: © William Belcher, U.S. Air Force

ISBN 978-90-6704-923-8 ISBN 978-90-6704-924-5 (eBook)
DOI 10.1007/978-90-6704-924-5

This Volume is also available as a journal product through Cambridge University Press. In addition to the electronic version published on www.springerlink, the Yearbook is also available online through the Cambridge Journals Online service.
Published by T.M.C. ASSER PRESS, The Hague, The Netherlands www.asserpress.nl
Produced and distributed for T.M.C. ASSER PRESS by Springer-Verlag Berlin Heidelberg

Printed on acid-free paper

Springer is part of Springer Science+Business Media (www.springer.com)

Contents

Part III Other Articles

In order to make the *Correspondents' Reports* immediately and widely accessible, they are now available online at

www.asser.nl/YIHL/correspondentsreports.

This brings the added benefit of making them fully searchable, thereby more easily serving the needs of scholars and practitioners.

Part I
The Tallinn Manual on the International Law Applicable to Cyber Warfare

Chapter 1
The Tallinn Manual and International Cyber Security Law

Wolff Heintschel von Heinegg

Contents

1.1 Introduction

In 2009, the NATO Cooperative Cyber Defence Centre of Excellence (CCD COE) in Tallinn, Estonia, established an "International Group of Experts" to conduct the first comprehensive examination of the international law governing cyber warfare. The group consisted of twenty international law scholars and practitioners, including senior military officers responsible for legal advice on cyber operations. Three organizations provided observers to the process: the International Committee of the Red Cross, NATO's Allied Command Transformation, and the

The author is Charles H. Stockton Professor of International Law, U.S. Naval War College; Professor of International Law, Europa-Universität Viadrina, Frankfurt (Oder).

W. Heintschel von Heinegg (✉)
U.S. Naval War College, Newport, RI, USA
e-mail: wolff.vonheinegg.de@usnwc.edu

T. D. Gill et al. (eds.), *Yearbook of International Humanitarian Law 2012*,
Yearbook of International Humanitarian Law 15, DOI: 10.1007/978-90-6704-924-5_1,

United States Cyber Command. A team of technical experts provided advice throughout the process. The resulting product of the three-year process was the *Tallinn Manual on the International Law Applicable to Cyber Warfare*.[1]

The authority of the International Group of Experts is not to be exaggerated. All members participated in their personal capacity. Moreover, no attempt was made to ensure geographical representation. Instead, participants were selected based on their mastery of the relevant law or their sensitivity to the cyber contexts in which that law would be applied, or both. Although a number of States took the opportunity to informally provide feedback on drafts of the *Tallinn Manual*, this was always done in an unofficial, non-attributable, and non-binding manner. Other international experts served as peer reviewers of the product, providing advice on revisions and corrections. Ultimately, all members of the International Group of Experts agreed with the formulation of the so-called "Rules" set forth in the Manual. They also agreed that the accompanying Commentary fairly explained how each rule was meant to be interpreted and applied, and fully captured any differences of opinion in that regard. Ultimately, the *Tallinn Manual* should be characterized as a consensus academic work by an international group of experts who devoted three years to identifying the *lex lata* applicable to cyber warfare.

In terms of scope, the *Tallinn Manual* addresses the *jus ad bellum, jus in bello,* and, to a lesser extent, the law of neutrality. It was felt that despite the malleability of the *jus ad bellum* in the cyber context, users of the Manual would be forced to consider both bodies of law, often in tandem, in order to evaluate most cyber situations. Indeed, as the project unfolded, it became clear that to fully understand the legal context of cyber warfare, some examination of sovereignty and State responsibility was also required.

While the *Tallinn Manual* addresses those cyber operations that are most severe, it must be acknowledged that the vast majority of cyber operations directed at a State (or entities on its territory) will not rise to the level of a use of force under the *jus ad bellum* or an armed conflict under the *jus in bello*. Accordingly, the CCD COE has commissioned a follow-up three-year project to examine State responses to cyber operations falling short of the use of force and armed conflict thresholds. Combined, the two products will address the full range of international cyber security law in a coherent fashion. This is essential, for until the latter is produced there may be a tendency to inappropriately view many cyber operations through the *Tallinn Manual*'s prism. After all, when one only has a hammer, most problems look like nails.

[1] Schmitt 2013.

1.2 The Tallinn Manual and the Security Dimension of Cyberspace

As noted, the *Tallinn Manual*'s focus on public international law, and therefore inter-State relations, does not accurately reflect the realities of cyberspace. This is especially so in light of its almost exclusive analysis of the *jus ad bellum* and the *jus in bello*. Indeed, in view of the centrality of cyberspace in modern life, current challenges to cyber security that affect the private sphere, business, and civil society would appear to have been riper for examination than the rules and principles of international law regarding the use of force or armed conflict. For the average person, for instance, cybercrime is of far greater concern than the 'high politics' of international relations. Moreover, the economic benefits derived from digital information and communications infrastructure are growing at an unparalleled rate. Despite these realities, recent events such as the Stuxnet incident illustrate the importance of the security dimension that underlies the *Tallinn Manual*.

1.2.1 The Private, Economic and Social Dimension

Although unforeseen by its creators, today cyberspace (the globally-interconnected digital information and communications infrastructure) has become a "backbone of economic growth" and a "critical resource that all economic sectors rely upon."[2] There are virtually no economic activities in modern societies that are not dependent on cyberspace.[3] In some cases, the dependence is total, as with the financial and banking industries. Dependency, of course, creates vulnerability, a particular concern with respect to critical infrastructure such as that associated with the energy (electricity and water) and transport sectors. Moreover, in many States the seamless functioning of cyberspace has become a precondition to social intercourse and the exercise of democratic rights.

The rapid development of digital information and communications infrastructure can be attributed to the fact that it offers business opportunities and private

---

[2] EU 2013, p. 2. See also U.S. President 2011, p. 3: "Digital infrastructure is increasingly the backbone of prosperous economies, vigorous research communities, strong militaries, transparent governments, and free societies." Cyberspace has been defined as "the interdependent network of information technology infrastructures, [which] includes the Internet, telecommunications networks, computer systems, and embedded processors and controllers in critical industries." See National Security Presidential Directive 54/Homeland Security Directive 23 (NSPD-54/HSD-23).

[3] DoD July 2011, p. 1: "U.S. and international businesses trade goods and services in cyberspace, moving assets across the globe in seconds. In addition to facilitating trade in other sectors, cyberspace itself is a key sector of the global economy. Cyberspace has become an incubator for new forms of entrepreneurship, advances in technology, the spread of free speech, and new social networks that drive our economy and reflect our principles."

amenities that the global community has widely embraced. In view of the profits involved, the creation of "digital infrastructure's architecture was driven more by considerations of interoperability and efficiency than of security."[4] The resulting openness, interoperability and ubiquity created dangerous vulnerabilities. As the European Union has noted, "Cybersecurity incidents, be it intentional or accidental, are increasing at an alarming pace and could disrupt the supply of essential services we take for granted such as water, healthcare, electricity or mobile services."[5] In light of the vulnerabilities, cybercrime[6] is an especially grave threat.[7]

In view of both the criticality of cyberspace to economic and social well-being and the pervasive threat of cybercrime, it is unsurprising that cyber security strategies tend to concentrate on preserving fundamental freedoms, privacy, information flow, and economic viability[8] by defending (critical) cyber infrastructure against malicious and criminal activities. Their shared goals include global interoperability, network stability, reliable access, multi-stakeholder governance, and cybersecurity due diligence.[9] The means to achieve these goals include network protection, law enforcement (including cyber forensics), and Internet governance.[10]

Despite its military roots, the Internet has become a venue for private commercial and other non-governmental entities, such as internet service providers (ISP's), the Internet Corporation for Assigned Names and Numbers (ICANN), cyber security providers, and even individuals. Information and communications networks are largely owned and operated by the private sector, both nationally and internationally. This being so, the private sector plays "a leading role"[11] in the field of cyber security.

---

[4] Cyberspace Policy Review 2009, p. iii.

[5] EU 2013, p. 3. See also DoD July 2011, p. 4: "Cyber threats to U.S. national security go well beyond military targets and affect all aspects of society. Hackers and foreign governments are increasingly able to launch sophisticated intrusions into the networks and systems that control critical civilian infrastructure. Given the integrated nature of cyberspace, computer-induced failures of power grids, transportation networks, or financial systems could cause massive physical damage and economic disruption."

[6] 'Cybercrime' refers to "a broad range of different criminal activities where computers and information systems are involved either as a primary tool or as a primary target. Cybercrime comprises traditional offences (e.g. fraud, forgery, and identity theft), content-related offences (e.g. on-line distribution of child pornography or incitement to racial hatred) and offences unique to computers and information systems (e.g. attacks against information systems, denial of service and malware)." See EU 2013, p. 3.

[7] See U.S. President 2011, p. 13: "In the case of criminals and other non-state actors who would threaten our national and economic security, domestic deterrence requires all states have processes that permit them to investigate, apprehend and prosecute those who intrude or disrupt networks at home or abroad. … all key tenets of the Budapest Convention on Cybercrime." See also Cyberspace Policy Review 2009, p. 1.

[8] U.S. President 2011, p. 5.

[9] Ibid., p. 10.

[10] Ibid., p. 17 *et seq.*

[11] EU 2013, p. 2.

In this environment, the role of States has often been to foster cooperation with and among these private actors. Although States do engage in regulatory activities, both national and international, they tend to assiduously avoid interference with the economy and social cyber actors, who are often motivated by a desire to minimize governmental regulation and control.

1.2.2 The Public and Military Dimension

It would be inaccurate to conclude that States play no role in cyber security. On the one hand, States can facilitate private efforts to enhance cyber security. Moreover, States have the power and legitimacy to "safeguard access and openness, to respect and protect fundamental rights online and to maintain the reliability of the Internet."[12] On the other hand, States use, and will continue to use, cyberspace for genuinely governmental purposes, including military purposes. Thus, they have a vested interest in dealing with cyber vulnerabilities.

Conflict between States will soon be reflected in cyberspace.[13] It has become evident that "governments are seeking to exercise traditional national power through cyberspace"[14] and that a "growing array of state and non-state actors are compromising, stealing, changing, or destroying information and could cause critical disruptions."[15] Today, "both state and non-state actors possess the capability and intent to conduct cyber espionage and, potentially, cyber attacks ..., with possible severe effects."[16] The United States Cyberspace Policy Review summarized the threat as consisting of "continued exploitation of information networks and the compromise of sensitive data, especially by nations, leave the United States vulnerable to the loss of economic competitiveness and the loss of the military's technological advantages. As the Director of National Intelligence (DNI) recently testified before Congress, 'the growing connectivity between information systems, the Internet, and other infrastructures creates opportunities for attackers to disrupt telecommunications, electrical power, energy pipelines, refineries, financial networks, and other critical infrastructures.' The Intelligence Community assesses that a number of nations already have the technical capability to conduct such attacks."[17]

---

[12] Ibid.

[13] U.S. President 2011, p. 4.

[14] Ibid., p. 9.

[15] Cyberspace Policy Review 2009, p. iii.

[16] White House 2012, p. 3.

[17] Cyberspace Policy Review 2009, p. 2, referring to: Director of National Intelligence, *Annual Threat Assessment of the Intelligence Community for the Senate Armed Services Committee*, Statement for the Record, March 10, 2009, p. 39.

State-based cyber threats have generated efforts to increase the resiliency of critical cyber infrastructure. They have also led to the consideration of State-to-State responses. Perhaps most notably, President Obama has announced that the United States has "the right to use all necessary means—diplomatic, informational, military, and economic—as appropriate and consistent with applicable international law, in order to defend our Nation, our allies, our partners, and our interests."[18] Therefore, the U.S. armed forces are taking steps to ensure they "have all necessary capabilities in cyberspace to defend the United States and its interests," including the ability to respond militarily in cyberspace.[19] Self-defense against cyber operations may also be conducted through resort to conventional armed force. It must be emphasized that exercise of the right of self-defense is not limited to actual cyber attacks that cause death, injury, destruction or damage. Any State attempting "to prevent the President from exercising traditional national security options by threatening or implying the launch of a crippling cyber attack against the United States … would be taking a grave risk."[20] For the United States, the right of self-defense matures whenever there is a hostile act, or demonstration of hostile intent, of sufficient gravity. Such acts "may include significant cyber attacks directed against the U.S. economy, government or military."[21] Similarly, a "particularly serious cyber incident or attack could constitute sufficient ground for a Member State [of the European Union] to invoke the EU Solidarity Clause (Article 222 of the Treaty on the Functioning of the European Union)."[22]

There is a genuinely military dimension to cyberspace. Information and communications technology has both opened new possibilities for military actions, while presenting the armed forces with difficult challenges. It is no exaggeration to observe, "national security is being redefined by cyberspace" because contemporary military operations "depend upon cyberspace for mission success."[23]

Today, advanced armed forces use cyberspace "to enable … military, intelligence, and business operations, including the movement of personnel and material and the command and control of the full spectrum of military operations."[24] The ability "to use cyberspace for rapid communication and information sharing in support of operations is a critical enabler."[25] In response, the United States will

[18] U.S. President 2011, p. 14.

[19] DoD November 2011, p. 2. See also White House 2012, p. 4.

[20] DoD November 2011, p. 3.

[21] Ibid., p. 4.

[22] EU 2013, p. 19. Interestingly, the Draft Strategy does not refer to Article 42(7) of the Treaty on European Union, although that would have benn the provision of first choice with regard to a "particularly serious cyber attack".

[23] DoD July 2011, p. 13. See also Lynn 2010, p. 101.

[24] DoD July 2011, p. 1.

[25] Ibid., p. 2. See also White House 2012, p. 5: "Modern armed forces cannot conduct high-tempo, effective operations without reliable information and communication networks and assured access to cyberspace and space."

"invest in the capabilities critical to ... prevailing in all domains, including cyber."[26] Cyberspace has become a 'fifth domain/dimension' of warfare.[27]

The use of, and dependence on, digital information and communications infrastructure creates a degree of vulnerability that forces the military to take measures to ensure the resiliency of their cyber infrastructure.[28] For instance, the establishment of the U.S. Cyber Command (USCYBERCOM) was in part an effort to manage cyberspace risk.[29] Effective cyber defense not only requires knowledge of the offensive cyber capabilities of potential adversaries, but also the capability of deterring attack through the possession of offensive capabilities. It is therefore unsurprising that the U.S. Department of Defense asserts it possesses "the capability to conduct offensive operations in cyberspace to defend our Nation, Allies and interests."[30]

1.2.3 The Tallinn Manual's Approach

For a period of roughly ten years, there was a widely-held view that cyberspace "is not a physical place—it defies measurement in any physical dimension or time space continuum. It is a shorthand term that refers to the environment created by the confluence of cooperative networks of computers, information systems, and telecommunication infrastructures commonly referred to as the World Wide Web."[31] Some commentators concluded that cyberspace eluded the traditional rules and principles of international law and that therefore an urgent need existed for new rules specifically designed for State conduct in the 'fifth domain.'

Such conclusions often characterize new technologies. However, only in rare cases are they justified. Wide-spread agreement now exists that the "same laws and norms that apply in other areas of our day-to-day lives apply also in the cyber domain."[32] In their cyber activities, States must therefore abide by the existing rules and principles of international law. While the unique characteristics of the digital information and communications infrastructure may require certain adaptations and modifications, the "development of norms for state conduct in

[26] White House, 2012.

[27] DoD July 2011, p. 5: "...treating cyberspace as a domain is a critical organizing concept for DoD's national security missions. ... DoD must ensure that it has the necessary capabilities to operate effectively in all domains—air, land, maritime, space, and cyberspace." See also White House 2012, p. 8, stressing the determination "to ensure the United States, its allies, and partners are capable of operating in A2/AD, cyber, and other contested operating environments." 'A2/AD' stands for Anti-Access Area-Denial (A2AD) in military domains and in cyberspace.

[28] DoD July 2011, p. 6 *et seq.*

[29] Ibid., p. 5.

[30] DoD November 2011a, b, p. 5.

[31] Wingfield 2000, p. 17.

[32] EU 2013, p. 3.

cyberspace does not require a reinvention of customary international law, nor does it render existing international norms obsolete."[33] This position is in accord with the International Court of Justice's Advisory Opinion on the Legality of Nuclear Weapons,[34] which held that the *jus ad bellum* applies "to any use of force, regardless of the weapons employed"[35] and that the conduct of armed hostilities is governed by international humanitarian law as soon as there exists an (international) armed conflict.[36]

It is incontestable that the law of self-defense applies to certain cyber operations. Similarly, there is no doubt as to the full applicability of international humanitarian law to cyber operations,[37] if they either rise to the level of an armed conflict or they are taken in the course of an armed conflict and qualify as 'attacks' under that law, and if they are conducted by members of the armed forces, members of organized armed groups or civilians directly participating in hostilities. These axioms do not resolve whether particular cyber operations constitute a use of force or an armed attack. Nor do they provide the complete guidance to members of armed forces who are actively engaged in an armed conflict involving cyber operations.

At times, cyber strategies and practice will deviate from the strict boundaries of international law. For instance, it would be naïve to believe that States will refrain from conducting cyber operations merely because the issue of attributability has not been definitively resolved in a manner that would satisfy a domestic or international court. The so-called Stuxnet incident demonstrates that governments may sometimes take advantage of the opportunities presented by cyber technology even when the operation in question might qualify as a prohibited use of force. Clearly, there is a need for sober and in-depth analysis of international law in general, the *jus ad bellum* and the *jus in bello* in particular, to provide States the guidance they need when pursuing national and international security interests in or through cyberspace. The *Tallinn Manual* seeks to offer just such an analysis.

---

[33] U.S. President 2011, p. 9. See also EU 2013, p. 15: "The EU does not call for the creation of new international legal instruments for cyber issues."

[34] International Court of Justice, *Legality of the Threat or Use of Nuclear Weapons*, Advisory Opinion, I.C.J. Rep., 226 (July 8, 1996).

[35] Ibid., para 39.

[36] Ibid., paras 74 *et seq.*

[37] DoD November 2011, p. 5: If directed by the President, DoD will conduct offensive cyber operations in a manner consistent with the policy principles and legal regimes that the Department follows for kinetic capabilities, including the law of armed conflict." EU 2013, p. 16: "If armed conflicts extend to cyberspace, International Humanitarian Law and, as appropriate, Human Rights law will apply to the case at hand." See also: DoD November 2011, p. 1: "[C]yberspace operations are … governed by all applicable domestic and international legal frameworks, including the protection of civil liberties and the law of armed conflict."

1.3 The Tallinn Manual and International Cyber Security Law

The *Tallinn Manual* does not claim to be the blueprint for an international convention on the use of force in or through cyberspace. But is there a body of law that deserves to be characterized as "international cyber security law" and, if so, how does the *Tallinn Manual* contribute to it?

1.3.1 The Tallinn Manual: A "Subsidiary Means for the Determination of Rules of Law"?

In view of the composition of the International Group of Experts and of the drafting process, the *Tallinn Manual* might qualify as a "subsidiary means for the determination of rules of law" in the sense of the International Court of Justice Statute's Article 38 (1) (d). It is, after all, a publication of what the expert participants agreed to by consensus with regard to the rules and principles of international law applicable to cyberspace. However, the label should not be attached too readily.

Each of the experts was hand-selected and most had worked intensively in the area of (cyber) security law. Moreover, they hailed from "various nations." The fact that they came from predominantly Western countries (the "North") and therefore did not represent the world's various legal cultures is not necessarily an obstacle to an application of Article 38 (1) (d). As has been noted, "one must admit that, as unfortunate as it is, the main doctrinal 'production' still comes from the North and more particularly from a handful of countries where international law has gained a rather high degree of sophistication."[38]

Still, the *Tallinn Manual* is not, and does not claim to be, a "subsidiary means for the determination of rules of law." This is not because the International Court of Justice has only rarely relied upon the "teachings of publicists", nor because the Manual's value is open to question.[39] Rather, the *Tallinn Manual* does not meet the requirements of Article 38 (1) (d) because its object and purpose is not to establish the existence of (new) rules of customary international law or to contribute to the progressive development of international law. The majority of rules and principles identified and analyzed were already recognized as belonging to customary international law. Hence, there was no need for in-depth scrutiny, evaluation, and classification of State practice. The few rules that the experts did not consider to be customary in nature were so identified and they have been

---

[38] Pellet 2006, p. 792 (MN 323).

[39] In the *Lotus* Case, the Permanent Court of International Justice seems to have had doubts "as to what their value may be from the point of view of establishing the existence of a rule of customary law". The SS Lotus, PCIJ, Ser. A, No. 10, p. 26.

limited in their scope of applicability to the Parties to the respective treaties from which they derive.

The *Tallinn Manual* is instead a restatement and analysis of the *lex lata*—no more, no less. Its unique feature is the application of the *lex lata* to a relatively new technological environment. The experts have merely identified possible State conduct in and through cyberspace, interpreted the applicable rules of international law, and provided solutions based upon a methodologically sound procedure. As with any interpretive endeavor, the findings of the experts can be challenged. States may even reject them as contrary to either their national and international security interests or their understanding of the law.

In that the Manual was produced through consensus by a group of experts, its black letter rules are an appropriate tool for States to employ in shaping their conduct in and through cyberspace. Moreover, it offers States normative options because the Commentary accompanying each rule clearly identifies those issues on which the experts were divided with respect to interpretation and application. In a sense, the *Tallinn Manual* is akin to the *San Remo Manual*[40] on the law of naval warfare and of the *AMW Manual*[41] on the law of air and missile warfare. Like those works, it intentionally examined issues about which States are concerned and for which they seek solutions. For instance, the U.S. Department of Defense identified the "issue of third-party sovereignty to determine what to do when the U.S. military is attacked, or U.S. military operations and forces are at risk in some other respect, by actions taking place on or through computer or other infrastructure located in a neutral country". Similarly, it highlighted the "issue of the legality of transporting cyber 'weapons' across the Internet through the infrastructure owned and/or located in neutral third countries without obtaining the equivalent of 'overflight right'."[42] These are matters that are dealt with extensively in the *Tallinn Manual*'s section on neutrality. Similarly, uncertainty exists as to the precise applicability of international humanitarian law to military operations in cyberspace, as well as to what cyber operations qualify as a use "use of force" under the *jus ad bellum*.[43] The existence of such uncertainty highlights the value of the *Tallinn Manual*.

1.3.2 The Tallinn Manual as Part of "International Cyber Security Law"?

It is obvious that the *Tallinn Manual* deals with important international law aspects of cyber security. Whether it can be considered as forming part of international

40 Doswald-Beck 1995.

41 HPCR 2009.

42 DoD November 2011, p. 8.

43 Ibid., p. 9.

cyber security law depends upon the definition of the term "international cyber security law." Fashioning the definition necessitates a brief look at the meaning of the terms "cyber security" and "cyber security policy."

"Cyber Security" refers to "the safeguards and actions that can be used to protect the cyber domain, both in the civilian and military fields, from those threats that are associated with or that may harm its interdependent networks and information infrastructure. Cyber-security strives to preserve the availability and integrity of the networks and infrastructure and the confidentiality of the information contained therein."[44] "Cyber security policy" includes "strategy, policy, and standards regarding the security of and operations in cyberspace, and encompasses the full range of threat reduction, vulnerability reduction, deterrence, international engagement, incident response, resiliency, and recovery policies and activities, including computer network operations, information assurance, law enforcement, diplomacy, military, and intelligence missions as they relate to the security and stability of the global information and communications infrastructure."[45] Rules and principles of international law that contribute to the aims of 'cyber security policy' accordingly comprise "international cyber security law."

It would be premature to suggest that "international cyber security law" has become a distinct branch of international law. Moreover, "cyber security in general, and cyber operations in particular, fit into a wide range of paradigms, ranging from (internet) governance to warfare."[46] The assorted cyber security strategies demonstrate the impossibility of drawing clear dividing lines between the economic and social aspects of cyberspace on the one hand and the policy and military aspects on the other. The necessity of a multi-stakeholder approach and public–private-partnership vis-à-vis cyber security has blurred the traditional distinction between the public and a purely private spheres. Activities and operations in cyberspace are therefore subject to a wide range of international law rules that derive from neither the *jus ad bellum strictu* sensu nor of the *jus in bello*. For instance, State responses to cyber-attacks may have to be evaluated in the light of international telecommunications law, international trade law,[47] space law, international finance law, and international human rights law.[48] Consequently, "international cyber security law" is a collective term that encompasses rules and principles derived from multiple branches of international law.

Although the term "international cyber security law" denotes a cross-sectional area of international law, the *Tallinn Manual*'s rules belong to the panoply of norms encompassed by the label "international cyber security law."

---

44 EU 2013, p. 3, fn 4.

45 Cyberspace Policy Review 2009, p. 2.

46 Ducheine et al. 2012, p. 110 *et seq*.

47 Interference with foreign service providers may violate obligations under the GATS.

48 See also EU 2013, p. 3: "The same laws and norms that apply in other areas of our day-to-day lives apply also in the cyber domain." See also Ducheine et al. 2012, p. 111 *et seq*.

1.3.3 The Potential Impact of the Tallinn Manual on International Cyber Security Law

Like-minded States agree that the "establishment of international cyberspace norms will … serve to strengthen cyberspace for the benefit of all."[49] They are determined "to work internationally to forge consensus regarding how norms of behavior apply to cyberspace, with the understanding that an important first step in such efforts is applying the broad expectations of peaceful and just interstate conduct to cyberspace."[50] By clarifying the scope of applicability of existing norms of international law governing the use of force, both prior to and during an (international) armed conflict, the *Tallinn Manual* fosters those efforts. Thus, a first fundamental contribution to the emergence and development of international cyber security law as a distinct branch of international law has been taken. At the very least, the Manual will serve as a basis for discussion in the process of achieving international consensus on the *jus ad bellum* and *jus in bello* applicable to State conduct in and through cyberspace.

An evaluation of the *Tallinn Manual* from a more cynical perspective could, however, give rise to concerns. Cyberspace is a highly complex domain in which the traditional distinction between the public and the private spheres no longer appears tenable. The very architecture of the globally-interconnected digital information and communications infrastructure, and the fact that modern societies have become so dependent on highly vulnerable critical infrastructure (including energy, banking and finance, transportation, communication, and the Defense Industrial Base[51])—seems to auger against the sectorial (and selective) approach to cyber security that underlies the *Tallinn Manual*. In other words, with its focus on the *jus ad bellum* and the *jus in bello,* the Manual might contribute to the fragmentation of 'international cyber security law' as a new branch of law.

Of particular note is the fact that both State and non-State actors—including organized criminals, terrorists, politically-motivated hackers, and others—possess the capabilities and intent to conduct cyber operations that could severely affect a State's economy and its water, healthcare, electricity, communications, and supply services.[52] Since such threats can no longer be clearly separated from each other, the only viable and sustainable solution is a holistic and coherent legal approach devoid of the traditional borders between rules applicable to the conduct of States and non-State actors. International law is far from the relatively coherent international legal order it was until the 1970's. The rapid progressive development of international law through treaty law has generated a multitude of international legal regimes that, to a certain extent, enjoy a life of their own. International trade

---

49 DoD July 2011, p. 2.

50 U.S. President 2011, p. 9.

51 DoD July 2011, p. 1.

52 EU 2013, p. 3.

law and international environmental law are but two examples for the said diversification and expansion of international law.[53] Rules of a highly technical nature, special treaty organs, and specialized international organizations increasingly seem disconnected from general international law. In particular, specialized institutions function through, *inter alia*, new mechanisms, sometimes with disregard for other applicable rules and principles of international law. Although international cyber security law, if it develops into a distinct branch of international law, may contribute to a further fragmentation of international law, a coherent legal approach would at least prevent sub-fragmentation. The international rules and principles agreed upon to counter cybercrime could then serve as guidelines for a new branch of international law that would deserve to be characterized "international cyber security law."

The fragmentation of international law is a phenomenon that reflects the desire of States to cleanly regulate particular aspects of their international relations. This trend will continue. It is therefore highly probable that in view of the urgency felt by governments regarding cyber issues, cyber security law will soon become a distinct branch of international law. The like-minded States are already determined to "work internationally to forge consensus regarding how norms of behavior apply to cyberspace."[54] Convinced that "international cyberspace norms will enhance the stability and predictability of State conduct in cyberspace," States are pursuing "bilateral and multilateral engagements to develop further norms that increase openness, interoperability, security, and reliability."[55]

It is doubtful that the sectorial/selective approach adopted in the *Tallinn Manual* will indelibly fragment (a prospective) "international cyber security law." States see the on-going efforts to clarify the *jus ad bellum* and the *jus in bello* as merely "an important first step"[56] in the overall process of international cyber security norm creation. It is unquestionable that the *Tallinn Manual*'s findings on various matters will eventually be supplemented by additional rules that will facilitate coherent legal approach. Coherence implies that international cyber security law would form a unified whole that enables States to preserve and enhance cyber security against all identified threats. It is typical that States initially concentrate on select, usually fundamental, rules and principles that are subsequently refined and supplemented to address a given issue in its entirety.

An important caveat exists. While the *Tallinn Manual* rules may become an integral part of a future "international cyber security law," they must not be allowed to replace concepts that distinguish between the private and the public spheres. In particular, any assimilation of State conduct to criminal conduct ought

---

53 For some of the issues of the fragmentation of international law see International Law Commission, Report on the 57th session (2 May–3 June and 11 July–5 August 2005), Chapter XI, UNGA, Official Records, Sixtieth Session, Supplement No. 10 (UN Doc. A/60/10).

54 U.S. President 2011, p. 9.

55 DoD November 2011, p. 5 *et seq.*

56 U.S. President 2011, p. 9.

to be avoided. The mere facts that both employ similar methods and means which may have similar effects does not justify abandoning this long-standing distinction. For instance, it would be a grave mistake if the military was subject to the same rules as private companies, individuals or non-State actors.

The decision by States to resort to the use of armed force remains an accepted "continuation of politics by other means"[57]—it is a fact of life. It would be naïve to believe that the contemporary United Nations system of collective security has been sufficiently developed to abolish the use of force in international relations. There are situations in which even the most peace-loving government may come to the conclusion that it must use its armed forces to achieve a given political goal. Such situations are not limited to the exercise of the inherent right of self-defense or to the enforcement of UN Security Council resolutions. The use of military force may also be the last resort when it comes to terminating gross and systematic violations of human rights[58] or to suppressing substantial organized crime. Governments will continue to make use of their armed forces for legitimate—and sometimes illegitimate—purposes. If, however, governments wish to preserve the military option, the operations of their (regular) armed forces must be judged on the basis of legal rules specifically designed for the conduct of States, i.e., the *jus ad bellum* and the *jus in bello*. If governments accepted the application of a unified body of international rules on cyber security that no longer distinguishes between State conduct on the one hand and the conduct of non-State actors on the other hand, the military option would simply be unavailable.

To reiterate, a coherent legal approach to cyber security is not jeopardized by the private–public distinction. Coherency does not exclude sub-systems or sub-regimes that have a limited and separate scope of applicability. In their entirety, the rules serve the same purpose—preserving and enhancing cyber security.

1.4 Concluding Remarks

The *Tallinn Manual*'s rules and interpretations may not be shared by everyone, but they represent the consensus view of a select group of scholars and practitioners who thoroughly analyzed the *lex lata*. As such, the *Tallinn Manual* will contribute to the legal discourse by serving as a basis upon which further scholarly work can build. Moreover, States should welcome the *Tallinn Manual* as a starting point in the process of forging agreement with other States on the applicability and scope of the rules and principles of international law governing the use of force and the conduct of hostilities in and through cyberspace.

---

57 Clausewitz 1832/34.

58 For the legality or illegality of humanitarian intervention see Byers and Chesterman 2003, pp. 177–203; Franck 2003, pp. 204–231. See also the statements on the Kosovo Campaign by Henkin et al. 1999, pp. 824–862.

Of course, the *Tallinn Manual* merely covers one, although highly relevant, facet of international cyber security law. This focus is adequate because a clarification of the applicability of the *jus ad bellum* and of the *jus in bello* to operations in and through cyberspace was overdue. Hence, the present contribution is far from criticizing the underlying approach. Any criticism by this author would in any event be quite odd since he actively and directly participated in the work of the Group of Experts and in the final drafting of the Manual. Still, much more needs to be done. International cyber security law is not a self-contained, established and highly-developed legal regime. For the time-being it is but a label for a legal cross-sectional area consisting of a panoply of rules and principles derived from most diverse fields of international law whose principal applicability to cyberspace and whose concurrence have not yet been fully analyzed. The same holds true for the role of the various stakeholders and for the critical issue of balancing democratic and economic freedoms on the one hand and security interests on the other hand.

References

Byers M, Chesterman S (2003) Changing the Rules about Rules? Unilateral Humanitarian Intervention and the Future of International Law. In: Holzgrefe J, Keohane R (eds.) (2003) Humanitarian Intervention, Cambridge University Press, Cambridge, pp 177–203.

Clausewitz C (1832/34) Vom Kriege, Book I, Section 24.

Cyberspace Policy Review (2009) Cyberspace Policy Review: Assuring a Trusted and Resilient Information and Communications Infrastructure http://www.whitehouse.gov/assets/documents/Cyberspace_Policy_Review_final.pdf. Accessed 22 May 2013.

DoD (Department of Defense U.S) (July 2011)Strategy for Operating in Cyberspace http://www.defense.gov/news/d20110714cyber.pdf. Accessed 22 May 2013.

DoD (Department of Defense U.S) (November 2011) Cyberspace Policy Report - A Report to Congress Pursuant to the National Defense Authorization Act for Fiscal Year 2011, Section 934 http://www.defense.gov/home/features/2011/0411_cyberstrategy/docs/NDAA%20Section%20934%20Report_For%20webpage.pdf. Accessed 22 May 2013.

Doswald-Beck L (ed.) (1995) San Remo Manual on International Law Applicable to Armed Conflicts at Sea. Cambridge University Press, Cambridge.

Ducheine P, Voetelink J, Stinissen J, Gill T (2012) Towards a Legal Framework for Military Cyber Operations. In: Ducheine P, Osinga F, Soeters J (ed) (2012) Cyber Warfare: Critical Perspectives. T.M.C. Asser Press, The Hague, pp 101–128.

EU (2013) Draft Cybersecurity Strategy of the European Union: An Open, Safe and Secure Cyberspace. Brussels.

Franck T (2003) Interpretation and Change in the Law of Humanitarian Intervention. In: Holzgrefe J, Keohane R (eds.) (2003) Humanitarian Intervention. Cambridge University Press, Cambridge pp 204–231.

HPCR (Harvard Program on Humanitarian Policy and Conflict Research) (2009) Manual on International Law Applicable to Air and Missile Warfare. Bern.

Henkin L, Wedgwood R, Charney J, Chinkin C, Falk R, Franck T, Reisman W (1999) 93 AJIL, pp 824–862.

Lynn W (2010) Defending an New Domain. 89 Foreign Affairs, pp 97–108.

Pellet A (2006) Article 38. In: Zimmermann A, Tomuschat C, Öllers-Frahm K (ed) The Statute of the International Court of Justice—A Commentary, Oxford University Press, pp 677–792

http://www.alainpellet.eu/Documents/PELLET%20%202006%20%20Article%2038%20of%20the%20Statute%20of%20the%20ICJ.pdf. Accessed 22 May 2013.
Schmitt M (2013) Tallinn Manual on the International Law Applicable to Cyber Warfare. Cambridge University Press, New York.
U.S. President (2011) International Strategy for Cyberspace. Washington, D.C.
White House (2012) Sustaining U.S. Global Leadership: Priorities for 21st Century Defense. http://www.defense.gov/news/defense_strategic_guidance.pdf. Accessed 22 May 2013.
Wingfield T (2000) The Law of Information Conflict: National Security Law in Cyberspace. Aegis Research Corp, Falls Church.

Chapter 2
The Tallinn Manual on the International Law Applicable to Cyber Warfare: A Commentary on Chapter II—The Use of Force

Nicholas Tsagourias

Contents

2.1 Introduction

Cyberspace and cyber technology are increasingly used by states and individuals for peaceful purposes, but they are also employed maliciously. Cyber attacks—that is, the use of cyber technology to attack a state's infrastructure—are perhaps one of the most serious threats currently facing states. Although not all cyber attacks are warlike, some of them may indeed be so, which immediately gives rise to the

The author is Professor of International Law, University of Sheffield.

N. Tsagourias (✉)
University of Sheffield, Sheffield, UK
e-mail: n.tsagourias@sheffield.ac.uk

T. D. Gill et al. (eds.), *Yearbook of International Humanitarian Law 2012*,
Yearbook of International Humanitarian Law 15, DOI: 10.1007/978-90-6704-924-5_2,

question of whether the current legal regulation of the use of force (*jus ad bellum*) applies to such attacks. *The 'Tallinn Manual' on the International Law Applicable to Cyber Warfare* responds to this question by mapping out the *jus ad bellum* and *jus in bello* rules that apply in such circumstances. The statement of the Rules is accompanied by a Commentary which clarifies the content of those rules, and explains their application in the specific context of cyber war.

In the following, I will present and critically comment on the *jus ad bellum* rules found in Chapter II of the *Tallinn Manual:* that is, Rules 10–19. The aim of this commentary is to draw attention to certain important but contested issues, identify jurisprudential ambiguities, and where possible offer alternative views.

2.2 The Rules

2.2.1 Rule 10: Prohibition of Threat or Use of Force

According to Rule 10, 'A cyber operation that constitutes a threat or use of force against the territorial integrity or political independence of any state, or that is in any other manner inconsistent with the purposes of the United Nations, is unlawful.'

This rule is a reflection of Article 2(4) of the UN Charter, but also of customary international law.[1] Although the application of this rule to cyber war is in principle undisputed, its scope is subject to debate. According to the Manual, the prohibition of the threat or use of force binds members of the United Nations (UN) and, as a customary rule it also applies to states that are not members of the United Nations but does not apply to non-state actors unless their acts are attributable to a state, pursuant to the law of state responsibility.[2] In this respect, the Manual adopts a state-oriented approach as far as the prohibition of the threat or use of force is concerned but, as will be seen later, it accepts that a non-state actor can be the author of an armed attack and, consequently, the target of self-defence action. If an armed attack by a non-state actor is in fact a use of force, albeit a grave one, a non-state actor can also be the author of a less grave use force. Indeed, as the Report of the Secretary-General's High-level Panel on Threats, Challenges and Change acknowledged, non-state actors are able and willing to use force against states.[3] One could thus say that the prohibition of the threat or use of force should apply to

---

[1] For the application of Article 2(4) to cyber attacks see Waxman 2011, p. 421; Roscini 2010, pp. 102–109; Barkham 2001, pp. 57, 69–73, 79–80.

[2] Rule 10, para 5. See also Simma et al. 2012, pp. 213–4. For attribution see Rule 6 and accompanying text.

[3] As it was stated there: 'Al-Qaida is the first instance—not likely to be the last—of an armed non-state network with global reach and sophisticated capacity. Attacks against more than 10 Member States on four continents … have demonstrated that Al-Qaida and associated entities pose a universal threat to the membership of the United Nations and the United Nations itself.'

non-state actors even if their act is not attributed to a state because, otherwise, a legal lacuna will appear in that such uses of force will not be caught by the prohibition. This may challenge the whole legal edifice established by the UN Charter because, as the International Court of Justice (ICJ) put it, '[t]he prohibition against the use of force is a cornerstone of the United Nations Charter'.[4]

It is true that the ICJ has included indirect uses of force within the meaning of Article 2(4)[5] and the attribution criteria may be interpreted more extensively in order to cover the activities of non-state actors, but, still, there may be situations where non-state actors act independently of states.

It is for this reason that in the opinion of the present commentator, non-state actors or at least those showing some form of organisation should be viewed as direct addressees of the customary rule prohibiting the threat or use of force. To explain: the rule will apply to non-state actors because their act–the threat or use of force–affects a fundamental state right encapsulated in Article 2(4) of the UN Charter and in customary law namely, the right of a state to be free from the threat or use of force.[6]

A related question not dealt with in the Manual is whether international organisations are bound by the rule prohibiting the threat or use of force. International Organisations, as subjects of international law, are bound by customary law[7] and, consequently, they are bound by the customary version of this rule. When it comes to NATO, whether it is bound by the rule depends on whether it has legal personality, which is perhaps the case if the ICJ's criteria in the *Reparations for Injuries* Advisory Opinion are taken into account.[8] Yet, even if it does not have legal personality, it will be bound by the rule as addressee of the law according to what was said above or because its members are bound by the rule.

According to the Manual, the phrase 'or in any manner inconsistent with the purposes of the United Nations' catches all threats or uses of cyber force—even those that are not against the territorial integrity or political independence of a state.[9] To the extent that the UN has many purposes—from peace and security to human rights and self-determination—and to the extent that different purposes may clash with each other, whether the prohibition contained in this rule is 'all-inclusive' can be debated. The Manual recognises this, but does not take a position as to whether other uses of force (for example, for humanitarian purposes) can be lawful, thus affecting the authority of this statement.

(Footnote 3 continued)
A More Secure World: Our Shared Responsibility, Report of the Secretary-General's High-level Panel on Threats, Challenges and Change, UN Doc. A/59/565 (2004), para 146.

4 *Congo v. Uganda*, para 148.

5 *Nicaragua*, para 228.

6 Tsagourias 2011, pp. 327–328; Wedgwood 1999, p. 26.

7 *WHO/Egypt*, para 37.

8 *Reparations for Injuries*, pp. 178–9.

9 Rule 10, para 2.

2.2.2 Rule 11: Definition of Use of Force

According to this rule, 'A cyber operation constitutes a use of force when its scale and effects are comparable to non-cyber operations rising to the level of a use of force.'

How 'force' is defined is of critical importance, but it is one of the perennial questions that affect the scope of the rule prohibiting the threat or use of force. The Manual rejects an instrument-based approach to force and adopts an effects-based one.[10] This reflects the widely held opinion, which decouples force from the instrument that produces it.[11] Prohibited force is thus any force, including cyber force, that produces harmful effects in the form of human death or injury and/or physical damage, and which are equivalent to those produced by military force.[12]

The immediate question is whether cyber operations against critical state infrastructure that do not cause physical harm but which severely disrupt the functioning of the state can be equated to a use of force within the meaning of Article 2(4). The Manual gives the impression that such cyber operations fall outside Article 2(4) by excluding economic or political coercion from the definition of force.[13] It relies for this on the *travaux préparatoires* and on the General Assembly's Friendly Relations Declaration. However, the possibility of qualifying cyber operations that seriously affect critical state infrastructure as uses of force should not be dismissed easily. For example, the manipulation of a state's economic data may have serious repercussions on the state's economic and political well being, which may not translate into immediate death or destruction, but may nevertheless be serious in view of the reliance of modern states on information technology. This can have the same effect as the one which can be produced by the physical destruction of a state's economic institutions. Why should the physical destruction of a state's main economic institutions be a use of force and not their functional paralysis?

On closer scrutiny, the Manual is not as categorical as it appears. For example, when it discusses the proposed factors that states may take into account in order to qualify a cyber force as unlawful use of force, it says, with regard to severity (which is presented as the most important factor) that the more the consequences impinge on critical national interests, the more they will contribute to the depiction of a cyber operation as a use of force and, in such a case, the scope, duration and intensity of consequences are of critical importance.[14] Indeed, the criterion of severity measures the various consequences of the attack, including its physical consequences, but not

---

[10] Rule 11, paras 1 and 8.

[11] *Nuclear Weapons*, para 39.

[12] Rule 11, paras 1–8. According to Simma's commentary of the UN Charter, physical force of a non-military nature can be covered by Article 2(4) or Article 51 only within narrow limits. Simma et al. 2012, p. 210.

[13] Ibid., para 2.

[14] Ibid., para 9.

only them. Thus, in the example given above, an attack on a state's financial institutions that causes serious disruption would warrant any such attack being qualified as a use of force irrespective of whether it produced physical damage.[15]

Be that as it may, the Manual introduces a *de minimis* threshold of 'scale and effects' in order to distinguish acts that qualify as use of force for Article 2(4) purposes from those that do not qualify as such.[16] It relies for this on the ICJ's judgment in the *Nicaragua Case*.[17] According to the Manual, the gravest uses of force would constitute an armed attack triggering the right of self-defence, whereas lesser uses of force would constitute violations of Article 2(4).[18] However, with no further explanation or criteria for measuring the gravity of a particular use of force, the margin of appreciation is rather broad.

The Manual recognises this problem and mentions a number of factors that states may take into account in order to determine whether a cyber attack qualifies as use of force. These factors are the following: severity; immediacy, directness, invasiveness, measurability of effects, military character of the operation, state involvement, and presumptive legality.[19] These factors, with some adaptations, have been promulgated by Professor Schmitt in past publications on the matter, yet no proof has been offered as to whether states actually do take them into account when determining the existence of a use of force.[20] That notwithstanding, and as is stated in the Manual, these factors are neither exhaustive nor legal.[21] Whether they provide any guidance is also conjectural. This becomes apparent if the aforementioned factors are applied to the 'Stuxnet worm' attack on Iran's nuclear reactor. Regarding the criterion of 'severity', it has been reported that the attack damaged or destroyed approximately 1,000 centrifuges; but whether this is severe depends on what is the *de minimis* threshold. It has also been reported that the attack set back the Iranian nuclear programme by several years, but this is not equivalent to physical destruction which is what is apparently required by the Manual for the designation of an operation as a use of force; neither did it have a debilitating effect on Iran's nuclear programme, which continues, although it did constitute a serious disruption.[22]

---

[15] The US shares the view that 'high level disruption' qualifies as a use of force; see Gorman and Barnes 2011: 'One idea gaining momentum at the Pentagon is the notion of "equivalence." If a cyber attack produces the death, damage, destruction or high-level disruption that a traditional military attack would cause, then it would be a candidate for a "use of force" consideration, which could merit retaliation.'

[16] Rule 11, paras 1, 6–7.

[17] *Nicaragua*, paras 191, 195; see also *Oil Platforms*, paras 51, 64.

[18] Rule 11, para 6.

[19] Ibid., para 9.

[20] Schmitt 1999, p. 914; Schmitt 2011, pp. 776–578; Ziolkowski 2012.

[21] Rule 11, para 7.

[22] Kirkup et al. (26 February, 2013) Iran's 'Plan B' for a nuclear bomb. The Telegraph, https://www.telegraph.co.uk/news/worldnews/middleeast/iran/9896389/Irans-Plan-B-for-a-nuclear-bomb.html. Accessed 28 February 2013.

With regard to the criterion of 'immediacy' (according to which states will qualify a cyber operation as use of force if it is likely to produce immediate results) there was a hiatus between the insertion of the vulnerability, the uploading of the payload and the damage caused.[23] Regarding 'directness', which is about the direct causal relationship between the act and the harmful effects, the destruction of the centrifuges was the direct effect of Stuxnet, but the operation included many stages, with the insertion of the vulnerability being the initial act. If the harmful effect is however the delay in Iran's nuclear programme, Stuxnet may be a factor, but that delay is perhaps more due to sanctions.[24] It should be noted at this juncture that the criterion of immediacy and directness complicate any assessment because the most serious consequences of a cyber operation may be indirect and non-immediate. Moreover, the indirect and non-immediate consequences may have been the primary aim of the operation. For example, whereas the immediate and direct effect of a cyber operation may be the destruction or corruption of a particular system, the long term and indirect effects of that operation may be extremely grave because of all the other systems that are linked to the affected system.

'Invasiveness' is about the degree of intrusion into the target state and its cyber systems. In this regard, there is no doubt that the Stuxnet attack satisfied this criterion. 'Measurability of effects' is about the ability to measure the destructive effects of the operation. This is the case as far as the destruction of the Iranian centrifuges is concerned, but it is difficult to measure the overall harm inflicted on Iran's nuclear programme. Moreover, if the consequences are mostly indirect, this criterion is difficult to be satisfied. 'State involvement' is another beclouded criterion because of the difficulties in attributing cyber activities to states, due to the fact that cyber attacks can be anonymous, multi-staged or be 'spoofing' cyber attacks.[25] As far as the Stuxnet attack is concerned, no state or other entity assumed responsibility, although suspicion fell on certain states. Finally, regarding the criterion of 'presumptive legality', it is true that it is difficult to legally justify the destruction of the centrifuges but Iran, for its own reasons, did not claim that it violated Article 2(4).[26]

However, it should be noted that it is not always easy to distinguish between lawful and unlawful cyber operations. For example, the insertion of vulnerability may be an unlawful intervention but it may also be an act of espionage, which is not prohibited by international law.[27] In view of the above, it cannot be said with

[23] Foltz 2012, p. 44.

[24] For example, see SC Res 1929 (2010).

[25] Clark and Landau 2010, p. 25. Boebert 2010, p. 41; Knake (July 15, 2010) Untangling Attribution: Moving to Accountability in Cyberspace, Council on Foreign Relations; Tsagourias 2012, pp. 229–245. 'Spoofing' is when the attacker falsifies his/her identity.

[26] Hollis (January 25, 2011) Could Deploying Stuxnet Be a War Crime? OpinioJuris.org. http://opiniojuris.org/2011/01/25/could-deploying-stuxnet-be-a-war-crime/. Accessed 26 February 2013. Brown Brown 2011, pp. 70–73.

[27] Lin 2010, pp. 78–79.

certainty that the Stuxnet incident constituted a use of force according to these criteria.

Applying now these factors to the 2007 Distributed Denial of Service (DDoS) attacks on Estonia, it may be doubted that they amount to a use of force. Their severity (in view of the duration and scope of the attack) was limited, and their harmful effect was limited and containable; the invasiveness of the attack was superficial and whereas there were some direct consequences, other consequences—economic or financial—were rather remote. Moreover, state involvement was never proven. That having been said, the view that the attacks on Estonia constituted a use of force has also been offered.[28]

The inclusion of these factors in the Manual introduces a policy dimension to assessments of what constitutes a use of force for Article 2(4) purposes[29] but they do not offer any more clarity or certainty. Neither does the inclusion of a *de minimis* threshold. As a result, in most cases, assessments are bound to be contested.

This does not mean that acts which do not fall within the meaning of Article 2(4) will be legal; they may amount to an unlawful intervention, as the Manual correctly recognises.[30] Intervention is a very broad concept[31] and prohibited intervention is any dictatorial interference in a state's affairs.[32] What defines intervention, therefore, and distinguishes it from mere interference, is the element of coercion,[33] in that the intervention makes a state do something that it would not otherwise do. As the ICJ put it, non-intervention is protecting the 'political integrity' of states.[34] Thus, even if the attacks on Estonia were not a use of force for Article 2(4) purposes, they could amount to unlawful intervention because their aim was to change the Estonian government's decision to relocate a Soviet era statue, provided however that they were attributed to a state. This means that, in order for a certain cyber operation to qualify as an unlawful intervention, state attribution is needed and this is very difficult to establish in cyberspace for the reasons mentioned above. That said, there are still questions that remain unanswered. One question is whether actions by non-state actors that cannot be attributed to a state could amount to unlawful intervention whereas the other question is whether forcible actions by non-state actors which fall bellow the *de minimis* threshold of Article 2(4) amount to unlawful intervention.[35]

[28] Schmitt 2011, pp. 569, 577.

[29] Schmitt 2012.

[30] Rule 10, paras 6–10 and Rule 1, para 7. See also Buchan 2012, p. 212.

[31] Bull, 1984. Declaration on Principles of International Law Concerning Friendly Relations and Cooperation Among States in Accordance with the Charter of the United Nations (1970) G.A Res. 2625 (XXV); *Nicaragua*, para 246.

[32] Jennings and Watts 2008, p. 428.

[33] *Nicaragua*, para 205.

[34] Ibid, para 202.

[35] *Congo v. Uganda*, para 160.

Because the rule on non-intervention relates to the use of force and gives rise to many intricate questions particularly when applied to cyberspace, the Manual should perhaps have included a separate rule and commentary on 'non-intervention'.

The Manual deals with the question of how a state should respond to uses of force falling within Article 2(4).[36] According to the Manual, the victim state can resort to non-forcible countermeasures (including cyber ones) or invoke the plea of necessity.[37]

Countermeasures are necessary and proportional reactions to illegal acts and their aim is to induce compliance with international law.[38] Although the Manual speaks of non-forcible countermeasures, the view was also expressed that when a state suffers a use of force it can resort to forcible countermeasures.[39] Opinions concerning the lawfulness or permissibility of forcible countermeasures differ. According to some legal commentators, forcible countermeasures are illegal[40] but others take a more nuanced approach. In his 1972 study, and after a thorough analysis of state practice, Bowett opined that forcible reprisals are illegal *de jure* but accepted *de facto*.[41] It has also been claimed that such forcible countermeasures are forms of self-defence against an initial armed attack which are below the maximal use of force permitted by self-defence.[42] As far as international jurisprudence is concerned, although the ICJ in the *Nicaragua Case* opined that a state that suffers a use of force below the threshold of an armed attack can take proportional countermeasures, it did not specify whether they can involve the use of force.[43] It was only with regard to third states that the Court said that they cannot take countermeasures involving the use of force. In the *Oil Platforms Case*, Judge Simma in his Separate Opinion was sympathetic to the view that a state may resort to 'proportional countermeasures' of a military nature in order to respond to a use of force below the threshold of an armed attack.[44]

From the preceding discussion, it transpires that there is some degree of uncertainty as to the legal status of forcible countermeasures. It should be noted, however, that the availability of forcible or non-forcible countermeasures needs to

---

36 Rule 10, para 6 and Rule 11, para 8.

37 Rule 11, para 11 and Rule 9.

38 Rule 9, paras 2, 3. Draft Articles on Responsibility of States for Internationally Wrongful Acts, *in* Report of the Int'l Law Comm'n, 53d Sess., Apr. 23-June 1, July 2-Aug. 10, 2001, UN DOC. A/56/10; GAOR, 56th Sess., Supp. No. 10 (2001), 324, arts. 49–54 (hereinafter ASR). Also *Gabčíkovo-Nagymaros* Project (*Hungary/Slovakia*), pp. 55–56; *Nicaragua* para 249.

39 Rule 9, para 5.

40 Gray 2008, pp. 195–198; Roscini 2010, pp. 113–114.

41 Bowett 1972, p. 1.

42 Dinstein 2010, paras 661–674.

43 *Nicaragua*, paras 210, 249. See Diss. Op. Judge Schwebel, ibid, para 175. *Ethiopia/Eritrea Award*, paras 11–12.

44 Diss. Op. Judge Simma in *Case Concerning Oil Platforms*, paras 13–15. Judge Kooijmans is rather noncommittal. Diss. Op. Judge Kooijmans, ibid., paras 52 and 62. See also J. Hargrove 1987, pp. 135, 141; Gazzini 2006, p. 138.

be considered in relation to what was said above about the application of the rule prohibiting the use of force to non-state actors. If the rule applies to non-state actors as advocated here, a state that has suffered a use of force by a non-state actor which is not attributed to another state can take non-forcible and, perhaps, even forcible countermeasures against the non-state actor which violated the referent obligation. Otherwise, states will have no protection.

In addition to countermeasures, a state may also invoke the plea of necessity[45] and take measures—including cyber ones—to protect itself against unlawful uses of force, provided that the measures are the only means available to safeguard its affected interests.[46] Yet the question is whether necessity can justify forcible measures. As the Manual says, this is highly uncertain.[47] However, there have been instances where necessity has been invoked in order to justify the use of force in order to avert a humanitarian catastrophe, for example.[48] Moreover, Article 25 ARSIWA (Articles on the Responsibility of States for Internationally Wrongful Acts) does not say that such measures should not involve the use of force, but that the plea of necessity is not intended to cover conduct that is regulated by primary rules such as the rules on the use of force.[49] This is correct because necessity falls under the secondary rules on state responsibility. The question then is not whether the use of force is lawful or unlawful according to the primary rules on the use of force but whether, at a secondary level, responsibility for an unlawful use of force can be excused by necessity. It is submitted that if the conditions laid down in Article 25 ASRIWA or in customary law are satisfied, necessity can excuse uses of force that are outside the use-of-force regime.[50] In this case what may cause some difficulties is the balancing criterion included in Article 25 according to which the wrongful act should not 'seriously impair an essential interest of the State or States towards which the obligation exists, or of the international community as a whole'. That said, it should be pointed out that it is not settled whether the balancing test represents customary international law[51] and, additionally, that in this case we are faced with two equivalent interests: the sovereignty of the victim state and the sovereignty of the target state. To the extent that the rule prohibiting the use of force is not *jus cogens*, balancing these interests is a difficult exercise and as was said 'in the event of incommensurable social values or interests, one state's *safeguarded* essential interest will often be another's *seriously impaired* essential interest'.[52]

---

45 Rule 11, para 11 and Rule 9. Also see Article 25 ASR.

46 Rule 9, paras 10–12.

47 Ibid., para 10.

48 UN Doc. S/PV.3988 (24 March 1999) [as per UK Representative]; *Legality of Use of Force*; Dutch Advisory Council on International Affairs and the Advisory Committee on Issues of Public International Law Dutch Advisory Council on International Affairs and the Advisory Committee on Issues of Public International Law 2008, pp. 307–308.

49 Article 25 ASR, para 21, p. 185.

50 Tsagourias 2010, pp. 39–42.

51 Sloan 2012, p. 447.

52 Ibid, p. 488.

The Manual also deals with the issue of the indirect use of cyber force.[53] For this it relies once more on the ICJ's *Nicaragua* judgment, which in its turn relied on the Friendly Relations Declaration.[54] For the Court, arming and training a guerrilla force would amount to a use of force, but supplying funds would not.[55] There is a further ambiguity in the Manual, which to some extent is not of its own making. More specifically, the question is whether training or arming groups constitute prohibited uses of force in themselves, or only when those assisted go on to use force. In the *Nicaragua Case* the Court oscillates between the two interpretations, whereas the Friendly Relations Declaration ascribes to the latter view. According to the Manual 'providing an organised group with malware and the training necessary to use it to carry out cyber attacks against another State'[56] would qualify as a use of force whereas in the paragraph that immediately follows it says that providing sanctuary coupled with other acts such as providing substantial support or cyber defences could in certain circumstances be a use of force.[57] In the view of the present commentator, there will be an indirect use of force only when the assisted group goes on to use force.

2.2.3 Rule 12: Definition of Threat of Force

According to Rule 12, 'A cyber operation, or threatened cyber operation, constitutes an unlawful threat of force when the threatened action, if carried out, would be an unlawful use of force.'

This rule reflects the ICJ's definition of unlawful threat of force as laid down in its *Nuclear Weapons* Advisory Opinion.[58] Accordingly, all threats of force other than the threat to use force by way of self-defence or in accordance with Chapter VII of the UN Charter are unlawful.[59] However this definition is not free from difficulties. In the first place, there is uncertainty as to the legal status of certain uses of force, for example, the use of force for humanitarian purposes. Second, even with regard to permitted uses of forces, there are still questions about the scope of self-defence and to what extent it applies to an imminent threat of an attack, an issue that will be discussed later. Third, it is difficult to assess the lawfulness of a threat to use cyber force by way of self-defence if the proportionality and necessity of the projected self-defence action cannot be assessed at the time of the threat.[60] For example, threatening a state with annihilation in the

[53] Rule 11, paras 4–5.

[54] *Nicaragua*, para 228 with reference to Friendly Relations Declaration, paras 8 and 9.

[55] Ibid, para 228; *Congo v. Uganda*, paras 164–165.

[56] Rule 11, para 4.

[57] Ibid., para 5.

[58] *Nuclear Weapons*, para 47.

[59] Rule 12, para 3.

[60] *Nuclear Weapons*, para 2C of the dispositive and para 48.

exercise of the right to self-defence will apparently breach the principle of proportionality, but the Court in the *Nuclear Weapons* Advisory Opinion was not able to 'conclude definitely' whether this is also the case when the very survival of the state is at issue.[61]

For an unlawful threat to exist, there is no requirement that a specific demand accompany the threat,[62] although coercion is the essence of the prohibited threat.[63] It is true that a threat of force—irrespective of whether it is accompanied by a specific demand—brings pressure to bear on the target state, and restricts its freedom of action. It is also true to say that the threat can be implicitly or explicitly communicative in nature.[64] A threat can be communicated through words, conduct or behaviour. Whether this is so depends on many factors, and it is contextual. The Manual gives an example of a state which aggressively develops its cyber capabilities in a climate of tension with another state. This will not be an unlawful threat of force according to the Manual but what will be an unlawful threat of force is the announcement that the acquired cyber capabilities will be used to that end.[65] In the view of the present commentator, the answer cannot be so categorical because it all depends on the context within which the particular conduct takes place which will include a number of historical, political, military, as well as a variety of other factors. If such factors are taken into account, there may be good reasons to infer that the acquisition or development of cyber capabilities constitutes a threat of force. For example, had the Stuxnet virus been detected earlier, whether its insertion into Iran's nuclear operation programme could constitute a threat of force would depend on the context within which that cyber operation took place, and the context was that of declarations or statements by certain states that force might be used against Iran. That shows that determinations as to whether there is a threat of force are subjective and, more than that, they are based on information and evidence which is not always conclusive or easy to verify. As a result, the content of the prohibition cannot be fixed, instead its very existence may increase the propensity of states to use force to counter threats of cyber force or threats of cyber attacks, particularly if anticipatory self-defence is permitted.

2.2.4 Rule 13: Self-Defence Against Armed Attack

According to Rule 13, 'A State that is subject to a cyber operation that rises to the level of an armed attack may exercise its inherent right of self-defence. Whether a cyber operation constitutes an armed attack depends on its scale and effects.'

---

61 Ibid, para 2E of the dispositive and paras 96–97.

62 *Contra* Brownlie 1963, p. 364; Sadurska 1988, p. 242.

63 Rule 12, para 4.

64 Ibid.

65 Ibid.

The Manual follows the ICJ's categorisation of uses of force into grave and less grave ones,[66] with self-defence being permitted only in response to a cyber operation that is equivalent to an armed attack. A cyber use of force is an 'armed attack' if its scale and effects are grave.[67] However, as the Manual notes, the ICJ did not provide any explanation as to how the gravity of the attack can be measured[68] neither does the Manual provide any further clarification. As a result, any determination is bound to be contested. For example, some members of the International Group of Experts viewed the Stuxnet attack on Iran's nuclear programme as an armed attack[69] whereas, by implication, others did not view it as an armed attack and, more importantly, Iran did not claim that it was even a use of force. The determination of what constitutes a cyber attack for self-defence purposes becomes even more complicated by the fact that the Manual introduces a *de minimis* threshold even for Article 2(4) uses of cyber force. If no criteria exist to distinguish between grave and less grave uses of force, and if all reasonably foreseeable consequences[70] need to be taken into consideration when determining the effects of the attack, the risk is that any cyber force of some significance may very well be labelled an armed attack and be met with defensive force in view also of the fact that, according to the Manual, a state cannot use force in response to a use of force which is below the threshold of an armed attack. The question is whether such disparity can be remedied by aligning the use of force in Article 2(4) with the 'armed attack' in Article 51. This is the US position[71] but there is still doctrinal resistance to such alignment and support for a differentiated approach.[72]

Yet, the boundaries between Article 2(4) and Article 51 are blurred by the adoption of the 'accumulation of events' theory. According to the Manual, a series of cyber incidents that individually are below the threshold of an armed attack but are perpetuated by the same author and are showing a certain pattern can cumulatively qualify as an armed attack and trigger the right of self-defence.[73] The question is whether this has been stated *de lex lata* or *de lege ferenda*. In the *Oil Platforms Case* the ICJ took into account a series of attacks in order to establish

---

[66] *Nicaragua Case*, paras 191, 193–195, 211, 237; *Oil Platforms*, para 51. See also Rule 10, para 6 and Rule 11, para 8.

[67] Rule 13, paras 3–6. See also Dinstein 2002, p. 100.

[68] *Nicaragua Case*, para 195; Rule 13, para 7.

[69] Rule 13, para 13.

[70] Ibid., para 10.

[71] Rule 11, para 7. International Law in Cyberspace, Remarks, Harold Hongju Koh, Legal Advisor of the Department of State, International Law in Cyberspace, USCYBERCOM Inter-Agency Legal Conference (Sept. 18, 2012), available at http://www.state.gov/s/l/releases/remarks/197924.htm. Accessed 27 May 2013. See also Greenwood Greenwood 2012, para 12.

[72] Simma et al. 2012, pp. 1401–1403. It has been commented that the main reason for rejecting such alignment is the need to avoid escalation of the conflict which is a policy consideration. Yet, one needs to take into account the danger of escalation from the part of the author of the use of force if no tangible response is available.

[73] Rule 13, para 8.

whether there was an armed attack,[74] and it did the same in the *Congo v. Uganda Case*[75]; but it did not pronounce on this issue because it rejected the existence of an armed attack for other reasons. Legal commentators have been more sympathetic to the view that the sum of low intensity attacks may constitute an armed attack for self-defence purposes[76] yet judges and other legal commentators have rejected the 'accumulation of events' theory.[77] If the view that a state cannot use force in response to a use of force that is below the threshold of an armed attack is formally the correct one, then the accumulation of events theory compensates for the differentiated treatment of uses of force in international law.

A number of other issues concerning self-defence are left unsettled in the Manual. One such issue is whether an attack that does not produce physical consequences, or an attack on critical state infrastructure can be qualified as an armed attack for self-defence purposes. The International Group of Experts was divided as to whether such attacks would constitute armed attacks,[78] but, as was said previously in the context of the use of force, it will not be unreasonable to treat a debilitating or hugely disruptive attack on critical state infrastructure as an armed attack for self-defence purposes.[79]

Another issue is whether attacks by non-state actors that are not attributed to a state can constitute an armed attack for purposes of self-defence.[80] For the majority of the International Group of Experts, such attacks can trigger the right to self-defence, but a minority did not agree with this view. The latter's view is supported by the ICJ which opined on many occasions that only a state can be the author of an armed attack.[81] The ICJ's opinion was however criticised by other judges in their dissenting opinions.[82] It is submitted that the majority's view is the correct one because both Article 51 UN Charter and the customary law of self-defence going back to the Caroline case[83] suggest that non-state actors can be the authors of an armed attack. Security Council (SC) Resolutions 1368 and 1373 (2001) which qualified the Al Qaeda attacks as an armed attack and recognised the

---

[74] *Oil Platforms*, para 64.

[75] *Congo v. Uganda*, paras 146–147.

[76] Dinstein 2010, paras 547–549; Simma et al. 2012, p. 1409; Greenwood 2012, para 13.

[77] Judge Simma in *Oil Platforms*, para 14; Gazzini 2006, p. 192; Lubell, 51.

[78] Rule 13, para 9.

[79] Sharp 1999, p. 129 *et seq.*; Jensen 2002, pp. 221–229; Tsagourias 2012, p. 231. *Contra* Dinstein 2002, pp. 99–119.

[80] Rule 13, paras 15–17.

[81] *Palestinian Wall*, para 139; *Congo v. Uganda*, para 146.

[82] *Palestinian Wall*, para 139; *Contra* Sep. Op. Judge Higgins ibid, paras 33–34; Sep. Op. Judge Kooijmans, ibid, paras 35–36 and Decl. Judge Burgenthal, ibid, para 6 in *Palestinian Wall*. See also *Congo v. Uganda*, para 146. *Contra* Diss. Op. Judge Kateka, ibid, para 34 and Diss. Op. Judge Kooijmans, ibid, para 28 and Diss. Op. Judge Simma, para 11 in *Congo v. Uganda*, See also Greenwood 2012, paras 16–17.

[83] If the *Caroline* case is viewed as the source of the modern law on self-defence, it involved non-state actors.

inherent right of self-defence seem to support this view. The question that remains is whether the non-state actor should have a certain degree of organisation in order to be the author of the attack or whether even a single individual can be considered the author of the attack.[84] Because neither the potential of non-state actors nor the level of technological development can be predicted, a case-by-case assessment may be more appropriate.

2.2.4.1 Attribution

From the preceding discussion, it transpires that attribution is a critical component of the use of force regime because it determines who will be the target of counter force. The Manual discusses the applicable attribution criteria in the section on state responsibility. According to the Manual, attributable to a state are all uses of force committed by its organs,[85] by persons or organs empowered to exercise governmental authority,[86] or by persons or groups under the instruction, direction or control of the state.[87] With regard to the latter standard, there is disagreement as to whether the requisite threshold is that of 'effective control'—as the ICJ opined in the *Nicaragua* and *Bosnia Genocide* cases[88]—or whether the requisite threshold is 'effective control' in the case of individuals and unorganised groups and 'overall control' in the case of organised groups, as the ICTY opined in the *Tadić* case.[89] The Manual does not state its position on the issue.[90] This is regrettable because, as was said, attribution is crucial to the use of force. Moreover, it is not settled whether the applicable attribution criteria are only those contained in the law of state responsibility. It should be recalled that the ICJ has accepted that different attribution criteria may apply to different situations.[91] After the '9/11' attacks and particularly in relation to terrorist attacks, the attribution criteria of 'toleration' and 'unwillingness' have been mentioned[92] and the ICJ was quite receptive to them in the *Congo v. Uganda* Case.[93] Consequently, if a state tolerates groups that go on to launch cyber attacks on another state, or is unwilling to suppress their activities, the attacks will be attributed to that state which will then become the target of self-defence action. The Manual does not deal with the question of whether additional

---

84 Rule 13, para 18.

85 Rule 6, paras 6–7.

86 Ibid., para 8.

87 Rule 6, para 9.

88 *Nicaragua*, paras 116–117; *Bosnia Genocide*, paras 402–406.

89 *Tadić* (Appeal), 15 July 1999, para 131.

90 Rule 6, para 10.

91 *Bosnia Genocide*, paras 404–405; Tsagourias 2010, pp. 29–39; Ruys 2010, pp. 491–93.

92 Letter from the Permanent Representative of the United States of America to the United Nations addressed to the President of the Security Council (7 October 2001) S/2001/946 (2001). Simma et al. 2012, p. 1418; Tams 2009, pp. 359, 384–387; Tsagourias 2012, pp. 240–1.

93 *Congo v. Uganda*, paras 147, 301.

attribution criteria exist, but instead considers the question of whether a state can take direct action against groups located in another state or against groups that use assets located in another state when the attacks are not attributed to that state according to the attribution criteria enumerated in the Manual. For the majority of the International Group of Experts, the victim state can take self-defence action against non-state actors when the state is unwilling or unable to suppress their activities provided that certain procedural requirements are satisfied. A minority of the Group was of the opinion that it is impermissible to do so.[94] When a state is unable to control non-state actors, it stands to reason that non-state actors become the direct targets of self-defence[95] but when a state is unwilling to control them, it is important in my view to consider whether there is state complicity in the attack.[96] As was opined, what will be determinative is to what extent state involvement has made the attack possible.[97] However, any assessment is complicated by the fact that non-state actors may use state infrastructures to launch their attack. Rule 7 on state responsibility provides that '[t]he mere fact that a cyber operation has been launched or otherwise originates from governmental cyber infrastructure is not sufficient evidence for attributing the operation to that State but is an indication that the State in question is associated with the operation'. This means that there may be situations where the attack can be attributed to the state if evidence exists, for example, that the state tolerates such attacks to be launched from its infrastructure or willingly fails to safeguard its governmental cyber infrastructure. Yet, even when the state is genuinely unable to control non-state actors that use its infrastructure and self-defence action is to be taken against the specific non-state actor, the question is whether it is possible to contain the action as not to target at the same time the state or states whose infrastructure has been infiltrated by the non-state actor.

2.2.5 Rule 14: Necessity and Proportionality

According to Rule 14, 'A use of force involving cyber operations undertaken by a State in the exercise of its right of self-defence must be necessary and proportionate.'

The principles of necessity and proportionality are part of the customary law of self-defence.[98] As far as necessity is concerned, it answers the question of whether the use of force by way of self-defence is the only available means of effectively

---

[94] Rule 13, paras 22 and 23.

[95] Even in this case, it has been claimed that the attack should be attributed to the state under a very broad attribution criterion of 'manifestly unable to prevent large-scale attacks'. Simma et al. 2012, p. 1419.

[96] For discussion of attribution criteria in the context of terrorism and for rejection of the complicity criterion see Trump 2011, pp. 34–62.

[97] Simma et al. 2012, p. 1416.

[98] *Nicaragua*, paras 176, 194, 237; *Nuclear Weapons*, para 41; *Oil Platforms*, paras 51, 73, 76–78; *Congo v. Uganda*, para 147. Simma et al. 2012, pp. 1423–1427; Gardam 2004.

repelling the attack. To what extent the criterion of necessity is of any practical significance depends on whether self-defence is a reaction to an ongoing attack, where the requirement of necessity is perhaps *ipso facto* satisfied, or whether it is a reaction to an immediate or prospective attack, where the necessity of self-defence can be assessed against other means of preventing the attack. It should be noted however that the principle of necessity does not require the exhaustion of all available peaceful means, but the necessity of self-defence is determined by the aim of the self-defence action which the other measures cannot meet.[99]

Proportionality has to do with the intensity, scale, scope and duration of the self-defence action measured against its aim. Proportionality can be quite elastic depending on whether the objective of the self-defence action is to repel the attack, to prevent future attacks, or to eliminate the source of the threat.

From the above it transpires that necessity and proportionality are not 'strict and objective criteria', as the ICJ said,[100] but rather flexible and contextual ones; and as the Manual says, they are judged from the perspective of the victim-state.[101]

This leads to the next question, which is whether the necessity of self-defence is eclipsed once the SC intervenes. It should be recalled that according to Article 51 of the UN Charter, self-defence is a provisional right until the Security Council takes measures necessary to maintain international peace and security. The Manual recognises the authority of the SC to expressly divest a state of its right of self-defence and to take measures in parallel with self-defence, but it does not say, in the absence of a clear SC decision, what measures can divest a state from its right to self-defence, and who determines that the right has become redundant.[102] It will be in line with the rationale behind Article 51 and the United Nations collective security system to say that the necessity of self-defence will cease to apply only when the SC takes effective measures that will substitute for the right of self-defence.[103] Regarding the question of who determines that the measures are necessary, both the SC and the victim-state can do so: the SC because it has that power under the Charter and the state because the right to self-defence is an individual right. This means that assessments may differ but, unless there is a clear SC determination, the state's assessment should prevail. For example, although the SC urged parties to the conflict in the Democratic Republic of the Congo to conclude a cease-fire,[104] the call was ignored but they were not divested of their right to self-defence.[105] In order to avoid misunderstandings, often the SC, when acting under Chapter VII, also recognises the right to self-defence.[106]

---

99 Rule 14, para 2. See also *Congo v. Uganda*, para 148.

100 *Oil Platforms*, para 73.

101 Rule 14, para 4. Greenwood 2012, paras 24–29.

102 Rule 17, paras 2–3.

103 See also Article 5(2) NATO.

104 SC Res 1258 (1999); SC Res 1304 (2000).

105 *Congo v. Uganda*, para 304.

106 SC Res 661 (1990); SC Res 1368 (2001), 1373 (2001).

2.2.6 Rule 15: Imminence and Immediacy

Rule 15 provides that the right to use force in self-defence arises if a cyber armed attack occurs or is imminent. It is further subject to a requirement of immediacy.

The majority of the International Group of Experts took the view that self-defence is permissible if the cyber attack is imminent, with imminence being interpreted under the *Caroline* formula as 'necessity of self-defence: instant, overwhelming, leaving no choice of means and no moment of deliberation',[107] but the Manual also mentions the views held by others according to which self-defence is permissible only if an armed attack has already been launched or at least when it is incipient.[108] This gives rise to questions as to whether Rule 15 reflects the current state of the law on anticipatory self-defence or is stated *de lege ferenda*. It is submitted that it reflects current law.[109] As the UN High-Level Panel Report on Threats, Challenges and Change states 'a threatened State, according to long-established customary international law, can take military action as long as the threatened attack is imminent, no other means would deflect it, and the action is proportionate.'[110] Thus, to give an example, self-defence action can be taken when cyber operations to disable a state's command and control systems, or its air defences are deemed to be preparatory of a conventional or a cyber attack.

The critical question is how imminence is interpreted. The majority of the International Group of Experts rejected the temporal criterion in the interpretation of imminence and adopted the 'last window of opportunity' standard, according to which a state can resort to self-defence the moment it judges that a failure to act will hinder its capacity to effectively defend itself when the attack is finally launched.[111] Taking into consideration factual as well as temporal criteria is reasonable and inevitable, due to the nature of cyber weapons.[112] It however becomes apparent that self-defence action can be taken long before the attack is about to occur, and thus the line between anticipatory and preventive self-defence (that is, defensive action against a prospective attack) collapses. For example,

---

107 30 B.F.S.P., 196–8.

108 Rule 15, paras 2 and 3. For example, see Gray 2008, p. 160, Dinstein 2010, paras 538–542.

109 Bowett 2008, pp. 188–9; Schachter 1984, pp. 1620, 1634–5; Greenwood 2012, paras 41–51; Roscini 2010, 120–123; Simma et al. 2012, pp. 1421–1424.

110 *A More Secure World: Our Shared Responsibility*, UN Doc A/59/565 (2004) paras 188 and 189–192.

111 Rule 15, para 4.

112 *The Chatham House Principles of International Law on the Use of Force in Self Defence*, 2006, p. 968: 'Factors that may be taken into account include: the *gravity* of the threatened attack; whether what is threatened is a catastrophic use of Weapons of Mass Destruction (WMD); *capability*, for example, whether the relevant State or terrorist organisation is in possession of WMD, or merely of material or component parts to be used in its manufacture; and the *nature* of the attack including the possible risks of making a wrong assessment of the danger. Other factors may also be relevant, such as the geographical situation of the victim State, and the past record of attacks by the State concerned.'

when is the 'last window of opportunity' if the technological or other capabilities of the affected state are also taken into account?

The Manual introduces some form of safeguard when it says that the prospective attack should not be speculative, but the decision to attack must have matured.[113] Whether the decision has matured can be inferred from acts, behaviours, statements and, crucially, from intelligence information, though it is always difficult to draw definite conclusions from such evidence. For example, if the Stuxnet attack is placed in the context of bellicose statements against Iran, could the inference be made that the decision to use force has matured?

This indicates that critical to assessments of imminence, and to the distinction between anticipatory and preventive self-defence, is the availability and probity of information, but information about another state's capabilities or intentions may be difficult to collect or to verify, and in any case information will be secret. Therefore, decisions as to whether the threshold of imminence has been reached will be political, and, as the Manual says, depend on the 'reasonableness of the victim-State's assessment of the situation'.[114]

Regarding the criterion of immediacy, it requires that the self-defence action should be in close proximity to the initial attack. Once more this requirement is contextual. One should take into account preparations preceding the self-defence action, political or other processes to find a solution, or investigations to identify the author of the attack. Thus, the boundaries of immediacy may be extended.

2.2.7 Rule 16: Collective Self-Defence

Rule 16 provides that the right of self-defence may be exercised collectively. Collective self-defence against a cyber operation amounting to an armed attack may only be exercised at the request of the victim-state and within the scope of the request.

This rule reflects customary international law, as the ICJ opined in the *Nicaragua Case*.[115] Lending assistance to a state only at its request and within the scope of the request is explicable by the fact that, otherwise, the assisting state's action will constitute unlawful intervention or unlawful use of force against the state that is assisted, or against the state that becomes the target of that action. Moreover, according to the Manual, both the victim-state and the one providing assistance need to be satisfied that an armed attack is underway or imminent.[116] International law traditionally required evidence only from the victim-state to

---

[113] Rule 15, para 7.

[114] Ibid., para 6.

[115] *Nicaragua* (Merits), paras 195, 199, 211, 232; but see Diss, Op. Judge Schwebel, para 221 *et seq.*; Diss. Op. Judge Jennings, paras 544–6; *Oil Platforms*, para 51.

[116] Rule 16, para 2.

establish that it suffered an armed attack.[117] Thus, it is not clear whether the statement that the assisting state needs to be satisfied that an armed attack is underway or imminent is presented as legal requirement or as good practice. In the view of the present commentator, it is good practice and politically expedient in light also of the fact that collective self-defence is a discretionary right and not a duty on the part of the assisting state.

2.2.8 Rule 17: Reporting Measures of Self-Defence

According to Rule 17, 'Measures involving cyber operations undertaken by States in the exercise of the right of self-defence pursuant to Article 51 of the United Nations Charter shall be immediately reported to the United Nations Security Council.'

As the Manual notes, reporting is not a requirement under customary international law,[118] but non-reporting is a violation of Article 51. It then goes on to say that a state that fails to report its action is not divested from its right to self-defence. This is because reporting is a procedural and not a substantive requirement, but if the Nicaragua judgment is to be followed, a report may be used as evidence that the action was not in self-defence.[119]

2.2.9 Rule 18: United Nations Security Council

According to Rule 17, should the United Nations Security Council determine that an act constitutes a threat to the peace, breach of the peace, or act of aggression, it may authorise non-forceful measures, including cyber operations. If the Security Council considers such measures to be inadequate, it may decide upon forcible measures, including cyber measures.

This rule reaffirms the powers of the SC under Chapter VII of the UN Charter. As is well known, the SC has broad and discretionary powers of appreciation under Article 39 and the SC has interpreted the concept of threat to the peace quite dynamically, adapting it to new threats. Furthermore, the SC has determined that not only specific events but also situations may be a threat to the peace. Consequently, a specific cyber operation, or cyber threats in general, may be deemed by the SC to fall within Article 39 and trigger further action. The SC may therefore adopt specific measures under Articles 41 and 42, and it may also adopt general measures of a legislative nature. It should be recalled that the SC adopted

[117] Nicaragua, paras 195, 199; *Oil Platforms*, paras 51 and 57.

[118] Nicaragua, para 199.

[119] Ibid, paras 200 and 235.

legislative resolutions to respond to the threat that terrorism[120] or weapons of mass destruction[121] posed to international peace and security, filling in the international legislative void. The power of the SC in this regard is very important, because in the absence of a comprehensive and binding regime concerning cyber threats, the SC can fill in the void by promulgating legislative resolutions.

The Manual is quite brief and enigmatic as to whether international law provides any limits to the SC action.[122] It states that a decision by the SC to disregard rules of international law should not be taken lightly but under no circumstances may the SC deviate from *jus cogens*. It is widely accepted that in addition to *jus cogens*, the SC is bound by the UN Charter and by customary international law to the extent that it is relevant to its activities.[123] It is also widely held that Article 103 does not invalidate states' international law obligations, but suspends them only for as long as it is necessary in order to give effect to the SC resolution.[124] As recent case law also shows, courts reconcile ostensibly conflicting obligations imposed on states by the SC and by other sources and it is only in those situations where no reconciliation can be achieved that Article 103 is used.[125]

2.2.10 Rule 19: Regional Organisations

Rule 19 provides that international organisations, arrangements, or agencies of a regional character may conduct enforcement actions, involving or in response to cyber operations, pursuant to a mandate from, or authorisation by, the United Nations Security Council.

This rule reflects the provisions of Chapter VIII of the UN Charter and more specifically Articles 52 and 53. The Manual does not provide a definition of what is 'regional'—but no such definition is provided in the Charter either. It appears that the Charter distinguishes regional organisations from collective self-defence organisations in that regional organisations can act only under SC authority[126] whereas a collective self-defence organisation can use force even without such authorisation.[127] Such a distinction, if it ever existed, is however artificial. Whether SC authorisation is needed depends on the activities of the organisation and

---

[120] SC Res 1373 (2001).

[121] SC Res 1540 (2004).

[122] Rule 18, para 8.

[123] Reparations 180; *WHO/Egypt*, para 37.

[124] De Wet and Vidmar 2012, p. 19; M. Wood, 'The UN Security Council and International Law', First Lecture, *The Legal Framework of the Security Council*, Hersch Lauterpacht Memorial Lectures 2006, para 55, available at www.lcil.cam.ac.uk/Media/lectures/pdf/2006_hersch_lecture_1.pdf. Accessed 27 May 2013.

[125] Al-Jedda v. *UK*; *Nada v. Switzerland.* Simma et al. 2012, pp. 2110–2137.

[126] Article 53 UN Charter, Simma et al. 2012, pp. 1500–1505.

[127] Compare Articles 51 and 53 of UN Charter.

not on its formal designation.[128] Thus, NATO—which defines itself as a collective self-defence organisation[129]—will need SC authorisation if it acts outside its collective self-defence mandate but will not need such authorisation if it acts in collective self-defence. That said, there will always be debate and disagreement as to whether the particular action is defensive or not.

Another point of contention is what constitutes "enforcement action". According to the Manual, enforcement action comprises both article 41 (non-forcible) and article 42 (forcible) measures.[130] Even if there is some support for such broad interpretation of enforcement action,[131] one needs to distinguish the case where the SC utilises regional organisations for enforcement action from the case where regional organisations act autonomously.[132] When the SC utilises (mandates) regional arrangements for enforcement action,[133] it can involve both Article 41 and Article 42 measures. However, when regional organisations decide to act autonomously, authorisation is required only when their action involves the use of force.[134] This is because of the central place of the rule prohibiting the use of unilateral force coupled with the centralisation and institutionalisation of the use of force regime in the Charter[135] and, because international law permits states or regional organisations to take non forcible measures if that is provided in their constitutive documents. For example, the EU, as a regional organisation, can and does impose sanctions under SC mandate but also autonomously.[136]

Another question that is left unanswered is whether regional organisations can operate only within their region. When regional organisations are mandated or authorised by the SC, they can operate outside their region. This involves both coercive and non-coercive action. Any conflict that may exist with the provisions of their constitutive treaties which may restrict the geographical scope of their activities will be settled on the basis of Article 103, according to which the obligations under the Charter—including SC resolutions—supersede other conventional obligations. With regard to non-forcible measures, regional organisations can act outside their region provided that their constitutive treaties allow them to do so and provided that these measures are permitted by international law. For example, the EU has imposed sanctions on non-EU states such as Belarus, China, Moldova, Myanmar, Uzbekistan and Zimbabwe.[137] That said, this issue is

---

[128] Simma et al. 2012, pp. 1451–3.

[129] Article 5 NATO.

[130] Rule 19, para 3.

[131] See for example the relevant discussion in Simma et al. 2012, pp. 1481–1484.

[132] See Article 53(1) UN Charter.

[133] Ibid.

[134] Simma et al. 2012, pp. 1484, 1500–1505.

[135] Article 2(4) and Chapter VII of the UN Charter.

[136] European Commission, Sanctions or Restrictive Measures 2008.

[137] OJ 2006, L 101/5-10; European Council, 'Declaration' (27 June 1989); OJ 2008, L 51/23-25; OJ 2006, L 116/77-97; OJ 2007, L 295/34-39; OJ 2004, L 50/66-72.

to a large extent rendered moot in cyberspace because of its borderless character and its interconnectivity.

2.3 Conclusion

As has become apparent from the preceding exposition, the Manual applies the current legal framework on the *jus ad bellum* formed by UN Charter law and customary international law to cyber war. This is quite reassuring, because the term 'cyber war' could invite thoughts that the existing legal regime is incapable of coping with this new and yet unknown terrain. That having been said, whereas the stated rules in the abstract do not raise any questions, the commentary that accompanies them reveals that there exist different views about the scope and content of these rules in general and even more so when applied to cyber war. Consequently, it is not always clear whether the Manual projects *lex lata* or *lex ferenda.*[138] Furthermore, it is not always clear whether the statement of the rules has taken into account the technological aspects of 'cyber' or the unique features of cyberspace. Yet, the value of the Manual is that by setting out the *jus ad bellum* rules that apply to cyber war and by exposing their interpretative vicissitudes, it may contribute in subsequent years to the clarification and solidification of the rules in light of subsequent state practice and technological advances.

References

Cases,

ICJ

Case Concerning Application of the Convention on the Prevention and Punishment of the Crime of Genocide (Bosnia and Herzegovina v. *Serbia and Montenegro)* Judgment of 26 February 2007, (2007) 2007 ICJ, *(Bosnia Genocide).*

Case Concerning Armed Activities on the Territory of the Congo (Democratic Republic of the Congo v. *Uganda)* Judgment of 19 December 2005, (2005) ICJ Rep. *(Congo* v. *Uganda).*

Case Concerning Legality of Use of Force (Yugoslavia v. *Belgium)* Verbatim Record, 10 May 1999, CR 99/15.

Case Concerning Military and Paramilitary Activities in and against Nicaragua (Nicaragua v. *United States of America)*, Judgment of 27 June 1986, [1986] ICJ Rep. 14 *(Nicaragua).*

Case concerning Oil Platforms (*Islamic Republic of Iran v. United States of America*), Judgment of 6 November 2003, (2003) ICJ Rep. 161 (*Oil Platforms).*

Gabčíkovo-Nagymaros Project (Hungary/Slovakia), Judgment of 25 September 1997, (1997) ICJ Rep. 7 *(Hungary/Slovakia).*

---

138 Manual, page 21.

Interpretation of the Agreement of 25 March 1951 between the WHO and Egypt, Advisory Opinion of 20 December 1980, (1980) ICJ Rep. 67 *(WHO/Egypt)*.
Legal Consequences of the Construction of a Wall in the Occupied Palestinian Territory, including in and around East Jerusalem, Advisory Opinion of 9 July 2004, (2004) ICJ Rep.136 *(Palestinian Wall)*.
Legality of the Threat or Use of Nuclear Weapons, Advisory Opinion of 8 July 1996, (1996) ICJ Rep. 227 *(Nuclear Weapons)*.
Reparation for Injuries Suffered in the Service of the United Nations, Advisory Opinion of 11 April 1949, (1949) ICJ Rep. 174 *(Reparation for Injuries)*.

ECtHR

Al-Jedda v. *The United Kingdom,* Application No. 27021/08, Judgment of 7 July 2011 *(Al-Jedda)*
Nada v. *Switzerland*, Application No. 10593/08, Judgment, 12 September 2012.

ICTY

Prosecutor v. *Dusko Tadić*, Appeal Judgement, ICTY Case No. IT-94-1-A, 15 July 1999 (*Tadić Appeal Judgment 1999*).

Arbitral Awards, Eritrea Ethiopia Claims Commission

Partial Award, *Jus Ad Bellum, Ethiopia's Claims 1–8 between The Federal Democratic Republic of Ethiopia And The State of Eritrea* (2005) (Ethiopia/Eritrea Award).

Books, Articles and Internet Sources

Barkham (2001) Information Warfare and International Law on the Use of Force. New York University Journal of International Law and Politics 34:57–113.
Buchan R (2012) Cyber Attacks: Unlawful Uses of Force or Prohibited Interventions? Journal of Conflict and Security Law 17:212–227.
Boebert E (2010) A Survey of Challenges in Attribution. In Proceedings of a Workshop on Deterring Cyberattacks: Informing Strategies and Developing Options for US Policy. National Research Council, National Academies Press, pp 41–54.
Bowett D (1972) Reprisals Involving Recourse to Armed Force. American Journal of International Law 66:1–36.
Bowett (2009) Self-Defence in International Law. The Lawbook Exchange, ltd. Originally published: Praeger, New York (1958).
Brownlie I (1963) International Law and the Use of Force by States. Oxford University Press, Oxford.
Brown G (2011) Why Iran Didn't Admit Stuxnet Was an Attack. Joint Force Quarterly, NDU press, Washington 63:70–73.
Bull H (1984) Intervention in World Politics. Clarendon Press, Oxford.
Clark D and Landau S (2010) Untangling Attribution. In Proceedings of a Workshop on Deterring Cyberattacks: Informing Strategies and Developing Options for US Policy. National Research Council, National Academies Press, pp 25–40.

Chatham House Principles of International Law on the Use of Force in Self-Defence. (2006) International and Comparative Law Quarterly, 55:963–972.

Dinstein Y (2002) Computer Network Attacks and Self-defence. In: Schmitt and O'Donnell, Computer Network Attack and International Law. International Law Studies – Naval War College 76:99–119.

Dinstein Y (2010) War, Aggression and Self-Defence. Cambridge University Press.

Dutch Advisory Council on International Affairs and the Advisory Committee on Issues of Public International Law (2008) Netherlands Yearbook of International Law, T.M.C. ASSER Press, The Hague.

European Commission, Sanctions or Restrictive Measures (2008) http://eeas.europa.eu/cfsp/sanctions/index_en.htm. Accessed 26 February 2013.

Foltz A (2012) Stuxnet, Schmitt Analysis, and the Cyber "Use-of-Force" Debate, Joint Force Quarterly 67:40. http://www.au.af.mil/au/awc/awcgate/jfq/foltz_stuxnet_schmitt_oct2012.pdf, Accessed 28 February 2013.

Gardam J (2004) Necessity, Proportionality and the Use of Force by States. Cambridge University Press, Cambridge.

Gazzini T (2006) The Changing Rules on the Use of Force in International Law. Manchester University Press, Manchester.

Gorman S and Barnes J (2011) Cyber Combat: Act of War. The Wall Street Journal.

Gray C (2008) International Law and the Use of Force, 3rd ed., Oxford University Press, Oxford.

Greenwood C (2012) Self-Defence. Max Planck Encyclopedia of Public International Law online.

Hargrove J (1987) The Nicaragua Judgment and the Future of the Law of Self-Defence, American Journal of International Law 81:135–143.

Jennings R, Watts A (2008) Oppenheim's International Law. Vol 1 Peace. 9th edn, Oxford University Press, Oxford.

Jensen E (2002) Computer Attacks on Critical State Infrastructure: A Use of Force Invoking the Right of Self-Defence. Stanford Journal of International Law, 38:207–240.

Lin H (2010) Offensive Cyber Operations and the Use of Force. Journal of National Security Law and Policy 4:63–86.

Lubell N (2010) Extraterritorial Use of Force Against Non-State Actors. Oxford University Press, Oxford.

Roscini M (2010) World Wide Warfare—Jus ad Bellum and the Use of Cyber Force. 14 Max Planck Yearbook of United Nations Law 14:85–130.

Ruys T (2010) 'Armed Attack' and Article 51 of the UN Charter: Evolutions in Customary Law and Practice. Cambrige University Press, Cambridge.

Sadurska R (1988) Threats of Force. American Journal of International Law 82:239 *et seq.*

Schmitt MN (1999) Computer Network Attack and the Use of Force in International Law: Thoughts on a Normative Framework. Columbia Journal of Transnational Law, 37:885–937.

Schmitt MN (2011) Cyber Operations and the *Jus Ad Bellum* Revised. Villanova Law Review 56:576 *et seq.*

Schmitt MN (2012) The 'Use of Force' in Cyberspace: A Reply to Dr Ziolkowski. 4th International Conference on Cyber Conflict, available at http://www.ccdcoe.org/publications/2012proceedings/5_4_Schmidt_ResponseToZiolkowski.pdf. Accessed 26 February 2013.

Sharp WG (1999) Cyberspace and the Use of Force. Aegis Research Corporation, Falls Church.

Simma B, Khan D-E, Nolte G, Paulus A (ed) (2012) The Charter of the United Nations. Oxford University Press, Oxford.

Schachter (1984) The Right of States to Use Armed Force. Michigan Law Review 82:1620 *et seq.*

Sloan RD (2012) On the Use and Abuse of Necessity in the Law of State Responsibility. American Journal of International Law 106:447–508.

Tams C (2009) The Use of Force against Terrorists. European Journal of International law 20:359–397.

Trump K (2011) State Responsibility for International Terrorism. Oxford University Press, Oxford.

Tsagourias N (2010) Necessity and the Use of Force: A Special Regime. Netherlands Yearbook of International Law 41:11–44.

Tsagourias N (2011) Non-State Actors and the Use of Force. In D'Aspremont J (ed), Participants in the International Legal System: Theoretical Perspectives. Routledge, London, p 326 *et seq.*

Tsagourias N (2012) Cyberattacks, Self-defence and the Problem of Attribution. Journal of Conflict and Security Law 17:229–245.

Waxman (2011) Cyber-Attacks and the Use of Force: Back to the Future of Article 2(4). 36 Yale Journal of International Law 36:421 *et seq.*

Wedgwood R (1999) Legal personality and the role of non-governmental organisations and non-state political entities in the United Nations system. In Hofmann R (ed) (1999) Non-State Actors as New Subjects of International Law, Duncker & Humblot, Berlin, pp 21–36.

Wet E de, Vidmar J (2012) Hierarchy in International Law: The Place of Human Rights, Oxford University Press, Oxford.

Ziolkowski K (2012) *Jus ad bellum* in Cyberspace – Some Thoughts on the "Schmitt-Criteria" for Use of Force. 4th International Conference on Cyber Conflict, NATO CCD COE Publications, Tallinn. http://www.ccdcoe.org/publications/2012proceedings/5_3_Ziolkowski_IusAdBellumInCyberspace.pdf. Accessed 26 February 2013.

Chapter 3
Law in the Virtual Battlespace: The Tallin Manual and the *Jus in Bello*

Rain Liivoja and Tim McCormack

Contents

3.1 Introduction: Proactively Identifying the Applicable Law

Reports of cyber operations have increased so dramatically in recent years that they have become commonplace. The reality that most attacks to date have resulted in relatively benign consequences—inconvenience and offence through

Rain Liivoja is a Research Fellow and Project Director for the Law of Armed Conflict at the Asia Pacific Centre for Military Law, Melbourne Law School. He is also an Associated Research Fellow at the Erik Castrén Institute of International Law and Human Rights, University of Helsinki.Tim McCormack is Professor of Law and Associate Director of the Asia Pacific Centre for Military Law at the Melbourne Law School. He is also an Adjunct Professor of Law at the University of Tasmania Law School and the Special Adviser on International Humanitarian Law to the Prosecutor of the International Criminal Court in The Hague. The views reflected here are personal and do not reflect the position of the Prosecutor or of her Office.

R. Liivoja (✉) · T. McCormack
Melbourne Law School, Asia Pacific Centre for Military Law, Melbourne, Australia
e-mail: rliivoja@unimelb.edu.au

T. McCormack
e-mail: t.mccormack@unimelb.edu.au

T. D. Gill et al. (eds.), *Yearbook of International Humanitarian Law 2012*,
Yearbook of International Humanitarian Law 15, DOI: 10.1007/978-90-6704-924-5_3,

defacement of government websites and/or temporary suspension of access—only serves to heighten awareness of the damage that could result from much more serious attacks on networks controlling, for example, vital public transport and emergency infrastructure, the financial system and sensitive communications networks. The threat of apocalyptic consequences has galvanized States into proactive cyber defence measures—spawning an entirely new category of bureaucracy that until recently might readily have been cynically dismissed as manipulative fear-mongering to justify yet more human and financial resources allocated to the public sector.[1]

That governments should proactively mitigate emergent and potentially catastrophic risks is an *a priori* notion. Citizens of a State whose government did not take cyber defence seriously would be entitled to feel aggrieved—particularly in the aftermath of a serious cyber attack where the lack of proaction on the part of central authorities was exposed. In contrast, expectations should be significantly lower for any proactive clarification of the applicable international law. The making of new, or even the clarification of the content of existing, international law has tended to be more reactive—requiring a major catalyst to expose the need for either clarification or regulation. It has been rare in the history of international law for new development to pre-empt subsequent catastrophe.

It is in this respect that the advent of the *Tallinn Manual on the International Law Applicable to Cyber Warfare* should be warmly welcomed. The instigators of the Manual, working under the auspices of the NATO Cooperative Cyber Defence Centre of Excellence (CCD COE) in Tallinn, Estonia, have recognised the potential for cyber warfare with devastating consequences for the victims of attacks and have anticipated future contingencies. Indeed, the principal instigator of the Manual, Michael Schmitt, explains that he declined an invitation from the NATO CCD COE to speak at a cyber warfare conference because he was tired of 'boring conferences on cyber … [with lawyers talking about] how truly hard cyber is' and instead wanted to initiate a process to answer difficult legal questions on cyber warfare.[2] The Manual is the result of the CCD COE accepting that invitation and in it the authors of the Manual have proactively grappled with the issues rather than waiting to scramble to clarify the extent to which the law of armed conflict (LOAC) applies to cyber warfare after a major attack with severe and widespread consequences. The publication of the Manual will undoubtedly provoke a robust debate about the applicable law that would otherwise not have occurred—at least not as early as 2013—but for the Manual's publication.

[1] For example, the Australian Government recently announced the establishment of a new Cyber Security Centre. See <www.defence.gov.au/defencenews/stories/2013/Jan/0124.htm>. Accessed 31 May 2013.

[2] See Michael N Schmitt, 'Tallinn Manual: Part I', NATO Cooperative Cyber Defence Centre of Excellence (CCDCOE) 4th annual International Conference on Cyber Conflict (CyCon) June 5–8, 2012 in Tallinn, Estonia (see <http://www.youtube.com/watch?v=wY3uEo-Itso>). Accessed 31 May 2013.

The Tallinn Manual comprises two Parts—Part A dealing with cyber security and the *jus ad bellum,* and Part B with the *jus in bello* or LOAC. This contribution offers some comments on the latter part. We recognise, however, that the sheer range and variety of issues covered by the Manual makes it difficult for us to provide any comprehensive assessment. Also, we cannot easily summarise and contrast with the Manual the large number of thoughtful books and papers on the legal aspects of cyber warfare that have appeared during the last decade.[3] Thus, we will limit our observations to the methodology of drafting the Manual and to a few selected issues of substantive law that illustrate the difficulties in applying LOAC to cyber operations.

3.2 The Rise of LOAC Manuals

The Tallinn Manual is the fourth and most recent in a succession of manuals[4] over the last 20 years on the international law applicable to a particular modality of warfare. In the early 1990s, there was no conscious decision to initiate successive manuals. The inaugural contemporary model—the *San Remo Manual on International Law Applicable to Armed Conflict at Sea*, adopted in 1994—stood alone for more than a decade. But that original San Remo Manual proved to be so influential that it has spawned a flurry of recent similar exercises in relation to other theatres of military operation. In just six short years, the *San Remo Manual on the Law of Non-International Armed Conflict* (2006), the *Harvard Manual on the International Law Applicable to Air and Missile Warfare* (2009) and the *Tallinn Manual on the Law Applicable to Cyber Warfare* (2013) have all emerged.

The authors of the three more recent manuals have clearly drawn inspiration from the 1994 Naval Warfare Manual. The authors of the 2006 Non-International Armed Conflict Manual, for example, returned to the International Institute of Humanitarian Law in San Remo, the same 'host' institute for the 1994 Naval Warfare Manual, and produced their document under the same institutional auspices. The titles of the 2009 Harvard and 2013 Tallinn Manuals adopt precisely the form of the title of the 1994 Naval Warfare Manual. All three of the more recent manuals were prepared under the auspices of a host institution and all involved an invited group of subject matter experts who participated in the process in their personal, and not their national/institutional, capacities.

---

[3] For some of the early contributions, see Schmitt 2002b, Byström 2005. Recent significant publications include Tikk et al. 2010, Dinstein 2012, Hathaway et al. 2012, Harrison Dinniss 2012, Kodar 2012, Schmitt 2012, Turns 2012.

[4] We do not include national military law manuals here of which there have been many produced in the past 20 years. One of the more recent and better known is the 2004 *Manual on the Law of Armed Conflict* compiled by the UK Ministry of Defence. Here we are speaking of manuals developed under international auspices.

The commonalities across all four contemporary manuals are not restricted to issues of form or logistics but extend to the rationale for each of the manuals. Those involved in the preparation of the manuals have never claimed, nor could they, that their respective products constitute binding legal instruments. Instead the consistent refrain is that the manual is intended to reflect the respective experts' view(s) of the current state of the law in the relevant field. Louise Doswald-Beck, the editor of the published version of the 1994 Naval Warfare Manual for example, stated of that original initiative that:

> The Manual is not a binding document. In view of the extent of uncertainty in the law, the experts decided that it was premature to embark on diplomatic negotiations to draft a treaty on the subject. The work therefore concentrated on finding areas of agreement as to the present content of customary law, which were far more numerous than initially appeared possible. As a second step the experts discussed controversial issues with a view to reaching an agreed compromise on innovative proposals by way of progressive development. However, although the Manual was to contain provisions of this latter type, most of them were always meant to be an expression of what the participants believed to be present law.[5]

The sentiments here have been rearticulated in relation to other manuals since. The authors of the Tallinn Manual are likewise eager to dispel any notion that their product creates new law or in any way constitutes a legally binding instrument. Indeed, any such claim on their part would be delusional. The Manual reflects the views of the legal experts who participated in its drafting—all of whom were appointed in their personal capacities.[6] The most that the authors are prepared to claim in relation to the legal authority of the Manual is that, to the extent the Rules identified and articulated in the Manual reflect the current state of customary international law, all States are bound—not by the Rules in the Manual but by that customary international law.[7] There is a sense in which the Manual is more akin to a restatement of the law rather than to some legislative enactment. But even this analogy is not entirely accurate. As the authors themselves observe, there are as yet no treaties dealing specifically with the law applicable to cyber warfare so that there is no existing law to be restated. Instead, the Introduction to the Manual explains that:

> The International Group of Experts was unanimous in its estimation that both the *jus ad bellum* and *jus in bello* apply to cyber operations. Its task was to determine how such law applied and to identify any cyber-unique aspects thereof.[8]

Some of the initiators of the three more recent manuals might suggest that, unlike with the 1994 Naval Warfare Manual, there was no secondary objective of progressive development of the relevant field of law. However, the shared hope unquestionably is that the collective wisdom reflected in the manuals helps bring clarity where previously there was extensive misunderstanding, obfuscation or confusion.

---

[5] Doswald-Beck 1995, p. 587.

[6] *Tallinn Manual* 2013, p. 11.

[7] Ibid., pp. 5–6.

[8] Ibid., p. 5.

For all the commonalities the Tallinn Manual shares with the 1994 Naval Warfare Manual, for example, there is one disconcerting departure. In the San Remo expert process, there was clearly a commitment to diversity of views from all major regions of the world. Despite the predominance of white, first-world experts—from North America, Western Europe and Australasia (Australia or New Zealand), the experts also came from Eastern Europe (Russia, Croatia), Asia (China, Japan, Singapore), the Middle East (Egypt, Iran, Israel) and Latin America (Argentina). In contrast, every single one of the experts involved in the preparation of the Tallinn Manual is white and either from North America, Western Europe or Australasia. The sole exception involves one of the two technical experts who is Estonian (it is, after all, the Tallinn Manual) from Eastern Europe.[9]

3.3 Structure and Approach of the Tallinn Manual

Part B of the Tallinn Manual, dealing with *jus in bello*, follows a logical structure: it addresses, in turn, the LOAC generally; the conduct of hostilities; protected persons, objects and activities; occupation; and neutrality. The scope of the Manual is very comprehensive; there are no glaring omissions in terms of the range of legal issues and their application to cyber operations.

The basic approach of the Manual is also difficult to criticise. The Manual commences with an articulation of the applicable Rule and then follows with commentary to each specific rule explaining the rationale for the particular formula adopted and substantiating it with reference to primary customary international law sources. The Commentary duly notes any disagreements as to the formulation of the rule that may have existed among the International Group of Experts. Hence, any criticism of a particular rule is readily deflected by reference to the Commentary which regularly includes the observation that the rule does nothing more than reflect the views of the majority in the International Group of Experts. Occasionally, of course, the Commentary explains that the experts were unanimous in their views but often there were divergent views—sometimes only a small minority held a divergent view while at other times the implication seems to be that the minority view was much more widely held. It is not the case that the Commentary simply states the majority view and refers to the fact of differing opinions. Instead, there is an admirable commitment to summarising the range of views articulated in such a way that even divergent views are respected.

Some specific examples are indicative of the general approach. With respect to the definition of an international armed conflict, the experts disagreed as to whether an international armed conflict could exist between a State and a non-State organized armed group acting transnationally.[10] The majority, whose view is reflected in Rule 22, thought that it could not. Also, while the experts agreed that there must exist a

[9] Ibid., x–xi.

[10] Ibid., Commentary to Rule 22, para 9.

nexus between a cyber activity and an armed conflict in order for that activity to be governed by LOAC, they differed as to the nature of the required nexus.[11] These examples suggest that some of the disagreements within the International Group of Experts related not to a specific aspect of applying LOAC to cyber operations but to fundamental, conceptual issues which constitute bases for disagreement by LOAC experts generally. For these sorts of disagreements, it perhaps would be more surprising if the International Group of Experts expressed unanimity.

Other grounds for disagreement are more specific to cyber operations. One good example arises in relation to the requisite factors for the existence of a non-international armed conflict: (i) a threshold level of intensity and (ii) sufficient 'organization' for non-State armed groups to constitute parties to a non-international armed conflict. In relation to the 'intensity' threshold, the Commentary to Rule 23 explains in relevant part that:

> The International Group of Experts struggled with the question of whether non-destructive cyber operations conducted during civil disturbances or in connection with other acts of violence not qualifying as a non-international armed conflict can tip the scale and cause the hostilities to rise to the level of an armed conflict. For instance, assume an organised armed group has orchestrated civil disturbances. Although destruction of property is involved, such destruction is insufficiently severe to meet the intensity criterion for non-international armed conflict. The International Group of Experts reached no consensus as to whether non-destructive but severe cyber operations satisfy the intensity criterion.[12]

In relation to the requisite degree of 'organisation', cyber operations raise the spectre of a coordinated group that never meets physically but which organises its activities virtually. The Commentary to Rule 23 explains that a majority of the experts 'agree that the failure of members of the group physically to meet does not alone preclude it from having the requisite degree of organisation'.[13] This finding immediately raises the question whether a lack of physical contact precludes effective implementation of LOAC—one of the indices of the requisite degree of 'organisation'. The Commentary somewhat forlornly states that '[t]he International Group of Experts was divided as to whether such difficulty would bar qualification as an organised armed group'.[14]

3.4 Cyber Operations as Hostilities and the Principle of Distinction

When cyber operations first caught the eye of humanitarian lawyers, a recurrent question was whether such operations could be subject to LOAC to begin with. But a consensus developed quite rapidly that neither the novelty of technology

[11] Ibid., Commentary to Rule 20, para 5.

[12] Ibid., Commentary to Rule 23, para 10.

[13] Ibid., para 13.

[14] Ibid., para 14.

involved nor the immediate lack of kinetic force would exempt cyber operations from the reach of the existing law. As for the former consideration, it is, after all, a well-accepted principle that novel means and methods of warfare must be assessed in light of the existing principles of LOAC[15] and that they do not escape scrutiny simply because they post-date the law.[16] Also, biological and chemical weapons are subject to the same LOAC discourse as other means and methods of warfare despite the lack of a distinctive 'bang'. Cyber operations quickly came to be seen as a type of a military operation whose legality must largely be assessed on the basis of its foreseeable effects and consequences. Accordingly, the widely shared view among commentators now appears to be that once an armed conflict is underway, LOAC regulates the conduct of any cyber operations undertaken within that conflict just as it regulates the use of other means and methods of warfare.[17] This view finds categorical reflection in Rule 20 of the Manual which provides that '[c]yber operations executed in the context of an armed conflict are subject to the law of armed conflict', although, as already noted, there is uncertainty as to the precise meaning of 'in the context of'.

Whether cyber operations themselves can trigger an armed conflict and thereby bring LOAC into operation has been a contentious issue. The Manual answers this question largely in the affirmative when it comes to international armed conflicts but takes a more nuanced position as regards non-international conflicts. As far as international armed conflicts are concerned, Rule 22 of the Manual defines them as inter-State 'hostilities, which may include or be limited to cyber operations'. This language clearly suggests that cyber operations that amount to hostilities would be sufficient to bring LOAC into effect. This interpretation is confirmed by the Commentary, which expresses the unanimous view of the International Group of Experts that 'cyber operations alone might have the potential to cross the threshold of international armed conflict'.[18] Rule 23 of the Manual defines non-international armed conflicts as 'protracted armed violence, which may include or be limited to cyber operations', between certain armed groups. Despite the similarities in language to the definition of international armed conflicts, this definition continues by emphasising the need for the confrontation to reach a 'minimum level of intensity' and for the armed groups to have 'a minimum degree of organisation' for LOAC to apply. The Commentary suggests that, in light of these two requirements, 'cyber operations in and of themselves will only in exceptional cases amount to non-international armed conflict'.[19]

With respect to international armed conflict, the question nevertheless remains as to what kind of cyber operations would amount to 'hostilities' and trigger the

[15] See Article 36, Additional Protocol I.

[16] See *Legality of the Threat or Use of Nuclear Weapons (Advisory Opinion)* [1996] ICJ Reports 226.

[17] See, e.g., Melzer 2011, p. 4.

[18] *Tallinn Manual* 2013, Commentary to Rule 22, para 15.

[19] Ibid., Commentary to Rule 23, para 2.

applicability of LOAC. Certainly, a cyber operation amounting to an 'attack' (a concept discussed in some more detail below) would be capable of initiating an international armed conflict.[20] However, as the Manual itself repeatedly points out, 'hostilities' is a broader term than 'attack'. For example, the loss of protection suffered by a civilian due to direct participation in hostilities (encapsulated in Rules 29 and 35 of the Manual) does not require the perpetration of an attack—other 'actions ... will satisfy this criterion so long as they negatively affect the enemy militarily'.[21] The question therefore arises whether, and if so what kind of, cyber operations falling below the intensity of an attack could nonetheless trigger an armed conflict. Unfortunately the Manual does not provide much guidance on this point.[22]

We now come to arguably the most critical *jus in bello* aspect of the Manual—the definition of an armed cyber attack. The notion of 'attack' is a key concept of the Manual and LOAC more generally. The law governing the conduct of hostilities is essentially concerned with who and what may be attacked and by what means and methods. Accordingly, the definition of 'attack' is critical for the interpretation and application of large parts of the Manual and indeed indicative of the broader conceptualisation of cyber warfare by the International Group of Experts. The implications for the applicable law from this single determination are profound and so we allocate a significant proportion of our analysis to the Manual's approach to the definition of a cyber attack precisely because so much turns on this issue.

According to Article 49(1) of Additional Protocol I, an 'attack' means an act of 'violence against the adversary, whether in offence or in defence'. So defined, 'attack' is a term of art—the ICRC's Commentary on the Additional Protocols duly explains that, in the context of LOAC, 'attack' should not be given the ordinary meaning of 'striking the first blow', but equated to 'combat action' more broadly.[23] However, the Commentary does not attempt to explain what 'violence' means or, for that matter, what 'combat action' entails.

In academic discussions, two schools of thought have emerged as to what should be regarded as an attack in the cyber context. Michael Schmitt and Yoram Dinstein, among others, draw inspiration from the notion of violence. They take the view that cyber operations qualify as attacks for LOAC purposes when, as a minimum, they cause injury to persons or damage to physical objects.[24] Knut Dörmann takes a different position. He points out that the definition of a military object in Article 52(2) of Additional Protocol I refers to the neutralisation of an object as a possible outcome of an attack, leading him to conclude that disabling an object should also qualify as an attack.[25]

---

[20] Ibid., See Commentary to Rule 22, para 11.

[21] Ibid., Commentary to Rule 35, para 4.

[22] Cf. ibid., Commentary to Rule 22, paras 12–15.

[23] Pilloud and de Preux 1987, paras 1879–1880.

[24] Schmitt 2002a, pp. 376–377; Dinstein 2012, p. 264.

[25] Dörmann 2005, pp. 142–143.

The Manual takes the former approach. In Rule 30 it defines a cyber attack as a 'cyber operation, whether offensive or defensive, that is reasonably expected to cause injury or death to persons or damage or destruction to objects'. Nonetheless, there appears to have been some debate within the International Group of Experts as to whether interference with the functionality of an object could amount to an attack in the absence of physical destruction. According to the Commentary, the majority took the view that such interference qualifies as damage, and thus the operation constitutes an attack, 'if restoration of functionality requires replacement of physical components'; however, there was disagreement as to whether the requirement of damage was met where functionality could be restored by re-installing the operating system (i.e., 'replacement' of the software).[26]

In accordance with its general approach of insisting on physical detrimental effects, the Manual takes the position that the destruction of data qualifies as an attack only when it 'results in the injury or death of individuals or damage or destruction of physical objects'.[27] This approach is not entirely unproblematic. Permanent destruction of data can have significant ramifications, even though falling short of physical violence. For example, wiping out the data in the entire State's banking system or patent database by means of a computer virus may have far more deleterious consequences than the physical destruction of a single data centre. Yet, under the Manual, the former would be an attack only if it can be demonstrated that some physical injury occurred, whereas the second is undoubtedly an attack. This peculiarity is remedied slightly by the admission that causing 'serious illness and severe mental suffering that are tantamount to injury'[28] would qualify as an attack. Thus terrorising the civilian population by means of cyber operations might rise to the level of attack. Accordingly, were the cyber operations against the banking system serious enough to cause widespread panic among the population, the argument could be made that the mental suffering of the civilians was such as to qualify the operation as an attack.

The Manual arguably fails to take the destruction of data and the value of digital assets sufficiently seriously. To a large extent this reflects the current conceptual framework of LOAC, which has not entirely caught up with the development of the concepts of intellectual property and intangible assets.[29] But the Manual's general position on the destruction of data seems curious in view of the fact that in Rule 82 it regards the destruction of digital cultural property perfectly governable by LOAC. Certainly, the use of the term 'property' in the context of cultural treasures may more readily allow for the incorporation of intangible assets, but the time has perhaps come to seriously consider whether an

---

[26] *Tallinn Manual* 2013, Commentary to Rule 30, para 10.

[27] Ibid., Commentary to Rule 30, para 6.

[28] Ibid., Commentary to Rule 30, para 8.

[29] See, e.g,, Schmitt 2011, p. 96, noting that 'data should not be characterized as an object in itself'. But see also US Department of Defense 2011, p. 4, recognising the threat to intellectual property as possibly the most pervasive cyber threat today.

'object' for the purposes of the targeting rules in LOAC necessarily needs to have corporeal existence.

3.5 Limitations on Cyber Operations Not Amounting to Attacks

Especially in view of the comparatively stringent interpretation of the notion of attack—which incidentally would mean that true cyber attacks would be few and far between—it becomes imperative to consider how LOAC regulates cyber operations that fall below this threshold.

Article 48 of Additional Protocol I codifies the principle of distinction by stipulating that parties to a conflict 'shall direct their operations only against military objectives'. This suggests that military operations undertaken in the context of an armed conflict which do not amount to attacks, should nonetheless be conducted against military objectives alone. Schmitt has argued otherwise. Largely relying on the fact that Article 48 appears in the context of a series of provisions that prohibit specific types of attack, he has suggested that cyber operations 'are permissible against non-military objectives, such as the population'.[30] This position has been criticised by other commentators as inconsistent with the express language of Additional Protocol I and the fact that other provisions of the Protocol use the term 'operations' in a sense wider than 'attack'.[31]

The Manual adopts Schmitt's position. It stipulates in Rule 31 that '[t]he principle of distinction applies to cyber attacks' and the Commentary largely reiterates Schmitt's views.[32] At the same time, the Manual adopts the principle of precaution found in Article 57(1) of Additional Protocol I[33] by stipulating in Rule 52 that '[d]uring hostilities involving cyber operations, constant care shall be taken to spare the civilian population, individual civilians, and civilian objects'. The Commentary to this Rule expressly states that hostilities are not limited to (cyber) attacks.[34] How these rules and their interpretations should be reconciled remains something of a mystery. On the one hand, it appears permissible to direct cyber operations short of an attack against the civilian population, but on the other hand, parties to the conflict must, in the words of the Commentary, 'be continuously sensitive to the effects of their activities on the civilian population and civilian objects, and to seek to avoid any unnecessary effects thereon'.[35]

---

30 Schmitt 2002a, p. 378.

31 See Harrison Dinniss 2011.

32 *Tallinn Manual* 2013, Commentary to Rule 31, para 5.

33 'In the conduct of military operations, constant care shall be taken to spare the civilian population, civilians and civilian objects.'

34 *Tallinn Manual* 2013, Commentary to Rule 52, para 2.

35 Ibid., Commentary to Rule 52, para 4.

3.6 Military Occupation and Neutrality

Since LOAC developed in response to events in actual physical battlespaces (on land, on or under the sea, in the air) the notion that attacks can be undertaken virtually, albeit with devastating physical consequences, raises the spectre of at least some novel consequences for the application of LOAC. Two examples in the Manual are illustrative of the ways in which cyber warfare impacts upon the specific rules of the *jus in bello*—the law of military occupation and the law of neutrality.

In relation to military occupation, the authors of the Manual are quick to point out that there is no legal concept of the occupation of cyberspace.[36] Military occupation occurs where the military forces of one State exercise effective authority and control over all or part of the physical territory of a foreign State without the territorial State's consent.[37] Occupation ends whenever the hostile military force ceases to exercise effective authority and control over foreign physical territory and it necessarily follows that occupation does not exist in the absence of the unauthorized exercise of authority over foreign physical territory.[38] The Manual claims correctly that 'cyber operations cannot alone suffice to establish or maintain the degree of authority over territory necessary to constitute occupation'[39] and, instead, discusses the application of LOAC rules to cyber operations conducted by the occupying power (to establish or to maintain the occupation) or to operations conducted against the occupying power (to disrupt its occupation). So, in relation to the law of military occupation, the advent of cyber warfare is not a game changer because an occupation is so fundamentally dependent upon physical reality—on the exercise of effective authority over physical foreign territory. Cyber warfare may well raise some novel legal issues in the day-to-day administration of an occupation, but it does not challenge the enduring relevance of the existing legal framework.

The law of neutrality, like the law of military occupation, only applies in situations of international armed conflict.[40] Neutrality regulates the relationships between a State (or States) that has (have) chosen to remain 'neutral'—to not join the armed conflict on either side—and the parties to the international armed conflict. The authors of the Manual explain three distinct objectives of the law of neutrality to:

> (i) protect neutral states and their citizens against the conflict's harmful effects; (ii) safeguard neutral rights, such as engaging in commerce on the high seas; and (iii) protect parties to the conflict against action or inaction on the part of neutral states that benefits their enemy.[41]

---

[36] See ibid., Chapter VI, 'Occupation', para 3.

[37] Article 42, 1907 Hague Regulations.

[38] Ibid.

[39] Ibid.

[40] See, e.g., Heintschel von Heinegg 2012.

[41] *Tallinn Manual* 2013, Chapter VII, 'Neutrality', para 3.

The Manual concedes that the historical development of the law of neutrality was predicated upon physical acts of entry into or exit from a State's territory. The emergence of virtual reality challenges such basic assumptions. Neutral States are obliged, for example, not to allow the use of their physical territory for belligerent acts in support of one or more parties to an international armed conflict[42] but the exercise of effective control over physical territory (demarcated by recognised international borders) is rendered far less relevant in cyberspace where the entire globe is interconnected. Now, for example, 'a single email message sent from belligerent territory may be routed through neutral cyber infrastructure before reaching its intended destination; the sender or owner of the neutral cyber infrastructure cannot necessarily control the route it takes'.[43] The Manual's commentary to Rule 93 explicitly proposes a teleological approach to interpretation of the 1907 Hague Convention V by: 'adapting the object and purpose of Hague Convention V to cyber operations, a neutral State may not allow a party to the conflict to use its pre-existing cyber infrastructure on neutral territory for military purposes or to establish any new cyber infrastructure for such purposes'.[44]

The authors of the Manual urge caution in any adoption of automatic presumptions of violation of obligations by neutral States in relation to cyber traffic routed through their physical infrastructure. The rationale for this expression of caution is that a violation of a neutral State's obligations requires an element of fault—that in the absence of any malice on the part of a neutral State in relation to a belligerent use of its cyber infrastructure, there is no notion of strict liability. The articulation of Rule 93 introduces a fault element that is not explicit in Article 5 of Hague Convention V: a neutral State 'may not *knowingly* allow the exercise of belligerent rights by the parties to the conflict from cyber infrastructure located in its territory or under its exclusive control'. In the Commentary to Rule 93 the Manual explains the prevailing view of the International Group of Experts that the knowledge element (actual or construed) reflects customary international law.

3.7 Concluding Remarks

The process adopted in the Manual is to state the rule of international law as it applies to cyber operations and then to provide extensive commentary on that rule. The Commentary reflects any disagreement between the experts and regularly identifies the majority view as well as any minority views. That approach is helpful and welcome.

---

42 See Article 5 (prohibiting neutral States from allowing any of the acts referred to in Articles 2-4) of Hague Convention (V) Respecting the Rights and Duties of Neutral Powers and Persons in Case of War on Land, 18 October 1907, (1908) 2 AJIL Supp. 117–127, *entered into force* 26 January 1910.

43 *Tallinn Manual* 2013, Chapter VII, 'Neutrality', para 4.

44 Ibid., Commentary to Rule 93, para 2.

But the extent of any articulation of alternative views of the law applicable to a particular aspect of cyber warfare is limited to the selected experts and those experts are not representative of the nations of the world. Given the extent of allegations of Russian and Chinese cyber attacks for example, it seems particularly restrictive not to have included experts from both nations. One can perhaps understand the sensitivities of a lack of enthusiasm on the part of the host institution for the project—the Tallinn-based NATO Cyber Co-operative Defence Centre of Excellence—for Russian expert involvement in the preparation of the Manual. Estonia, of all countries, knows more of the potential damage from cyber-attack in the aftermath of their 2007 experiences. But any such sensitivity about Russian involvement in the process does not explain the lack of Chinese (or other Asian, Latin American, Middle Eastern or African) participation in Manual drafting process. This palpable lack of diversity among the expert group must raise questions about just how comprehensive the views canvassed in the Commentary really are.

In any event, the editors of the Manual and the International Group of Experts involved in its drafting have done a valuable service in developing a comprehensive statement of the applicability of LOAC to cyber operations. While we think that this statement reflects some imperfections, the existence of such a consolidated work has undoubted value. Some parallels can be drawn with the ICRC's *Customary International Humanitarian Law* study: while the study has been subjected to all manner of criticism, it has become a convenient starting point for discussions of the customary status of various LOAC rules. With respect to the application of LOAC to cyber operations, the Tallinn Manual is likely to become such a 'standard work', raising the profile of the issues it covers and serving as a catalyst for further study and debate.

References

Byström K (ed) (2005) *International Expert Conference on Computer Network Attacks and the Applicability of International Humanitarian Law, 17–19 November 2004, Stockholm, Sweden: Proceedings of the Conference*. Swedish National Defence College, Stockholm.

Dinstein Y (2012) 'The Principle of Distinction and Cyber War in International Armed Conflicts', *Journal of Conflict & Security Law* 17:261–277.

Dörmann K (2005) 'The Applicability of the Additional Protocols to Computer Network Attacks: An ICRC Approach', in Byström K (ed.), *International Expert Conference on Computer Network Attacks and the Applicability of International Humanitarian Law, 17–19 November 2004, Stockholm, Sweden: Proceedings of the Conference*. Swedish National Defence College, Stockholm, 139–153.

Doswald-Beck L (1995) 'San Remo Manual on International Law Applicable to Armed Conflict at Sea', *International Review of the Red Cross* no 309, 35:583–594.

Harrison Dinniss HA (2011) 'Attacks and Operations: The Debate over Computer Network "Attacks"', presented at *New Technologies, Old Law: Applying International Humanitarian Law in a New Technological Age*, Hebrew University of Jerusalem, 28–29 November 2011.

Harrison Dinniss HA (2012) *Cyber Warfare and the Laws of War*. Cambridge University Press, Cambridge.

Hathaway OA, Crootof R, Levitz P, Nix H, Nowlan A, Perdue W, and Spiegel J (2012) 'The Law of Cyber-Attack', *California Law Review* 100:817–885.

Heintschel von Heinegg W (2012) 'Neutrality in Cyberspace', in Czosseck C, Ottis R and Ziolkowski K (eds), (2012) *4th International Conference on Cyber Conflict: Proceedings*. NATO CCD COE Publications, Tallinn, 35–46.

Kodar E (2012) 'Applying the Law of Armed Conflict to Cyber Attacks: From the Martens Clause to Additional Protocol I', in Liivoja R and Saumets A (eds), *The Law of Armed Conflict: Historical and Contemporary Perspectives*, Tartu University Press: Tartu, 107–132.

Manual on International Law Applicable to Air and Missile Warfare (2009) Harvard Program on Humanitarian Policy and Conflict Research.

Manual on the Law of Non-International Armed Conflict (2006) International Institute of Humanitarian Law, San Remo.

Melzer N (2011) 'Cyber Operations and Jus in Bello', *Disarmament Forum* no 4, 3–17.

Pilloud C and de Preux J (1987) 'Protocol I—Article 49—Definition of Attacks and Scope of Application', in Sandoz Y, Swinarski C, Zimmermann B (eds), *Commentary on the Additional Protocols to the Geneva Conventions*. ICRC & Martinus Nijhoff, Geneva, 601–608.

San Remo Manual on International Law Applicable to Armed Conflicts at Sea (1994) International Institute of Humanitarian Law, San Remo.

Schmitt MN (2002a) 'Wired Warfare: Computer Network Attack and Jus in Bello', *International Review of the Red Cross* no 846, 84:365–399.

Schmitt MN (ed) (2002b) *Computer Network Attack and International Law*. Naval War College Press, Newport, RI.

Schmitt MN (2011) 'Cyber Operations and the *Jus in Bello*: Key Issues', in Pedrozo RA and Wollschlaeger DP (eds), *International Law and the Changing Character of War*. Naval War College Press, Newport, RI, 89–110.

Schmitt MN (2012) 'Classification of Cyber Conflict', *Journal of Conflict and Security Law* 17:245-260.

Tallinn Manual on the International Law Applicable to Cyber Warfare (2013) Cambridge University Press, Cambridge.

Tikk E, Kaska K and Vihul L (2010) *International Cyber Incidents: Legal Considerations*. CCD COE Publications, Tallinn.

Turns D (2012) 'Cyber Warfare and the Notion of Direct Participation in Hostilities', *Journal of Conflict and Security Law* 17:279–297.

UK Ministry of Defence (2004) *The Manual of the Law of Armed Conflict*. Oxford University Press, Oxford.

US Department of Defense (2011) *Strategy for Operating in Cyberspace*.

Part II
Child Soldiers and the Lubanga case

Chapter 4
Between Consolidation and Innovation: The International Criminal Court's Trial Chamber Judgment in the *Lubanga* Case

Sylvain Vité

Contents

Sylvain Vité teaches Human Rights Law at Bilkent University in Ankara, Turkey. The author would like to thank Yvette Issar for her support in editing this article.

S. Vité (✉)
Bilkent University, Ankara, Turkey
e-mail: sylvain_vite@hotmail.com

T. D. Gill et al. (eds.), *Yearbook of International Humanitarian Law 2012*,
Yearbook of International Humanitarian Law 15, DOI: 10.1007/978-90-6704-924-5_4,

4.1 Introduction

The judgment delivered by Trial Chamber I of the International Criminal Court on 14 March 2012 in the case of *The Prosecutor v. Thomas Lubanga Dyilo*[1] was welcomed by a number of experts as a landmark decision.[2] Not only was the judgment the first ever adopted by the Court, thus marking a new step in the operationalization of the Rome Statute, but it also provided an opportunity for addressing a number of procedural and substantive issues that are essential to the progressive development of both international criminal and humanitarian law.

This chapter does not seek to provide a comprehensive analysis of all these issues.[3] It focuses instead on the core of the judgment, i.e., the definitions of the war crimes for which Thomas Lubanga Dyilo was convicted (Sect. 4.3). The Trial Chamber found that the accused was guilty of conscripting and enlisting children under 15 into an armed group, namely the *Forces Patriotiques Pour la Libération du Congo* (UPC/FPLC), and of using them to participate actively in hostilities. These crimes occurred in the Ituri region of the Democratic Republic of the Congo from September 2002 to August 2003. This article also examines how the Trial Chamber addressed the preliminary question of the characterization of the situation during the relevant period (Sect. 4.2). The judgment provides essential insight into the Trial Chamber's understanding of the notion of armed conflict within the framework of the Rome Statute.

4.2 Characterization of the Situation

A detailed part of the *Lubanga* judgment analyzed the nature of the context in which the relevant facts occurred. The Trial Chamber looked into whether the situation could be characterized as an armed conflict, and if so, whether this conflict should be classified as international or non-international. This is a necessary prerequisite for determining whether the jurisdiction of the Court extended to cover the facts of the case, and also, which of the two potentially relevant Articles of the Rome Statute applied to the situation. The Chamber stressed that "[t]he relevant

[1] International Criminal Court, Trial Chamber I, Situation in the Democratic Republic of the Congo in the case of *The Prosecutor v. Thomas Lubanga Dyilo*, 14 March 2012, ICC-01/04-01/06-2842.

[2] *See, e.g.*, Committee on the Rights of the Child, *Press statement—Committee on the Rights of the Child welcomes the ICC ruling in the Lubanga Case,* Geneva, 15 March 2012; Office of the Special Representative of the Secretary-General for Children and Armed Conflict, *SRSG Coomaraswamy welcomes the International Criminal Court's first verdict—the conviction of Thomas Lubanga for child recruitment*, 14 March 2012.

[3] For a comprehensive review of the legal issues addressed in the *Lubanga* judgment, see Ambos 2012, pp. 115–153.

Elements of Crimes require that the alleged criminal conduct 'took place in the context of and was associated with an [...] armed conflict'" (para 531).

The Trial Chamber embarked on its analysis by first employing interpretative efforts to clarify the notion of armed conflict. It recalled the fact that neither the Rome Statute nor the Elements of Crimes provide a definition of this notion (para 531). Likewise, there is no such definition under existing treaties of international humanitarian law, although the existence of an armed conflict is required to trigger the application of these treaties, setting limits as to their scope of application (para 532). The Trial Chamber then turned to international jurisprudence seeking further guidance on this matter, and paid special attention to the case law of the ICTY. The Trial Chamber endorsed, in particular, the Tribunal's well-known definition, which states that "an armed conflict exists whenever there is a resort to armed force between States or protracted violence between governmental authorities and organized armed groups or between such groups within a State" (para 533).[4] This definition has been used by a number of other international bodies since,[5] and its adoption in the *Lubanga* judgment further confirms a now well-established trend.

Having established this broader framework, the Trial Chamber then developed a more detailed analysis in three main steps: it reaffirmed the legal basis for distinguishing between international and non-international armed conflicts (Sect. 4.2.1); it examined whether the context of the case under consideration represented a non-international armed conflict, in which case Article 8(2)(e)(vii) of the Rome Statute would apply (Sect. 4.2.2); after responding positively to the previous question, it evaluated whether the intervention of foreign forces during the period under examination had "internationalized" the conflict, in which case Article 8(2)(b)(xxvi) of the Statute would apply (Sect. 4.2.3).

4.2.1 *Categories of Armed Conflicts*

The distinction between international and non-international armed conflicts, which dates back to the origin of the law of armed conflicts, has been challenged by scholars on a number of occasions.[6] In this debate, the Trial Chamber took a very clear position. It stated that "the international/non-international distinction is not only an established part of the international law of armed conflict, but more importantly it is enshrined in the relevant statutory provisions of the Rome Statute framework" (para 539). The Trial Chamber did not rely solely on the Rome Statute to support this statement (which would have been sufficient for the

---

[4] ICTY, *Prosecutor v. Tadić*, Case no. IT-94-1-AR72, Appeals Chamber, Decision on the Defense Motion for Interlocutory Appeal on Jurisdiction, 2 October 1995, para 70.

[5] *See, e.g.*, Commission of Inquiry on Lebanon, Report pursuant to Human Rights Council resolution S-2/1, A/HRC/3/2, 23 November 2006, para 51; ICRC 2008.

[6] *See., e.g.*, Dupuy and Leonetti 1979, p. 258; Reisman and Silk 1988, p. 465. More recently, see also Stewart 2003, pp. 313–349.

purposes of its judgment), but it also insisted that the distinction is a fundamental feature of international humanitarian law. Despite the growing convergence of the two legal frameworks governing each category of armed conflict, significant differences indeed remain. The most important difference relates to the combatant privilege, which only applies in international armed conflicts. Those enjoying this privilege are entitled to immunity from domestic prosecution for lawful acts of war. If captured by the enemy, they are considered prisoners of war and, as such, must be released and repatriated without delay after the end of hostilities.[7] They are not, however, immune from prosecution for war crimes and other violations of international humanitarian law. In non-international armed conflicts, combatant privilege does not exist. Those participating in hostilities remain subject to prosecution for violations of domestic law even if they fully respect the rules of international humanitarian law.

Pursuing this reasoning, the Trial Chamber also recognized that different types of armed conflicts may occur at the same time and on the same territory, depending on the nature of the parties involved in particular confrontations (para 540). If, for instance, foreign States become involved in an existing non-international armed conflict, any of the following different scenarios may be envisaged: Fighting may take place between the forces of the territorial State and those of an intervening State, between intervening States taking action on both sides of the front line, between government forces (of the territorial State or of a third State) and non-governmental armed groups or between such groups only. In other words, as the Trial Chamber confirmed, international and non-international armed conflicts may "coexist" within the same territory (para 540). The Trial Chamber thus implicitly recognized that different legal frameworks may apply to the distinct conflicts occurring in such situations. Inter-State confrontations are governed by the law of international armed conflict, whereas other scenarios are subject to the law of non international armed conflict.

This approach is based on well-established international jurisprudence. The Trial Chamber itself invoked the judgment of the International Court of Justice (ICJ) in the Nicaragua Case (1986) (para 540, note 1644), which laid the basis for the theory of a fragmented application of international humanitarian law. In its analysis of the conflict, the ICJ differentiated between, on the one hand, the conflict opposing the Nicaraguan government and the armed opposition ("the Contras") and, on the other, the conflict opposing that same government and the United States of America.[8] Other international bodies, such as the ICTY, have applied this theory since then.[9]

---

[7] GCIII, Article 118(1).

[8] ICJ, *Military and Paramilitary Activities in and against Nicaragua (Nicaragua v. United States of America),* Judgment, ICJ Reports 1986, para 219. See Vité 2009, p. 86.

[9] ICTY, *Prosecutor v. Tadić*, IT-94-1-A, Appeals Judgment, 15 July 1999, para 84. A number of scholars also support this approach (see Schindler 1982, pp. 255–264).

This approach suggests that foreign intervention in a purely internal armed conflict would not necessarily automatically confer an international character on such a conflict. The classification of the situation in this case will depend on the relationship between the intervening troops and the non-state armed groups that are parties to the conflict, and on the degree of influence the former may potentially exert over the latter. This is a key issue that the Trial Chamber further analyzed in another part of the judgment (see Sect. 4.2.3). However, before addressing this question, the Trial Chamber first assessed whether there was, in actual fact, an armed conflict of a non-international character occurring on the territory during the relevant period.

4.2.2 Non-international Armed Conflict

For this purpose, the Trial Chamber began its reasoning by providing its understanding of the notion of non-international armed conflicts within the meaning of Article 8(2)(f) of the Rome Statute. This is the provision that sets out the scope of application of the previous paragraph of the Statute (Article 8(2)(e)), which itself enumerates a list of serious violations of the laws and customs of war, including the conscription and enlistment of children under 15 into armed forces or groups, or their use to participate actively in hostilities (Article 8(2)(e)(vii)). Article 8(2)(f) states that the armed conflicts to which it applies are those "that take place in the territory of a State when there is protracted armed conflict between governmental authorities and organized armed groups or between such groups".

To fully understand this paragraph, it must be compared to Article 8(2)(d) of the Rome Statute, which defines the scope of application of another set of war crimes, namely "serious violations of article 3 common to the four Geneva Conventions of 12 August 1949" (Article 8(2)(c)). While both provisions deal with offences committed during "armed conflicts not of an international character", Article 8(2)(f), unlike Article 8(2)(d), requires an additional element, stating that such conflict must be "protracted".[10] This difference between the two provisions gives rise to the question of whether Article 8(2)(f), by referring explicitly to the criterion of duration ("protracted armed conflict"), merely clarifies the terms of para (2)(d), without creating a separate category of armed conflict, or whether it instead applies to a distinct category of non-international armed conflict, thus defining a distinct field of application for the list of crimes in Article 8(2)(e). This question has been debated amongst scholars, who hold diverging views on the matter.[11]

---

[10] For an analysis of the notion of non-international armed conflict under both provisions, see Dörmann Dörmann 2003, pp. 384–389 and 441–442.

[11] For a reminder of this debate, see Schabas 2010, pp. 205–206; Vité 2009, pp. 80–83; Sivakumaran 2009, pp. 371–380.

While it did not address this question directly, the Trial Chamber did make a number of comments, which serve to shed new light on this debate. It is important to note in this regard that the Chamber referred to Additional Protocol II governing non-international armed conflicts[12] as the main source for interpreting Article 8(2)(f). This is a coherent approach as this provision relates to a list of war crimes, which, to a certain extent, amount to violations of the Protocol. By contrast, Article 8(2)(d), as previously mentioned, focuses on serious violations of Article 3 common to the four Geneva Conventions of 1949. The Chamber's approach is also consistent with the drafting history of the Rome Statute. Article 8(2)(f) was originally conceived as a provision covering serious violations of Additional Protocol II. Explicit reference to the Protocol in the draft text of the provision was replaced during the negotiations with the notion of "protracted armed conflict".[13] This would therefore suggest that both Additional Protocol II and Article 8(2)(f) have an identical scope of application.

Although it adopted this approach, the Trial Chamber did not seem completely at ease with this reasoning. While referring to Additional Protocol II as the main legal source for interpreting Article 8(2)(f), it immediately stressed that this provision "only requires the existence of a 'protracted' conflict between 'organised armed groups'" (para 536). This implies that elements of the restrictive scope of application of Additional Protocol II should not be transposed to Article 8(2)(f). In the Chamber's views, these elements include the requirements that organized armed groups involved in the conflict must be "under responsible command" and "exercise such control over a part of [the] territory as to enable them to carry out sustained and concerted military operations and to implement this Protocol" (para 536).[14] It is surprising in this respect that the Trial Chamber did not mention another restrictive element, namely that Additional Protocol II only applies to armed conflicts opposing State armed forces and dissident armed forces or other organized armed groups. The Protocol does not extend to armed conflicts between such groups only. The Trial Chamber however implicitly admitted that this restrictive element is not part of Article 8(2)(f), when it referred to the jurisprudence of the ICTY as an additional source for clarifying the notion of armed

[12] Protocol Additional to the Geneva Conventions of 12 August 1949a, and relating to the Protection of Victims of Non-International Armed Conflicts (Protocol II), 8 June 1977.

[13] The wording of para (2)(f) is the outcome a compromise between delegations in favor of introducing a list of war crimes applicable to non-international armed conflicts and those against the introduction of such a list. An initial proposal in the direction of such a compromise was submitted by the 'Bureau of the Committee of the Whole' and consisted of limiting the field of application of the crimes mentioned in para (2)(e) by taking up the restrictive criteria elaborated in Article 1(2) of APII (A/CONF.183/C.1/L.59). As an agreement could not be reached on that proposal, Sierra Leone suggested the text of para (2)(f) that was ultimately retained, with a reference to the notion of "protracted armed conflict". The aim was to appease the delegations that were reluctant to introduce war crimes into the law of non-international armed conflict, while avoiding a threshold of application as high as that in APII. Other delegations were indeed opposed to inserting such a threshold in the Rome Statute (A/CONF.183/C.1/SR.35, para 8).

[14] Additional Protocol II, Article 1(1).

conflict for the purposes of the Rome Statute. The Tribunal has indeed clearly stated that non-international armed conflicts include those that involve "protracted violence between governmental authorities and organized armed groups *or between such groups* within a State" (emphasis added).[15]

Thus, while relying on Article 1 of Additional Protocol II as the main source for interpreting Article 8(2)(f) of the Rome Statute, the Trial Chamber nonetheless set aside some of the specificities of the Protocol, i.e., those requirements that result in a narrow scope of application of this instrument. It would seem that the Trial Chamber felt obliged to refer to Additional Protocol II in order to be consistent with the internal structure and drafting history of Article 8 of the Rome Statute, but that it simultaneously sought to ensure that both sub-para 2(d) and 2(f) of this provision are understood to address the same types of situations. Indeed Article 1 of Additional Protocol II without its restrictive elements has the same scope of application as Article 3 common to the four Geneva Conventions of 1949. The Trial Chamber's reasoning would therefore seem to support the views of those who consider that there is no difference between the thresholds of application of the two sub-paragraphs of the Rome Statute discussed above.

This conclusion is further confirmed in looking at the criteria used by the Trial Chamber to determine whether the situation under consideration actually amounted to an armed conflict in the sense of Article 8(2)(f). The Chamber stated that two conditions must be fulfilled in this regard, namely a certain level of "intensity", and the involvement of "organized armed groups" (para 536). In order to assess each of these conditions, the Chamber identified "factors" which could be potentially relevant, but which are not, in themselves, *sine qua non* requirements for determining the existence of intensity and organization. These factors include, for instance, the "command structure and rules" of a group, or its "ability to plan military operations and put them in effect" (organization). They also include "the seriousness of attacks and potential increase in armed clashes", or "their spread over territory and over a period of time" (intensity) (paras 537–538). These two conditions and the related factors are taken from the jurisprudence of the ICTY to which the Trial Chamber makes explicit reference.[16] Yet these criteria were developed by the Tribunal in order to distinguish non-international armed conflicts "from banditry, unorganised and short–lived insurrections, or terrorist activities, which are not subject to international humanitarian law".[17] They relate to all forms of non-international armed conflicts, and as such,

---

[15] ICTY, *Prosecutor v. Tadić*, IT-94-1-AR72, Decision on the Defense Motion for Interlocutory Appeal on Jurisdiction, 2 October 1995, para 70.

[16] The Trial Chamber explains that the lists of factors provided in its judgment are not exhaustive. Other factors may be found in case law of the ICTY. See ICTY, *Prosecutor v. Boškoski et al.*, IT- 04-82, Trial Judgment, 10 July 2008, paras 173–206. See also ICTY, *Prosecutor v. Limaj et al.*, IT-03-66-T, Trial Judgment, 30 November 2005, paras 83–174; ICTY, *Prosecutor v. Haradinaj et al.*, IT-04-84-T, Trial Judgment, 3 April 2008, paras 37–60.

[17] ICTY, *Prosecutor v. Limaj et al.*, ibid., para 84.

are not meant to define a specific category among these conflicts corresponding to a higher threshold of application.[18]

As for the facts, the Trial Chamber noted that the military wing of the *Forces Patriotiques Pour la Libération du Congo* (UPC/FPLC), the armed group for which Thomas Lubanga Dyilo was commander-in-chief, "was organised with a leadership structure that was capable of training troops as well as imposing discipline, and it carried out sustained military operations in Ituri during the relevant timeframe" (para 543). It further noted that the FPLC had been engaged in prolonged hostilities against other organized armed groups during the period of the charges (paras 544–547). Lastly, the Trial Chamber remarked that no "peaceful settlement" between the parties had been reached despite international efforts to put an end to the conflict (para 548). It therefore concluded that the conditions necessary to classify these confrontations as a non-international armed conflict were fulfilled during the relevant period (para 550).

However, the characterization of the situation in the *Lubanga* judgment did not end with this analysis. The Trial Chamber went further, with a view to determining whether the involvement of foreign forces had affected the nature of the situation, potentially turning it into an international armed conflict.

4.2.3 Internationalization of a Non-international Armed Conflict

An international armed conflict[19] may occur in two different ways: (i) when States directly resort to armed force against each other; and (ii) when a State exercises a sufficient amount of control over a non-state armed group, which is itself a party to an armed conflict involving another State. The Trial Chamber, citing Pre Trial Chamber II, in this way noted that "an international armed conflict exists in case of armed hostilities between States through their respective armed forces or other actors acting on behalf of the State" (para 541).

Though the formulation of the Trial Chamber is correct in distinguishing these two forms of international armed conflict, the statement that such situations are characterized by "armed hostilities" may be misleading, as this may be interpreted as requiring an excessively high threshold of violence. The general view is that international armed conflicts, as opposed to non-international armed conflicts, do not require a particular threshold of armed violence to be reached. The ICRC commentary to the Geneva Conventions of 1949 defines an international armed conflict as "[a]ny difference arising between two States and leading to the

[18] This conclusion was already anticipated by Sivakumaran on the basis of the decision of the Pre-Trial Chamber I on the confirmation of charges; see Sivakumaran 2009, pp. 377–380.

[19] Rome Statute, Article 8(2)(a) and (b).

intervention of armed forces".[20] It further explains that "[i]t makes no difference how long the conflict lasts, or how much slaughter takes place".[21] The ICTY also reminds us that an international armed conflict exists, "whenever there is a resort to armed force between States".[22] The Tribunal further specifies that "*le recours à la force armée entre Etats suffit en soi à déclencher l'application du droit international humanitaire*".[23] It is true however, that this position has recently been challenged. Some argue that a distinction must be made between international armed conflicts (reaching a certain level of intensity) and other expressions of hostility between States, such as minor "incidents", "border clashes" or "skirmishes".[24] The Trial Chamber could therefore have expounded on its views on this issue, given its use of the phrase "armed hostilities between States".

It is not disputed however, that an assessment of the level of violence is necessary to determine whether foreign intervention has led to internationalization of internal armed conflicts. In such cases, the characterization of the situation as an international armed conflict requires the following two steps: first, it must be shown that the conditions of "organization" and "intensity" necessary to establish the existence of a non-international armed conflict have been met; second, it must be demonstrated that the level of control exercised by foreign forces over an organized armed group is sufficient to conclude that the conflict is, in fact, a confrontation between States. In other words, the classification of such a situation as an international armed conflict supposes a pre-existing non-international armed conflict, which in turn implies that the required threshold of intensity has been met.

As for the nature of the control exercised over the armed group, the Trial Chamber relied fully on the criteria developed by the ICTY. The Chamber considered that "the 'overall control' test is the correct approach" (para 541). Quoting the ICTY, it confirmed that the armed conflict becomes international when the foreign State "*has a role in organising, coordinating or planning the military actions* of the military group, in addition to financing, training and equipping or providing operational support to that group" (para 541).[25]

Regarding the facts, the Trial Chamber noted that there were a number of simultaneous conflicts in the region during the period covered by the charges, some of them including the UPC/FPLC (para 543). It considered, however, that

---

[20] Pictet 1952, p. 32. This sentence was also quoted by Pre-Trial Chamber I in the confirmation of charges. (Pre-Trial Chamber I, *Prosecutor v. Thomas Lubanga Dyilo*, Decision on the confirmation of charges, ICC-01/04-01/06-803-tEN, 29 January 2007, para 207).

[21] Pictet 1952, p. 32. For further details on the notion of international armed conflict in international criminal law, see Dörmann 2003, pp. 23–28.

[22] ICTY, *Prosecutor v. Tadić*, IT-94-1, Decision on the Defense Motion for Interlocutory Appeal on Jurisdiction, 2 October 1995, para 70.

[23] ICTY, *Prosecutor v. Delalić et al.* ("*Čelebići* Camp"), IT-96-21, Trial Judgment, 16 November 1998, para 184.

[24] This view was most notably developed in International Law Association 2010, pp. 28–32.

[25] This quote comes from ICTY, *Prosecutor v. Tadić*, IT-94-1-A, Appeals Judgment, 15 July 1999, para 137 (emphasis in the original).

there was no sufficient evidence supporting the view that the UPC/FPLC had acted under the "overall control" of any of the States involved in the relevant conflicts, namely Uganda, Rwanda or the Democratic Republic of the Congo (paras 551–567).[26] It thus concluded that "[s]ince the conflict to which the UPC/FPLC was a party was not 'a difference arising between two states' but rather protracted violence carried out by multiple non-state armed groups, it remained a non-international conflict notwithstanding any concurrent international armed conflict between Uganda and the DRC" (para 563). With this statement, the Trial Chamber changed the legal characterization of the facts adopted by the Pre-Trial Chamber I when confirming the charges. The latter had concluded that the conflict had been internationalized through the occupation of the Ituri region by the Ugandan army until 2 June 2003.[27]

4.3 Protection of Children Under 15

The most innovative developments in the *Lubanga* judgment relate to the criminalization of acts that seek to involve children as participants in armed conflict. The Trial Chamber undertook an in-depth analysis of Article 8(2)(e)(vii) of the Rome Statute, which states: "2. For the purpose of this Statute, 'war crimes' means: [...] (e) Other serious violations of the laws and customs applicable in armed conflicts not of an international character, within the established framework of international law, namely, any of the following acts: [...] (vii) *Conscripting or enlisting children under the age of fifteen years into armed forces or groups or using them to participate actively in hostilities*; [...]"(emphasis added).[28]

A large part of the judgment is dedicated to clarifying the meaning of the three types of criminal conduct referred to in this provision, and to assessing the extent to which these acts might be interconnected. To begin its analysis, the Trial Chamber recalled that the three relevant concepts are not defined in the Statutes, the Rules of Procedure or Evidence or the Elements of Crimes (para 600). The Trial Chamber therefore first endeavoured to provide its interpretation of the notions of conscripting and enlisting children under 15, and examined the relation between these two notions and the third, namely using children to participate actively in hostilities (Sect. 4.3.1). Secondly, the Trial Chamber provided its own

[26] This assessment has been questioned by K. Ambos. The author stresses that the Trial Chamber has itself recognized that parties to the non-international armed conflict had received support from States, namely the Democratic Republic of the Congo (providing support to the *Armée du people congolais* (APC)) and Uganda and Rwanda (providing support to the UPC/FPLC) (see Judgment, paras 553 and 554, 558) (Ambos 2012, pp. 115–153).

[27] Pre-Trial Chamber I, *Prosecutor v. Thomas Lubanga Dyilo*, Decision on the confirmation of charges, ICC-01/04-01/06-803-tEN, 29 January 2007, para 220.

[28] For detailed analyses of this provision, see Happold 2009 and Kurth 2010.

understanding of the third notion, and proposed new criteria for identifying those activities that amount to "active participation in hostilities" (Sect. 4.3.2).

With these objectives in view, the Trial Chamber recalled that the legal sources for interpreting Article 8(2)(e)(vii), as stipulated in Article 21 of the Statute, include "the established principles of the international law of armed conflict" adding that such interpretation must be "consistent with internationally recognized human rights" (para 600). More specifically, the Trial Chamber announced that it would rely on Article 4(3) of Additional Protocol II and Article 38 of the Convention on the Rights of the Child. Both instruments prohibit the recruitment of children under 15 and their participation in hostilities, although in different terms. Under the Protocol, all forms of participation in hostilities are prohibited without further specification, while the Convention only bans "direct" participation in hostilities.[29]

4.3.1 Conscripting or Enlisting Children into Armed Forces or Groups

With a view to clarifying the concepts of conscription and enlistment under Article 8(2)(e)(vii) of the Rome Statute, the Trial Chamber examined how these concepts relate to two other notions, namely "recruitment" (Sect. 4.3.1.1) and "use to participate actively in hostilities" (Sect. 4.3.1.2).

4.3.1.1 "Conscripting or Enlisting" Versus "Recruiting"

The Trial Chamber endorsed the definition proposed by Pre-Trial Chamber I,[30] according to which "'conscription' and 'enlistment' are both forms of recruitment, in that they refer to the incorporation of a boy or a girl under the age of 15 into an armed group, whether coercively (conscription) or voluntarily (enlistment)" (para 607). This definition indicates that there is no difference between the material scope of application of Article 8(2)(e)(vii) and that of the corresponding provisions of international humanitarian law and human rights law. "Conscripting" and "enlisting" are both forms of "recruitment", which is the notion used in these two legal frameworks, most notably in Additional Protocol II (Article 4(3)(c)) and the Convention on the Rights of the Child (Article 38(2)).[31] This is further confirmed

---

[29] Article 4(3)(c) of APII reads: "children who have not attained the age of fifteen years shall neither be recruited in the armed forces or groups nor allowed to take part in hostilities". Article 38(2) of CRC reads: "States Parties shall take all feasible measures to ensure that persons who have not attained the age of fifteen years do not take a direct part in hostilities".

[30] Pre-Trial Chamber I, *Prosecutor v. Thomas Lubanga Dyilo*, Decision on the confirmation of charges, ICC-01/04-01/06-803-tEN, 29 January 2007, para 246.

[31] International practice also shows that this prohibition has crystallized into customary international law, binding both States and non-state parties to armed conflicts. See Henckaerts

by the ICRC Commentary to Additional Protocol II, which states that "[t]he principle of non-recruitment also prohibits accepting voluntary enlistment".[32] The three bodies of law concerned therefore address the same practice, i.e. all forms of recruitment of children, even though different wording is used in the Rome Statute. There is no gap in the material scope of application of the rules prohibiting and punishing such conduct.[33]

While neither international humanitarian law nor human rights law envision consent-based recruitment of children under 15, the *Optional Protocol to the Convention on the Rights of the Child on the involvement of children in armed conflict* (OP-CAC) takes this practice into account for older children. This instrument prohibits States Parties from "compulsorily"[34] recruiting children under 18, but allows "voluntary recruitment" of such children under certain conditions.[35] The OP-CAC therefore follows the example of the Rome Statute in establishing two categories of recruitment.[36] It is not clear however whether these categories are fully identical under each of these instruments. While the OP-CAC refers to "compulsory" recruitment, the Trial Chamber preferred the notion of "coercive" recruitment. The Chamber did suggest however that both notions should have the same meaning in this context, stressing that the distinctive characteristic of conscription (as compared to enlistment) is "the added element of *compulsion*" (para 608) (emphasis added).

Concerning recruitment by non-state armed groups, however, the OP-CAC does not provide for such a distinction based on consent. It states that these groups "should not, under any circumstances, recruit or use in hostilities persons under

---

(Footnote 31 continued)
and Doswald-Beck 2005, pp. 482–485. For a different view on the notions used in the Rome Statute, see the dissenting opinion of Justice Robertson of the Special Court of Sierra Leone, who declared that "'(r)ecruitment' is a term which implies some active soliciting of 'recruits', i.e., to pressure or induce them to enlist: it is not synonymous with 'enlistment'" (Special Court for Sierra Leone, *Prosecutor v. Samuel Hinga Norman*, SCSL-2004-14-AR729E, Decision on preliminary motion based on lack of jurisdiction (child recruitment), 31 May 2004, Dissenting Opinion, para 27).

32 Sandoz et al. 1987, para 4557.

33 K. Ambos explains in this regard that "the interplay between (voluntary) enlistment and (compulsory) conscription prevents a punishability gap since any form of child recruitment (voluntary or not) is covered by the offence", Ambos Ambos 2012, p. 134. In this sense, see also Happold 2009, p. 587.

34 OP-CAC, Article 2.

35 For more details on the conditions and limits of voluntary recruitment by States into armed forces under the OP-CAC, see Article 3.

36 A similar distinction also exists under ILO *Convention 182 concerning the prohibition and immediate action for the elimination of the worst forms of child labour* (1999). This Convention mentions among the different forms of the worst forms of child labor "all forms of slavery or practices similar to slavery, such as the sale and trafficking of children, debt bondage and serfdom and forced or compulsory labour, *including forced or compulsory recruitment of children for use in armed conflict*" (emphasis added) (Article 3(a)).

the age of 18 years".[37] It allows no exception to the "straight 18 rule", although the exact implications of this rule have been discussed.[38] The OP-CAC further requires States Parties to take all feasible measures to prohibit and criminalize such practices by non-state armed groups.[39]

As for the reasons for separating "conscription" and "enlistment" of children in the Rome Statute, the Trial Chamber raised a somewhat audacious question. It examined whether the distinction between the two forms of recruitment is actually relevant for the purpose of criminal prosecution. External experts consulted on this question during the procedure gave a clear answer. One of them explained that "from a psychological point of view, children cannot give 'informed' consent when joining an armed group, because they have a limited understanding of the consequences of their choices; they do not control or fully comprehend the structures and forces they are dealing with; and they have inadequate knowledge and understanding of the short- and long-term consequences of their actions" (para 610). Perhaps even more categorically, the UN Special Representative of the Secretary-General for children and armed conflict clearly considers that "the line between voluntary and forced recruitment is [...] not only legally irrelevant but practically superficial in the context of children in armed conflict" (para 612). According to these experts, there is therefore no such thing as voluntary recruitment of children under 15. Any incorporation of such children into armed forces or groups therefore entails, to a certain extent, some form of coercion or deception.

While claiming to endorse these views, the Trial Chamber adopted a less straightforward position, creating confusion on the issue. On the one hand, it held that "it will frequently be the case that girls and boys under the age of 15 will be unable to give genuine and informed consent when enlisting in an armed group or force" (para 613). The Chamber therefore implied that, although "frequent", this is not necessarily always the case. It seemed to support the view that it may be possible in practice for children under 15 to genuinely consent to their recruitment. It thus suggested that the distinction between conscription and enlistment in the Statute is actually relevant.

On the other hand, the Chamber also declared that "the consent of a child to his or her recruitment does not provide an accused with a valid defence" (para 617).[40] The Chamber seemed to refer here to recruitment taken as a whole, irrespective of the two subcategories mentioned in Article 8(2)(b)(vii). This statement indicates that even though consent may be used in a specific case as a valid defense for the crime of conscription, as the lack of agreement is a constitutive part of the offense,[41]

[37] OP-CAC, Article 4.

[38] The nature of this prohibition, whether legally binding or not under the OP-CAC, has been debated. See Vité 2011, pp. 27–28.

[39] For further details on the OP-CAC, see Vandewiele 2006.

[40] This is also the position adopted by the Special Court for Sierra Leone. See for instance *Fofana and Kondewa*, SCSL-04-14-A, Appeals Chamber, 28 May 2008, para 140.

[41] For an interesting discussion on this point, see Ambos 2012, pp. 134–136.

those responsible for the incorporation of children into armed forces or groups would have to be prosecuted and punished anyway for enlistment.[42] The distinction based on the consent of the child thus does not appear to be relevant for the purpose of the judgment on the merits. It is significant in this regard that the Trial Chamber did not differentiate between conscription and enlistment when examining the facts of the case (para 759). It declared that the difference may be taken into consideration only at the following stage of the procedure, i.e., when determining the sentence and reparations (para 617).[43] The Trial Chamber therefore followed a more nuanced approach than the experts. It considered that free consent to recruitment by children under 15 is actually possible, although irrelevant in deciding whether the accused has committed a crime under Article 8(2)(e)(vii).

4.3.1.2 "Conscripting or Enlisting" Versus "Using to Participate Actively in Hostilities"

After emphasizing the close connection between the first two key concepts of Article 8(2)(e)(vii), the Trial Chamber examined the relation between these concepts and a third, namely the use of children under 15 to participate actively in hostilities. More precisely, the Chamber raised the question of whether the three offenses are characterized by a common purpose, i.e., the active participation of children in hostilities. It noted that the Rome Statute is not clear in this regard, as the last part of Article 8(2)(e)(vii) ("to participate actively in hostilities") could be interpreted as relating either to the three notions as a whole or to the last one only ("use"). Choosing the first interpretation, as suggested by the defense,[44] would considerably restrict the scope of application of the provision. In practice, children are very often recruited for purposes other than actual involvement in combat. The Trial Chamber suggested however, that the Elements of Crimes provides further guidance in this regard, as they draw a clearer separation between conscripting and

---

[42] See Graf 2012, p. 956.

[43] In its decision on the sentence of 10 July 2012, the Trial Chamber did not elaborate on this question (Trial Chamber I, *Situation in the Democratic Republic of the Congo in the case of the Prosecutor v. Thomas Lubanga Dyilo,* Decision on sentence pursuant to Article 76 of the Statute, ICC-01/04-01/06-2901, 10 July 2012). It simply indicated that criteria to assess the gravity of the crimes that were committed and thus to determine the sentence include "the nature of the unlawful behaviour and the means employed to execute the crime" (para 44). On this basis, Thomas Lubanga received different sentences for the crimes of conscripting and enlisting children under 15, respectively 13 and 12 years' imprisonment. In this gradation, the use of these children to participate actively in hostilities was considered the most serious crime and the related sentence was fixed at 14 years' imprisonment (para 98). These differences in sentencing were however criticized by Judge Odio Benito in her dissenting opinion annexed to the decision of 10 July 2012 (paras 24–27).

[44] The defense defines enlistment as "integration of a person as a soldier, within the context of an armed conflict, for the purposes of participating actively in the hostilities on behalf of the group" (ICC-01/04-01/06-2773-RED-tENG, para 34).

enlisting on the one hand and using children to participate actively in hostilities on the other. The first two offences are mentioned without further specification regarding their purpose, while active participation in hostilities is presented as a constitutive element of the third one only. The Chamber therefore concluded that "the status of a child under 15 who has been enlisted or conscripted is independent of any later period when he or she may have been 'used' to participate actively in hostilities, particularly given the variety of tasks that he or she may subsequently be required to undertake. Although it may often be the case that the purpose behind conscription and enlistment is to use children in hostilities, this is not a requirement of the Rome Statute" (para 609, see also para 620).[45] While the conclusion reached by the Trial Chamber is correct, the added value of resorting to the Elements of Crimes in this respect is not obvious. This instrument simply repeats what is already clear in the Rome Statute. The latter separates the different offences by using the word "or", as explained by the Chamber itself in the beginning of its reasoning.[46] The argument could therefore have been based on the plain wording of the Statute.

The Trial Chamber's conclusion, however, is extremely important for two main reasons. First it avoids any loopholes in the legal protection of children under 15 against conscription or enlistment. It ensures that all forms of recruitment can actually be prosecuted, whatever the purpose of the incorporation of the children into military structures. This position is in line with recent developments in international law related to the prevention of this phenomenon. A comprehensive approach to recruitment is followed most notably in the *Principles and Guidelines on Children Associated with Armed Forces or Armed Groups* (Paris Principles 2007). The use of the word "associated" in this instrument is intended to encompass all possible reasons for which children are integrated into armed forces or groups in practice. The Paris Principles apply to all children (in this case "any person less than 18 years of age in accordance with the Convention on the Rights of the Child"[47]) who have been recruited or used "in any capacity, including but not limited to children, boys, and girls used as fighters, cooks, porters, messengers, spies or for sexual purposes. It does not only refer to a child who is taking or has taken a direct part in hostilities".[48] Even though the Trial Chamber does not use the notion of "association" with armed forces or groups in its judgment,[49] its understanding of conscription and enlistment mirrors the definition given in the Paris Principles.[50]

---

[45] See Graf 2012, p. 959.

[46] On the same line, see Ambos 2012, p. 133.

[47] Paris Principles, para 2.0.

[48] Ibid., para 2.1.

[49] The Trial Chamber discusses the notion of association "with armed conflict" only (para 606).

[50] The Trial Chamber does not however answer the question whether recruitment for sexual purpose is included in Article 8(2)(e)(vii) of the Statute. Under the Paris Principles recruitment for such purpose is explicitly considered a form of "association" with armed forces or groups covered by the scope of application of this instrument.

The second reason that the Trial Chamber's interpretation is so important in practice is related to the third crime mentioned in Article 8(2)(e)(vii). The Chamber explains that the prohibition of the "use" of children for their active participation in hostilities does not require their previous conscription or enlistment (para 620). This means that seeking support from "civilians" under 15, i.e., children who are not members of armed forces or groups, for combat operations may amount to a war crime under Article 8(2)(e)(vii) of the Rome Statute. This happens in practice for instance when a boy or a girl living in the area of the hostilities is required, with or without coercion, to provide intelligence to the belligerents.

Thus, the recognition that both forms of recruitment on the one hand, and the "use" of children on the other, are separate offences ensures maximum protection for children against any form of involvement in military activities. This includes protection against recruitment for purposes other than combat, as well as against active participation in hostilities without previous incorporation into armed forces or groups.

4.3.2 Using Children to Participate Actively in Hostilities

The need to ensure the most comprehensive protection possible for children involved in armed conflict is also reflected in the reasoning that the Trial Chamber developed concerning the third offence of Article 8(2)(e)(vii) of the Rome Statute. The Chamber stressed that the crime of using children to participate actively in hostilities encompasses a range of activities, which are not limited to involvement in actual fighting. Quoting the *travaux préparatoires* of the Rome Statute, the Trial Chamber confirmed that "[t]he words 'using' and 'participate' have been adopted in order to cover both direct participation in combat and also active participation in military activities *linked* to combat such as scouting, spying, sabotage and the use of children as decoys, couriers or at military checkpoints. It would not cover *activities clearly unrelated to the hostilities* such as food deliveries to an airbase or the use of domestic staff in an officer's married accommodation" (emphasis added by the Trial Chamber).[51]

Thus, according to the Trial Chamber, "active participation in hostilities" for the purpose of Article 8(2)(e)(vii) is an intermediate notion between two other categories. On the one hand, it is broader than "direct participation in hostilities", as it includes some activities, which might be characterized as "indirect" participation in hostilities (Sect. 4.3.2.1). On the other hand, it does not include forms of

---

[51] UN Diplomatic Conference of Plenipotentiaries on the Establishment of an International Criminal Court, Report of the Preparatory Committee on the Establishment of an International Criminal Court, Draft Statute for the International Criminal Court, UN Doc. A/CONF.183/2/Add.1, 14 April 1998, p. 21, footnote 12.

support to armed forces or groups, which are "clearly unrelated to the hostilities" (Sect. 4.3.2.2).

4.3.2.1 "Active" Versus "Direct" Participation in Hostilities

The Trial Chamber stressed in its judgment that "[t]he use of the expression 'to participate actively in hostilities', as opposed to the expression 'direct participation' (as found in Additional Protocol I to the Geneva Conventions) was clearly intended to import a wide interpretation to the activities and roles that are covered by the offence of using children under 15 actively to participate in hostilities" (para 627). The Chamber further supported this statement by arguing that the notion of direct participation in hostilities is basically limited to functions "on the front line" (para 628).

This position, however, does not take into account that both the notions of active and direct participation in hostilities are not only used in relation to the involvement of children in military operations, but have broader implications both under international humanitarian law and criminal law. Common Article 3 to the Geneva Conventions of 1949 provides that all "[p]ersons taking no *active part in the hostilities*" (emphasis added) must be treated humanely in all circumstances. Similarly, the personal scope of application of Article 8(2)(c) of the Rome Statute covers "persons taking no active part in the hostilities". In addition, both treaty and customary international humanitarian law provide that civilians are protected against attack during armed conflict "unless and for such time as they take *a direct part in hostilities*" (emphasis added).[52] In the same way, the war crimes listed in the Rome Statute include, both in relation to international and non-international armed conflicts, "[i]ntentionally directing attacks against the civilian population as such or against *individual civilians not taking direct part in hostilities*" (emphasis added) (Article 8(2)(b)(i) and 8(2)(e)(i)).

Therefore, it is surprising that the Trial Chamber chose not to take these provisions and related practice into account, or even to mention them, in giving its own interpretation of the notions of active and direct participation in hostilities within the framework of Article 8(2)(e)(vii) of the Rome Statute. This is particularly surprising as the "chapeau" to this provision describes the crimes thereafter listed as "serious violations of the laws and customs applicable in armed conflicts not of an international character, *within the established framework of international law*" (emphasis added). This suggests that the Trial Chamber should have at least discussed this framework before proposing its own interpretation of the provision. This would have been particularly welcome, as its interpretation partly differs from the conclusions of recent in-depth research and expert discussions on these notions in the framework of the law governing the conduct of hostilities in armed conflict.

---

[52] API, Article 51(3); APII, Article 13(3); Henckaerts and Doswald-Beck 2005, r 6.

Relevant work on this issue includes, most notably, the *Interpretive Guidance on the Notion of Direct Participation in Hostilities under International Humanitarian Law* (Interpretive Guidance) issued by the ICRC in 2009.[53] This document draws on a variety of sources, such as the *travaux préparatoires* of relevant treaties, international jurisprudence, military manuals, and legal doctrine. In addition, it is based on discussions held during a series of meetings involving the participation of experts from different backgrounds.[54] It expresses, however, the ICRC's view on this topic and does not necessarily reflect the unanimous views of participants.

If examined in the light of the ICRC's Interpretive Guidance, the Trial Chamber's reasoning is based at once on a broad definition of the notion of active participation in hostilities, as well as a narrow understanding of the notion of direct participation in hostilities. This interpretation may have undesirable consequences. It carries first the risk of a loss of protection for the children whose situation is addressed in Article 8(2)(e)(vii). Second, it may allow the prosecution, under the Rome Statute, of acts which are not prohibited under international humanitarian law.

It is, of course, not possible to give a comprehensive account of the legal argumentation and conclusions contained in the Interpretative Guidance in the limited framework of this article. Suffice it to stress first that this document recalls that persons "taking no active part in the hostilities," in the sense of Article 3 common to the Geneva Conventions of 1949, are mentioned in the equally authentic French text of the same provision as persons "qui ne participent pas *directement* aux hostilities" (emphasis added). This suggests that the terms "direct" and "active" were intended to have the same meaning at the time of the adoption of the Conventions. The ICRC confirms that these terms "refer to the same quality and degree of individual participation in hostilities".[55]

The broader understanding adopted by the Trial Chamber for the notion of "active" participation in hostilities is thus confusing and may potentially have a negative impact on the children that Article 8(2)(e)(vii) intends to protect. This interpretation may be used to justify extending the circle of persons who can be the object of legitimate attacks under international humanitarian law.[56] In addition, it also tends to limit the number of individuals protected by Article 3 common to the Geneva Conventions and Article 8(2)(c) of the Rome Statute, as these provisions apply to persons taking "no" active part in the hostilities.[57] The Special Court for

[53] Melzer Melzer 2009.

[54] Ibid., p. 9.

[55] Ibid., p. 43. See also M. Happold, who reaches the same conclusion on the basis of Resolution 2675 of the UN General Assembly and jurisprudence of the ICTY and ICTR. Happold 2009, pp. 594–595.

[56] Graf 2012, p. 963.

[57] Urban 2012.

Sierra Leone had already remarked in this regard that "an overly expansive definition of active participation in hostilities would be inappropriate as its consequence would be that children associated with armed groups lose their protected status as persons *hors de combat* under the law of armed conflict".[58]

Additionally, according to the Interpretive Guidance, an act amounting to "direct participation in hostilities" is composed of three cumulative elements: a) it must be likely to reach a certain threshold of harm, b) there must be "a relationship of direct causation between the act and the expected harm", and c) it must be "specifically designed to directly cause the required threshold of harm in support of a party to the conflict and to the detriment of another" (belligerent nexus).[59] With regard to the second requirement (direct causation), the ICRC further explains that the expected harm must be brought about "in one causal step".[60] Such a relationship of direct causation is present not only in cases where the act itself is intended to reach the required threshold of harm, but also when it is an integral part of a coordinated military operation designed to reach this threshold.[61] This means that the notion of "direct participation in hostilities" is not limited solely to the use of weapons during combat operations. It also includes conduct which, taken in isolation, would not meet the required threshold of harm, but which, in conjunction with other acts, would contribute to reaching that threshold.[62]

As a consequence, the definition adopted by the ICRC is broader than the one used by the Trial Chamber. Some acts amounting to "direct participation in hostilities" under the *Interpretive Guidance* would not be considered as such by the Chamber. Conduct comprising acts such as scouting, spying, or sabotage, which are mentioned as "active participation in military activities *linked* to combat" in the *Lubanga* judgment, would certainly amount to "direct participation in hostilities" under the criteria proposed by the ICRC.[63]

Without further explanation, the position adopted by the Trial Chamber on this point raises a number of questions. It is not clear whether this position suggests that a legal concept could be interpreted in different ways when used in relation to distinct provisions of the same legal instrument. If so, this would imply that the International Criminal Court would have to give a certain meaning to the notion of "direct participation in hostilities" to interpret Articles 8(2)(e)(vii) and 8(2)(b)(xxvi) (use of children under 15) on the one hand, and a separate distinct

[58] Special Court for Sierra Leone, *Prosecutor v. Sesay, Kallon, Gbao (RUF Case)*, SCSL-04-15-T, Judgment, Trial Chamber I, 2 March 2009, para 1723.

[59] Melzer 2009, pp. 46–64.

[60] Ibid., p. 53.

[61] Ibid., pp. 51–55.

[62] Ibid., pp. 54–55. Example of such conduct include "the identification and marking of targets, the analysis and transmission of tactical intelligence to attacking forces, and the instruction and assistance given to troops for the execution of a specific military operation"; see Melzer Meler 2009, p. 55.

[63] See Urban 2012.

meaning to the same notion as it appears in Articles 8(2)(b)(i) and 8(2)(e)(i) (principle of distinction in the conduct of hostilities) on the other. The alternative, i.e., a single, consistent understanding of the notion of "direct participation in hostilities" in the framework of the Rome Statute, would be problematic. It would confirm the existence of different interpretations of this notion under international criminal law and international humanitarian law respectively. This would have unwelcome practical consequences. Combatants targeting civilians would risk being prosecuted and sentenced by the International Criminal Court, in application of Articles 8(2)(b)(i) or 8(2)(e)(i) of the Statute, while such conduct would not necessarily be prohibited under international humanitarian law. This would happen each time that acts carried out by these civilians would be considered as amounting to "direct participation in hostilities" under international humanitarian law, but not under the Rome Statute.[64]

These uncertainties are unfortunate, especially because comparing "active" and "direct" participation in hostilities was not necessary for the purposes of the judgment. It would have been sufficient to clarify the distinction between acts that amount to "active" participation in hostilities, and those that do not, i.e. those that are "clearly unrelated to the hostilities". In other words, it would have been sufficient to focus the analysis on the threshold of application of the third offense mentioned in Article 8(2)(e)(ii) of the Rome Statute.

4.3.2.2 "Active Participation in Hostilities" Versus "Activities Clearly Unrelated to the Hostilities"

With respect to this threshold of application, the Trial Chamber noted that the "decisive factor [...] in deciding if an 'indirect' role is to be treated as active participation in hostilities is whether the support provided by the child to the combatants exposed him or her to real danger as a potential target" (para 628). The Chamber thus identified the following two "combined factors" to determine when the use of a child under fifteen amounts to a war crime under the Rome Statute: a) the child's support to combatants; b) the "level of consequential risk" the child is exposed to (para 628). The Chamber further explained in this regard that assessments of particular situations, informed by these two criteria, must be made "on a case-by-case basis" (para 628). The use of these two combined factors is in line with the view that the notion of "active participation in hostilities" is not limited to front line functions. These factors allow for a broad definition of this notion, as they potentially include activities that are rather remotely linked to the hostilities. One could therefore ask whether the Trial Chamber perhaps went too far down this path.

With regard to the first factor, the concept of "support" seems so broad that it may include almost all forms of contact that a child may have with armed forces or

64 Ibid.

groups. The Trial Chamber recognized that, in practice children "are involved in a myriad of roles that support combatants" (para 628). Activities carried out in this regard do not need to be likely to reach a certain threshold of harm, as would be the case with the notion of "direct participation in hostilities".[65] Moreover, the Trial Chamber did not seek to define any particular causal relationship between such activities and actual combat operations. Neither did it require that the children concerned have any particular intention to play, or even awareness of playing, a role in the hostilities. "Support to combatants" is sufficient, regardless of the ultimate purpose of the concerned activities. Therefore the first criterion used by the Trial Chamber does not help to differentiate between activities amounting to "active participation in hostilities" and those that are "clearly unrelated to the hostilities".

The second factor proposed by the Trial Chamber provides further guidance in this regard. It identifies the level of risk to the children resulting from the support to combatants as the relevant link between the use of children and the hostilities. It is not clear, however, how such risk must be assessed in practice or, in the words of the Chamber, how to determine when a child is exposed to "real danger as a potential target" (para 628). It may be argued first that children taking an active part in hostilities should include at the very least those that are legitimate military targets under international humanitarian law. These are members of regular State armed forces (with the exception however of medical and religious personnel)[66] or of other armed groups or units belonging to the State, as well as members of dissident armed forces or other organized armed groups.[67] In addition, as previously mentioned, legitimate military targets also include civilians taking a direct part in hostilities, for the duration of such participation only.

Second, the Trial Chamber's reference to the "level of consequential risk" also suggests that "active participation in hostilities" includes persons who cannot be considered legitimate targets under international humanitarian law, but who are in such a situation as to make them potential victims of an attack in practice. This could include a category of children who are not members of State armed forces, dissident armed forces or other organized armed groups, but who are in another way "associated with" such forces or groups. Their use would constitute a war crime each time that they were exposed to a certain level of risk on the basis of criteria that must still be specified. One relevant criterion in this regard could be, for instance, the level of proximity to military objectives. The use of a child under

[65] Melzer 2009, p. 47.

[66] GCI, Article 24-26; GCII, Article 36; GCIV, Article 20; API, Article 15; Henckaerts and Doswald-Beck 2005, r 3 and 25.

[67] According to the ICRC, individual membership in an organized armed group other than dissident armed forces includes any person assuming "a continuous function for the group involving his or her direct participation in hostilities" ("continuous combat function"); see Melzer 2009, pp. 21–25, 32–34.

15 would amount to a war crime under the Rome Statute each time that such use occurs in the vicinity of a military objective.[68]

It is not obvious, however, that Article 8(2)(e)(vii) of the Rome Statute should really apply to this last category. Relevant conduct may be so remotely linked to the hostilities that it may hardly be categorized as "active participation". The reason for this is that the second factor used by the Trial Chamber does not focus on the nature of the activities carried out by the children, but rather on the context in which these activities take place or, in other words, on factual elements resulting in the risk that the children are exposed to real danger as potential targets. The definition of "active participation in hostilities" therefore depends on the circumstances surrounding every single situation, opening the notion up to include almost any form of support given to armed forces or groups.

The Chamber itself seems to be hesitant in this regard. Its approach based on the two factors discussed above appears to be at odds with the categories presented in the beginning of its analysis, namely "direction participation in hostilities", "active participation in hostilities", and "activities clearly unrelated to the hostilities". Using these factors means that it is not possible to identify, in the abstract, activities belonging to the third category. Yet, the Trial Chamber gives examples of such activities, namely "food deliveries to an airbase or the use of domestic staff in an officer's married accommodation". Following the logic presented with regard to the two factors, such activities could, however, amount to "active participation in hostilities" depending on the resulting "level of consequential risk" involved. These activities may indeed take place close to combat areas, where risks of being targeted are high.

The lack of clarity on this point is similarly evident in elements of the Trial Chamber's analysis of the facts of the case. With regard to domestic work for instance, the Chamber first made a clear reference to the two combined factors. It stated that domestic work amounted to a war crime under the Rome Statute "when the support provided by the girl exposed her to danger by becoming a potential target" (para 882). However, in the same paragraph, the Trial Chamber also emphasized that the girls concerned were used for domestic work, "in addition to the other tasks they carried out as UPC/FPLC soldiers, such as involvement in combat, joining patrols and acting as bodyguards". It is therefore unclear whether the Trial Chamber considered that domestic work as such might amount to "active participation in hostilities" if it involved risks of being targeted, or whether this is the case in this instance because the girls were also involved in other activities acquiring the required threshold of danger.[69]

---

[68] See Article 58(a) of API, which requires Parties to international armed conflicts to endeavor to remove civilians under their control "from the vicinity of military objectives". See also Henckaerts and Doswald-Beck 2005, r 24.

[69] The same question was raised regarding the use of children for sexual purposes, but the Trial Chamber did not take a position on this issue, stressing that this practice was not included in the decision on the confirmation of charges (para 629). Judge Odio Benito however, in her separate and dissenting opinion, suggested that sexual violence should have been included in a

4.4 Conclusion

The *Lubanga* judgment was an occasion for the International Criminal Court to take a position on a number of crucial issues, thus providing legal guidance for its future work and for the development of international criminal law. With respect to some of these issues, the Trial Chamber drew on the well-established practice of other international jurisdictions, most notably the ICTY. It endorsed, for instance, the criteria and reasoning developed by the Tribunal to define non-international armed conflict, and to determine the point at which such a conflict could become international owing to foreign intervention. Thus, a significant contribution of the *Lubanga* judgment consists of importing such previous practice into the system of the Rome Statute.

The judgment is also important because the Trial Chamber settled certain issues that have recently been debated. It reaffirmed that the fundamental distinction between international and non-international armed conflicts remains an essential feature of both international criminal and humanitarian law. It also indicated that Articles 8(2)(d) and 8(2)(f) of the Rome Statute do not define different material scopes of application despite their differences in wording. The expression "protracted armed conflict" in Article 8(2)(f) therefore does not create a higher threshold of application for that provision.

The most innovative part of the judgment relates to the involvement of children in armed conflicts. The Trial Chamber clarified fundamental concepts and proposed new criteria for the application of the relevant provisions of the Rome Statute. It adopted a broad definition of the notions of conscription and enlistment, stressing that the purpose of the integration of children into armed forces or groups is not relevant. It thus followed an approach that is legally correct and certainly abides by the principle of the best interests of the child. On the other hand, its reasoning concerning the war crime of using children under 15 to participate actively in hostilities is subject to more controversy. This reasoning ignores recent key developments related to the notion of participation in hostilities (both active and direct) under international humanitarian law and may potentially weaken the protection enjoyed by these children under existing rules. Moreover, the two combined factors adopted by the Chamber do not appear to be precise enough to really facilitate the identification of a clear threshold of application of the relevant notion of Article 8(2)(e)(vii) of the Rome Statute, and may therefore undermine the predictability of this rule.

(Footnote 69 continued)
comprehensive legal definition of recruitment and active participation of children in hostilities, and as such should have been addressed in the *Lubanga* Judgment (paras 6–8). On this specific issue, see Aptel 2012; Graf 2012, pp. 965–966.

References

Documents

Geneva Convention (I) for the Amelioration of the Condition of the Wounded and Sick in Armed Forces in the Field, 12 August 1949 (CGI).

Geneva Convention (II) for the Amelioration of the Condition of Wounded, Sick and Shipwrecked Members of Armed Forces at Sea, 12 August 1949 (GCII).

Geneva Convention (III) relative to the Treatment of Prisoners of War, 12 August 1949 (GCIII).

Geneva Convention (IV) relative to the Protection of Civilian Persons in Time of War, 12 August 1949 (GCIV).

Protocol Additional to the Geneva Conventions of 12 August 1949, and relating to the Protection of Victims of International Armed Conflicts (Protocol I), 8 June 1977 (API).

Protocol Additional to the Geneva Conventions of 12 August 1949, and relating to the Protection of Victims of Non-International Armed Conflicts (Protocol II), 8 June 1977 (APII).

Convention on the Rights of the Child, 20 November 1989 (CRC).

Optional Protocol to the Convention on the Rights of the Child on the involvement of children in armed conflict, 25 May 2000 (OP-CAC).

Rome Statute of the International Criminal Court, 17 July 1998 (Rome Statute).

Literature

Ambos K (2012) The first judgment of the International Criminal Court (Prosecutor v. Lubanga): A comprehensive analysis of the legal issues. International Criminal Law Review 12(2):115–153.

Aptel C (2012) Lubanga decision roundtable: The participation of children in hostilities. Opinio Juris Blog: Opiniojuris.org/2012/03/18/lubanga-decision-roundtable-the-participation-of-children-in-hostilities. Accessed 7 December 2012.

Dörmann K (2003) Elements of war crimes under the Rome Statute of the International Criminal Court: Sources and commentary, Cambridge University Press, Cambridge.

Dupuy RJ, Leonetti A (1979) La notion de conflict armé à caractère non international. In: Cassese A (ed) The new humanitarian law of armed conflict, Editoriale scientifica, Naples, pp 258–276.

Graf R (2012) The International Criminal Court and child soldiers, An appraisal of the *Lubanga* judgment. Journal of International Criminal Justice 10:945–969.

Happold M (2009) Child recruitment as a crime under the Rome Statute of the International Criminal Court. In: Doria J, Gasser HP, Bassiouni C (eds) The legal regime of the International Criminal Court, Essays in honour of Professor Igor Blishchenko, Nijhoff, Leiden/Boston, pp 579–607.

Henckaerts JM, Doswald-Beck L (eds) (2005) Customary International Humanitarian Law, Volume I: Rules, Cambridge University Press, Cambridge.

ICRC (2008) How is the term "armed conflict" defined in international humanitarian law. www.icrc.org/eng/assets/files/other/opinion-paper-armed-conflict.pdf. Accessed 31 October 2012.

International Law Association, Committee on the Use of Force (2010) Final report on the meaning of armed conflict in international law. www.ila-hq.org/en/committees/index.cfm/cid/1022. Accessed 31 October 2012.

Kurth ME (2010) The recruitment and use of child soldiers: some reflections on the prosecution of a new war crime. In: Stahn C, Van Den Herik L. (eds) Future perspectives on international criminal justice, TMC Asser Press, The Hague, pp 475–497.

Melzer N (2009) Interpretive guidance on the notion of direct participation in hostilities under international humanitarian law, ICRC, Geneva.
Pictet JS (ed) (1952) Commentary (I) of the Geneva Convention for the amelioration of the condition of the wounded and sick in armed forces in the field, ICRC, Geneva.
Reisman WM, Silk J (1988) Which law applies to the Afghan conflict? American Journal of International Law 82:459–486.
Sandoz Y, Swinarski C, Zimmermann B (eds) (1987) Commentary on the Additional Protocols of 8 June 1977 to the Geneva Conventions of 12 August 1949, ICRC, Geneva.
Schabas WA (2010) The International Criminal Court: A commentary on the Rome Statute. Oxford University Press, Oxford.
Schindler D (1982) International humanitarian law and internationalized internal armed conflicts. International Review of the Red Cross 230:255–264.
Sivakumaran S (2009) Identifying an armed conflict not of an international character. In: Stahn C, Sluiter G (eds) The emerging practice of the International Criminal Court, Nijhoff, Leiden/Boston, pp 371–380.
Stewart J (2003) Towards a single definition of armed conflict in international humanitarian law: A critique of internationalized armed conflict, International Review of the Red Cross 85/850:313–349.
Urban N (2012) Direct and active participation in hostilities: The unintended consequences of the ICC's decision in Lubanga, EJIL Talk. www.ejiltalk.org/direct-and-active-participation-in-hostilities-the-unintended-consequences-of-the-iccs-decision-in-lubanga. Accessed 7 December 2012.
Vandewiele T (2006) Optional Protocol, The involvement of children in armed conflict, Nijhoff, Leiden/Boston.
Vité S (2009) Typology of armed conflicts in international humanitarian law: legal concepts and actual situations. International Review of the Red Cross 91/873:69-94.
Vité S (2011) Protecting children during armed conflict: international humanitarian law. Human rights and international discourse 5(1):14–39.

Chapter 5
The Effects of the *Lubanga* Case on Understanding and Preventing Child Soldiering

Mark A. Drumbl

Contents

On March 14, 2012, ICC Trial Chamber I issued its judgment convicting Thomas Lubanga Dyilo, a rebel leader in the Democratic Republic of the Congo (DRC). Lubanga was found guilty, as a co-perpetrator, of the war crimes of conscripting and enlisting children under the age of fifteen years and using them to participate actively in hostilities from early September 2002 to August 13, 2003, in a

The author is Class of 1975 Alumni Professor of Law and Director, Transnational Law Institute, Washington and Lee University. I extend my appreciations to Jillian Nyhof for research assistance and to the Frances Lewis Law Center for its support. Although much of its discussion is original, this chapter adapts, updates, and in many places directly excerpts portions of the following published work: Mark A. Drumbl, Reimagining Child Soldiers in International Law and Policy (OUP, 2012) (specifically parts of chapters 1, 2, and 5); Mark A. Drumbl, *Child Soldiers and Clicktivism: Justice, Myths, and Prevention*, 4:3 Journal of Human Rights Practice 481 (2012); and Mark A. Drumbl, *Lubanga Legacies?*, Opinio Juris Lubanga Decision Roundtable, *available at* http://opiniojuris.org/2012/03/19/lubanga-decision-roundtable-legacies/. Accessed 21 May 2013.

M. A. Drumbl (✉)
Transnational Law Institute, Washington and Lee University, Lexington, VA 24450, USA
e-mail: drumblm@wlu.edu

T. D. Gill et al. (eds.), *Yearbook of International Humanitarian Law 2012*,
Yearbook of International Humanitarian Law 15, DOI: 10.1007/978-90-6704-924-5_5,

non-international conflict in the DRC's Ituri region.[1] Lubanga was charged exclusively with child-soldier-related crimes. He had served as President of the *Union des patriotes congolais* (UPC) and Commander-in-Chief of the *Forces patriotiques pour la libération du Congo* (FPLC), the entities into which he had unlawfully conscripted, used, and enlisted children. His lengthy trial was punctuated with due process concerns regarding the disclosure of evidence, confidentiality agreements, the Office of the Prosecutor's (OTP) delegation of investigative responsibilities to intermediaries, and the reliability of witness testimony. A stay of proceedings had twice been ordered.

On July 10, 2012, ICC Trial Chamber I sentenced Lubanga—the ICC's first convict—to a prison term of fourteen years.[2] It deducted the six years that Lubanga had already spent in detention (his surrender to the ICC occurred on March 16, 2006) from the sentence. In dissent, Judge Odio Benito would have marginally increased the sentence by one year, to fifteen years. According to the Rome Statute and the Rules of Procedure and Evidence, Lubanga will be eligible for a sentence reduction, contingent upon his deportment as a prisoner, once he serves two-thirds of the term (namely, mid-2015).

Lubanga currently appeals both his conviction and sentence, while the OTP appeals the sentence.

On August 7, 2012, ICC Trial Chamber I issued its decision regarding the principles and procedures to be applied to reparations in the *Lubanga* case.[3] This was the third major decision issued in 2012 in the *Lubanga* proceedings.

Although Lubanga's guilty verdict represents a watershed for the ICC, his is not the first conviction by an internationalized tribunal for child-soldier-related offenses. The Special Court for Sierra Leone (SCSL) has been path-breaking in this regard, having convicted several militia leaders for such offenses. In 2012, sitting exceptionally in The Hague, it also convicted Charles Taylor, Liberia's former Head of State, on charges that—depending on the time and place—included aiding and abetting, and planning, the commission of child-soldier-related crimes.[4]

---

[1] *Lubanga* Trial Judgment 2012 (Judges Fulford (Presiding, from the United Kingdom), Odio Benito (Costa Rica), and Blattmann (Bolivia)). Lubanga's convictions were entered pursuant to Rome Statute articles 8(2)(e)(vii) and 25(3)(a). In December 2012, ICC Trial Chamber II acquitted another DRC defendant, Mathieu Ngudjolo Chui, of all charges, including the active use of child soldiers under the age of fifteen in an attack against the Bogoro village in Ituri on February 24, 2003 (under Rome Statute article 8(2)(b)(xxvi), which criminalizes this conduct when undertaken in international armed conflict). Trial Chamber II did not find that no crimes occurred during the attack but, rather, found that the Prosecution had not established beyond a reasonable doubt that Ngudjolo was responsible, per article 25(3) of the Rome Statute, for the crimes allegedly committed during the attack. International Criminal Court Press Release 2012.

[2] *Lubanga* Sentencing Judgment 2012.

[3] *Lubanga* Reparations Decision 2012. This is the ICC's first reparations decision.

[4] *Taylor* Sentencing Judgment 2012. Taylor appeals. In March 2012, George Boley, the former leader of the Liberian Peace Council, was ordered removed from the United States under the U.S. Child Soldiers Accountability Act of 2008. Cook 2012, p. 681. This Act stipulates the recruitment

This article unpacks the relationships between the Lubanga proceedings and how the international community conceptualizes, and strives to prevent, child soldiering. My central thesis is that the Lubanga proceedings reinforce, and curry, a stylized portrayal of the child soldier as a faultless passive victim, psychologically devastated, and irreparably damaged.[5] These portrayals emerge rather starkly in the penal proceedings; they are much less prominent in the reparative phase of the case.

The use of imagery, to be sure, is a powerful device to mobilize resources, secure convictions, and actualize denunciation. The motivations behind the dissemination of the image of the child soldier as passive and incapable are well-intended. That said, this image morphs into a narrative and set of expectations that fail to instantiate the best interests of actual or former child soldiers while also occluding the complex, and unsettling, realities of child soldiering. As I argue at length in my book *Reimagining Child Soldiers in International Law and Policy*, narrative imagery of passivity, victimization, jejunity, and lack of agency tendentiously incubate policy initiatives that ultimately fall short in terms of actual effectiveness.[6] This imagery may also disable former child soldiers, discourage their input in processes of post-conflict reconstruction, impair a full understanding of child soldiering, and hamper the development of a robust culture of juvenile rights.

International criminal trials serve important expressive, performative, and didactic functions. They galvanize public attention. These trials, however, also can spectacularize and essentialize. To posit that the adduced facts of the *Lubanga* case reflect the realities of child soldiering throughout Ituri or the DRC—let alone the rest of the world—is inaccurate and counterproductive. The coincidental overlap between the release of the *Lubanga* judgment and the viral success of the Kony 2012 video[7] further reinforces a number of sensationalized exaggerations in global public consciousness. These include: the Africanization of child soldiering; that child soldiering is caused by brutal armed rebel groups; that all child soldiers are abducted and forced to kill in the most heinous ways; that, post-conflict, psychological devastation is rampant; that all child soldiers are rescued by valiant international humanitarians; and that the archetypical child soldier is very young. While accurate in some instances, these beliefs—which have come to constitute conventional wisdom—are far from representative of the situations of all, or even most, child soldiers.

(Footnote 4 continued)
and use of child soldiers as a ground of deportability from the United States. Cook 2012, p. 682. Boley was the first person to be ordered removed pursuant to this legislation. Cook 2012, p. 681.

5 I mapped the currency of this portrayal in Drumbl 2012. In this article, I consider how the *Lubanga* judgment and sentence, which post-date publication of the book, reflect and nourish this narrative imagery.

6 Drumbl 2012.

7 Invisible Children 2012.

This Article proceeds through several steps. First, it defines the term child soldier. Second, it discusses how child soldiers are portrayed within the international legal imagination. Third, the on-the-ground realities of child soldiering are set out. The discussion, fourthly, then moves to a detailed analysis of the *Lubanga* trial and sentencing judgments, which are placed within the broader discursive and sociological contexts earlier discussed. This Article concludes with an overview and brief discussion of the *Lubanga* reparations decision.

5.1 Defining the Terms: Who is a Child Soldier?

It is a conventional and customary war crime only to enlist, use, or conscript children younger than fifteen. Nonetheless, a firm push—often called the Straight 18 advocacy position—is afoot that defines child soldiers as being under the age of eighteen. This push manifests itself in two pivotal non-binding instruments. The first instrument, the Cape Town Principles,[8] was generated at a conference on the demobilization and reintegration of child solders held at Cape Town in 1997. The second instrument, which emerged from a 2007 follow-up conference (in Paris), is referred to as the Paris Commitments. Endorsed by 105 states as of December 2012,[9] the Paris Commitments are accompanied by an important elaborative document known as the Paris Principles.

Although not formally binding upon states, these instruments have considerable professional, operational, and political currency. They indicate *de lege ferenda*. Trial Chamber I approvingly, and regularly, cited them—in particular, the Paris Principles—as guidance in the *Lubanga* reparations decision.[10] Adopting the age of eighteen as the terminal point of child soldiering meshes with internationalized, and putatively universal, understandings of when childhood ends and adulthood begins.[11] These understandings are chronological in nature, as opposed to liminally experiential.

Age is only one element determining who can be classed as a child soldier. The other element is situational—namely, what conduct or circumstances are considered part of child soldiering? Both the Cape Town and Paris Principles protect much more than only those persons younger than eighteen who carry weapons, engage in combat, or who take (or have taken) a direct part in hostilities. Also

---

[8] UNICEF 1997. A child soldier is 'any person under 18 years of age who is part of any kind of regular or irregular armed force or armed group in any capacity, including but not limited to cooks, porters, messengers and anyone accompanying such groups, other than family members;' and explicitly including girls recruited for sexual purposes and forced marriage; and affirming that the definition 'does not, therefore, only refer to a child who is carrying or has carried arms.'

[9] UNICEF 2012.

[10] In the *Lubanga* criminal proceedings, the prosecution submitted that the definition of child soldiers includes all persons under the age of eighteen. *Lubanga* Trial Judgment 2012, para 574.

[11] Convention on the Rights of the Child 1989, Article 1.

included are children used for auxiliary activities (for example, portering, spying, and cooking) and children forced into sexual servitude. The impetus among policymakers is to discourage distinctions from being drawn between children who serve as combatants and children who do not or who do so only incidentally. One motivation in this regard is to ensure inclusiveness toward both girl and boy soldiers. Accordingly, and responsively, official nomenclature has drifted away from *child soldier* as initially set out and defined in the Cape Town Principles. The move is now toward thc somewhat tongue-tying *children associated with armed forces or armed groups*, defined in the Paris Principles to cover:

> Any person below 18 years of age who is or who has been recruited or used by an armed force or armed group in any capacity, including but not limited to children, boys, and girls used as fighters, cooks, porters, messengers, spies or for sexual purposes. It does not only refer to a child who is taking or has taken a direct part in hostilities.[12]

Whereas *armed forces* refer to official state militaries, *armed groups* refer to non-state entities distinct from those forces (notably, rebel militias, dissident factions, and insurgents). For ease of language and economies of space, in this article I use the term 'child soldier' but understand it to comport with the 2007 Paris Principles definition cited above. The determination of who I consider a child soldier arises not at the point of exit from militarized life, but at the point of entry. Hence, a *former child soldier* is a person who was initially associated with armed forces or armed groups while under the age of eighteen, even if he or she is eighteen or older at the time of release, demobilization, escape, or rescue.

In terms of formal binding law, when it comes to armed groups, the recruitment of anyone younger than eighteen is unlawful,[13] although—as mentioned previously—when it comes to sanctions it is not yet customary or conventional international law in such instances to ascribe individual penal responsibility for the recruitment of fifteen, sixteen, or seventeen-year-olds.[14] In the case of national armed forces, the push is to permit recruitment at the benchmark age of eighteen.[15] A minority of states still permit voluntary enlistment of sixteen or seventeen-year-olds in armed forces or reserves.[16] A non-exhaustive list of such states includes: seventeen years (Australia, Austria, Azerbaijan, Cape Verde, China, Cuba, France, Germany, Ireland [with a further exception to sixteen in the case of apprentices], Israel, Italy, Luxembourg, Netherlands, New Zealand, Poland, and United States); sixteen-and-a-half years (Singapore); and sixteen years (Bangladesh, Belize, Canada, Egypt, El Salvador, India, and the United Kingdom)[17]. Voluntary enlistment of minors into

---

[12] UNICEF 2007, prin. 2.1.

[13] Optional Protocol 2000, Article 4(1).

[14] Straight 18 aspirations endeavor to expand this prohibition to cover all children, that is, all persons younger than eighteen. The Redress Trust 2006, p. 1; United Nations 2006, sec. 5.30, p. 23.

[15] Optional Protocol 2000, Article 3(1).

[16] This is permitted by declaration. *id*, articles 3(2)–3(3).

[17] Drumbl 2012, p. 138 (directly drawn there from).

armed forces is subject to strict conditions and is generally preclusive of engagement in hostilities. In any event, these children, according to the Paris Principles, are child soldiers.

Pursuant to Rome Statute article 26, the ICC lacks jurisdiction over anyone under the age of eighteen. Hence, the ICC cannot investigate or prosecute a fifteen, sixteen, or seventeen-year-old alleged to have committed acts of genocide, war crimes, or crimes against humanity. This leads to a troubling gap. There is no criminal responsibility at the ICC for the adult recruiter who conscripts fifteen, sixteen, or seventeen-year-olds, and the ICC cannot hold these conscripts responsible for their conduct. An incentive may therefore arise to recruit persons in this age cohort. This is particularly disturbing because, as I discuss below, this age cohort demographically corresponds to the clear majority of persons classed as child soldiers.

International law's predilection with chronological binaries places a heavy burden on all soldiers aged eighteen or older. They bear the full weight of legal responsibility when they commit international crimes. They do so despite the fact they operate in the exact same context as many child soldiers, and despite neuroscientific research that suggests that the brain continues to develop well past the age of eighteen. The law, therefore, may indulge those under the age of eighteen while being exigent in its approach to those eighteen or older. Advocacy groups that emphasize chronological bright lines end up protecting too much, and too little, at the same time. Emphasis on these binaries also risks neglecting the fact that persons aged eighteen or older suffer tremendously in conflict and are not *ipso facto* more resilient than their counterparts younger than eighteen. Children abducted into armed groups do not axiomatically suffer greater psychosocial harm than similarly abducted young adults. By turning to the bright line of eighteen, and endeavoring to prohibit conscription only below that line, international efforts leave untouched the conscription of persons over the age of eighteen.

To be sure, about 40 % of child soldiers world-wide are estimated to be in Africa, but child soldiering truly is a global phenomenon. Child soldiers are found on every continent. In Colombia, for example, some 18,000 children remain militarized.[18] Popular discourse tends to downplay that Western children become militarized and may also suffer human rights violations.[19] In 2008, it was estimated that military recruitment of children and their use in hostilities 'still takes place in one form or another in at least 86 countries and territories worldwide.'[20]

Nor is child soldiering caused only by non-state rebel groups. Many child soldiers certainly are found within the ranks of such armed groups, but state actors also incorporate children into armed forces. Burma (Myanmar) is presently the largest state recruiter of child soldiers. Child Soldiers International, looking only at

---

[18] International Center for Transitional Justice 2012.

[19] For example, Australia recently released documents detailing hundreds of cases of physical and sexual abuse of minors—dating back decades—in its national armed forces. Siegel 2012, p. 2.

[20] Coalition to Stop the Use of Child Soldiers 2008, p. 12.

armed forces for which states are responsible, found that seventeen states used child soldiers between January 2010 and June 2012.[21]

Child soldiering is an active concern in Libya, Iraq, Yemen, Mali,[22] Syria,[23] South Sudan, and Afghanistan. In December 2012, UNICEF estimated that 'tens of thousands of children are still involved in violent conflicts around the world.'[24] Moreover, a broad swath of countries are seeking (and at times struggling) to re-integrate large numbers of former child soldiers, including Sierra Leone, Uganda, Liberia, Nepal, Sri Lanka, Timor-Leste, and, as well, the DRC.

5.2 Images of Child Soldiers

Transnational discourse typifies child soldiers in a variety of images. These portraits engage with the public, but Myriam Denov is right to point out that they also inordinately simplify the complex lives and experiences of child soldiers.[25] In this regard, I would add, these images may poorly serve their subjects.

One image is that of a very young child—a guileless naïf—hued as clueless and dependent. This image presents the child soldier as a helpless object manipulated locally by adult malevolence, yet at the same time to be rescued transnationally by adult humanitarianism. It portrays child soldiers as forced into service, forced to fight, and forced to kill. Its visuals are of deranged militias that steal children from their families and tear them from their communities. Within such militias, these children become neutered mechanical means used to fulfill nefarious ends over which they have no input. They are no more than 'instruments of war' and 'the weapon of choice'[26]—putty in malevolent hands. In another influential account, that of eminent human rights activist Roméo Dallaire, child soldiers are portrayed as an 'end-to-end weapon system' and as 'tools;' what is more, children 'are vulnerable and easy to catch, just like minnows in a pond,' with the involved adults depicted as 'evil.'[27] This image melds with and, in turn, disseminates a narrative—now transposed into law and policy—through which child soldiers are construed first and foremost as victims.[28] In terms of on-the-ground practice, however, the conceptual understanding of child soldiers principally as victims

[21] Child Soldiers International 2012, p. 11.

[22] Lloyd-George 2012.

[23] Jørgensen 2012, para 2.

[24] UNICEF 2012.

[25] Denov 2010, pp. 5–14.

[26] Otunnu 2000, pp. 48–49. Otunnu served as the UN Special Representative for Children and Armed Conflict from 1997 to 2005.

[27] Dallaire 2010, pp. 3, 12, 15, 150. This book also refers to former child soldiers as 'immature souls in small bodies.'

[28] McKnight 2010, p. 137. '[T]he actions of States and courts with regard to former child soldiers must reflect the post-conflict reality that these children are victims and not perpetrators.'

tends toward operational interventions that essentialize their victimhood. This first image, therefore, typifies the child soldier as a *faultless passive victim*.

A second image, which synergizes with the victim narrative, is that of child soldiers as *irreparable damaged goods*. Pursuant to this image, child soldiers are tormented and scarred. They form part of a 'lost generation.'[29] This image captures the pain of militarized life and the concomitant physical and emotional injuries. Yet it does so at the cost of overlooking the resilience of former child soldiers and children in war zones generally. This depiction defines expectations and sets parameters. Constructions of the child soldier as psychologically devastated and pilfered by conflict, for example, have spurred the preeminence of medicalized trauma and psychotherapeutical recovery models in post-conflict programming.

A third image—somewhat antiquated, yet still in circulation—posits the child soldier as a *hero*, whose valor flows from fighting for a just cause that resists oppression or from demonstrating patriotism. In contradistinction to the faultless passive victim image, the hero image plays up the independence, conviction, nobility, bravery, and enterprise of the child soldier. This portrayal also may venerate military service, however, and feed into pernicious norms of masculinity and hyper-aggression. It can lead to a parlous situation for the unpopular side. In Timor-Leste, for example, 'children who fought on the side of independence were considered heroes [while] [t]hose who fought on the opposing side were stigmatized, and some were later targeted.'[30]

A final image appears in journalistic accounts, political grandstanding, and national security circles. This image stylizes the child soldier as *demon and bandit*: irredeemable, baleful, and sinister. This flawed image comports with an alarming policy output, namely, the pointlessness of investing in the rehabilitation of former child soldiers. Pursuant to this depiction, the child soldier is a ticking time-bomb, bad seed, and warped soul incorrigibly determined to kill with alacrity.[31] The United States, for example, had cast Omar Khadr, a child associated with Al Qaeda as very dangerous, despite his youth, so as to justify his becoming the subject of harsh military commission proceedings. Khadr, fifteen years old at the time of his capture in 2002 by American forces in Afghanistan, was finally repatriated from Guantanamo Bay to Canada on September 29, 2012, to serve out the remainder of his sentence following a plea agreement.

These four images are not equals. Hierarchy and ordinality can be theorized among them with regard to their operational influence in shaping conventional wisdom within the international legal imagination.

---

[29] Singer 2006, p. 44.

[30] UNICEF 2010, p. 47 (citation omitted).

[31] Denov 2010, p. 6; Wessells 2006, p. 45. Wessells notes that 'this portrayal contradicts much evidence and does injustice to the rich interplay between personal and situational influences on decisions to become soldiers.'

The faultless passive victim image has achieved widespread traction within—and is avidly disseminated by—influential intergovernmental organizations and UN agencies, along with NGOs and other actors that populate global civil society.[32] It has consequently come to dominate international discourse. Applied top-down in a wide-range of places, this portable image forms part of transnational rule of law discourse and technique. Although projections of this image by communities of conscience have become more refined over time, its core attributes persist and, in fact, are hardening into law and policy. This portrait scripts official conversations about child soldiers. Accordingly, these conversations become conformist and stilted.

Within post-conflict societies guided by international judicialization and administration efforts, policy initiatives generated by the faultless passive victim imagery presuppose and designate local child soldiers as programmed to commit terrible abuses over which they have neither appreciation nor control. Child soldiers are seen as forcibly coerced into military service and, in the case of atrocity-producing conflicts, compelled to commit horrific human rights abuses.[33] As a group, and *ipso facto* as individuals, they are taken to lack any volition. Seen as 'faceless,' they 'have not yet developed a concept of justice.'[34] Accordingly, former child soldiers cannot plausibly play active roles in transitional justice mechanisms—such as truth commissions and reintegrative ceremonies—that examine their agency, authorship, or role in violence. The international legal imagination's propensity is to generically ease a potential three-dimensional status of child soldiers as perpetrators, witnesses, and victims into a two-dimensional portrayal of child soldiers as victims and witnesses alone.[35] In response, I advance the normative claim that transitional justice initiatives other than criminal trials, in

[32] *Cf.* Utas 2003, pp. 7–8; Boyden and Berry 2004, pp. xi, xv; Ben-Ari 2009, p. 13.

[33] For a typical presentation, see Spiga 2010, p. 192 ('It is common knowledge that children are often forced to take up arms and have little choice on whether or not to enlist; after their recruitment, they are coerced to commit actions, of which—in most cases—they have little understanding.'). Although not the doing of global civil society, the turn to victimhood narratives to thwart punitive policies and retributive measures can be selective. Owing to state behavior, the political suitability of these narratives correlates to whom, exactly, the conduct of the child soldiers aggrieves. A center/periphery divide emerges. Transnational conceptions of faultlessness do not fully reach children from the periphery who commit atrocious acts against Westerners. Whereas the child perpetrator targeting Africans tends to be held as a mindless captive of purposeless violence, the child perpetrator targeting Westerners tends to be held as an intentional author of purposeful violence.

[34] Dallaire 2010, pp. 3, 138 (also describing some child soldiers as 'zombies').

[35] For example, the International Center for Transitional Justice, while advocating for greater involvement of children in transitional justice processes, carefully circumscribes the space available for such participation through its call for 'strategies [...] that create a safe space for children and youth to participate in proceedings both as victims and members of transitional societies.' International Center for Transitional Justice 2012, p. 3. See also in terms of best practices, UNICEF 2007, prins. 3.8 (also adding the stipulation that child participation must be by informed consent of both the child and parent or guardian where appropriate and possible) and 8.16.

particular truth commissions and endogenous mechanisms, can help facilitate reintegration and reconciliation in cases of the minority of child soldiers implicated in the completion of acts of atrocity.[36]

The faultless passive victim image is often paired with the evocation of former child soldiers as irreparably damaged by their experiences, the second image I identified. This twinning of victimization with dilapidation is promoted, as this article will demonstrate, in and by the *Lubanga* penal proceedings.

In the end, all extreme images are at best partial prints that occlude more than they clarify. Child soldiers are heterogeneous in their experiences, expectations, and paths to (and from) militarization. Remedial initiatives, therefore, should be contextual, rather than preordained. They should be evidence-based as opposed to belief-driven.

5.3 Realities of Child Soldiering

Surely apposite in individual cases, the totalized portrayal of the child soldier as a faultless passive victim devastated by conflict is also unduly reductive.

Although the standard image is of the very young child staggering under the weight of automatic weaponry and sinking into baggy fatigues, most child soldiers are not young children—most are adolescents, with many aged fifteen, sixteen, or seventeen. Many former child soldiers, upon demobilization, are well into their twenties or, even, thirties.

Popularized discourse tends to portray child soldiers as boys, but as many as 40 percent of child soldiers may be girls.[37] Girl soldiers already are poorly served by extant programming that under-appreciates the specific gender-based reintegrative challenges they face, such as recovery from abhorrent sexual violence[38] and forced marriage perpetrated not only by male adult commanders but also by boy soldiers and, at times, even by female commanders and other girl soldiers. Girl soldiers face elevated risks of HIV/AIDS and sexually transmitted diseases.[39] Girl soldiers who become pregnant rarely receive prenatal care, thereby exposing them to significant health concerns including what is believed to be high rates of maternal mortality.[40] Girl soldiers who survive childbirth and become mothers may face great challenges (as do their children), including when it comes to social reintegration in post-conflict phases.[41]

---

[36] I remain skeptical of the value of retributive criminal trials as justice mechanisms to assess the conduct of former child soldiers. Drumbl 2012, pp. 21–22, 178–180.

[37] Wessells 2006, p. 9 (citing a 2005 Save the Children Report).

[38] To be clear: boys, too, are sexually abused.

[39] Wessells 2006, p. 116; WHO 2009.

[40] Ibid, pp. 100, 117.

[41] Ibid 2006, p. 101.

Another myth is that all child soldiers are abducted and forcibly conscripted. Although abduction reflects the experiences of some child conscripts, including in jurisdictions whose tragedies are being investigated and prosecuted by the ICC, worldwide most child soldiers are neither abducted nor forcibly conscripted: significant numbers of child soldiers, in fact, exercise some (at times considerable) initiative in coming forward to enroll.[42] Nor is it the case that abduction was a dominant (or even a preponderant) mode of recruitment in the DRC,[43] though—depending on the armed force or group in question—it was in other conflicts, such as with the Lord's Resistance Army (LRA) in Northern Uganda. The motivations of those child soldiers who exhibit initiative in coming forward to serve are varied and should be explored. Young people may step forward to join armed forces or groups, or perform functions therein, to achieve political goals, topple dictators, acquire training, effect economic gains, serve their community, and make the best of a bad situation. Environmental factors and situational constraints—which include poverty, insecurity, lack of education, socialization into violence, and broken families—certainly inform their decisions to enlist.[44] Children's engagement with these factors, however, can be more usefully understood as interactive and negotiated processes of negative push and affirmative pull instead of unilateral processes of suppression. In other cases, child recruits deceive their parents and other commanders. They conceal their age, travel great distances, and persevere tenaciously in their quest to associate with armed forces or groups. These children, too, count as child soldiers. They may join despite community and family exhortations to the contrary. These youth may believe their participation will lead to a better future. After all, although armed groups may seek to undermine legitimate governments through macabre methods, they may also serve as engines of protest against illegitimate rulers, state authoritarianism, and kleptocratic dictatorship.

Youth volunteerism, however controversial and often chimerical, simply cannot be wished away—it needs to be recognized in order to develop effective preventative and rehabilitative mechanisms. Yet there is a profound tendency among distinguished international activists to view youth volunteerism as illusory or impossible in periods of armed conflict, and to predetermine that no child has the capacity to volunteer or to consent to serve—whether innately or because of

[42] See e.g., Singer 2006, p. 61 ('[R]oughly two of every three child soldiers have some sort of initiative in their own recruitment.'); Wessells 2004, p. 514 ('The best evidence available indicates that significant numbers of children join armed groups without explicit coercion …'); Rosen 2007, pp. 298–299 ('[T]he vast majority of child soldiers are not forcibly recruited or abducted into armed forces and groups.'); International Labour Office 2003, p. viii; Schmidt 2007, p. 49 ('A number of recent studies from Sub-Saharan Africa show that the majority of children and young people join armed groups voluntarily for a number of reasons.'); UNICEF 2002, p. 19.

[43] Drumbl 2012, p. 64 (citing two surveys on voluntary recruitment in the DRC that found that volunteerism was the most common form of recruitment, and discussing youth motivations in joining); see also ibid, p. 83.

[44] Brett and Specht 2004; Drumbl 2012, p. 79.

nightmarish circumstances, or both.[45] In this vein, Radhika Coomaraswamy, the distinguished UN Special Representative of the Secretary General on Children and Armed Conflict, submitted in the *Lubanga* trial that, for the purpose of the criminal culpability of the adult recruiter, 'the line between voluntary and forced recruitment' is 'legally irrelevant' and 'practically superficial' in the case of children.[46] However, this line remains quite relevant to developing post-conflict transitional policies insofar as abductees experience different reintegrative needs than youth who had voluntarily enlisted. Recognition of these differences better serves rehabilitative, restorative, and reconciliatory ends.

What child soldiers actually say about their experiences may contrast with how international observers broadcast those experiences. In interviews, for example, former child soldiers often describe themselves as having volunteered for service.[47] Some interviewers respond by discounting all such statements. They thereby massage complex data to fit a simple pre-existing theory. P.W. Singer—whose work on child soldiers has received considerable traction—finds the notion of voluntary recruitment 'misleading,' in part because children are 'of an age at which they are not capable of making mature decisions.'[48] Helping hands may prefer to believe that child soldiers are ignorant of the absence of choice in their lives and lack the cognitive capacity for discernment. This strategy, however well-intentioned, may prove demeaning, while also depleting the informational record and leading to misguided recommendations. This strategy foreshadows presenting youth as inanimate objects of study, rather than vibrant sources of information. Although assertions of volunteer service made by child soldiers should not be immunized from contextual analysis, I believe it is wrong to summarily dismiss them. Young people may understand volunteerism within the context of their lives and apply it fairly to themselves.

Dismissing what adolescents have to say owing to their putative immaturity contrasts sharply with assumptions of juvenile capacity and autonomy that animate other areas of law and policy. For example, when it comes to bioethical debates regarding consent to medical treatment and access to reproductive rights and technologies, in many jurisdictions adolescents tend to be presumed competent. International human rights law highlights that adolescents can exercise rights of freedom of association and expression. So, too, does international family law as regards to custodial determinations. Protective policies predicated upon children being constructed as enfeebled before and during conflict may counterproductively result in children persistently being treated as enfeebled after conflict. I remain skeptical that atrophied delineations of capacity, and the notion that adolescents

[45] Hart 2006, p. 7 ('The authors of global accounts of 'child soldiers'… have little time for the idea that children may be capable of exercising any real measure of choice about recruitment….[T]he very notion of voluntary recruitment is largely an illusion.').

[46] *Lubanga* Trial Judgment 2012, para 612.

[47] A number of OTP child witnesses in *Lubanga* stated that they had joined voluntarily. See Easterday 2009.

[48] Singer 2006, p. 62.

categorically require infantilizing rules to protect them, actually promote the aspiration to engage them robustly as full members of society. Moreover, many persons initially recruited as children age into adulthood during conflict or before they feasibly can enroll in post-conflict programming. In these instances, the tendency to infantilize may become perceived by them and the community as particularly ill-fitting.

In contradistinction to often graphic media representations, significant numbers of youth classified as child soldiers neither fight nor carry weapons.[49] Of great salience is the fact that most child soldiers are not implicated in serially committing acts of atrocity proscribed by international criminal law.[50] When it comes to those child soldiers who are implicated in such crimes, the conventional wisdom is that they all are forced to do so by commanders and, hence, operate under extreme duress; that they are incapacitated by compelled ingestion of narcotics and alcohol; that they are brainwashed and re-socialized by the endemic violence that envelops them; and that they are plagued with fears of brutal punishment. This dominant account, to be sure, explains many acts of atrocity perpetrated by persons under the age of eighteen. Despite their frequency, however, these explanations cannot be universalized. It is imprudent to wish away the fact that not all child soldiers materially implicated in acts of atrocity actually conform to this explanatory account. Considerable heterogeneity arises among child soldiers with regard to their relationship to violence that, in turn, underscores the ongoing relevance of disposition, choice, and residual discretion to exceed or subvert command authority. Furthermore, regardless of why they did it and the circumstances thereof, the fact remains that the acts of child soldiers do impose staggering consequences upon the lives of others, including children.

Nor is it self-evident that child soldiers are rescued by humanitarians—in particular, Western humanitarians—nor, for that matter, by anyone. Escape is much more prevalent than commonly believed. In Northern Uganda, for example, the vast majority of initially abducted child soldiers exited the LRA—a terribly invidious organization—on their own initiative, whether through escape or by abandoning the group.[51]

What about mental health issues? In the *Lubanga* proceedings, considerable reliance was placed on an expert report (and related testimony) of Dr. Elisabeth Schauer, a distinguished psychologist and director of Vivo International (an

---

[49] Wessells 2006, p. 71 ('Contrary to popular conceptions, many child soldiers never fight, and many neither carry their own weapon nor know how to use one.').

[50] Drumbl 2012, pp. 82–85.

[51] Annan et al. 2006, pp. vii, 53; Annan et al. 2009, p. 642 (reporting that 80 % of abductees from northern Acholi districts exited the LRA by escape, with the remainder being rescued or released); Blattman and Annan 2010, p. 883 ('Eighty-four percent of abductees eventually escaped, usually in an unsupervised moment such as the heat of battle.').

NGO).[52] This report, relied upon in both the trial and sentencing judgments, paints a grim picture of the mental health of former child soldiers. Schauer emphasized the prevalence of post-traumatic stress disorder (PTSD) among former child soldiers. She connected PTSD to an array of other impairments, including poor performance in school and on cognitive tests, depression, dissociation, derealisation, and suicide. She underlined the need for therapy to target brain dysfunction and implored that more attention be accorded to mental health.

Schauer's research, however probative for the ICC, is not the only research on the topic of the mental health of former child soldiers. Evidence from various other sources, which I explore elsewhere, suggests that the psychological health of former child soldiers may not be as imperiled as is commonly claimed.[53] This research—which does not appear to have materially influenced Trial Chamber I—reveals the resilience, tenacity, agility, and strength of former child soldiers.

In the end, although PTSD therapy should form part of post-conflict programming for child soldiers, overstating its relevance may yield interventions that mesh neither with their needs nor with those of the community. Community welfare is not necessarily fostered by individualized psychotherapeutic approaches, especially when pursued to the detriment of traditional reintegration mechanisms. These mechanisms often nest in an understanding of repairing war trauma as a collective journey rather than personal endeavor and involve restorative works, cleansing ceremonies, and reunification rituals.

In short, dominant imagery of child soldiers as passive, clueless victims, as demolished, dehumanized tools of war, robotically programmed to kill in purportedly senseless African wars belies a much more sublime, humanistic, and granular reality of resilience, agency, potential, and globality.

5.4 The *Lubanga* Criminal Proceedings and Portrayals of Child Soldiers

Overall, the *Lubanga* criminal case—beginning with the Prosecution's submissions, to the trial judgment, and ending with the sentencing judgment—invokes, and further embeds, the prevailing image of child soldiers as faultless passive victims devastated by the effects of their conflict experiences. In some occasional

[52] Vivo International is 'an independent non-profit organization' that is an 'alliance of professionals experienced in the fields of psychotraumatology, international health, humanitarian aid, scientific laboratory and field research, sustainable development and human rights advocacy.' *See* http://www.vivo.org/about_vivo/who_is_who_in_vivo/index_eng.html. Accessed 21 May 2013. At trial, Dr. Schauer testified that Vivo International 'concentrate[s] on post-traumatic stress disorder, depression, suicidality'; she 'attended this court at the express invitation of the Judges.' *Lubanga* Trial Transcript April 2009, p. 81 lines 14–15, p. 97 lines 18–19.

[53] Drumbl 2012, pp. 53–57.

instances, however, the judgments do approach child soldiering in a more nuanced and humanistic manner, while still firmly denouncing the practice, which is a promising move and salutary balance that should be encouraged.

5.4.1 Trial Proceedings and Judgment

According to Michael Wessells, depicting former child soldiers as 'emotionally crippled and damaged for life' risks emphasizing 'deficits,' while overlooking the reality that child soldiers 'exhibit considerable resilience.'[54] Such depictions may garner sympathy, but they also enfeeble. Yet in his opening statement in the *Lubanga* trial, former ICC Chief Prosecutor Moreno-Ocampo portrayed the former child soldiers as indelibly wounded and as prisoners of their past:

> They cannot forget the beatings they suffered; they cannot forget the terror they felt and the terror they inflicted; they cannot forget the sounds of their machine guns; they cannot forget that they killed; they cannot forget that they raped and that they were raped.[55]

It is one thing to recognize the painful personal histories of child soldiers in Ituri who had initially been recruited while under the age of fifteen. It is quite another, however, to immobilize them statically in relation to the harms they have suffered. Moreno-Ocampo's tactic to highlight those former child soldiers who have since turned to drugs to cope, who have become prostitutes, and who are orphaned and jobless—all part of his opening statement—ultimately collectivizes frailty. Drawing attention to those who suffer the most may, in turn, desolately define the group as asphyxiated by suffering and hamstrung by despondency.

As part of their goal to accentuate the moral culpability of adult recruiters or users, criminal prosecutions amplify how post-traumatic stress syndrome debilitates former child soldiers. Nuance stands at cross-purposes with the prosecutorial imperative to convict and, following conviction, to secure a lengthy sentence. These imperatives, however understandable, create an incentive to depict the victims—in this case, the former child soldiers—as being as chronically devastated, dependent, and weak. After all, the more hapless their situation, the more the perpetrator marred their lives, and the more heinous the crime. But do the former child soldiers see themselves so sullenly? If not, then, this effort to depict devastation may represent an appropriation of the voices of former child soldiers that, in turn, further nourishes victimcy instead of empowering them to surpass their situation. If they can never be free of the abuses, there is no relief from the abuser. If they can never get better, then funding rehabilitative programs might become perceived as a case of throwing money at an intractable problem—meaning that donors may not be inclined to do it any longer. In short, if convicting perpetrators

[54] Wessells 2006, p. 4.

[55] Moreno-Ocampo, *Lubanga* Trial Transcript January 2009, p. 2.

becomes inextricably entwined with tropes of youth helplessness, prosecutions may well incarcerate a few adults while perpetuating gerontocracy and hampering the development of a robust culture of active youth as social actors and political players.

More immediately, the credibility of child soldiers as witnesses may be impaired by their typification as faultless passive victims lacking in capacity.[56] These portrayals, after all, may jaundice external perceptions of the veracity of their recollections when they testify against others or claim reparations. In *Lubanga*, disturbingly, the OTP's negligent failure to properly supervise the intermediaries it had used in its investigations ultimately contributed to the possibility that these intermediaries may have improperly influenced the testimony of some child soldier witnesses, leading Trial Chamber I to find that much of their testimony was unreliable and, moreover, to void their victim status.[57] In faulting the OTP in this regard, Trial Chamber I underscored how these former child soldiers were 'vulnerable to manipulation.'[58] Yet, in this instance, the manipulation came from the very people tasked to protect the child soldiers by prosecuting Lubanga. Helping hands proved unhelpful. The consequences for these former child soldiers were very real, as was the impact on the trial itself. In light of the constriction of credible witness testimony, Trial Chamber I concentrated on video and documentary sources. The result was to scale back the opportunity for former child soldiers to empower themselves by authenticating the realities of child soldiering in Lubanga's militias through their own voices and testimonials. Instead, the public impression gleaned from the testimony of several of the former child soldiers is one of contradiction, distortions, untruths, vacillations, and implausibility.[59]

The *Lubanga* trial judgment is very long (nearly 600 pages). Much of it is concerned with establishing the crime base, determining the accused's individual criminal responsibility, and assessing his contribution to the common plan. Slightly over one hundred pages of the judgment, moreover, involve discussion of the intermediaries.

The trial judgment, however, also clarifies the scope of the war crimes of conscripting and enlisting children under the age of fifteen into armed forces or groups or using them to participate actively in hostilities. Although conscription

---

[56] Moreno-Ocampo argued that Lubanga 'stole the childhood of the victims by forcing them to kill and rape. [He] victimised children before they ever had the chance to grow up into full human beings who could make their own decisions.' Moreno-Ocampo, *Lubanga* Trial Transcript 2012 ibid., p. 29.

[57] Judge Odio Benito, in dissent, would not have voided their victim status despite her findings with regard to the unreliability of their testimony for the purposes of Lubanga's criminal trial. Intermediaries are 'individuals and organizations working in the field that act as liaisons between the ICC, including the Office of the Prosecutor, and individuals and communities.' See Women's Initiatives for Gender Justice 2012.

[58] *Lubanga* Trial Judgment 2012, para 482.

[59] Women's Initiatives for Gender Justice 2012, note 76.

and enlistment are separate offenses,[60] with the former involving compulsion and the latter involving the enrollment of children who volunteer to join,[61] Trial Chamber I emphasized how the consent of the child can never be a defense. As a matter of establishing criminal responsibility, therefore, it does not matter whether the child was forcibly abducted or was enlisted after coming forth to volunteer.[62] This difference, then, is one without distinction or relevance when it comes to ascertaining penal responsibility. Trial Chamber I therefore followed the views of the Special Representative, as discussed previously, along with antecedent SCSL judgments and Pre-Trial Chamber I's January 2007 decision to confirm the charges against Lubanga. Trial Chamber I also directly invoked the views of the expert witness Elisabeth Schauer in concluding that from a 'psychological point of view children cannot give "informed" consent when joining an armed group.'[63] According to Dr. Schauer, as affirmed by Trial Chamber I, this is because they have 'limited understanding of the consequences of their choices; they do not control or fully comprehend the structures and forces they are dealing with; and they have inadequate knowledge and understanding of the short- and long-term consequences of their actions.'[64] Trial Chamber I did state, however, that manner of recruitment may be taken into consideration in sentencing or reparations; hence, an abductor might be punished more harshly than a commander who enrolls child volunteers.[65] Ultimately, as discussed *infra*, Trial Chamber I's subsequent majority sentencing judgment did differentiate—albeit only slightly—along these lines.

The *Lubanga* trial judgment also examines the question of what, exactly, using a child to participate actively in hostilities actually means.[66] The majority approach focused on whether the 'support provided by the child to the combatants exposed him or her to real danger as a potential target.'[67] This approach, however broad, may obscure the reality that some child soldiers may face the prospect of greater harm from members of their own side (whether adult leaders, mid-level

[60] *Lubanga* Trial Judgment 2012, para 609.

[61] Ibid. paras 607–608.

[62] Insofar as much of the evidence adduced in the trial related to enlistment of volunteers, the legal irrelevance of this fact was clearly pertinent. At times, the Trial Judgment refers to the 'voluntary' nature of the recruitment. It explicitly uses quotation marks around the term, ostensibly to denote skepticism at the possibility that the recruitment could actually be voluntary.

[63] *Lubanga* Trial Judgment 2012, para 610.

[64] Ibid. (noting also that 'Ms. Schauer (CHM-0001) concluded that children lack the capacity to determine their best interests in this particular context.'). Accordingly, for Trial Chamber I, 'it will frequently be the case that girls or boys under the age of 15 will be unable to give genuine and informed consent when enlisting in an armed group or force.' Ibid. para 613.

[65] Ibid., para 617. To be clear: 'the consent of a child to his or her recruitment does not provide an accused with a valid defence.'

[66] This prohibition is not dependent upon the concerned children having been previously conscripted or enlisted into armed forces or armed groups.

[67] *Lubanga* Trial Judgment 2012, para 628.

officials, and fellow children) than from the enemy side.[68] Harms arising from sexual violence, enslavement, and abusive punishment come to mind.[69] Judge Odio Benito took up this point in her separate and dissenting opinion.[70] To be clear, conscription of girls and boys into armed forces or armed groups for sexual exploitation would definitely constitute unlawful conscription.[71]

In any event, regardless of the benefits of not distinguishing the roles of the children (i.e., as sex slaves, porters, cooks, active combatants, or persons committing atrocities) for the purposes of securing criminal convictions of adults on child-soldier-related offenses, such distinctions matter greatly in terms of crafting tailored reintegration and restoration programs for former child soldiers.[72]

5.4.2 Sentencing Judgment

Trial Chamber I sentenced Lubanga to a total term of fourteen years.[73] Specifically, the majority concurrently sentenced him to thirteen years' imprisonment for the crime of conscription, twelve years for the crime of enlistment, and fourteen years for the crime of using children to participate actively in hostilities.[74] These distinctions, however mild, are pertinent insofar as they recognize that the three offenses may differ in terms of inherent gravity. Sentencing is an often overlooked aspect of international criminal law. This is regrettable, insofar as penological determinations can inject some nuance, context, and granularity into the adjudication of atrocity crimes. The *Lubanga* judgments, however, did not distinguish

---

[68] The majority rejected the submissions of Special Representative Coomaraswamy that the focus should be on whether the child served an 'essential support function' to the group. Ibid, para 626. That said, and however well-intentioned, it is deeply discomfiting to intimate that sexual exploitation could constitute an 'essential support function' for armed groups along the lines of cooking, providing health care, spying, portering, and communicating messages.

[69] The majority of Trial Chamber I felt constrained on due process grounds to exclude evidence of sexual violence as a form of use in hostilities since the facts thereof were not included in the confirmation of charges decision. Ibid., para 630.

[70] *Lubanga* Sentencing Judgment 2012 dissent, paras 15–21.

[71] Jørgensen 2011, para 54.

[72] Ibid., para 22. Curiously, according to Jørgensen, the *Lubanga* judgment 'skirts' the issue of addressing the crimes committed by child soldiers against civilians as part of their use to actively participate in hostilities, 'placing emphasis instead on the use of children in support roles, for example as bodyguards […].' Ibid., para 32 (see also para 63 ['The approach in *Lubanga* meant that the issue of crimes committed by children and complicity in those crimes by adults also remained unexplored.']).

[73] The Trial Chamber did not impose a fine in addition to the prison term, 'given the financial situation of Mr Lubanga.' *Lubanga* Sentencing Judgment 2012, para 106.

[74] Ibid., para 98. In this regard, the judges departed from Prosecutor Moreno-Ocampo's opening statement submission that no 'distinction as to gravity' arises between conscripting children, enlisting them, or using them to participate actively in hostilities. Moreno-Ocampo, *Lubanga* Trial Transcript January 2009, pp. 9–10.

the evidence related to enlistment of volunteers, on the one hand, and conscription by coercion, on the other and, in this regard, failed to develop a nuanced record of the realities of child soldiering in the UPC/FPLC that, in turn, could better justify differential sentencing for Lubanga depending on gravity.

Judge Odio Benito, in dissent, 'firmly disagree[d] with the Majority's decision to impose a differentiated sentence to the convicted person as regards the crimes of enlistment, conscription and use to participate actively in the hostilities.'[75] According to Judge Odio Benito, each of the three crimes results in damage to the victims and their families regardless whether the initial recruitment was voluntary or compulsory and regardless whether the children were used actively to participate in hostilities or not.[76]

Trial Chamber I began its sentencing judgment with a summary of the applicable provisions of the Rome Statute and the Rules of Procedure and Evidence. It then assessed whether it could consider, for the purposes of sentencing, facts and circumstances extending beyond those described in the confirmed charges.[77] Trial Chamber I held that evidence admitted for sentencing 'can exceed the facts and circumstances set out in the Confirmation Decision, provided the defence has had a reasonable opportunity to address them.'[78] Also as a preliminary matter, it concluded that aggravating factors are to be established beyond a reasonable doubt, while mitigating circumstances are to be established on a balance of probabilities.[79] Any factors to be taken into account when assessing the gravity of the crime are not to be considered as aggravating circumstances (and *vice versa*).[80]

The gravity of the crime is a principal factor in determining sentence. On this note, Trial Chamber I determined Lubanga's crimes to be 'undoubtedly very serious.'[81] It emphasized how conscription involves compulsion and how children actively used in hostilities become exposed to 'real danger as potential targets.'[82] The Trial Chamber noted that '[t]he vulnerability of children mean [*sic*] that that they need to be afforded particular protection that does not apply to the general population, as recognised in various international treaties.'[83]

The sentencing judgment evokes the imagery of Lubanga's child victims—the only victims, given the narrowness of the charges—as vulnerable and passive. It prioritizes and excerpts from Dr. Schauer's expert submissions, entitled in written form 'The Psychological Impact of Child Soldiering' and also presented in oral

---

75 Ibid., para 3 dissent.

76 Ibid., para 25 dissent.

77 Ibid., para 27.

78 Ibid., para 29. It found that these conditions were satisfied in the *Lubanga* case.

79 Ibid., paras 33–34.

80 Ibid, para 35.

81 Ibid., para 37.

82 Ibid., para 37.

83 Ibid., para 37 (lengthy footnote omitted).

testimony at trial.[84] Elements of Dr. Schauer's work that are viewed as probative to Trial Chamber I's sentencing analysis include her submissions that '[a]mong a number of at risk populations, children of war and child soldiers are a particularly vulnerable group and often suffer from devastating long-term consequences of experienced or witnesses acts of violence' and that conflict experiences 'can hamper children's healthy development and their ability to function fully even once the violence has ceased.'[85] Noting that the purpose of the prohibition against the use of child soldiers is to protect children, in this case under the age of fifteen, from the risks associated with armed conflict,[86] Trial Chamber I specifically included among these the 'inevitable risk of being wounded or killed.'[87] Trial Chamber I relied upon Dr. Schauer's written submissions and testimony to determine that 'a significant number of the children who were interviewed had developed the debilitating mental health condition known as post-traumatic stress disorder.'[88] The interviews in question arose within 'studies carried out with former child soldiers in various countries including Uganda and the DRC between 2004 and 2008.'[89] According to Dr. Schauer, 'the post-traumatic stress tends to persist, possibly for the remainder of the individual's life.'[90] Trial Chamber I noted that '[a] significant percentage of the former child soldiers who were the subject of the study had abused drugs or alcohol; they suffered from depression and dissociation; and some demonstrated suicidal behaviour.'[91] The fact that this important thread of evidence arose from studies that included jurisdictions and armed groups well beyond Lubanga's in the DRC raises the specter of legality concerns. These concerns, however, do not appear in the sentencing judgment.

Trial Chamber I relied upon Dr. Schauer's emphasis on the frequency of 'severe forms of multiple psychological disorders' among child soldiers.[92] Trial Chamber I also excerpted from her written submissions that former child soldiers 'have little skills to handle life without violence,' that they show 'ongoing aggressiveness within their families and communities even after relocation to their home villages,' and that 'psychological exposure and suffering from trauma can cripple individuals and families even into the next generations.'[93] Trial Chamber I held that '[s]tudies indicate that abduction and the consequent trauma have a negative impact on their

---

[84] Ibid., paras 38–39.

[85] Ibid., para 39 (internal quotations omitted).

[86] Ibid., para 38.

[87] Ibid., para 40.

[88] Ibid., para 40.

[89] Ibid., para 40. Dr. Schauer's testimony involved extensive reference to data from Northern Uganda, as well as other jurisdictions.

[90] Ibid., para 40.

[91] Ibid., para 41.

[92] Ibid., para 40 (internal quotations omitted).

[93] Ibid., para 41 (internal quotations omitted).

[*n.b.* former child soldiers'] education and cognitive abilities.'[94] I would add, however, that the prevalence of abduction into the UPC/FPLC likely did not constitute a dominant recruitment mechanism; the incidence thereof is lower than into groups such as the RUF or LRA.[95] In fact, UN Special Representative Coomaraswamy gave evidence that 'many of the children she had spoken with voluntarily joined armed groups because of their circumstances.'[96] When discussing this evidence in the sentencing judgment, Trial Chamber I immediately discounted its relevance by remarking that 'the consent of a child to recruitment does not constitute a valid defence to any of the crimes.'[97] Trial Chamber I also noted how, according to Dr. Schauer, children who have 'been child soldiers for a significant period of time usually do not demonstrate "civilian life skills."'[98] In sum, the dire nature of the consequences (the 'damage caused') of the illicit recruitment on the victims—that is, the children and their families—is intimately connected to the gravity of the crime.[99]

Dr. Schauer merits great commendation for her tireless and herculean efforts on behalf of children affected by armed conflict. A tricky question arises, nonetheless, when eminent academics/professionals also coordinate non-governmental activist organizations. This question, which arises generally in national legal systems as well, relates to whether advocates, no matter how principled, should serve as experts. If they do so, then, what effects might arise for the legality of the system of international justice?[100] Upon the due process rights of the accused? Looking beyond activism and advocacy, what is the ICC saying, epistemologically, when it relies on the research of one discipline, in this case child psychology? What does this suggest more broadly about the sources of information that comprise conventional wisdom about child soldiering? Child psychology and the reports of human rights groups play a dominant role in shaping our understanding of child soldiering. As I have argued elsewhere, a number of other disciplines have much to say about militarized youth, yet these other disciplines—for example ethnography, anthropology, adolescent neurobiology, and feminist studies—do not get much traction within the international legal imagination.[101] Research emerging from these disciplines may—depending on the specific context—suggest a less frail and more engaged reality of child soldiers as social navigators.

---

[94] Ibid., 2012, para 41.

[95] Drumbl 2012, pp. 66–69 (LRA), and 64–65 and 70–74 (Sierra Leone, including the RUF, but noting the prevalence of enlistment of child volunteers into the CDF).

[96] *Lubanga* Sentencing Judgment 2012, para 43. She noted that this was frequently 'as a matter of pure survival'.

[97] Ibid.

[98] Ibid., para 42.

[99] Ibid., para 44.

[100] *Cf* Schabas 2012 ('Perhaps we are too uncritical in listening to experts, who are in fact child rights advocates, and their claims about the impact of war on child psychology.').

[101] Drumbl 2012, pp. 11–12, 52–53, 61–101.

In the *Taylor* trial judgment, relatedly, the SCSL Trial Chamber cited approvingly from an expert report prepared for the Prosecution, as well as the research of the Coalition to Stop the Use of Child Soldiers (now Child Soldiers International), Amnesty International, and Human Rights Watch.[102] When fact-finding by advocacy organizations becomes relied upon by international judges, it is all the more important for the fact-finders to cleave data collection/presentation from advocacy and, in turn, to rely on neutral, dispassionate, and empirically rigorous scientific methodologies. Else, confirmation bias or normativity may settle into—and, however well-intentioned, distort—the fact-finding process, only to become subsequently authenticated as judicial truths.

Returning to the *Lubanga* sentencing judgment, Trial Chamber I also identified the large-scale, significant, and widespread nature of child soldier recruitment into and use by the UPC/FPLC as indicative of the gravity of the crimes. Trial Chamber I did not 'reach[] conclusions to the criminal standard, namely beyond reasonable doubt, as to the precise number, or proportion, of the recruits who were under 15 years,' but determined that 'the involvement of children was widespread.'[103] Finally, as to gravity, the sentencing judgment also linked Lubanga's degree of participation and intent,[104] his position of authority,[105] and his individual circumstances (namely, that he 'is clearly an intelligent and well-educated individual'),[106] to the gravity of the crimes.

No aggravating circumstances were established. The majority held that 'the evidence does not support a conclusion beyond reasonable doubt that the punishment of children below 15 years of age occurred in the ordinary course of the crimes for which Mr. Lubanga has been convicted.'[107] Nor was it 'demonstrated that the individual punishments [...] were the responsibility of Mr. Lubanga.'[108] In terms of sexual violence, the majority was cabined by—and 'strongly deprecate[d]'—the former Prosecutor's decision not to apply (and, in fact, to oppose) to include sexual violence or sexual slavery at any stage during the proceedings.[109]

---

[102] *See e.g.*, *Taylor* Sentencing Judgment 2012, paras 1359, 1360, 1361, 1410, 1436, 1541, 1553, 1566, 1568, 1575, 1581, 1598, 1600 (not a complete list).

[103] *Lubanga* Sentencing Judgment 2012, para 50.

[104] Ibid., para 97.

[105] Lubanga 'agreed to, and participated in, a common plan to build an army.' *Lubanga* Sentencing Judgment 2012, para 52. Although in the trial judgment Trial Chamber I 'did not conclude that Mr. Lubanga meant to conscript and enlist boys and girls under the age of 15 into the UPC/FPLC and to use them to participate actively in hostilities,' it did conclude that Lubanga 'was aware that, in the ordinary course of events, this would occur.' Ibid., para 52. Hence, Lubanga was convicted as a 'co-perpetrator who made an essential contribution to the common plan.' Ibid.

[106] Ibid., para 56.

[107] Ibid., para 59 (also concluding: '[N]othing suggests that Mr Lubanga ordered or encouraged these punishments, that he was aware of them or that they can otherwise be attributed to him in a way that reflects his culpability.').

[108] Ibid.

[109] Ibid., para 60.

Although the majority felt itself entitled to consider sexual violence in determining sentence, it also felt, based on the 'totality of the evidence,' that it was 'unable to conclude that sexual violence against the children who were recruited was sufficiently widespread that it could be characterised as occurring in the ordinary course of the implementation of the common plan for which Mr. Lubanga is responsible.'[110] Hence, sexual violence 'cannot properly form part of the assessment of his culpability for the purposes of sentence.'[111] Trial Chamber I did not consider the age of the child recruits as relevant to aggravation, because their age had already informed determinations of gravity.[112] The majority also found unproven the allegation, in aggravation, that Lubanga 'deliberately discriminated against women in committing these offenses.'[113]

Turning to mitigating factors, Trial Chamber I found that Lubanga's hope that peace would return to Ituri once he had secured his military objectives was 'only of limited relevance' insofar as, 'in order to achieve his goals, he used children as part of the armed forces over which he had control.'[114] The Trial Chamber also firmly emphasized Lubanga's notable and consistent cooperation with the Court, and that he 'was respectful and cooperative throughout the proceedings, notwithstanding some particularly onerous circumstances.'[115]

In dissent, Judge Odio Benito challenged the majority's decision to 'disregard' the damage to the victims and their families wrought by the harsh punishments and sexual violence.[116] Judge Odio Benito agreed with the majority that there were no aggravating circumstances, but would have considered this evidence in terms of the gravity of the crimes. Judge Odio Benito felt the punishments and sexual violence, and the resultant damage, had been proven beyond a reasonable doubt. She also invoked Dr. Schauer's expert evidence, which she found 'fundamental to determine the damage that the crimes for which Mr. Lubanga has been convicted cause on the lives of the young victims and their families.'[117] Judge Odio Benito underscored how Dr. Schauer noted that 'the post-traumatic stress disorder may affect victims for their entire lives.'[118] Judge Odio Benito emphasized the intergenerational aspects of the effects of these crimes.[119] The fact the victims were

[110] Ibid., para 74. 'Moreover, nothing suggests that Mr Lubanga ordered or encouraged sexual violence, that he was aware of it or that it could otherwise be attributed to him in a way that reflects his culpability.' Ibid.

[111] Ibid., para 75.

[112] Ibid., para 78.

[113] Ibid., para 81.

[114] Ibid., para 87.

[115] Ibid., paras 91, 97.

[116] Ibid., dissent, para 2; *See also* ibid. dissent, para 22 (noting that 'these acts resulted in serious and often irreparable harm to the victims and their families').

[117] Ibid. dissent, para 9.

[118] Ibid.

[119] Ibid. *See also* ibid. dissent, para 19 ('Children born as a result of the sexual violence suffered by girls who were recruited are also deeply affected by these crimes and this is what was defined

under the age of fifteen additionally for Judge Odio Benito would be germane to determining sentence as an 'exacerbating factor[]:'

> [B]ecause of their age, many of the victims may never be able to be fully repaired for the harm they suffered and still continue to suffer. Their childhood was deeply affected by these crimes that have scarred their lives and those of their families forever.[120]

In the end, and after her powerful dissent, Judge Odio Benito would have sentenced Lubanga to fifteen years' imprisonment, this being one year longer than the majority, broken down as fifteen years, concurrently, for each of the enlistment, conscription, and use charges.

Lubanga's fourteen-year sentence is lower than that of other persons convicted internationally on child-soldier-related charges.[121] Trial Chamber I actively canvassed these other sentences in its deliberations. It noted that the SCSL has entered seven convictions in four cases for the crime of using child soldiers under the age of fifteen.[122] In two of these cases, separate sentences were issued on the child-soldier-related convictions. First, in the *RUF* case, Issa Sesay was awarded a fifty-year sentence and Morris Kallon a thirty-five-year sentence.[123] In the *RUF* case, when it came to determining the '"exceptionally high'" gravity of the criminal acts, the SCSL emphasized the large-scale nature of the use of child soldiers (including to commit gruesome atrocities), the prevalence of abduction, the cruel training, the very young age of some of the recruits, and the druggings.[124] Second, Trial Chamber I also considered the seven-year sentence issued to Allieu Kondewa for child soldiering crimes in the *CDF* (Civil Defence Forces) case,[125] although this specific conviction was ultimately quashed on appeal.

Charles Taylor's fifty-year global sentence, not discussed by Trial Chamber I, did not separately address the child soldier crimes.[126] In Taylor's case, SCSL Trial Chamber II mentioned the harms visited upon the former child soldiers when it discussed gravity in its sentencing judgment, although it did not do so extensively. For example, SCSL Trial Chamber II underscored the public stigma and the often

(Footnote 119 continued)
by expert Ms Schauer as the "transgenerational effects", which in her words "cripple individuals and families even into next generations."').

[120] Ibid. dissent, para 20.

[121] Lubanga's sentence comes in under, but not too far off, the average sentence at the ICTY, in cases involving murder and rape, but, as William Schabas observes, it also reflects 'the sort of sentence that domestic courts might give to a mid-level drug trafficker.' Schabas 2012.

[122] Ibid., para 12.

[123] Ibid, para 13. Sesay and Kallon received 52 years and 40 years in total, respectively, on all convictions.

[124] Ibid.

[125] Ibid., para 15.

[126] *Taylor* Sentencing Judgment 2012. The principal circumstance in aggravation of Taylor's sentence was his status as Head of State.

'irreparable' alienation suffered by former child soldiers, as well as the scarification of their bodies.[127] It also concluded that '[p]articularly reprehensible were the crimes committed against vulnerable groups', for example:

> Child soldiers, both boys and girls, had their innocence stolen and were forced to commit murders, rapes and mutilations at a very young age, their lives permanently marred by these traumatic experiences.[128]

In the *Taylor* trial judgment, it had been noted that the Prosecution evidence related 'almost entirely' to forcible conscription of children 'in circumstances of coercion.'[129]

In conclusion, the OTP bumped up against palpable limits in terms of the traction generated by its submissions regarding the gravity of the crimes for which Lubanga had been charged and convicted. The OTP, after all, had requested a 30-year sentence.[130] The OTP emphasized the devastation of the former child soldiers, which resonated with Trial Chamber I, but resulted only in what can best be described as a middling sentence.

5.5 Conclusion

Doubts have been raised whether Lubanga's case ought to have been prosecuted by the ICC. Lubanga had, after all, been in custody in the DRC on charges of genocide and crimes against humanity.[131] The case was admissible before the ICC because the OTP went forward with the child-soldier-related charges alone. This singularity of focus was supposed to simplify the case, but matters proved to be much more complicated in practice. Moreover, this singularity meant that the foulest instances of the conduct, to wit, the mass murders, abductions, and sexual violence perpetrated within and by the UPC/FPLC were not independently

---

[127] Ibid., para 71 (noting also that '[t]he Defence aptly described "the pain of lost limbs, the agony of not only rape in its commonly understood sense, but also the rape of childhood, the rape of innocence, possibly the rape of hope"' (footnote omitted)). See also ibid., para 72 ('Witness TF1-143 was 12 years old when he and 50 other boys and girls were captured by RUF rebels in September 1998 in Konkoba. The rebels turned him into a child soldier after carving the letters "RUF" on his chest. Having been told to amputate the hands of those who resisted him, this 12 year-old subsequently used a machete to amputate the hands of men who had refused to open the door of their shop. When ordered on a food-finding mission to rape an old woman they found at a farmhouse, the boy cried and refused, for which he was punished.' [footnotes omitted]).

[128] Ibid., para 75.

[129] *Taylor* Trial Judgment 2012, para 1363.

[130] *Cf* Rome Statute 1998, Article 77(1) (providing that the ICC may sentence a convict to '[i]mprisonment for a specified number of years, which may not exceed a maximum of 30 years' or '[a] term of life imprisonment when justified by the extreme gravity of the crime and the individual circumstances of the convicted person').

[131] Schabas 2012.

prosecuted. Eastern DRC was, and still is, among the most dangerous places in the world for women: electing not to prosecute rampant sexual violence in such a high-profile inaugural trial certainly transmitted a callous message. Prosecuting Lubanga only for conscription, enlistment, or use failed to reflect the full array of indignities that the child soldiers (and adults) had endured and, in turn, the harms the child soldiers (and adults) inflicted on communities. In fact, in a 2009 decision, ICC Trial Chamber I ruled that persons harmed by the conduct of children under the age of fifteen could not be considered direct or indirect victims for the purpose of participating in the criminal proceedings against Lubanga.[132] Manifestation of victim status was reserved for the child recruits (direct victims), regardless of their conduct, and their family members (indirect victims). All told, as Jørgensen eloquently concludes:

> The ghosts of more than one group of "invisible" victims may haunt the first completed trial before the ICC; those who suffered at the hands of child soldiers and those who suffered more because they were girls, and the next generation of children born of forced marriage.[133]

It is easy to blame a handful of crazed commanders for child soldiering. But this ease of blame fails to deracinate the many structural factors that conspire to facilitate child soldiering, including the small arms trade, self-interested behavior of foreign states, the aspirations of militarized youth, labor-market forces, and illegal export of pilfered natural resources. Justice for child soldiers, moreover, requires much more than sporadic criminal convictions of stigmatized adult recruiters. It requires reintegrating child soldiers into communities. It requires listening to former child soldiers and their priorities, which often include education, conflict resolution, community reintegration, physical rehabilitation, and jobs—not far away, languid trials or medicalized psychotherapy. It requires restoration for persons affected by the violent acts of child soldiers.

The reparative aspects of the *Lubanga* proceedings, which now follow, may redress some of these gaps while also diversifying the kinds of remedies available for systematic human rights abuses. On this latter note, the August 2012 *Lubanga* reparations decision portends a promising approach. In this decision, Trial Chamber I noted that reparations are not to be limited only to the small group of victims who participated in the trial and those who applied for reparations; it also supported collective reparations so as to avoid stigmatizing former child soldiers.[134] Despite stating that restoring the victim to the *status quo ante* will often be 'unachievable,'[135] Trial Chamber I overall struck an optimistic tone that empowers, as opposed to disables, former child soldiers. It emphasized the need to

---

[132] *Lubanga* Indirect Victims Decision 2009 (excluding from the category of indirect victims persons who suffered harm resulting from the later conduct of the direct victims). The OTP did not support this interpretation.

[133] Jørgensen 2012, para 64.

[134] *Lubanga* Reparations Decision 2012, paras 187, 219, 274.

[135] Ibid., para 223.

develop the former child soldiers' 'personalities, talents and abilities to the fullest possible extent'[136] and the need to consider their views when decisions are made about reparations (which, in this case, largely will be the province of the Trust Fund for Victims). On this note, Trial Chamber I recommended that the Trust Fund for Victims retain a team of 'multidisciplinary experts' to assist in assessing harms, effects, and identifying appropriate forms of reparations (hopefully this will pluralize the involved disciplines, persons, and perspectives).[137] Trial Chamber I took a view of rehabilitation that included much more than psychotherapy and mental health counseling.[138] It did not go so far, however, as to explicitly support the funding of transitional justice ventures (focusing on the child soldiers as witnesses, victims, and actors) to facilitate the reintegration of former child soldiers who committed acts of atrocity, nor did it explicitly discuss what to do about the victims (survivors, both children and adults, and the families of those killed) by child soldiers. Nonetheless, with a critical nod to the limited categories of victims who were eligible to participate in the *Lubanga* case owing to the limited scope of the OTP's charges, Trial Chamber I opined that '[r]eparations should secure, whenever possible, reconciliation between the convicted person, the victims of the crimes and the affected communities.'[139]

In sum, it seems that the very same Trial Chamber, when called upon to discuss reparations, was liberated from much of the disabling imagery that scripted its determination of judgment and sentence in the criminal proceedings against Lubanga.

References

Annan J, Blattman C, and Horton R (2006) The State of Youth and Youth Protection in Northern Uganda: Findings from the Survey for War Affected Youth (report prepared for UNICEF Uganda).

Annan J, Brier M, and Aryemo F (2009) From 'Rebel' to 'Returnee': Daily Life and Reintegration for Young Soldiers in Northern Uganda. Journal of Adolescent Research 24:639–667.

Ben-Ari E (2009) Facing Child Soldiers, Moral Issues, and "Real Soldiering": Anthropological Perspectives on Professional Armed Forces. Scientia Militaria: South African Journal of Military Studies, 37(1):1–24.

Blattman C and Annan J (2010) The Consequences of Child Soldiering. Review of Economics and Statistics 92(4):882–898.

Boyden J and de Berry J (2004) Introduction. In: Jo Boyden and Joanna de Berry (eds) Children and Youth on the Frontline: Ethnography, Armed Conflict and Displacement. Berghahn Books.

---

[136] Ibid., para 213.

[137] Ibid., paras 264–265.

[138] Ibid., paras 232–236.

[139] Ibid., para 193.

Brett R and Specht I (2004) Young Soldiers: Why They Choose to Fight. Lynne Rienner Publishers, Boulder.
Child Soldiers International (2012) Louder Than Words: An Agenda for Action to End State Use of Child Soldiers. Child Soldiers International, London.
Coalition to Stop the Use of Child Soldiers (2008) Child Soldiers Global Report 2008. Coalition to Stop the Use of Child Soldiers, London.
Cook J R (2012) Contemporary Practice of the United States: Liberian Removed from United States for Human Rights Abuses. American Journal of International Law 106:680–685.
Dallaire R (2010) They Fight Like Soldiers, They Die Like Children. Random House Canada, Toronto.
Denov M (2010) Child Soldiers: Sierra Leone's Revolutionary United Front. Cambridge University Press, Cambridge.
Drumbl M A (2012) Reimagining Child Soldiers in International Law and Policy. Oxford University Press, New York.
Easterday J (15 May 2009) Expert Reports on the Psychological Impact of Child Soldiering. http://www.lubangatrial.org/2009/05/15/expert-reports-on-the-psychological-impact-of-child-soldiering/. Accessed 22 May 2013.
Hart J (2006) Saving children: What role for anthropology? Anthropology Today 22(1):5–8.
International Center for Transitional Justice (12 August 2012) Colombia: Hay 18.000 menores en grupos armados y bandas. http://ictj.org/es/news/colombia-hay-18000-menores-en-grupos-armados-y-bandas. Accessed 15 August 2012.
International Labour Office (2003) Wounded Childhood: The Use of Children in Armed Conflict in Central Africa.
Invisible Children (5 March 2012) KONY 2012. http://www.youtube.com/watch?v=Y4MnpzG5Sqc. Accessed 22 May 2013.
Jørgensen N (2012) Child Soldiers and the Parameters of International Criminal Law. Chinese Journal of International Law 11(4):657–688.
Lloyd-George W, Inter Press Service (4 May 2012) Child Soldiers Used in Mali Conflict. http://allafrica.com/stories/201205041186.html. Accessed 8 May 2012.
Lubanga Trial Transcript (2009) Situation in the Democratic Republic of the Congo in the Case of Prosecutor v. Thomas Lubanga Dyilo, Trial English Language Transcript, Case No. ICC-01/04-01/06 (7 April 2009).
Lubanga Indirect Victims Decision (2009) Situation in the Democratic Republic of the Congo in the Case of Prosecutor v. Thomas Lubanga Dyilo, Decision on "Indirect Victims," Case No. ICC-01/04-01/06 (8 April 2009).
Lubanga Trial Judgment (2012) Situation in the Democratic Republic of the Congo in the Case of Prosecutor v. Thomas Lubanga Dyilo, Trial Judgment, Case No. ICC-01/04-01/06 (14 March 2012).
Lubanga Sentencing Judgment (2012) Situation in the Democratic Republic of the Congo in the Case of Prosecutor v. Thomas Lubanga Dyilo, Decision on Sentence, Case No. ICC-01/04-01/06 (10 July 2012).
Lubanga Reparations Decision (2012) Situation in the Democratic Republic of the Congo in the Case of Prosecutor v. Thomas Lubanga Dyilo, Decision establishing the principles and procedures to be applied to reparations, Case No. ICC-01/04-01/06 (7 August 2012).
McKnight J (2010) Child Soldiers in Africa: A Global Approach to Human Rights Protection, Enforcement and Post-Conflict Reintegration, African Journal of International and Comparative Law, 18(2):113–142.
Moreno-Ocampo L, Opening Statement in Situation in the Democratic Republic of the Congo in the Case of Prosecutor v. Thomas Lubanga Dyilo, Trial English Language Transcript, Case No. ICC-01/04-01/06 (26 January 2009) [Lubanga Trial Transcript].
Otunnu O (2000) Keynote Address: The Convention and Children in Situations of Armed Conflict. In: Lisa Carlson et al. (eds) Children in Extreme Situations, LSE Development Studies Institute, London.

Taylor Sentencing Judgment (2012) Prosecutor v. Charles Ghankay Taylor, Case No. SCSL-03-01-T (18 May 2012).

The Redress Trust (2006) Victims, Perpetrators or Heroes? Child Soldiers Before the International Criminal Court. http://www.redress.org/downloads/publications/childsoldiers.pdf. Accessed 22 May 2013.

Rosen D (2007) Child Soldiers, International Humanitarian Law, and the Globalization of Childhood. American Anthropologist 109(2):296–306.

Schmidt A (2007) Volunteer Child Soldiers as Reality: A Development Issue for Africa. New School Economic Review 2(1):49–76.

Siegel M (16-17 June 2012) Report Details Sex Abuse of Minors in Australian Forces, International Herald Tribune.

Singer P W (2006) Children at War. University of California Press, Berkley.

Spiga V (2010) Indirect Victims' Participation in the Lubanga Trial. Journal of International Criminal Justice 8:183–198.

United Nations (20 November 1989) Convention on the Rights of the Child, U.N. Doc. A/RES/44/25 (entered into force 2 September 1990) [Convention on the Rights of the Child].

United Nations (1998) Rome Statute of the International Criminal Court. http://untreaty.un.org/cod/icc/statute/romefra.htm. Accessed 22 May 2013).

United Nations (25 May 2000) Optional Protocol to the CRC on the involvement of children in armed conflict, U.N. Doc. A/RES/54/263 (entered into force 12 February 2002) [Optional Protocol].

United Nations (2006) Integrated Disarmament, Demobilization and Reintegration Standards (IDDRS). http://pksoi.army.mil/doctrine_concepts/documents/UN%20Guidelines/IDDRS.pdf. Accessed 22 May 2013.

UNICEF (April 1997) Cape Town Principles and Best Practices. http://www.unicef.org/emerg/files/Cape_Town_Principles(1).pdf. Accessed 22 May 2013.

UNICEF (2002) Adult Wars, Child Soldiers: Voices of Children Involved in Armed Conflict in the East Asia and Pacific Region.

UNICEF (February 2007) The Paris Principles: Principles and Guidelines on Children Associated with Armed Forces or Armed Groups. http://www.unicef.org/emerg/files/ParisPrinciples310107English.pdf. Accessed 22 May 2013.

UNICEF Innocenti Research Centre in cooperation with the International Center for Transitional Justice (August 2010) Children and Truth Commissions. http://www.unicef-irc.org/publications/pdf/truth_commissions_eng.pdf. Accessed 22 May 2013.

UNICEF (3 December 2012) Five new countries endorse the Paris commitments to end the use of children in conflict. http://childrenandarmedconflict.un.org/press-releases/five-new-countries-endorse-the-paris-commitments-to-end-the-use-of-children-in-conflict/. Accessed 22 May 2013.

Utas M (2003) Sweet Battlefields: Youth and the Liberian Civil War. Lindblom & Co., Stockholm.

Vivo, who is who in vivo. http://www.vivo.org/about_vivo/who_is_who_in_vivo/index_eng.html. Accessed 25 January 2013.

Wessells M (2004) Psychosocial Issues in Reintegrating Child Soldiers. Cornell International Law Journal 37:513–525.

Wessells M (2006) Child Soldiers: From Violence to Protection. Harvard University Press, Cambridge.

Women's Initiatives for Gender Justice (August 2012) Legal Eye on the ICC Special Issue # 3. http://www.iccwomen.org/news/docs/WI-LegalEye8-12-FULL/LegalEye8-12.html. Accessed 14 August 2012.

World Health Organization (2009) Bulletin of the World Health Organization: Healing Child Soldiers. http://www.who.int/bulletin/volumes/87/5/09-020509/en/. Accessed April 18, 2013.

Further Reading

Drumbl M A (2012) Child Soldiers and Clicktivism: Justice, Myths, and Prevention, Journal of Human Rights Practice 4(3):481–485.

Drumbl M A (3 March 2012) Lubanga Decision Roundtable: Lubanga Legacies? http://opiniojuris.org/2012/03/19/lubanga-decision-roundtable-legacies/. Accessed 22 May 2013.

International Center for Transitional Justice (2012) Engaging Children and Youth in Transitional Justice Processes: Guidance for Outreach Programs. http://ictj.org/sites/default/files/ICTJ-Report-Childrens-Outreach-Guidelines-Nov2012.pdf. Accessed 22 May 2013.

International Criminal Court (18 December 2012) ICC Trial Chamber II acquits Mathieu Ngudjolo Chui. http://www.icc-cpi.int/en_menus/icc/press%20and%20media/press%20releases/news%20and%20highlights/Pages/pr865.aspx. Accessed 3 March 2013.

Schabas W (13 July 2012) Lubanga Sentenced to Fourteen Years. http://humanrightsdoctorate.blogspot.nl/2012/07/lubange-sentence-to-fourteen-years.html. Accessed 16 July 2012.

Chapter 6
Sexual Violence Against Children on the Battlefield as a Crime of Using Child Soldiers: Square Pegs in Round Holes and Missed Opportunities in *Lubanga*

Joe Tan

Contents

The author is a Lawyer in the Human Dignity Trust, London. Former Legal Advisor, Pre-Trial Chamber, Special Tribunal for Lebanon and Former Legal Assistant to the Special Advisor on International Humanitarian Law at the International Criminal Court. The author acknowledges the support of Professor Timothy McCormack and the Melbourne Law School, University of Melbourne and is grateful for the insightful comments of Valentina Azarov and Lachezar Yanev on previous versions of this article as well as those of the anonymous reviewers. Any errors remain solely the responsibility of the author. All views are strictly personal and do not represent the position of the United Nations or the International Criminal Court.

J. Tan (✉)
Human Dignity Trust, London, UK
e-mail: joewtan@gmail.com

T. D. Gill et al. (eds.), *Yearbook of International Humanitarian Law 2012*,
Yearbook of International Humanitarian Law 15, DOI: 10.1007/978-90-6704-924-5_6,

6.1 Introduction

On 14 March 2012, the International Criminal Court ('ICC') delivered its historic and much anticipated first judgment in the case of *Prosecutor v Thomas Lubanga Dyilo*.[1] The Accused in the case was charged and convicted of conscripting and enlisting children under the age of 15 into armed forces or groups and using those children to participate actively in hostilities. While the ICC was not the first international court to have done so, having been beaten to this distinction by the Special Court for Sierra Leone ('SCSL'),[2] it is an important judgment nonetheless for providing some much needed clarification on the law. One of the more significant contributions of the *Lubanga* judgment was the recognition of the crime of 'using'[3] children to participate actively in hostilities as an offense in its own right, distinct from the 'recruitment' crimes of conscripting or enlisting children into armed forces or groups. All three crimes are referred to in the single provision of Article 8(2)(e)(vii) of the *Rome Statute* ('child soldiers provision'). The case is unique due to the Prosecution's attempt to run the novel argument that acts of sexual violence (rape, forced marriages and sexual slavery) by commanders against girls—primarily 'child soldiers'[4] but also civilians—constituted the crime of using child soldiers.

Section 6.2 of this article begins with an overview of how the prosecution of Mr. Lubanga was undertaken and progressed. Notably, sexual violence came to attain prominence haphazardly and belatedly in the proceedings rather than by way of any deliberate case theory properly investigated, pleaded and particularized in the Document Containing the Charges from the outset. Bound by charges of conscription, enlistment and use of child soldiers as confirmed by the Pre-Trial Chamber, the Prosecution found itself in the difficult position of pursuing a sexual violence case with the blunt instrument of the child soldiers provision. Misconceptions in the SCSL, which saw the crime of use conflated with conscription/enlistment, were also repeated by the Prosecution in *Lubanga*.

As outlined in Sect. 6.3, the findings of a divided Trial Chamber revealed a stark divergence on the issue of the capacity of the child soldiers provision to encompass sexual violence. A majority refused to entertain the Prosecution's case on sexual violence as a form of use of child soldiers—albeit, on a technicality for

---

[1] ICC, *Prosecutor v Thomas Lubanga Dyilo*, ICC-01/04-01/06, Trial Judgment, 14 March 2012 (hereinafter '*Lubanga* Trial Judgment').

[2] SCSL, *Prosecutor v Brima, Kamara and Kanu*, SCSL-04-16-T, Trial Judgment, 20 June 2007 (Trial Chamber) (hereinafter: '*AFRC* Trial Judgment').

[3] For the sake of brevity, the shorthand term 'use' or 'using' is adopted in this article from time to time to refer to the use of children under fifteen years of age to participate actively in hostilities.

[4] For the sake of brevity, the commonly known term 'child soldiers' is adopted in this article to refer to children under the age of fifteen years who have been conscripted or enlisted into armed forces or groups or used to participate actively in hostilities.

not disclosing or referring to the facts and circumstances as required by the *Rome Statute*.[5]

In Sect. 6.4, the vigorous dissent of the minority decision, which did fully engage with the Prosecution's submissions, is analyzed and critiqued. The minority relied heavily on international human rights law ('IHRL') and 'soft law' to expand the scope of the crime of using child soldiers to include forms of sexual violence. The author develops the principal submission that these IHRL and 'soft law' norms were overstated at the expense of international humanitarian law ('IHL'). In fact, such an approach by the minority had the distortive effect of *decreasing* the level of protection available to sexual exploited girls under IHL and opening up a protection gap. In order to preserve the integrity of IHL, an interpretation of Article 8(2)(e)(vii) consistent with the notion of 'active participation in hostilities' in IHL should be maintained. It is submitted further that the proper approach in dealing with sexual violence against children is not by way of the child soldier provision, but rather via the ample specific sexual offense provisions listed in the *Rome Statute* as war crimes and crimes against humanity, which should be charged cumulatively in addition to any child soldiers offense.

Finally in Sect. 6.5, two missed opportunities that escaped the attention of both the majority and minority decisions in *Lubanga* are addressed. First, a more plausible argument that sexual violence possibly constitutes 'conscription' rather than the use of child soldiers. Conscription, unlike the crime of use, is not burdened by the qualification 'active participation in hostilities' and does not require an inquiry into the form of activity engaged in by the child. Secondly, the use of child soldiers to commit crimes of sexual violence against other female civilian children was not fully explored. This arises, for instance, in cases where child soldiers are ordered to abduct a civilian girl and bring her back to camp for the commander to sexually exploit. These oversights were, in part, due to a failure to appreciate the distinction between the crimes of conscription, enlistment and use of child soldiers.

6.2 Sexual Violence Prosecution Through the Back Door

Sexual violence is viewed by some as a 'defining characteristic' of the conflict in the eastern Democratic Republic of the Congo ('DRC').[6] Indeed, the UN Secretary-General's Special Representative on Sexual Violence in Conflict, Margot Wallström, famously singled out the eastern DRC as the 'rape capital of the

---

[5] *Rome Statute of the International Criminal Court*, opened for signature 17 July 1998, 2187 UNTS 90 Article 74 (entered into force 1 July 2002) ('Rome Statute').

[6] Letter from Women's Initiative for Gender Justice to Luis Moreno-Ocampo, August 2006, available at: http://www.iccwomen.org/news/docs/Prosecutor_Letter_August_2006_Redacted.pdf (hereinafter: 'Letter from Women's Initiative for Gender Justice to Luis Moreno-Ocampo').

world'.[7] Certainly, it had been well documented that rape as a weapon of war had been systematically utilized against women and girls (some as young as 12 years of age) by all parties to the conflict in the eastern district of Ituri, including Lubanga's armed militia groups, the *Union des Patriotes Congolais* (Union of Congolese Patriots) and the *Forces patriotiques pour le libération du Congo* (Patriotic Force for the Liberation of Congo) ('UPC/FPLC').[8] These reports identified, in particular, the problem of sexual violence against girls abducted by militia groups in the DRC.[9]

The vexed issue of sexual violence came to be one of the most contentious and controversial aspects of the *Lubanga* proceedings. As the foregoing outline will demonstrate, the problematic issue of sexual violence was compounded by a series of complications in the carriage of the case. This included the Prosecution's vacillating positions on the inclusion of sexual violence, a significant technical error in omitting to describe the facts and circumstances of sexual violence in the Document Containing the Charges, inadequate investigations and a case theory which failed to appreciate the distinction between conscription, enlistment and the use of child soldiers.

6.2.1 Pre-trial Phase

In September 2003, Luis Moreno-Ocampo, then Prosecutor of the ICC, announced his intention to commence an investigation on the DRC situation.[10] Based on reports by States, international organizations and non-governmental organizations, the Prosecutor expressly recognized the DRC situation was characterized by 'a pattern of rape, torture, forced displacement and the illegal use of child soldiers'.[11] Yet, on 10 February 2006, the Prosecution obtained an arrest warrant against Lubanga which only contained charges for the crime of conscripting, enlisting and using children to participate actively in hostilities and omitted any

---

[7] UN News Centre, 'Tackling sexual violence must include prevention, ending impunity—UN official', 27 April 2010 available at http://www.un.org/apps/news/story.asp?NewsID=34502.

[8] United Nations Security Council, 'Special report on the events in Ituri, January 2002-December 2003' under cover of letter dated 16 July 2004 from the Secretary-General addressed to the President of the Security Council, UN Doc. S/2004/573 (2004), paras 37, 80 and 108. For investigations conducted by other international human rights organizations, see also, Amnesty International 2004; Human Rights Watch 2005, pp. 19–20.

[9] Amnesty International 2003, pp. 8–9; Save the Children Fund 2005, pp. 11–16; Coalition to Stop the Use of Child Soldiers 2004, p. 52.

[10] ICC, 'The Office of the Prosecutor of the International Criminal Court opens its first investigation', (Press Release, 23 June 2004) available at http://www.icc-cpi.int/en_menus/icc/press%20and%20media/press%20releases/2004/Pages/the%20office%20of%20the%20prosecutor%20of%20the%20international%20criminal%20court%20opens%20its%20first%20investigation.aspx.

[11] Ibid.

mention of acts of sexual violence whatsoever.[12] This was despite repeated acknowledgement of the prominence of sexual violence in the eastern DRC where Lubanga and his armed groups operated.[13] Within the ICC's jurisdiction *ratione materiae*, Article 8(2)(e) of the *Rome Statute*—which formed the basis of the charges and ultimately the conviction in the *Lubanga* judgment—defines a 'war crime' to mean *inter alia*:

> Other serious violations of the laws and customs applicable in armed conflicts not of an international character, within the established framework of international law, namely, any of the following acts:
>
> …
>
> (vii) Conscripting or enlisting children under the age of fifteen years into armed forces or groups or using them to participate actively in hostilities.

Article 8(2)(b)(xxvi) is the similarly worded counterpart applicable in international armed conflicts.[14]

When challenged by civil society groups as to whether any serious investigations into gender-based crimes had been conducted at all, the Prosecution responded to criticisms by explaining that there was insufficient time to include gender-based crimes. Instead, it insisted that 'evidence of gender-based crimes was insufficient because either the evidence did not exist or… crimes of rape and other forms of sexual violence committed by the UPC were opportunistic and not conducted on a large scale'.[15]

Furthermore, on assuming office, Moreno-Ocampo adopted a policy of short, 'focused investigations' examining only a 'sample' of crimes committed, which would purportedly be 'reflective of the gravest incidents and the main types of victimization'.[16] This approach of conducting 'limited scope' investigations and prosecutions was justified by the Prosecution as a means to avoid the exhaustive investigations and long proceedings at the *ad hoc* Tribunals for the Former Yugoslavia and Rwanda but the inadequate resourcing of investigations was

---

[12] *Prosecutor v Lubanga*, ICC-01/04-01/06, Warrant of Arrest, 10 February 2006 (Pre-Trial Chamber I).

[13] Prosecutor Luis Moreno-Ocampo, *Third Session of the Assembly of States Parties to the Rome Statute of the International Criminal Court* (Address delivered at the Third Session of the Assembly of States Parties, The Hague, 6 September 2004); ICC, *Report of the International Criminal Court*, UN Doc A/60/177 (2005), para 37; ICC, *Report on the activities of the Court*, ICC Doc ICC-ASP/4/16, Assembly of States Parties, Fourth Session, 28 November to 3 December 2005, para 53: 'The Office of the Prosecutor is investigating the situation in the Democratic Republic of the Congo, which involves allegations of thousands of deaths by mass murder and summary execution since 2002, as well as large-scale patterns of rape, torture and use of child soldiers.'

[14] Article 8(2)(b)(xxvi) of the *Rome Statute* is identical in all relevant aspects to Article 8(2)(e)(vii), save for the substitution of the words 'the national armed forces' instead of 'armed forces or groups'. The analysis in this article applies *mutatis mutandis* to international armed conflicts.

[15] Letter from Women's Initiative for Gender Justice to Luis Moreno-Ocampo, p. 5.

[16] ICC Office of the Prosecutor, *Report on Prosecutorial Strategy*, September 2006, pp. 5–6.

subject to criticism by civil society groups.[17] Short cuts taken in investigations ultimately had an adverse impact on both the strength of the prosecution case and the length of proceedings.[18]

In any event, the Prosecution was resolute in staying its course and pressed on. On 28 August 2006, the Prosecution filed the "Document Containing the Charges" accusing Thomas Lubanga Dyilo of the war crimes of conscripting, enlisting or using child soldiers.[19] No charges or factual particulars of sexual crimes were included. Nor was there any reference made to acts of sexual violence against girl child soldiers at the subsequent confirmation hearing before the Pre-Trial Chamber.

6.2.2 The Trial Phase

The next *volte face* occurred at the opening of the trial two and a half years after the filing of the Document Containing the Charges. Surprisingly, the Prosecution launched into highly detailed submissions in its opening address on the evidence it intended to lead on forms of sexual violence committed by commanders and boy soldiers including instances of rape, sexual slavery and forced marriage. Indeed, it appeared that in highlighting his determination that 'in this International Criminal Court, the girl soldiers will not be invisible',[20] the Prosecutor intended to construct the case on child soldiers, with sexual violence as its centerpiece. Hence on the issue of rape, the Prosecution submitted in its opening address:

> [A] child told us how during fighting at Lipri the commanders: *'really encouraged us to rape women, and the commanders will send [us] to look for women. So we took them and brought them to the camp and then we did those bad things'*.[21]
>
> Let me address the particular issue of sexual violence in the context of child recruitment and the fate of girl soldiers enlisted, conscripted, and used in combat by Thomas Lubanga's militia. In the camps child soldiers were exposed to the sexual violence perpetrated by Thomas Lubanga's men in unspeakable ways. As I said before, *young boys were instructed to rape. In the training camps, girl soldiers were the daily victims of rape by the commanders* … One of our witnesses will describe how he observed *daily examples of his commanders raping girl soldiers*.[22]

---

[17] International Federation for Human Rights (FIDH), *The Office of the Prosecutor of the ICC—9 Years On* (2011), p. 10.

[18] An over-reliance on UN reports and intermediaries and refusal to disclose their details to the defense resulted in two separate stays of the proceedings. The use of intermediaries also had an adverse impact on the credibility of many Prosecution witnesses leading to the exclusion of their testimonies from the final judgment by the Trial Chamber.

[19] *Prosecutor v Lubanga*, ICC-01/04-01/06, Document Containing the Charges, Article 61(3)(a), 28 August 2006.

[20] *Prosecutor v Lubanga*, ICC-01/04-01/06, Transcript of Proceedings, (Trial Chamber I) (hereinafter '*Lubanga* Trial Transcript'), 26 January 2009, p. 13, lines 7–8.

[21] Ibid., p. 10, lines 8–10 (emphasis added).

[22] Ibid., p. 11, lines 17–13 and line 4 (emphasis added).

On the issue of sexual slavery:

> The victims have endured physical and psychological harm and still have traces of… this moral damage today, stigmatisation for one. In particular, *young girls were subjected to sexual violence, sometimes even sexual slavery*.[23]

Likewise on forced marriage:

> You will hear that as soon as the girl's breasts started to grow, Thomas Lubanga's *commanders could select them as their forced wife. "Wife" is the wrong word … they were sexual slaves* … You can still meet many of them in the Democratic Republic of Congo. *Some of them kept as so-called wives by the commanders* … These girl combatants are left on the margins of many disarmament, demobilisation and reintegration project.[24]

Needless to say, during the course of the trial itself, evidence emerged from witnesses who testified of widespread and systematic sexual violence and abuse of girls in camps, most frequently by commanders but also by other soldiers. Some of the girls were as young as 12 years of age.[25] Some had fallen pregnant resulting in abortions[26] and there were instances of multiple abortions.[27] New girl recruits were raped almost immediately during training by their trainers and commanders, irrespective of their age.[28] Other testimonies alluded to sexual slavery and girls being taken as 'wives' by commanders who were kept at home to tend to the commander's domestic and sexual needs.[29]

However, three critical aspects hampered the Prosecution's case from the very start. First, the omission in particularizing the facts or circumstances of sexual violence in the Document Containing the Charges proved fatal. This technical defect meant that the Trial Chamber was hamstrung in being able to issue any findings on alleged acts of sexual violence as Article 74 of the *Rome Statute* prohibits any final decision from exceeding the facts and circumstances described in the Document Containing the Charges.

Shortly after the Prosecutor's opening statement, the Legal Representatives of Victims attempted taking matters into their own hands to rectify the defect by filing an application requesting the Trial Chamber to add further charges of war crimes and crimes against humanity for sexual slavery and other forms of sexual violence, pursuant to regulation 55 of the Regulations of the Court.[30] The Prosecution opposed the application, arguing that it would cause unfairness to the

---

23 Ibid., p. 39, lines 25–40, line 3 (emphasis added).

24 Ibid., p. 11, lines 17–13, line 4 (emphasis added).

25 *Lubanga* Trial Transcript, 9 July 2009, p. 35, lines 17–23 (Witness P-0046).

26 Ibid., p. 31, lines 2–4 (Witness P-0046).

27 Ibid., p. 38, lines 11–14 (Witness P-0046).

28 Ibid., p. 16, lines 1–13 (Witness P-0016).

29 *Lubanga* Trial Transcript, 3 February 2009, p. 254, lines 8–11 (Witness P-0038); p. 78, lines 11–79, line 7 (Witness P-0055); p. 18, lines 18–17, line 4 (Witness P-0016).

30 *Prosecutor v Lubanga*, ICC-01/04-01, Joint Application of the Legal Representatives of the Victims for the Implementation of the Procedure under Regulation 55 of the Regulations of the Court, Case No ICC-01/04-01/06, 22 May 2009 (Trial Chamber). It was argued that regulation

accused if he was tried and convicted on this basis.[31] While the application was successful at first instance,[32] it was subsequently overturned by the Appeals Chamber.[33] Moreover, as the Prosecutor conceded before the Appeals Chamber,[34] Article 61(9) of the *Rome Statute* prevented the addition of charges after the confirmation stage was complete, and most definitely once the trial was underway.[35] This places a heavy burden on the Prosecution to ensure that investigations are thorough and complete, and pleadings are correctly settled at the outset of each case. Despite the Appeals Chamber's findings, the Prosecution pressed on obliviously by continuing to lead evidence and make submissions on sexual violence until the very close of proceedings.

The second feature of significance in the Prosecution's strategy, and probably of central importance to its case, was the contention that forms of sexual violence against child soldiers constituted a form of 'use' of the child to participate actively in hostilities.[36] Radhika Coomaraswamy, the UN Special Representative of the Secretary-General on Children and Armed Conflict ('UN Special Representative'),

(Footnote 30 continued)
55, in part, conferred the power on the Court to allow it to change the legal characterization of the facts during proceedings unconstrained by Article 74 of the *Rome Statute*.

[31] *Prosecutor v Lubanga*, ICC-01/04-01, Prosecution's Application for Leave to Appeal the "Decision giving notice to the parties and participants that the legal characterization of the facts may be subject to change in accordance with Regulation 55(2) of the Regulations of the Court", 12 August 2009 (Trial Chamber I) paras 22–23. See also, *Prosecutor v Lubanga*, ICC-01/04-01/06, Prosecution's Further Observations Regarding the Legal Representatives' Joint request Made Pursuant to Regulation 55, 12 June 2009.

[32] A majority of the Trial Chamber (Judge Adrian Fulford, dissenting) allowed the application. See, *Prosecutor v Lubanga*, ICC-01/04-01, Decision giving notice to the parties and participants that the legal characterization of the facts may be subject to change in accordance with Regulation 55(2) of the Regulations of the Court, 14 July 2009 (Trial Chamber I) and *Prosecutor v Lubanga*, ICC-01/04-01/06, Decision issuing a second corrigendum to the "Minority opinion on the 'Decision giving notice to the parties and participants that the legal characterization of facts may be subject to change in accordance with Regulation 55(2) of the Regulations of the Court'", 31 July 2009 (Trial Chamber I).

[33] *Prosecutor v Lubanga*, ICC-01/04-01/06, Judgment on the appeals of Mr Lubanga Dyilo and the Prosecutor against the Decision of Trial Chamber I of 14 July 2009 entitled "Decision giving notice to the parties and participants that the legal characterization of the facts may be subject to change in accordance with Regulation 55(2) of the Regulations of the Court", 8 December 2009 (Appeals Chamber) (hereinafter '*Lubanga* Regulation 55 Appeal Decision'). The Appeals Chamber confirmed that the entirety of regulation 55 had to be read subject to Article 74: see paras 89–93.

[34] *Lubanga* Regulation 55 Appeal Decision, para 55.

[35] Article 61(9), *Rome Statute*: 'After the charges are confirmed and before the trial has begun, the Prosecutor may, with the permission of the Pre-Trial Chamber and after notice to the accused, amend the charges. If the Prosecutor seeks to add additional charges or to substitute more serious charges, a hearing under this article to confirm those charges must be held. After commencement of the trial, the Prosecutor may, with the permission of the Trial Chamber, withdraw the charges.'

[36] *Prosecutor v Lubanga*, Prosecutor's Closing Brief, Case No. ICC-01/04-01/06, 1 June 2011 (hereinafter '*Lubanga* Prosecution Closing Brief') paras 142–143.

enlisted as a key expert witness for the Prosecution, argued further that 'active participation' for the purposes of Article 8(2)(e)(vii) could be determined by 'whether the child's participation served an *essential support function* to the armed force or armed group during the period of conflict.'[37] In doing so, the UN Special Representative stressed that a case-by-case approach was warranted in applying the 'essential support function' standard.[38]

Borrowing directly from 'soft law' human rights instruments relating to the reintegration of child soldiers into the community, the UN Special Representative acknowledged that the 'essential support function' standard 'deliberately moves away from a rigid definition of child soldiers as exclusively armed combatants and recognizes all children "participating in and *associated with* armed groups and forces" as victims of these crimes'.[39] If accepted, this would bring Article 8(2)(e)(vii) into line with the conception of a 'child associated with armed groups and forces' preferred by soft-law standards such as the *Principles and Guidelines on Children Associated with Armed Groups or Armed Forces*, commonly known as the 'Paris Principles'.[40] Accordingly, essential support functions were proposed to include, without limitation, cooks, porters, nurses, spies, messengers, administrators, translators, radio operators, medical assistants, public information workers, youth camp leaders and, most critically, 'girls and boys used for sexual exploitation'.[41]

Thirdly, the distinction between the three separate offenses of conscription, enlistment and use was not fully recognized or appreciated. In all fairness, this was not assisted by the rather ill drafted provision in Article 8(2)(e)(vii), which rolls up the concepts of conscription, enlistment and use and is beset by ambiguity. The language 'conscripting or enlisting children under the age of fifteen years into armed forces or groups or using them to participate actively in hostilities' leads the

---

37 *Prosecutor v Lubanga*, Written Submissions of the United Nations Special Representative of the Secretary-General on Children and Armed Conflict Submitted in Application of Rule 103 on the Rules of Procedure and Evidence, Case No ICC-01/04-01/06, 18 March 2008 (hereinafter 'UN Special Representative Submissions'), para 21. This standard is developed from the UN Integrated Disarmament, Demobilization and Reintegration Standards 2006. (hereinafter: '*Integrated Disarmament, Demobilization and Reintegration Standards*'). These standards relate to women's and girls' eligibility for reintegration assistance after being involved with armed forces or groups.

38 UN Special Representative Submissions, para 21. See also, Sivakumaran 2010, p. 1019.

39 UN Special Representative Submissions, para 22 (emphasis added).

40 UNICEF 2007 (hereinafter: 'Paris Principles'), p. 7.

41 UN Special Representative Submissions, para 23. See also, UNICEF 1997 (hereinafter 'Cape Town Principles'), p. 12 ('Definitions'). The Cape Town Principles were adopted in April 1997 at a symposium led by UNICEF on the Prevention of Recruitment of Children into the Armed Forces and on Demobilization and Social Reintegration of Child Soldiers in Africa. Among other things it was agreed that a 'child soldier' includes 'girls recruited for sexual purposes and for forced marriage'. The Cape Town Principles were subsequently reviewed and confirmed by the Paris Principles.

observer to query whether it speaks of one,[42] two (recruitment crimes of conscription/enlistment on one hand and use on the other)[43] or three distinct crimes. In particular, the wording 'using *them*' begs the question as to whether usage is referable only to children already conscripted or enlisted previously, rather than being a distinct and independent offense in its own right.

The exact provision, replicated in the Statute of the SCSL,[44] resulted in jurisprudence that failed to shed light on the matter. Instead, conscription and enlistment on the one hand, was repeatedly conflated with use and the provision as a whole was conceived not only as a single crime, but one by which acts of conscription or enlistment were interdependent with the use of children in hostilities. Hence in the seminal trial of *Prosecutor v Brima, Kamara and Kanu* ('*AFRC* Trial Judgment'), which witnessed the first ever conviction for the crime of recruiting child soldiers, the Trial Chamber observed that '[t]he *actus reus* of the *crime* [in the singular] can be satisfied by "conscripting" or "enlisting" children under the age of 15, or by "using" them to participate actively in hostilities'.[45] Moreover, conscription was held to 'encompass acts of coercion, such as abductions and forced recruitment ... committed *for the purpose of* using them to participate actively in hostilities'.[46]

Similarly, at various points of the *Lubanga* proceedings, the Prosecution exhibited a tendency to conflate the recruitment crimes (conscription/enlistment) with use. Hence in his very opening statement at the commencement of trial, Moreno-Ocampo submitted:

> [D]uring the course of this trial my office will make it its mission to ensure that Thomas Lubanga is held criminally responsible for the atrocities committed against those little girl soldiers when he *enlisted and conscripted them to be used as sexual prey* when he used them in combat.[47]

This oversight in the Prosecution's case theory was evident as the concepts of recruitment and use continued to be indistinguishable and adopted interchangeably,

---

[42] Ambos 2012, p. 133; Schabas 2010, p. 252.

[43] Sivakumaran 2010, pp. 1011–1012.

[44] SCSL Statute, Article 4(c).

[45] *AFRC Trial Judgment*, para 733 (emphasis added). See also, SCSL, *Prosecutor v Fofana and Kondewa*, SCSL-04-14-A, Judgment, 28 May 2008 (Appeals Chamber), para 139 where it was observed: 'The *actus reus* requires that the accused recruited children by way of conscripting or enlisting them or that the accused used children to participate actively in hostilities.'

[46] SCSL, *Prosecutor v Norman*, SCSL-2004-14-AR72(E), 31 May 2004, Decision on Preliminary Motion Based on Lack of Jurisdiction (Child Recruitment), Dissenting Opinion of Justice Robertson (Appeals Chamber) (hereinafter '*CDF* Child Recruitment Decision Dissent'), para 1: Justice Robertson opined, that use was the 'more serious alternative' to enlistment involving, 'taking the more serious step, *having conscripted or enlisted them*, of putting their lives directly at risk in combat' (emphasis added). Followed in *AFRC* Trial Judgment, para 734; SCSL, *Prosecutor v Sesay, Kallon and Gbao*, SCSL-04-15-T, Judgment, 2 March 2009 (Trial Chamber) (hereinafter '*RUF* Trial Judgment'), para 1695.

[47] *Lubanga* Trial Transcript, 26 January 2009, p. 11, lines 17–13, line 4 (emphasis added).

particularly in the crucial final stages of its case. Hence, in adopting the 'essential' support or function test proposed by the UN Special Representative, the Prosecution submitted in its final closing brief that sexual violence conduct perpetrated against young girl soldiers constituted use but then confused this with the concept of recruitment. Consequently, it was submitted:

> **Active Participation**
>
> The term 'child soldiers' commonly refers to children under the age of 18 [sic] who partake in an armed group or force, regular or irregular, in any capacity. It is not restricted to children who actively fight. It also includes children whose roles are *essential* to the functioning of the armed group, such as those working as cooks, porters, messengers, as well as girls *recruited for sexual purposes and forced marriage*.[48]

During the ensuing final oral submissions, however, the Prosecution proceeded to refer at various points to sexual violence solely as a crime of 'recruitment':

> The Prosecution submits that the war crime of enlisting and conscripting children under the age of 15 … encompasses all the acts suffered by the child during the training and during the time they were forced to be a soldier. *This interpretation is particularly relevant to capture the gender abuse, a crucial part of the recruitment of girls.* The Prosecution requests the Chamber to make clear that *these girls … are not the wives of, of commanders. They are also the victims of the crimes of recruitment* and have to be particularly protected … by this Court.[49]

When the Prosecutor was queried by Judge Odio Benito on the critical issue of how sexual violence could have any bearing in light of the constraints of Article 74, the language of conscription and use was again used interchangeably in his response:

> We believe the facts are that the girls were abused, *used as sexual slaves and raped.* We believe this suffering is part of the suffering of *conscription* … We allege that [these acts were] linked … with the *conscription … Gender crimes were committed as part of the conscription of girls—in the militias* … That is why the Prosecutor decided to confine the charges—*to present the suffering and the sexual abuse and the gender crime suffered by the girls in the camps just as conscription*, showing this gender aspect of the crime.[50]

The failure to properly appreciate the distinction between conscription/enlistment crimes and the crime of use is an issue that goes beyond mere theoretical interest. As submitted further below, while sexual violence is inappropriately characterized as 'use' (Sects. 6.4.1 and 6.4.2), a case of greater merit could have been made for the harms of sexual exploited child soldiers, most of whom had been abducted, to be captured under the crime of conscription (Sect. 6.5.1).

---

48 *Lubanga* Prosecution Closing Brief, para 139 (emphasis added).

49 *Lubanga* Trial Transcript, 25 August 2011, p. 10, lines 4–11.

50 Ibid., p. 53, lines 19–54, line 22.

6.3 Findings in the *Lubanga* Trial Judgment

The *Lubanga* Trial Judgment is welcome for bringing some much-needed clarity to the terminological and conceptual uncertainty surrounding Article 8(2)(e)(vii). The Trial Chamber construed the disjunctive 'or', referred to twice in the provision, but particularly preceding the 'use' limb, as clearly delineating each of the three limbs—conscription, enlistment and use—so that each are to be considered a separate criminal offense in their own right.[51] Specifically, the Chamber unanimously held that the crime of use must be able to be applied independently from the recruitment crimes of conscription and enlistment, and *vice versa*.[52]

Having established the distinctive nature of the crime of using child soldiers, it remained necessary to determine its content and limits. Critically, the crime of use (unlike conscription and enlistment) is qualified by the further requirement that the child must be used to 'participate actively in hostilities' in order for criminal liability to attach. On this point and the issue of sexual violence in the *Lubanga* proceedings, Trial Chamber I was divided in very significant respects.

6.3.1 The Majority Decision

Ultimately, the majority of the *Lubanga* Trial Chamber (comprising of Judges Fulford and Blattmann) adopted the 'risk' test noting that 'the extent of the potential danger faced by a child soldier will often be unrelated to the precise nature of the role he or she is given'.[53] The Chamber held that the decisive factor in deciding if an 'indirect' role constitutes 'active participation in hostilities' is 'whether the support provided by the child to the combatants exposed him or her to real danger as a potential target'.[54] Additionally, given the vastly different types of roles that may be performed by children used by armed groups, the Chamber held that a determination of whether a particular activity constitutes 'active participation' can only be made on a case-by-case basis.[55]

The *Lubanga* Trial Chamber adopted and developed a version of the test articulated by the SCSL in the *AFRC* Trial Judgment that an accused who 'put … at sufficient risk' a child who was used in hostilities would be criminally liable.[56] On that basis, the use of a child to guard a diamond mine amounted to active

[51] *Lubanga* Trial Judgment, para 609. See also, Smith 2004, p. 1144; Sivakumaran 2010, p. 1012.

[52] Ibid., para 620.

[53] Ibid., para 628.

[54] Ibid.

[55] Ibid.

[56] Ibid. This formulation is wider than Justice Robertson's finding in *obiter* that use entails putting their lives 'directly at risk in combat': *CDF* Child Recruitment Decision Dissent, para 5.

participation in hostilities.[57] Diamond mining figured prominently in the Sierra Leone cases because diamonds were mined and sold to raise revenue to finance war efforts. Child soldiers were armed and ordered to kill anyone who tried to escape or take diamonds away from the area.[58] Diamond mines became highly contested and strategic locations in the conflict and therefore potential military targets as armed groups fought for their control. Consequently, it is understandable that placing child guards at these locations put them in direct danger of being caught in hostilities.[59]

Commendably, the *Lubanga* Trial Chamber steered a prudent course by refraining from endorsing other broader tests espoused in the Sierra Leone jurisprudence such as the formulation that 'any labour or support that gives effect to, or helps maintain, operations in a conflict constitutes active participation'.[60] Even more broadly, the *AFRC* Trial Chamber suggested, as a second standard, that regardless of the specific duties of the children, the mere 'presence of children in locations where crimes were widely committed' could constitute a violation of the use offense.[61] This sufficed, for example, to render the use of child soldiers at the AFRC Secretariat unlawful, simply because this was a location where crimes had been committed.[62]

Yet, despite adopting the risk test, the majority of the Trial Chamber in *Lubanga* concluded that it was bound by a previous ruling of the Appeals Chamber that, pursuant to Article 74 of the *Rome Statute*, the Trial Chamber's final decision is forbidden from exceeding the factual allegations described in the Document Containing the Charges.[63] As the majority observed, '[f]actual allegations potentially supporting sexual slavery are simply not referred to at any stage in the Decision on the Confirmation of Charges'.[64] Accordingly, it declined to entertain any request by the Prosecution to consider the issue of whether sexual violence may properly be included within the scope of 'using [children under the age of fifteen] to participate actively in hostilities' as a matter of law, as well as any such evidence or submissions in support.

---

[57] *RUF* Trial Judgment, para 1725; ICC, *Prosecutor v Lubanga*, Decision on the Confirmation of Charges, Case No ICC-01/04-01/06, 29 January 2007 (Pre-Trial Chamber I) (hereinafter '*Lubanga* Confirmation Decision'), para 263.

[58] SCSL, *Prosecutor v Charles Ghankay Taylor*, SCSL-03-01-T, Judgment, 18 May 2012 (Trial Chamber) (hereinafter '*Taylor* Trial Judgment'), para 1458.

[59] Ibid., para 1459.

[60] *AFRC* Trial Judgment, para 737. On this basis, carrying loads for the fighting faction, finding or acquiring food, carrying ammunition or equipment, acting as decoys, carrying messages, making trails or finding routes were found to constitute 'active participation' in hostilities.

[61] *AFRC* Trial Judgment, para 1267.

[62] Ibid.

[63] *Lubanga* Regulation 55 Appeal Decision.

[64] *Lubanga* Trial Judgment, para 630.

6.3.2 The Minority Decision

In a separate decision dissenting on the issue of sexual violence, Judge Odio Benito agreed with the risk test espoused by the majority, but insisted that this did not go sufficiently far enough. Rather, Judge Odio Benito noted that the protection afforded by Article 8(2)(e)(vii) extended also to the risk of children being a target of their 'own' armed group. These groups were responsible for recruiting and ultimately subjecting the children to mistreatment in ways that were incompatible with, and in violation of, children's fundamental rights.[65] Critically, Judge Odio Benito accepted the broader 'essential' support standard in declaring that as a matter of law:

> Sexual violence is an intrinsic element of the criminal conduct of 'use to participate actively in the hostilities'. Girls who are used as sex slaves or 'wives' of commanders or other members of the armed group provide essential support to the armed groups.[66]

Judge Odio Benito criticized the majority's failure to make such a declaration which rendered 'invisible' this critical aspect of the case, namely, the systematic and 'intrinsic' feature of sexual violence in Article 8(2)(e)(vii). While adopting the 'essential support' standard advocated by the Prosecution, the case-by-case approach submitted by the UN Special Representative and adopted by the majority was rejected as being discriminatory.[67] As Judge Odio Benito observed:

> Sexual violence and enslavement are in the main crimes committed against girls and their illegal recruitment is often intended for that purpose (nevertheless they also often participate in direct combat.) If the war crimes considered in this case are directed at securing their physical and psychological well being, then we must recognize sexual violence as a failure to afford this protection and sexual violence as acts embedded in the enlisting, conscription and use of children under 15 in hostilities. It is discriminatory to exclude sexual violence which shows a clear gender differential impact from being a bodyguard or porter which is mainly a task given to young boys. The use of young girls and boys bodies by combatants within or outside the group is a war crime and as such encoded in the charges against the accused.[68]

In seeking to overcome the constraints of Article 74(2) of the *Rome Statute*, Judge Odio Benito drew the distinction between the legal definition of the crimes (of enlistment, conscription and use of children under the age of 15 to participate actively in hostilities) on the one hand, and on the other hand, the evaluation of evidence presented in the case within the limits of the facts and circumstances required to substantiate the alleged crimes.[69] In Judge Odio Benito's view, the legal definition incorporating the sexual violence conduct could be articulated

---

[65] Ibid., Separate Opinion of Judge Odio Benito, para 19.

[66] Ibid., para 20.

[67] Ibid., paras 15–16.

[68] Ibid., para 21.

[69] Ibid., para 5.

independently of the evaluation of any evidence tendered in trial, or the scope of the charges brought against the accused.[70]

On this basis, according to Judge Odio Benito, it was impermissible for the Chamber to simply decline to declare a 'comprehensive legal definition of the crime [of use] and leave it open to a case-by-case analysis or to the limited scope of the charges brought against the accused'.[71] On the contrary, it was necessary, and indeed a 'duty' of the Chamber to pronounce a wider, more comprehensive definition that explicitly encompassed and envisaged sexual violence and abuse within the purview of the crime of use 'regardless of the impediment of the Chamber to base its decision pursuant to art 74(2) of the [Rome] Statute'.[72] Failure to do so was a 'step backwards in the progressive development of international law' denounced Judge Odio Benito.[73]

Furthermore, Judge Odio Benito criticized the majority's approach in declining to articulate a comprehensive legal definition of use, as being contrary to the 'object and purpose' of the *Rome Statute*,[74] contrary to internationally recognized human rights[75] and as being discriminatory contrary to Article 21(3). Judge Odio Benito claimed that the majority addressed only one purpose of the trial, namely, to decide on the guilt or innocence of an accused, and overlooked another purpose of attending to the harm suffered by victims as a result of the crimes within the jurisdiction of the Court.[76]

6.4 Critique of the Minority Decision

The findings of the *Lubanga* Trial Chamber majority being, in effect, a non-finding on the ability of Article 8(2)(e)(vii) to encompass sexual violence, potentially leaves open many questions which may be revisited on another future occasion. The vigorous dissent of Judge Odio Benito in particular raises further issues of

---

70 Ibid., para 6.

71 Ibid., para 7.

72 Ibid., para 17.

73 Ibid., para 7.

74 Citing Article 31(1), *Vienna Convention on the Law of Treaties*.

75 Citing 'soft law' such as the Cape Town Principles and Paris Principles as well as African Union, *Solemn Declaration on Gender Equality in Africa*, adopted June 2006. Citing also, international treaties: Article 38, *Convention on the Rights of the Child*; *International Labour Organization (ILO) Convention (No 182) concerning the prohibition and immediate action for the elimination of the worst forms of child labour*, opened for signature 17 June 1999, 2133 UNTS 161, Article 3 (entered into force 19 November 2000); *Optional Protocol to the Convention on the Rights of the Child on the Involvement of Children in armed conflict*, opened for signature 25 May 2000, 2173 UNTS 222 (entered into force 12 February 2002); *African Charter on the Rights and Welfare of the Child*, OAU Doc CAB/LEG/24.9/49 (1990), Article 22 (entered into force 29 November 1999).

76 *Lubanga* Trial Judgment, Separate Opinion of Judge Odio Benito, para 8.

concern that were insufficiently addressed by the majority and remain unresolved. The central question at issue is: should activities involving the sexual exploitation of children involved with armed forces (through rape, forced marriages and sexual slavery) constitute a prohibited use of that child in the 'active participation in hostilities'? IHL is silent on this issue while IHRL norms have rapidly progressed in recent times in favor of such an approach resulting in a normative discrepancy between the two bodies of law.

The following analysis seeks to confront this matter. In particular, it is submitted that the minority decision overstates the importance of IHRL and soft-law norms. These IHRL and soft-law norms expressly contemplate that the child soldier provision is inclusive of forms of sexual violence against children in accordance with a broader 'essential support' standard. However, the protective effect under IHL of those children is lessened as a result. This is because a finding that a sexually exploited child is 'actively participating in hostilities' leaves her (or him) exposed to an increased risk of being a legitimate target of attack by opposing forces—either permanently or on a temporary basis.

Moreover, the minority holding could be viewed as an unwarranted form of judicial activism in the context of other specific provisions in the *Rome Statute* of war crimes and crimes against humanity which address sexual violence. Certainly, the *Lubanga* judgment highlights a possible lacuna in IHL that might present a good case for States Parties to the Geneva Conventions to revisit this lag. However, in the context of prosecutions in international criminal law, a more restrained approach is advocated as unintended effects including the distortion of the protective objectives of IHL as a whole may result through mere judicial reform. In the meantime, to preserve the integrity of IHL as a self-contained system of legal protection, Article 8(2)(e)(vii) should be interpreted in a manner that remains faithful to IHL norms. In any event, an attempt to correct prosecutorial failings and defects from the bench is an insufficient justification in itself to extend the scope of otherwise well defined terms in IHL.

6.4.1 Human Rights Law and 'Soft-Law' Standards

Consensus has rapidly gathered momentum in the fields of IHRL and 'soft-law' standards since the mid-1990s on the specific issue of the use of children for purposes of sexual exploitation in armed forces. Spurred on by the pivotal 1996 Machel report on children in armed conflicts,[77] the international community has coalesced behind a number of norm setting initiatives to deal specifically with the multitude and ever expanding number of roles in conflicts which children are being used. The distinct impact of recruitment on girls, the activities and manner in

[77] Graça Machel, *The Impact of Armed Conflict on Children*, UN Doc A/51/306.Add. 1 (1996).

which they are used and their greater experience of sexual exploitation has justifiably been high on the agenda.

Hence in 1997, the adoption of the groundbreaking *Cape Town Principles* explicitly recognized for the first time, that the term 'child soldier' includes 'girls recruited for sexual purposes and for forced marriage'.[78] This soft-law standard was followed by an oblique reference in the preamble to the *Optional Protocol to the Convention on the Rights of the Child on the Involvement of Children in Armed Conflict* (2001) to the recognition of the 'special needs of those children who are particularly vulnerable to recruitment or use in hostilities contrary to this Protocol owing to their ...gender'.[79] Likewise, by 2003, the *Protocol to the African Charter on Human and People's Rights on the Rights of Women in Africa* also required States Parties to 'take all necessary measures to ensure that no child, especially girls under 18 years of age ... is recruited as a soldier'.[80] Most recently, in 2007, the *Cape Town Principles* were revisited and reconfirmed in the form of the *Paris Principles*.[81]

Each of these abovementioned soft-law standards and IHRL treaties were relied on in the minority decision,[82] but none more so than the adoption of the *UN Integrated Disarmament, Demobilization and Reintegration Standards* ('IDDRS'). Developed in 2006 to deal specifically with women's and girls' eligibility for reintegration assistance on their removal from armed forces. In light of this objective, it is understandable and desirable that a broad standard should be adopted to maximize the coverage for affected girls and women. The criterion that was settled upon for determining the eligibility for reintegration assistance was whether the women and girls were involved in providing an 'essential support function' to an armed force. As previously mentioned, the UN Special Representative submitted that the *Lubanga* Trial Chamber should adopt this standard of 'essential support function' and read it into the concept of 'active participation in hostilities' in Article 8(2)(e)(vii) when ascertaining the type of activities contemplated by the crime of use.[83]

The 'essential support function' standard, is far more extensive than what was envisaged by the drafters of the *Rome Statute*. The report of the Preparatory Committee on the Establishment of an International Criminal Court ('PrepCom') contains the intention and understanding of the delegates in a footnote to a draft of

[78] Cape Town Principles, p. 12.

[79] *Optional Protocol to the Convention on the Rights of the Child on the Involvement of Children in armed conflict*, opened for signature 25 May 2000, 2173 UNTS 222 (entered into force 12 February 2002).

[80] Article 11, *Protocol to the African Charter on Human and People's Rights on the Rights of Women in Africa*, OAU Doc CAB/LEG/66.6, adopted on 11 July 2003 (entered into force 25 November 2005).

[81] Paris Principles, paras 6.28–6.29.

[82] *Lubanga* Trial Judgment, Separate Opinion of Judge Odio Benito, p. 2, n. 4.

[83] UN Special Representative Submissions, para 21.

the *Rome Statute* settled at the penultimate meeting at Zutphen, in The Netherlands, just prior to the Rome Diplomatic Conference:

> The words 'using' and 'participate' have been adopted in order to cover both *direct participation in combat* and also *active participation in military activities linked to combat* such as scouting, spying, sabotage and the use of children as decoys, couriers or at military checkpoints. It would not cover activities *clearly unrelated to the hostilities* such as food deliveries to an airbase of [sic] the use of domestic staff in an officer's married accommodation. However, use of children in a *direct support function* such as acting as bearers to take supplies to the front line, or activities at the front line itself, would be included within the terminology.[84]

It may appear that the intention of the drafters of the Rome Statute in adopting this text ('Zutphen text') was to make clear that a wider scope of use was envisaged in settling on the use of the wording 'active' in Article 8(2)(e)(vii), as opposed to the commonly understood IHL notion of 'direct participation' in combat.[85] Yet, on closer inspection, great care was taken in ensuring that there was still a closely-held relationship between an impugned activity and combat or military activities. Hence, the Zutphen text establishes a hierarchy of participation and four distinct levels are discernible in descending order of proximity to combat or hostilities:

(a) direct participation in combat;
(b) active participation in 'military activities linked to combat';
(c) direct support functions (with reference to examples limited solely to 'front line' activities); and
(d) activities clearly unrelated to hostilities.

The very clear intention of the drafters as discerned from the Zutphen text was to delineate a bright line rule on the types of activities that constitute 'active participation in hostilities'. In light of this, the only option available to the Prosecution in *Lubanga* was to ask the Court to effectively ignore the terms which limited active participation to 'military activities linked to combat' and '*direct* support functions' in favor of a much broader standard of 'essential support function' derived from soft law instruments such as IDDRS.

As the UN Special Representative herself expressly conceded, the 'essential support function' standard deliberately moves away from a rigid definition of child soldiers, as exclusively armed combatants, and recognizes all children 'participating in and *associated with* armed groups and forces' as victims of these crimes.[86] Furthermore, the UN Special Representative highlighted soft law

[84] UN Diplomatic Conference of Plenipotentiaries on the Establishment of an International Criminal Court, *Report of the Preparatory Committee on the Establishment of an International Criminal Court, Draft Statute for the International Criminal Court*, UN Doc A/CONF.183/2/Add.1 (1998), para 21 (emphasis added).

[85] *See e.g.*, Article 77(2), API which prohibits children being used to take a 'direct part in hostilities'.

[86] UN Special Representative Submissions, para 21.

instruments such as the *Cape Town Principles* which expressly recognize that the term 'child soldier' includes 'girls recruited for sexual purposes and for forced marriage'.[87]

It is contended that the UN Special Representative's submission is, with respect, misconceived in its attempt to impart a gloss on the text of Article 8(2)(e)(vii) derived from 'soft law' provisions in the human rights field. The UN Special Representative argued that the Court should deliberately include any sexual violence, perpetrated in particular against girls, within its understanding of the crime of 'use':

> Because they are also wives and domestic aides, they either slip away, or are not brought forward for DDR programs. Commanders prefer to 'keep their women', who often father their children, and even if the girls are combatants, they are not released with the rest. Their complicated status makes them particularly vulnerable. They are recruited as child soldiers and sex slaves but are invisible when it comes to counting.[88]

This demonstrates the dangers and the inappropriateness of conflating distinct legal regimes that have different purposes and objectives. Ensuring that girls who are trapped in forced marriages or sexual slavery with armed groups are not disentitled from rehabilitation programs in the field is a commendable objective justifying expansive standards such as the 'essential support' function. However, this is not a consideration relevant to the application of rules of international criminal law, and no conviction on such grounds could effectively advance this particular objective of protecting girls for the purposes of rehabilitation and reintegration. More significantly, as will be discussed further below, it runs counter to the fundamental IHL objective of preventing children from being legitimate objects of attack in armed conflicts.

The UN Special Representative attempts to find further support for her argument in the SCSL Trial Chamber's seemingly broad ruling in the *AFRC* case that '[a]ny labour or support that gives effect to, or helps maintain, operations in a conflict constitutes active participation'.[89] What the UN Special Representative fails to acknowledge, however, is that this loosely worded test must be read in context with, and subject to, the often overlooked wording preceding it, namely, '"using" children to "participate actively in hostilities" encompasses putting their lives directly in risk *in combat*'.[90] The more appropriate test lies in this qualification, and not the often stated but selectively misquoted formulation put forward by the UN Special Representative. Indeed, the wording of the qualification accords with the risk test properly restated by the majority in the *Lubanga* Trial Judgment.

---

87 Reads: 'State Parties shall take all necessary measures to ensure that no child, especially girls under 18 years of age … is recruited as a soldier'; See, also, *Paris Principles*, p. 7 which reviewed the Cape Town Principles and confirmed the status of child soldier for all children used for sexual purposes.

88 UN Special Representative Submissions, at para 26.

89 *AFRC* Trial Judgment, paras 736–737.

90 Ibid.

6.4.2 The Primacy of International Humanitarian Law

The prohibition on the recruitment and use of child soldiers in IHL first appeared in the Additional Protocols to the Geneva Conventions adopted on 8 June 1977.[91] Since then, the parallel evolution of the prohibition on the recruitment and use of child soldiers within the two regimes of IHL and IHRL have progressed at different rates.[92] One such discrepancy that has been brought into sharp focus in *Lubanga* is whether the sexual exploitation of girl child soldiers by commanders and soldiers in the armed forces is able to be characterized as 'active participation in hostilities' by these girls. While the IHRL position clearly confirms this to be the case as outlined previously, it is submitted that IHL would be equally opposed resulting in a tension between the two bodies of law. Accordingly, a protection gap has seemingly opened as IHL lags behind its more progressive IHRL counterpart on this discrete issue of sexually exploited child soldiers. To appreciate the distinction between the approaches of these two distinct legal regimes, it is necessary to examine how IHL has interpreted the term 'active' participation in hostilities.

Despite appearances, there is little relevant difference in IHL between the concept of 'active participation in hostilities' and formulation 'direct participation in hostilities' adopted in the corresponding prohibition against child soldiers in Article 77(2) of *Additional Protocol II*. Guidance on this topic can be derived from the International Committee of the Red Cross' ('ICRC') most comprehensive study to date on the interpretation of the notion of 'direct participation in hostilities' in IHL. As the ICRC explains, the distinction between 'active' and 'direct' participation in hostilities is a superficial one. The concept of 'direct participation in hostilities' in fact evolved from the phrase 'taking no active part in hostilities' contained in common Article 3 of the *Geneva Conventions*.[93] While this discrepancy appears in the English text, the synonymous meaning attributed to 'active' and 'direct' in IHL is reinforced by consistent use of the phrase '*participent directement*' in the equally authoritative French text.[94] Indeed, this position has also been confirmed in international criminal law jurisprudence by the International Criminal Tribunal for Rwanda in the *Akayesu* case.[95] Significantly, on the

---

[91] Additional Protocol I, Article 77 (international armed conflicts); Additional Protocol II, Article 4(3)(c) (non-international armed conflicts).

[92] *See* e.g., differences in the prescribed ages limits protected by the respective child soldier provisions in IHL and IHRL: Additional Protocol II, Article 4(3)(c) (under 15 years) *cf Optional Protocol to the Convention on the Rights of the Child on the Involvement of Children in armed conflict*, opened for signature 25 May 2000, 2173 UNTS 222 (entered into force 12 February 2002), article 1 (under 18 years).

[93] Melzer 2009 ('ICRC Interpretive Guidance on Direct Participation in Hostilities'), p. 43.

[94] Ibid. See also, Article 32(3) of the *Vienna Convention on the Law of Treaties* 1155 UNTS 331 (entered into force on 27 January 1980) on the consistent interpretation of treaties authenticated in two or more languages.

[95] ICTR, *Prosecutor* v. *Jean-Paul Akayesu*, ICTR-96-4-T, Judgment, 2 September 1998 (Trial Chamber), para 629.

issue of the apparent discrepancy in terminology arising through the adoption of the term 'active' in Article 8(2)(2)(vii) of the *Rome Statute*, the ICRC recalls the PrepCom's Zutphen text and observes that the distinction there was in reality one between 'combat' and 'military activities linked to combat' rather than between 'active' and 'direct' participation.[96]

The ICRC concludes that to qualify as direct participation in hostilities (and by logical extension, active participation in hostilities as well), three cumulative criteria must be met. First, the act must be likely to adversely affect the military operations or military capacity of a party to an armed conflict, or alternatively to inflict death, injury, or destruction on persons or objects protected against direct attack ('threshold of harm').[97] Second, there must be a direct causal link between the act and the harm likely to result either from that act, or from a coordinated military operation of which that act constitutes an integral part ('direct causation').[98] Third, the act must be specifically designed to directly cause the required threshold of harm in support of a party to the conflict and to the detriment of another ('belligerent nexus').[99]

Without directly attributing reference to the ICRC's Interpretive Guidance on direct participation in hostilities, early international criminal law jurisprudence on the child soldier offense has gone some way towards developing standards closely aligned to the ICRC's three aforementioned criteria. In the ICC, the *Lubanga* Pre-Trial Chamber in its decision confirming the charges was required to grapple with the activity of using child bodyguards even though this was not expressly contemplated as a prohibited activity type in the Zutphen text.[100] Ultimately the Pre-Trial Chamber accepted that guarding military objectives (such as the military quarters of various units or bodyguards safeguarding the physical safety of military commanders) would constitute a form of prohibited activity. Relevantly, the Pre-Trial Chamber reasoned that this was because the act of being a bodyguard had a direct impact on the level of logistic resources and on the organization of

[96] ICRC Interpretive Guidance on Direct Participation in Hostilities, p. 43, n. 84. *Contra*, Cottier 2008, pp. 470–471. Cottier comments that the drafters of the *Rome Statute* intended to effect a clean break away from the conceptual IHL understanding of 'direct participation in hostilities' in adopting the term 'active'. In doing so, they consciously and deliberately chose to expand the prohibition to encompass a broader range of participation than that which falls under 'direct' participation.

[97] Ibid., pp. 47–50. The phrase 'direct participation in hostilities' is found also in the context of the prohibited targeting of civilians. In that context, direct participation in hostilities means 'acts of war which by their nature or purpose are likely to cause *actual* harm to the personnel and equipment of the enemy armed forces': Sandoz et al. 1986, p. 618, para 1943 (emphasis added). Similarly, 'hostile acts' are understood to mean acts which 'by their nature or purpose are intended to cause actual harm to the personnel and the equipment of the enemy armed forces': *See*, p. 618, para 1942.

[98] Ibid., pp. 51–58.

[99] Ibid., pp. 58–64.

[100] *Lubanga* Confirmation Decision, para 260.

operations required by the other party to the conflict.[101] This is akin to at least the ICRC's threshold of harm and direct causation criteria. Notably, this understanding by the Pre-Trial Chamber was also endorsed by the Trial Chamber in the *Lubanga* Trial Judgment.[102]

A requisite causal nexus was also evident in earlier SCSL jurisprudence including the *Taylor* Trial Judgment in its application of the risk test to the more contentious activity of food-finding missions. In the prior *RUF* Trial Judgment, the Trial Chamber held that unarmed children on food-finding missions did not amount to active participation in hostilities because 'although this activity supports the armed group in a general sense … it does not establish that the children openly carried arms while on such missions'.[103] However, the *Taylor* Trial Chamber was prepared to accept that to the extent food-finding missions may be considered 'activities linked to combat', it may constitute an unlawful 'use'. Nevertheless, it only arrived at this view after determining that there was 'a *clear link* between the mission and the hostilities'.[104] In the circumstances, where the food-finding mission was carried out in the context of children carrying arms and partaking in hostilities such as committing crimes against civilians, the Trial Chamber held that the link was a clear one.[105]

Carrying looted goods was another example of a borderline case. After being abducted from a village, one child was forced to carry rice and groundnut that the rebels had forcibly taken from civilians.[106] The Trial Chamber held that the removal and carrying away of looted goods from a village is a 'foreseeable and integral part of the appropriation of the private property of a civilian' which has a '*direct nexus* with the conflict'.[107] In contrast, activities considered *not* constituting 'use' included domestic chores such as laundering, cooking and cleaning in households of members of the armed forces as they were 'not related to the hostilities and do not directly support the military operations of the armed groups'.[108] In light of the three criteria established by the ICRC, this aspect of causation will require further development by the ICC in future cases.

In any event, as conceived in IHL, there is very little room for doubt that active participation in hostilities requires any prohibited activity to be closely related to combat or hostilities. In the circumstances it would be a stretch to submit that the use of girl soldiers for rape, enforced marriages and sexual slavery, is insufficiently connected to hostilities or combat in a direct way that would qualify as active

[101] Ibid., para 263.

[102] *Lubanga* Trial Judgment, para 622.

[103] *RUF* Trial Judgment, para 1743 (emphasis added).

[104] *Taylor* Trial Judgment, para 1479 (emphasis added).

[105] Ibid., para 1479; *cf* a negative finding based on the absence of arms carried by the children while on a food-finding mission: para 1493.

[106] Ibid., para 1542.

[107] Ibid., para 1546 (emphasis added).

[108] Ibid., paras 1477, 1522.

participation. This gives rise to a seemingly irreconcilable conflict between IHL and IHRL on this narrow but important aspect.

Much legal commentary and thought has gone into the ways of optimizing the level of protection to individuals, particularly civilians, through the complementary interpretation and application of IHL and IHRL.[109] In its *Nuclear Weapons Advisory Opinion*, the International Court of Justice ('ICJ') first opined that in situations of armed conflict, IHL as the *lex specialis*, displaced the *lex generalis* of IHRL.[110] Subsequently, in the *Wall Advisory Opinion*, ICJ softened its stance and clarified that IHRL may not be entirely displaced and could be applicable in situations of armed conflict. In doing so, it observed three situations wherein this relationship between IHL and IHRL was relevant: 'some rights may be exclusively matters of international humanitarian law; others may be exclusively matters of human rights law; yet others may be matters of both these branches of international law.'[111] Moreover, even where it is determined that IHL is the *lex specialis*, in the case where *lex generalis* norms of IHRL co-exist and serve to regulate the same field, the *lex generalis* still remains in the background and must be taken into account when interpreting the *lex specialis* in a manner that reduces any conflict and achieve maximum harmonization between the two legal regimes.[112]

The Rome Statute itself is consistent with the harmonization principle outlined above. The chapeau of Article 8(2)(e) specifically demands that any interpretation or consideration of the substantive crimes contained therein must be governed by 'the laws and customs applicable in armed conflict not of an international character, *within the established framework of international law*'. Secondly, Article 21, which establishes a hierarchy of the applicable governing law, requires the Court to apply, in the first place, the Statute, Elements of Crimes and Rules of Procedure and Evidence,[113] and in the second place, 'where appropriate, applicable treaties and the principles and rules of international law, including the established principles of the international law of armed conflict'.[114] This includes recognized rules of treaty interpretation such as Article 31(3)(b) and (c) of the *Vienna Convention on the Law of Treaties* which permits recourse to subsequent practice and other

[109] *See generally*, Draper 1971; Doswald-Beck and Vité 1993; Vinuesa 1998; Heinze 2004; Provost 2002.

[110] ICJ, *Legality of the Threat or Use of Nuclear Weapons*, Advisory Opinion, 8 July 1996, ICJ Reports 1996, para 25.

[111] ICJ, *Legal Consequences of the Construction of a Wall in the Occupied Palestinian Territory, Advisory Opinion*, 9 July 2004, ICJ Reports 2004, para 106.

[112] *Vienna Convention on the Law of Treaties*, Article 31(3)(c) which requires other rules of international law to be taken into account; Martin Koskenniemi, 'Fragmentation of International Law: Difficulties Arising from the Diversification and Expansion of International Law, Study Group of the Report of the International Law Commission', Fifty-sixth session, UN Doc A/59/10, paras 31 and 37.

[113] Article 21(a), Rome Statute.

[114] Article 21(b), Rome Statute.

relevant rules of international law. Additionally, the *travaux préparatoires* of the *Rome Statute* may assist as an interpretive aid in instances of ambiguity.[115]

Yet, each case where a conflict of norms in different legal regimes arises must be analyzed individually.[116] While in principle, IHRL norms should be available to assist in the interpretation of IHL and the Article 8(2)(e)(vii), the *Lubanga* case brings into sharp relief, one such situation and context where an irreconcilable conflict arises between IHL and IHRL. In such instance, it is submitted that IHL may well have the monopoly in regulating the use of child soldiers to actively participate in hostilities insofar as sexual violence against child soldiers is concerned.

Sassòli and Olson propose a persuasive proposal in resolving this type of stalemate that prioritizes the most detailed and adapted norm. As they suggest: 'It is the norm with the more precise or narrower material and/or personal scope of application that prevails. Precision requires that the norm explicitly addressing a problem prevails over the one that addresses it implicitly, the one providing the advantage of detail provides over the other's generality, and the more restrictive norm over the one covering the entire problem but in a less exacting manner'.[117]

In the discrete context of sexual violence against child soldiers, the problematic interpretation of 'active participation in hostilities' in Article 8(2)(e)(vii) should be guided exclusively by IHL as the more binding, comprehensive and detailed norm adapted for the situation. Prior to going into the specific justifications, it should be made clear at the outset that this is not a situation which calls for the intervention of IHRL to cure any protection gaps. Indeed, as discussed further in Sect. 6.5.1, the sexual exploitation of child soldiers is adequately dealt with through the crime of conscription. Moreover, as previously outlined, the position advanced by the Prosecution in *Lubanga* for an expansive reading of 'active participation in hostilities' to extend to 'essential support functions' is controversial due to its heavy reliance on non-binding soft-law standards and ambiguous human rights conventions.

Two main reasons, however, would support a prioritization of IHL to the exclusion of IHRL in interpreting the crime of use in Article 8(2)(e)(vii). The first approaches IHL holistically and takes into account the unintended consequences on child soldiers of an expansive reading, which includes sexual violence on child soldiers. An expansive reading affects the principles of distinction and civilian immunity from attack in particular and distorts the integrity of IHL. The second reason, which is explored in further detail in Sect. 6.4.3, relies on broader considerations of the *Rome Statute* and international criminal law, taking into account the specific provisions of sexual violence that already exist.

---

[115] Article 32 of the *Vienna Convention on the Law of Treaties*; ICC, *Situation in the Democratic Republic of the Congo*, ICC-01/04-168, Judgment on Prosecutor's Application for Extraordinary Review of Pre-Trial Chamber I's 31 March 2006 Decision Denying Leave to Appeal, 31 July 2006 (Appeals Chamber), para 33.

[116] Sassòli and Olson 2008, p. 604; Lindroos 2005.

[117] Sassòli and Olson 2008, p. 604.

With respect to the first justification, it should be borne in mind that a person who is deemed to be 'actively participating in hostilities', is performing the functions of a combatant. As such, for the duration in which that person is engaged in those combatant functions he or she is no longer entitled to the specific protections afforded to civilians under IHL—most importantly: immunity from attack.[118] The term 'direct', or indeed 'active', participation in hostilities generally gives effect to the principle of civilian immunity, which seeks to protect civilians from attacks by belligerents (as reflected in the in Article 8(2)(b)(i) and (e)(i) of the *Rome Statute*). Accordingly, the term tends to be construed in the narrowest possible terms in order to preserve the protected status of civilians in armed conflict.[119]

An unintended consequence of unduly enlarging the scope of Article 8(2)(e)(vii), therefore, is that it robs certain individuals of their civilian status and turns them into legitimate objects of attack. This significantly weakens the protection otherwise available to sexually exploited child soldiers under IHL. Ironically, this undercuts the object and purpose of Article 8(2)(e)(vii) and its underpinned IHL provisions of keeping children out of hostilities. This was expressly noted by the SCSL Trial Chamber in the *RUF* case when it stated that 'an overly expansive definition of active participation in hostilities would be inappropriate as its consequence would be that children associated with armed groups would lose their protected status as persons *hors de combat* under the law of armed conflict'.[120] Expanding the crime of 'use' to encompass sexual violence is a paradox that is ultimately a zero-sum game for victims. A young girl sexually exploited by a commander or soldier but otherwise not engaging in any other military activity directly linked to combat is placed at greater risk of being a legitimate enemy target and subject to attack simply because of her status has changed from civilian to 'soldier'.

6.4.3 *Specificity,* Nullum Crimen Sine Lege *and the 'Progressive Development of International Law'*

None of the aforementioned critiques should be construed as acceptance of the proposition that sexual exploitation of young girls associated with armed groups should be subject to impunity. However, a number of factors must be kept foremost in mind. First, the *Lubanga* proceeding was exclusively a prosecution of war crime charges. At the same time, where possible and appropriate, the widest available protection for children as civilians should be preserved. IHL does not

[118] Smith 2004, pp. 1144–1145.

[119] Garraway 2001, pp. 205–206.

[120] *RUF* Trial Judgment, para 1723. *See also*, Guibert and Blumenstock 2007, p. 381.

permit impunity for sexual violence, nor does it render such violence invisible. Likewise, modern international criminal law itself has evolved to a stage where sexual crimes, particularly against girls and women, are no longer 'invisible' contrary to the assertion of the minority view in *Lubanga*.

The second reason why an approach deferring to IHL's norms on the use of child soldiers should be adopted, despite its apparent silence on sexual violence, is that sexual violence is already regulated by other detailed provisions in the *Rome Statute*. It should not be forgotten that the exercise engaged in is the interpretation of the *Rome Statute*. IHL and IHRL are mere tools resorted to in service of that objective. Accordingly, the problem is a wider one involving the intersection of IHL, IHRL and the distinct regime of international criminal law. All three regimes should be harmonized as far as possible.

Addressing impunity for sexual violence crimes should have been properly dealt with by including charges of sexual crimes and particularizing the factual circumstances in full accordance with the requirements of Article 74. An application could have been made to file an amended Document Containing the Charges for confirmation by the Pre-Trial Chamber anytime prior to the start of the trial. The Trial Chamber saved its harshest criticism for the Prosecution's conduct in the *Lubanga* sentencing decision by making it clear that 'it strongly deprecates the attitude of the former Prosecutor [Luis Moreno-Ocampo] in relation to the issue of sexual violence' for not only failing to apply to include sexual violence or sexual slavery at any stage of the proceedings, including in the original charges, but actively opposing taking this step during the trial on the basis that it would cause unfairness to the accused.[121]

Notably, when the specificity of international criminal law is taken into account, a number of potential charges would have been available to the Prosecution in *Lubanga* based on the evidence in its possession. Those charges could have included:

(a) 'Sexual slavery', as a crime against humanity[122] and/or a war crime.[123]
(b) 'Inhuman treatment', as a war crime.[124]
(c) 'Cruel treatment', as a war crime.[125]
(d) Rape, as a crime against humanity[126] and/or a war crime.[127]

[121] *Prosecutor v Thomas Lubanga Dyilo*, ICC-01/04-01/06, Decision on Sentence pursuant to Article 76 of the Statute, 10 July 2012 (Trial Chamber I), para 60.

[122] Article 7(1)(g), *Rome Statute*.

[123] Article 8(2)(b)(xxii) or 8(2)(e)(vi), *Rome Statute*.

[124] Article 8(2)(a)(ii), *Rome Statute*.

[125] Article 8(2)(c)(i), *Rome Statute*.

[126] Article 7(1)(g), *Rome Statute*.

[127] Articles 8(2)(b)(xxii) or 8(2)(e)(vi), *Rome Statute*.

(e) 'Forced marriage' constituting the crime against humanity of 'other inhumane acts…intentionally causing suffering, or serious injury to body or to mental or physical health'.[128]

The approach and the disappointing consequences of presenting a focused or 'thematic prosecution'[129] in *Lubanga*, can be contrasted with the Sierra Leone cases which all included separate charges and particulars in the indictment of rape, sexual slavery and forced marriage in addition to the child soldier charges. As some have observed, this more comprehensive approach was deliberate to permit 'a complete picture of the fate of child soldiers, especially girls, to emerge'.[130]

IHRL principles and standards may be better suited to and are of greater assistance in developing the content of concepts such as the thresholds of 'inhuman treatment', 'cruel treatment' or 'inhumane acts causing suffering'. A further advantage of these crimes is that they do not fundamentally alter the victim's *status* from that of civilian to combatant, which is one of the unique side effects of Article 8(2)(e)(vii). It would not serve anyone's interests, however, including those of victims, to distort the construction of Article 8(2)(e)(vii) to accommodate a mistaken or defective prosecutorial strategy.

Secondly, the prosecution of accused in criminal proceedings takes place in the context of an international criminal court, rather than a court of human rights. International criminal law, and the *Rome Statute* itself, places paramount importance on fair trial guarantees for the accused. The minority opinion, lamented the 'step backwards in the progressive development of international law'[131] taken by the majority. It is arguable from a review of the historical development of the Additional Protocols and the *Rome Statute*, that the submissions made by the Prosecution in *Lubanga*, if accepted, would violate the fundamental principle of *nullum crimen sine lege*. This doctrine of legality forbids the retrospective application of criminal law to an accused's disadvantage, on the basis that laws should be specific, certain, foreseeable and accessible.[132] This absolute and non-derogable right, enshrined in Article 22 of the *Rome Statute*,[133] has the object and

[128] SCSL, *Prosecutor v Brima, Kamara and Kanu*, Judgment, SCSL-2004-16-A, 22 February 2008 (Appeals Chamber Judgment), para 202. In a landmark ruling, the Appeals Chamber, reversed the Trial Chamber below, holding that 'forced marriage' constituted a separate crime distinct from sexual slavery as a crime against humanity.

[129] Bergsmo and Cheah 2012, p. 2.

[130] Jørgensen 2012, p. 659.

[131] *Lubanga* Trial Judgment, Separate Opinion of Judge Odio Benito, para 7.

[132] *Veeber v Estonia (No 2)*, Application No 45771/99, Judgment, 21 January 2003 (European Court of Human Rights), para 11.

[133] Article 22, *Rome Statute* reads:

1. A person shall not be criminally responsible under this Statute unless the conduct in question constitutes, at the time it takes place, a crime within the jurisdiction of the Court.
2. The definition of a crime shall be strictly construed and shall not be extended by analogy. In case of ambiguity, the definition shall be interpreted in favor of the person being investigated, prosecuted or convicted.

purpose of providing an effective safeguard against arbitrary prosecution, conviction and punishment, and is the cornerstone of the accused's right to a fair trial.[134] In the event of any ambiguity, Article 22(2) clearly directs that the definition of any crime must be interpreted strictly and in favor of the accused.

While true that several groundbreaking developments have taken place, particularly with the recognition of sexual crimes, they have largely concerned crimes against humanity and genocide, these are not expressly constrained by IHL resulting in a greater scope for the application of IHRL arguments and standards.[135] The same was not warranted in the circumstances presented by *Lubanga*, which were limited to war crimes. The distinguished jurist Mohamed Shahabuddeen has noted that the principle of *nullum crimen* does not bar the 'progressive development of international law' through clarification of the rules of criminal liability by way of judicial interpretation from case to case, but only where the developed law is consistent with, and retains the essence of the original crime.[136] As the Appeals Chamber of the International Criminal Tribunal for the Former Yugoslavia ('ICTY') held in *Ojdanić*:

> [T]he principle of *nullum crimen sine lege* is, as noted by the International Military Tribunal in Nuremberg, first and foremost, a 'principle of justice' … This fundamental principle 'does not prevent a court from interpreting and clarifying elements of a particular crime'. Nor does it preclude the progressive development of the law by the courts. *But it does prevent a court from creating new law or from interpreting existing law beyond reasonable limits of acceptable clarification.* This Tribunal must therefore be satisfied that the crime or the form of liability with which an accused is charged was sufficiently foreseeable and that the law providing for such liability must be sufficiently accessible at the relevant time, *taking into account the specificity of international law when making the assessment.*[137]

(Footnote 133 continued)

3. This article shall not affect the characterization of any conduct as criminal under international law independently of this Statute.

[134] Articles 7 and 15, *European Convention for the Protection of Human Rights and Fundamental Freedoms*, opened for signature 4 November 1950, 213 UNTS 222, (entered into force 3 November 1953); Articles 4 and 15, *International Covenant for Civil and Political Rights*, opened for signature 19 December 1966, 999 UNTS 171, (entered into force 23 March 1976); see also, *Puhk v Estonia*, Application No 55103/00, Judgment, 10 February 2004 (European Court of Human Rights), para 24.

[135] ICTR, *Prosecutor v Jean-Paul Akayesu*, ICTR-96-4, Trial Judgment, 2 September 2009 (rape was recognized as a form of genocide).

[136] Shahabuddeen 2004, p. 1013. *See also*, *CR v United Kingdom* (1995) 335-C Eur Court HR (ser A) [34].

[137] ICTY, *Prosecutor v Ojdanić*, IT-99-37-AR72, Decision on Dragoljub Ojdanić's Motion Challenging Jurisdiction—Joint Criminal Enterprise, 21 May 2003 (Appeals Chamber), paras 37–38 (emphasis added and footnotes omitted). *See also*, ICTY, *Prosecutor v Delalić*, IT-96-21-A, Judgment, 20 February 2001 (Appeals Chamber), para 173; ICTY, *Prosecutor v Aleksovski*, Judgment, IT-95-14/1-A, 24 March 2000 (Appeals Chamber), para 127.

A blanket declaration, advocated by Judge Odio Benito, that as a matter of law, all forms of sexual violence against children participating in armed forces or groups constitute the use of those children to participate actively in hostilities is concerning. This goes beyond merely clarifying the law, but rather, creates new law, which arguably contravenes the principle of *nullum crimen*.

Judge Odio Benito's position is also difficult to reconcile with the expert *amicus* submissions of the UN Special Representative, which specifically advocated a case-by-case approach based on her Office's experience and expertise of female child soldiers in the field. No other party to the proceedings made any submission to the contrary. Indeed, as the Prosecution itself submitted:

> Girl soldiers, some aged 12 years, were used as cooks and fighters, cleaners and spies, scouts and *sexual slaves*. One minute they will carry a gun, the next minute they will serve meals to the commanders, the next minute the commanders will rape them.[138]

Moreover, as the UN Special Representative properly observed, a case-by-case approach is particularly apt and critical in the context of modern conflicts in which the nature of warfare differs depending on the group whereby children used in hostilities played multiple, fluid and changing roles. Based on the UN Special Representative's vast experience in the field, girl combatants in the DRC recounted their experience of being 'fighters one minute, a "wife" or "sex slave" the next, and domestic aides and food providers at another time'.[139] In other words, the reality of modern day conflicts is that most female child soldiers are not solely sex slaves or purely the subjects of sexual violence. On the contrary, they are bound to take part in direct or indirect military activities at some stage. These observations that clearly fall within the expertise of the UN Special Representative is where the real value of the *amicus* submissions lies. Judge Odio Benito's characterization of female child soldiers fails to accord with this reality. In going much further than what was submitted in the proceedings, it appears to be a reductionist and essentialist view of the actual experiences of female child soldiers as acknowledged by experts in the field and in academic literature.[140]

6.5 Missed Opportunities

In addition to the weaknesses inherent in the minority decision, other alternative approaches and issues of sexual violence were overlooked by both the majority and minority in the *Lubanga* judgment. One alternative to relying on the crime of using child soldiers may have been to characterize the acts of sexual violence as falling within the scope of the crime of recruitment. A second issue that was raised

---

[138] *Lubanga* Trial Transcript, 26 January 2009, p. 11, lines 17–13, line 4 (emphasis added).

[139] UN Special Representative Submissions, para 22.

[140] Drumbl 2012, pp. 7–8.

on the evidence was use of child soldiers to commit acts of sexual violence such as the abduction of girl civilians for the sexual exploitation by commanders. Defects in the Prosecution's case, such as the failure to distinguish between crimes of use and conscription and insufficient investigations, contributed to the oversight of these issues; however, they remain possible issues to address in future cases.

6.5.1 Sexual Violence as Conscription

One possible alternative argument could have been advanced that may have allowed the Prosecution to progress the law in a manner that might not have transgressed the *nullum crimen* rule. Depending on the available evidence, it could be argued that girl child soldiers, usually forcibly abducted, who experienced sexual violence had simply been conscripted. Conscription (or enlistment) does not require proof that the girls were 'actively participating in hostilities', making their function, whether for sexual purposes or not, irrelevant for establishing criminal liability. This is clearly supported by the *Lubanga* Trial Chamber's unanimous holding that 'the status of a child under 15 who has been enlisted or conscripted is independent of any later period when he or she may have been "used" to participate actively in hostilities, particularly given the variety of tasks that he or she may subsequently be required to undertake'.[141]

Unfortunately, this was not the focus of the Prosecution's arguments, despite the occasional slippage into language of 'recruitment' and 'conscription'. In not appreciating the distinction between conscription, enlistment and use, the Prosecution was unable to capitalize on the full benefit of the conscription offense. Had a clear delineation between conscription/enlistment and use been appreciated, this argument could have perhaps been made more forcefully. This approach would have meant that sexual violence would not have such a prominent role on criminal liability, although it may well have had an impact on sentencing.

Interestingly, the victims' legal representatives raised this very argument in the course of trial proceedings. As noted, the Trial Chamber, in an earlier decision allowed victims to participate in the proceedings, on the following basis:

> [i]t is not necessary… for this Chamber to engage in the critical question that otherwise arises in this application as to *whether the 'use' of children for sexual purposes alone, and including forced marriage, can be regarded as conscription or enlistment into an armed force*, or the use of that person to participate actively in hostilities… *the applicant has presented enough evidence to conclude prima facie, that she was abducted in the broad context of the systemic conscription* of children under the age of 15 into the military forces of the UPC.[142]

---

[141] *Lubanga* Trial Judgment, para 620.

[142] *Prosecutor v Lubanga*, Annex 1 to the Decision on the applications by victims to participate in the proceedings, Case No ICC-01/04-01/06, 15 December 2008 (Trial Chamber) para 103, cited in *Lubanga* Trial Judgment, para 599 (emphasis added).

The *Lubanga* Trial Chamber did not ultimately address this issue, as it was distracted largely by the controversy surrounding the crime of use but it potentially remains a live issue for the future. Of course, the greatest disadvantage of this approach is that the issue of sexual violence remains masked or, at the very least, muted and that narrative is only exposed at the sentencing stage. If condemnation of acts of sexual violence is the objective, cumulative charging of specific sexual offenses as war crimes and/or crimes against humanity is the most desirable course of action.

6.5.2 Using Child Soldiers to Commit Crimes of Sexual Violence

A clear distinction was also not drawn between two very different factual scenarios being presented to the Court, namely, sexual violence against girls within the armed forces on the one hand, in contrast to child soldiers used by being ordered to commit crimes of sexual violence. An illustration of the latter is the example of the child soldier who is ordered to go out to abduct a civilian girl and bring her back to the military camp to sexually gratify the commander. The child soldier (known as Witness 0294 in the proceedings) was a witness who testified that he was the bodyguard of a commander. His first duty was to guarantee the security of his commander wherever he went, but he had other duties as well. In particular, he testified that he was sent on errands to arrest people who could give the commander weapons, or money, and in some instances, girls so the commander could sleep with them. The Prosecution submitted in their closing oral statements, summarizing their case, that 'all these ways in which Witness 0294 was used ... is use to participate actively in hostilities'.[143]

When queried about this submission, the Prosecutor later returned to the point by arguing that 'ordering [boy child soldiers] to abduct girls in order to rape them is an order... to use children in hostilities'.[144] Although, this was summarily rejected by the bench, the principle underlying the submission has some merit. Unfortunately, in the case of *Lubanga*, there was little evidence presented in the Prosecution's case that rape of civilians was part of the common plan, adopted as a weapon of war as an intrinsic part of 'hostilities' rather than an isolated incident. This was reflective of how the Prosecution's case was hampered, in part, by the prosecutorial strategy of 'limited scope' prosecutions and deficient investigations.

By way of contrast, in the *Taylor* case, the SCSL Trial Chamber also considered evidence of a commander who ordered two child soldiers to capture a girl in the course of an attack on a village. The child soldiers captured her at gunpoint, stripped her naked and left her in a house for the commander. They then stood

---

143 *Lubanga* Trial Transcript, 25 August 2011, p. 15, line 23, p. 16, line 5.

144 Ibid., p. 55, lines 15–21.

guard at the door of the house while the commander raped her.[145] The *Taylor* Trial Chamber found that this incident constituted active participation in hostilities and the unlawful use of children in hostilities.[146] Similarly, in another incident, two young boy soldiers kidnapped girls aged eight to ten years in a village raid then detained and lived with them for sexual purposes. The *Taylor* Trial Chamber found that this also constituted use of children in hostilities.[147] The curiosity of this outcome may be that sexual violence, including 'sexual slavery', committed by young child soldiers would constitute their use to participate actively in hostilities. This is quite distinct from characterizing a child victim of sexual violence as a 'soldier' who is being used to actively participate in hostilities, solely by reason of being forcibly engaged in sexual acts.

The notable distinction between the *Taylor* and *Lubanga* cases is that the *Taylor* Trial Chamber was in a position to be able to find that the use of child soldiers themselves to commit crimes, such as rape, was 'related to hostilities and directly supports the military operations of the armed group'.[148] In particular, the *Taylor* Prosecution had demonstrated, and the Trial Chamber accepted, that the context of the Sierra Leone conflict was one of frequent and brutal acts of violence specifically directed against civilians as a hallmark of the operations of the armed rebel groups. The rapes occurred while the children were armed and in the company of adult fighters and commanders and in 'the prevailing context of guerrilla warfare'.[149] More significantly, the purpose of the crimes against ordinary civilians was to 'damage or harm the adversary by eradicating support for opposing forces, or destroying territory'.[150] This is akin to the ICRC's third 'belligerent nexus' test of 'an act specifically designed to directly cause the required threshold of harm in support of one party of the conflict to the detriment of another'. It is also a more fulsome and sophisticated argument than what was posed by the prosecution in *Lubanga*. However, it conceivably also requires proper investigations going beyond a 'limited scope' prosecution.

6.6 Conclusion

It is not disputed that by the added trauma of sexual violence, usually in addition to other regular functions in combat or combat-related roles, female child soldiers experience armed conflict differently, and arguably more oppressively, than their

---

145 *Prosecutor v Taylor*, SCSL-2003-01-T, Transcript of Trial Proceedings, (Trial Chamber), 5 May 2008, pp. 9008–9010; *Taylor* Trial Judgment, para 1561.

146 *Taylor* Trial Judgment, para 1565.

147 Ibid., para 1502.

148 Ibid., para 1565.

149 Ibid.

150 Ibid., para 1604. See also, *RUF* Trial Judgment, para 1722.

male counterparts. However, Articles 8(2)(e)(vii) and 8(2)(b)(xxvi) are not an all-encompassing panacea for every possible ill concerning the involvement of children in armed conflict. Relative to IHRL and 'soft-law' standards, which have evolved more rapidly, the narrower compass of IHL is concerned largely with the objective of preventing the active participation of children in hostilities. It may be that a lacuna has been identified in the substantive child soldier provisions in IHL, reflected in Article 8 of the *Rome Statute*, which lags behind normative standards established in IHRL insofar as sexual violence against girl child soldiers is concerned. However, the appropriate and preferable manner in dealing with this to minimize any protection gaps to child victims is to charge sexual offenses cumulatively using the specific pre-existing sexual violence provisions for rape, sexual slavery and forced marriages as war crimes and/or crimes against humanity. The IHL objectives for the protection of child soldiers *vis-à-vis* civilian targeting is finely balanced, and the wholesale grafting of IHRL standards upon IHL can have a distortive and unintended effect on the overall protection of those victims. In this regard, it is encouraging to see that lessons are being learned. Shortly after the issue of the *Lubanga* Trial Judgment but prior to the surrender of Bosco Ntaganda, another top commander of the UPC/FPLC, a second warrant of arrest adding charges of rape and sexual slavery as crimes against humanity was promptly issued to supplement child soldier charges in the first warrant.[151] A further lesson to be taken away from *Lubanga*, which remains less explicit on the face of the judgment, is the necessity for well-resourced and thorough investigations—another responsibility that falls squarely within the mandate of the Office of the Prosecutor. The strategy of 'focussed investigations' has proven to be a disappointing legacy. It is hoped, for the sake of the child soldiers and other child victims of sexual violence in armed conflicts, that further progress and improvements are achievable on this front.

References

Ambos K (2012) The First Judgment of the International Criminal Court (Prosecutor v Lubanga): A Comprehensive Analysis of the Legal Issues. International Criminal Law Review 12:115–153.

Amnesty International (2003) Democratic Republic of Congo—Children at War. https://www.amnesty.org/en/library/asset/AFR62/034/2003/en/123f1fc9-d699-11dd-ab95-a13b602c0642/afr620342003en.pdf. Accessed 30 May 2013.

Amnesty International (2004) Democratic Republic of Congo—Mass Rape—Time for Remedies. http://www.amnesty.org/en/library/asset/AFR62/018/2004/en/618e1ff2-d57f-11dd-bb24-1fb85-fe8fa05/afr620182004en.pdf (Accessed 30 May 2013)

Bergsmo M, Cheah W (2012) Towards Rational Thematic Prosecution and the Challenge of International Sex Crimes. In: Bergsmo M (ed) (2012) Thematic Prosecution of International Sex Crimes. Torkel Opsahl Academic EPublisher, Beijing.

[151] ICC, *Prosecutor v Bosco Ntaganda*, ICC-01/04-02/06, Decision on the Prosecution's Application Under Article 58, 13 July 2012.

Coalition to Stop the Use of Child Soldiers (2004) Child Soldiers Global Report, 2004. www.child-soldiers.org/user_uploads/pdf/globalreporttextweb7361911.pdf. Accessed 30 May 2013.

Cottier M (2008) Article 8(2)(b)(xxvi). In: Triffterer O (ed) Commentary on the Rome Statute of the International Criminal Court. Hart Publishing, Oxford, pp 470 *et seq.*

Doswald-Beck L, Vité S (1993) International Humanitarian Law and Human Rights Law. International Review of the Red Cross 293:94 *et seq.*

Draper G (1971) The Relationship Between the Human Rights Regime and the laws of Armed Conflict. Israel Yearbook of Human Rights 1:191–207.

Drumbl M (2012) Reimagining Child Soldiers in International Law and Literature. Oxford University Press, Oxford.

Garraway C (2001) Article 8(2)(b)(xxvi) – Using, Conscripting or Enlisting Children. In Lee R S (ed) (2001) The International Criminal Court: Elements of Crimes and Rules of Procedure and Evidence. Transnational Publishers, Incorporated.

Guibert N, Blumenstock T (2007) The First Judgement of the Special Court for Sierra Leone: A Missed Opportunity? The Law and Practice of International Courts and Tribunals, 6:367–391.

Heinze H (2004) On the relationship between human rights law protection and international humanitarian law. International Review of the Red Cross, 86:798 *et seq.*

Human Rights Watch (2005) Seeking Justice: The Prosecution of Sexual Violence in the Congo War. http://www.hrw.org/sites/default/files/reports/drc0305.pdf. Accessed 30 May 2013.

Jørgensen N (2012) Child Soldiers and the Parameters of International Criminal Law. Chinese Journal of International Law 11:657 *et seq.*

Lindroos A (2005) Addressing Norm Conflicts in a Fragmented System: the Doctrine of Lex Specialis. Nordic Journal of International Law 74:42 *et seq.*

Melzer N (2009) Interpretive Guidance on the Notion of Direct Participation in Hostilities under International Humanitarian Law ('ICRC Interpretive Guidance on Direct Participation in Hostilities').

Provost R (2002) International Human Rights Law and Humanitarian Law. Cambridge University Press, Cambridge.

Sandoz Y, Swinarski C, and Zimmermann B (eds) (1986) Commentary on the Additional Protocols of 8 June 1977 to the Geneva Conventions of 12 August 1986. Martinus Nijhoff Publishers, Dordrecht.

Sassòli M, Olson L M (2008) The Relationship Between International Humanitarian and Human Rights Law Where it Matters: Admissible Killings and Internment of Fighters in Non-International Armed Conflicts. International Review of the Red Cross 90:599 *et seq.*

Save the Children Fund (2005) Forgotten Casualties of War – Girls in armed conflict. http://resourcecentre.savethechildren.se/content/library/documents/forgotten-casualties-war-girls-armed-conflicts(Accessed 30 May 2013)

Schabas W (2010) The International Criminal Court: A Commentary on the Rome Statute. Oxford University Press, Oxford.

Shahabuddeen M (2004) Does the Principle of Legality Stand in the Way of Progressive Development of Law? Journal of International Criminal Justice 2:1007 *et seq.*

Sivakumaran S (2010) War Crimes before the Special Court for Sierra Leone: Child Soldiers, Hostages, Peacekeepers and Collective Punishments. Journal of International Criminal Justice 1009 8:1009–1034.

Smith A (2004) Child Recruitment and the Special Court for Sierra Leone. Journal of International Criminal Justice 2:1141–1153.

UNICEF (1997) Cape Town Principles and Best Practices: Adopted at the Symposium on the Prevention of Recruitment of Children Into the Armed Forces and on Demobilization and Social Reintegration of Child Soldiers in Africa (Cape Town Principles). http://www.unicef.org/emerg/files/Cape_Town_Principles(1).pdf (Accessed 30 May 2013)

UNICEF (2007) Principles and Guidelines on Children Associated with Armed Forces or Armed Groups (The Paris Principles). http://www.unicef.org/emerg/files/ParisPrinciples310107English.pdf. (Accessed 30 May 2013)

Vinuesa R (1998) Interface, correspondence and convergence of human rights and international humanitarian law. Yearbook of International Humanitarian Law 1:69–110.

Part III
Other Articles

Chapter 7
The Duty to Investigate Civilian Casualties During Armed Conflict and Its Implementation in Practice

Alon Margalit

Contents

The author is Research Associate, Hotung Programme for Law, Human Rights and Peace Building in the Middle East, SOAS, University of London; PhD Candidate, Institute of Advanced Legal Studies, University of London. I am grateful to Charles Garraway, Iain Scobbie, Tatyana Eatwell, Adrian Garcia, members of the Editorial Board and anonymous peer reviewers for their valuable comments on earlier drafts. Any errors are my own.

A. Margalit (✉)
University of London, London, UK
e-mail: am110@soas.ac.uk

T. D. Gill et al. (eds.), *Yearbook of International Humanitarian Law 2012*,
Yearbook of International Humanitarian Law 15, DOI: 10.1007/978-90-6704-924-5_7,

7.1 Introduction

Seeking to balance military necessity with humanitarian considerations, the Law of Armed Conflict (LOAC) restricts the manner in which force can be used during warfare and prohibits certain kinds of attacks. In order to protect civilians and civilian objects while pursuing attacks against combatants[1] and military objectives, LOAC prescribes strict targeting rules which are based on the principles of distinction, proportionality and precautions.[2] The investigation of civilian casualties that have occurred during armed conflict enforces (and reinforces) these targeting rules and serves a similar purpose—protecting the civilian population from the effects of military operations.

The present article discusses the circumstances which give rise to a duty to investigate civilian casualties. It considers whether and to what extent a State whose armed forces caused civilian causalities during combat is required—under LOAC—to investigate these incidents. While the starting point is the case where a suspected war crime is involved, the article also deals with the question whether there is a duty to investigate incidents which indicate a LOAC violation that does not trigger individual criminal responsibility, namely a suspected failure to take feasible precautions in attack. It further considers whether an obligation to investigate arises in each and every case of civilian casualties, notwithstanding they are not necessarily unlawful under LOAC.

The analysis continues with a discussion of how to investigate once it was determined that such a duty exists. In this context, the article distinguishes between a criminal investigation that is carried out by professional investigators and subject to strict rules of evidence acceptable in criminal proceedings, and a post-attack review, a generic term which refers to non-criminal investigations that do not aim to assign criminal responsibility, and thus are conducted in a more flexible and informal manner. Given that the state practice scrutinized for this article indicates that command investigations—post-attack reviews conducted by commanders from different levels of the chain of command—are commonly used to examine civilian casualties, the final section assesses whether these investigations are adequate under international law.

[1] The term 'combatants' is used in its generic meaning and does not imply the status of a combatant or of a prisoner of war in the context of an international armed conflict.

[2] Protocol Additional to the Geneva Conventions of 12 August 1949, and Relating to the Protection of Victims of International Armed Conflicts (Protocol I) (adopted 8 June 1977) 1125 UNTS 3 ('AP I') Articles 48, 51, 57. These fundamental rules form part of customary LOAC and thus apply during international and non-international armed conflicts, see Henckaerts and Doswald-Beck 2005 ('ICRC Study'), p. 25 (r 7), p. 37 (r 11), p. 46 (r 14), p. 51 (r 15).

7.2 Criminal Collateral Damage

It does not seem to be in dispute that States are obliged to investigate civilian casualties that allegedly involve war crimes, those incidents which are the result of prima facie deliberate attacks on civilians, indiscriminate and/or disproportionate attacks. A breach of the rule of distinction or proportionality is regarded as a serious violation of LOAC: it is enumerated as a grave breach of the 1977 Additional Protocol I to the Geneva Conventions (AP I) and as a war crime under the Rome Statute of the International Criminal Court (ICC).[3] The authoritative ICRC Commentary to the Geneva Conventions notes in relation to grave breaches that States wanted to draw up "as a warning to possible offenders a clear list of crimes whose authors would be sought for in all countries".[4]

Given the seriousness of these violations, the Geneva Conventions require States to search for persons alleged to have committed, or ordered to have committed, grave breaches of the Conventions[5] and this obligation is reiterated in AP I.[6] An investigation in relation to persons who are suspects of committing war crimes may also be initiated by the prosecutor of the ICC.[7] The principle that States must investigate possible war crimes committed by their armed forces, and when appropriate prosecute the suspects, is considered a norm of customary LOAC applicable in both international and non-international armed conflicts, and it has been repeatedly affirmed in state practice including in military manuals and by UN bodies.[8]

Accordingly, it is generally accepted that under LOAC, credible information suggesting that civilian casualties were caused as a result of a prima facie war crime compels the opening of a criminal investigation.[9] The fact that the

---

[3] Geneva Convention (IV) Relative to the Protection of Civilian Persons in Time of War (adopted 12 August 1949, entered into force 21 October 1950) 75 UNTS 287 ('Fourth Geneva Convention'), Article 147; AP I, Article 85; Rome Statute of the International Criminal Court (adopted 17 July 1998, entered into force 1 July 2002) 2187 UNTS 90 ('Rome Statute') Article 8.

[4] Uhler et al. 1958 ('ICRC Commentary on the Geneva Conventions') p. 597.

[5] Convention (I) for the Amelioration of the Condition of the Wounded and Sick in Armed Forces in the Field, Article 49; Convention (II) for the Amelioration of the Condition of Wounded, Sick and Shipwrecked Members of Armed Forces at Sea, Article 50; Convention (III) relative to the Treatment of Prisoners of War, Article 129; Fourth Geneva Convention, Article 146.

[6] AP I, Article 85(1); Sandoz et al. 1987 ('ICRC Commentary') pp. 973–974, 992.

[7] Rome Statue, Articles 8, 15.

[8] Henckaerts and Doswald-Beck 2005, pp. 607–609 (r 158) and the sources cited there; see also, for example, UNSC Res 1894 (2009), UNSC Presidential Statement S/PRST/2013/2 (12 Feb 2013), UNGA Res 64/10 (5 November 2009), UNGA Res 60/147 (16 December 2005) adopting the Basic Principles and Guidelines on the Right to a Remedy and Reparation for Victims of Gross Violations of International Human Rights Law and Serious Violations of International Humanitarian Law ('Basic Principles on the Right to a Remedy').

[9] Schmitt 2011, pp. 31, 79. The recently published Turkel Report has discussed the duty to investigate LOAC violations, focusing on the Israeli experience, and concluded that a *reasonable*

investigation needs to be of a criminal character is clear given that the commission of those acts triggers individual criminal responsibility and that suspects are exposed to prosecution and penal sanctions.[10] The ICRC Commentary emphasizes that States must ensure that the person suspected of committing a war crime is arrested and prosecuted and that "the necessary police action" is taken on the State's own initiative with all speed.[11]

7.3 Collateral Damage and an 'Ordinary' (Non-criminal) LOAC Violation

7.3.1 Suspected Failure of Precautions

Not every attack which resulted in civilian casualties indicates a violation of the principle of distinction or proportionality. An attack can be directed at a military objective and cause relatively small civilian loss that may not be excessive, or "clearly excessive" per the Rome Statute, taking into account the importance of the military target. But while being discriminate and proportionate, the civilian damage could have been avoided or minimized if only practically possible precautions had been taken, for instance, had smaller weapons been used, the time of the attack been changed or advance warning been given. Indeed while serious collateral damage is often followed by allegations that it was caused due to an indiscriminate and/or disproportionate attack—at times coupled with the demand for the opening of a criminal investigation—in many cases the issue is a failure of precautions, namely, the question whether feasible precautionary measures could have avoided civilian losses altogether or at least minimized them.

Consider the following examples: 13 civilians were killed and dozens more were injured in July 2002 in Gaza after Israel targeted Salah Shehadeh, the commander of the military wing of Palestinian Hamas, a high-value target who, according to Israel, was responsible for the death of hundreds of Israeli soldiers and civilians. Despite the high toll of civilian casualties, Israel persistently refused

(Footnote 9 continued)
suspicion or a *credible accusation* that a war crime has been committed gives rise to an obligation to open a criminal investigation, Turkel Commission 2013, p. 100. The Turkel Commission was established by the Israeli government to examine whether Israel's investigations practice conforms with the state's obligations under international law; see also Alon Margalit, 'Some Observations on the Turkel Report and the Investigation of Wrongdoing by the Armed Forces' (Turkel Commission 2013) EJIL: Talk! http://www.ejiltalk.org/some-observations-on-the-turkel-report-and-the-investigation-of-wrongdoing-by-the-armed-forces/. Accessed 22 May 2013.

[10] See n 5; Rome Statue, Articles 8, 25; Henckaerts and Doswald-Beck 2005, pp. 551–554 (r 151).

[11] Uhler et al. 1958, p. 593.

to open a criminal investigation of the attack.[12] A command investigation by senior officers of Israel's security forces took place and concluded that the operation was "correct and professional;" however, shortcomings were found in the information that had been available to the attacking force in relation to the presence of innocent civilians near Shehadeh.[13] A few years later, the incident was examined by civilian experts appointed by the Israeli government and the civilian Inquiry concluded that while the attack was not indiscriminate, nor disproportionate (as the resultant excessive collateral damage was not expected by those involved), questions arose with respect to the information gathered for "identifying and mapping the number of individuals that might get hurt in the close surroundings", and to whether the resultant collateral damage could have been avoided had more information been collected.[14]

In a 2003 report on Iraq, Human Rights Watch criticized the US over attacks during the invasion phase that resulted in dozens of civilian casualties.[15] But at the same time, it was acknowledged that these attacks were targeting high-value military objectives—senior members of the Iraqi leadership. Later in the organization's report, it becomes clear that the complaint did not concern distinction or proportionality aspects, but rather insufficient precautions in the targeting process. According to Human Rights Watch, the US attacks repeatedly failed to hit their targets as they were based on the identification and tracking of the target's location according to unreliable and imprecise information obtained from the signals of satellite phones.[16]

In September 2009, a US airstrike was called in by a local German commander to target Taliban insurgents in Kunduz province, Afghanistan. Whilst it was reported that about 70 insurgents were hit, the attack caused more than 30 civilian deaths.[17] German officials initially said that the airstrike was "military appropriate" but Amnesty International called for an urgent and transparent investigation claiming that an effective warning should have been given to local villagers before the attack.[18] A NATO investigation later confirmed that no warning was given as the German commander, fearing that fuel tanks hijacked by insurgents would be

---

[12] HCJ 8794/03 *Hess v Military Advocate General* (judgment of 23 December 2008) ('*Hess* Case'). For an unofficial English version see <http://www.adh-geneva.ch/RULAC/pdf_state/HCJ-decision-8794-03-1-.pdf>. Accessed 22 May 2013.

[13] IDF Spokesperson, *Findings of the Inquiry into the Death of Salah Shehadeh* (2 August 2002) http://www.mfa.gov.il/MFA/Government/Communiques/2002/Findings%20of%20the%20inquiry%20into%20the%20death%20of%20Salah%20Sh. Accessed 22 May 2013.

[14] Margalit 2012, p. 147.

[15] Human Rights Watch 2003, pp. 20–21.

[16] Ibid., pp. 24–26.

[17] Rajiv Chandrasekaran, 'NATO Says US Airstrike in Kunduz Killed 30 Civilians', *Washington Post* (5 September 2009).

[18] Amnesty International, 'German Government Must Investigate Deadly Kunduz Airstrikes' (30 October 2009) http://www.amnesty.org/en/news-and-updates/news/afghanistan-german-government-must-investigate-deadly-kunduz-airstrikes-20091030. Accessed 22 May 2013.

used to attack a nearby NATO camp, was not aware of the presence of civilians near the target and mistakenly identified civilians as insurgents.[19] The investigation further emphasized that the attack was based on lacking and misleading intelligence, and that there were alternative means, namely sending ground forces, to deal with the perceived threat.[20]

In all these illustrative cases, attacks were directed against military objectives with a clear military advantage. They complied with the principle of distinction, and plausibly also with the principle of proportionality as high-value targets were hit. Whilst these illustrative cases probably did not establish a prima facie violation that triggers individual criminal responsibility under LOAC, they had suggested a failure to take feasible precautions which at times was confirmed following an official investigation by the responsible State.

7.3.2 A Duty to Investigate

In comparison to a case where the principles of distinction and/or proportionality were allegedly violated, it is less clear whether an obligation to investigate arises when civilian casualties were caused due to a prima facie failure to take precautions. A breach of the duty of precautions is neither listed as a grave breach of the Geneva Conventions and AP I, nor as a war crime under the Rome Statute.[21] The ICRC Commentary explains that violations of the Geneva Conventions, other than grave breaches, are "minor offences or mere disciplinary faults which as such could not be punished to the same degree [as grave breaches]".[22] The issue here is whether LOAC imposes a duty to investigate collateral damage that does not indicate criminal wrongdoing but 'only' a non-criminal LOAC violation.

Indeed a failure to take precautions in attack is considered less serious than the deliberate targeting of civilians or launching an indiscriminate/disproportionate attack as it is characterized by the lack of foresight or negligence as opposed to criminal intent. Nonetheless, the ICRC Commentary clarifies that "failing to take the necessary precautions, particularly failing to seek precise information,

[19] John Goetz, 'NATO's Secret Findings: Kunduz Affair Report Puts German Defense Minister Under Pressure' *Spiegel* (19 January 2010) <http://www.spiegel.de/international/germany/nato-s-secret-findings-kunduz-affair-report-puts-german-defense-minister-under-pressure-a-672468-2.html>. Accessed 22 May 2013.

[20] Ibid.

[21] See Fourth Geneva Convention, Article 147; AP I, Article 85; Rome Statute, Article 8. While LOAC and International Criminal Law do not impose criminal responsibility on individuals for a failure of precautions, States might choose to do so and create additional grounds for responsibility in their domestic laws. For a discussion of criminal responsibility under International Criminal Law and under German domestic criminal law in the context of the September 2009 Kunduz incident discussed earlier, see Groeben 2010, pp. 469, 486–489.

[22] Uhler et al. 1958, p. 597.

constitutes culpable negligence punishable at least by disciplinary sanctions".[23] The fact that judicial or quasi-judicial proceedings, imposing civil or disciplinary liability, are the potential outcome of such a failure implies that some sort of investigation is required in order to ascertain the facts and collect evidence which will be used to hold these proceedings when appropriate.

7.3.2.1 Treaty-Law and Other Material

The argument that during armed conflict States are required to investigate cases of civilian casualties that do not suggest criminal behavior under LOAC may face some scepticism. Looking for additional support for such a legal duty, it is important to note that LOAC imposes a duty to investigate also LOAC violations that are neither grave breaches of the Geneva Conventions and AP I, nor war crimes punishable under the Rome Statute.[24] The obligation to investigate any LOAC violation essentially derives from the general undertaking by States, embodied in Common Article 1 of the Geneva Conventions, to respect—and in particular "to ensure respect"—for LOAC as a whole. This active duty includes the elements of applying the appropriate level of supervision in order to ensure that the State's armed forces abide by LOAC, as well as of enforcement when LOAC rules are not being complied with.[25] The investigation of suspected violations enforces and reinforces these rules; the message is that violations will not be tolerated and an official action will be taken in response, thus deterring potential violators.

In addition, the Geneva Conventions stipulate that States Parties "shall take measures necessary for the suppression of all acts contrary to the provisions of the present Convention other than the grave breaches".[26] The ICRC Commentary adds that this obligation "covers everything which can be done by a State to avoid acts contrary to the Convention being committed or repeated", and further emphasizes that less serious non-criminal breaches should be punishable by judicial or disciplinary means.[27]

AP I instructs States to ensure that military commanders, with respect to persons under their control, "suppress and report to competent authorities" breaches of the Geneva Conventions and of the Additional Protocol.[28] When commanders are aware of a possible breach of these instruments—any breach, not necessarily a criminal one—they must initiate such necessary steps to prevent

[23] Sandoz et al. 1987, p. 994.

[24] Turkel Commission 2013, pp. 99, 149; Cohen and Shany 2011, p. 37.

[25] Uhler et al. 1958, p. 16.

[26] Fourth Geneva Convention, Article 146; AP I, Articles 85(1), 86(1). For similar provisions in the 1949 Geneva Conventions, see n 5.

[27] Uhler et al. 1958, p. 594.

[28] AP I, Article 87(1).

violations, including, where appropriate, a disciplinary or penal action against the violators.[29] According to the ICRC Commentary, the term "to suppress" should be understood in a broad sense, and breaches of the Geneva Conventions and AP I, other than grave breaches, "can and should lead to administrative, disciplinary or even penal sanctions" in accordance with the severity of the breach.[30]

These obligations in the Geneva Conventions and AP I to ensure respect to LOAC as a whole and to suppress all LOAC violations form part of customary international law.[31] They determine that all breaches may lead to disciplinary or even judicial proceedings. As noted earlier, in order to hold such proceedings, an investigation of the suspected violation is required.

The special role of commanders in conducting the initial investigation of a possible LOAC violation is also indicative of a duty to investigate violations that do not necessarily amount to a grave breach or a war crime. The ICRC Commentary notes that "[commanders] are in a position to establish or ensure the establishment of the facts, which would be the starting point for any action to suppress or punish a breach".[32] This implies not only that an investigation (the establishment of the facts) is a legal duty following any suspected LOAC violation but also that on-scene commanders are authorized to conduct such an investigation.

An investigation in these circumstances is also seen as an adequate remedy by the law of state responsibility whose principles are generally regarded as customary international law.[33] Bearing in mind that customary LOAC prescribes that a State which is responsible for a LOAC violation is required to make full reparations for the loss or injury caused by its actions,[34] it is recalled that according to the law of state responsibility, full reparation following an internationally wrongful act may include more than paying compensation. The satisfaction element of reparation requires the responsible State to provide "acknowledgement of the breach, an expression of regret, a formal apology or another appropriate modality", and commentary states that "[m]any possibilities exist, including due inquiry into the causes of an accident resulting in harm or injury".[35] Soft law based on the customary principles of state responsibility specifies that victims who suffered damage following a breach of an international obligation may be provided with appropriate remedies such as compensation,

---

[29] Ibid., Article 87(3).

[30] Sandoz et al. 1987, p. 975.

[31] See Henckaerts and Doswald-Beck 2005, p. 495 (r 139) as well as p. 558 (r 153) and especially at p. 562 ("Failure to punish subordinates who commit war crimes can result from a failure to *investigate* possible crimes and/or failure to *report* allegations of war crimes to higher authorities").

[32] Sandoz et al. 1987, p. 1022.

[33] Crawford 2008, para 65.

[34] The Hague Convention (IV) Respecting the Laws and Customs of War on Land and its Annex: Regulations Concerning the Laws and Customs of War on Land, 18 October 1907, Article 3; AP I, Article 91; Henckaerts and Doswald-Beck 2005, p. 537 (r 150).

[35] International Law Commission 2001, p. 106 (article 37).

apology or an account of the events that led to their victimization.[36] Therefore conducting an investigation in response to a certain incident which involves a possible LOAC violation is not only instrumental for establishing liability and providing an appropriate remedy, but it also has a remedial quality in and of itself.

7.3.2.2 State Practice

The procedures adopted in state practice that will be presented below are consistent with an obligation to investigate suspected violations of LOAC notwithstanding that they do not seem to be criminal violations, and more specifically with the duty to examine credible information regarding a failure to take feasible precautions. While this state practice is in no way comprehensive, it does support the existence of such a duty and provides some insights on the way it is implemented.

In US practice, the common mechanism for reviewing civilian casualties caused by its armed forces is command investigations which are carried out by on-site commanders or by Investigating Officers appointed by the chain of command.[37] Civilian deaths in Iraq and Afghanistan caused by US soldiers may constitute a 'reportable incident' which is reported and investigated in accordance with the Department of Defense Directive 2311.01E:

> All reportable incidents committed by or against US personnel, enemy persons, or any other individual are reported promptly, investigated thoroughly, and, where appropriate, remedied by corrective action.[38]

A 'reportable incident' is defined as "a possible, suspected, or alleged violation of the law of war, for which there is credible information…",[39] and thus it also covers violations that do not trigger criminal responsibility under LOAC. Upon obtaining information about a 'reportable incident', US military regulations instruct the commander of the unit involved to conduct a preliminary inquiry.[40]

---

[36] Basic Principles on the Right to a Remedy (n 8 above) Article 24.

[37] Judge Advocate General's Legal Center and School 2008, p. 99. These investigations follow the procedures prescribed by the Dept. of Army, 'Army Regulations 15-6 Procedures for Investigating Officers and Boards of Officers' 2006 ('AR 15-6 Investigations') http://www.apd.army.mil/pdffiles/r15_6.pdf. Accessed 22 May 2013; Following a Freedom of Information Act request by the American Civil Liberties Union (ACLU), the US Administration disclosed some investigation reports by Investigative Officers who examined civilian casualties allegedly caused by US personnel in Iraq and Afghanistan, see 'ACLU Releases US Army Documents that Depict American Troops' Involvement in Civilian Casualties in Iraq and Afghanistan' (4 September 2007) <http://www.aclu.org/national-security/aclu-releases-us-army-documents-depict-american-troopsE2%80%99-involvement-civilian-casua>. Accessed 22 May 2013.

[38] DoD 2006, s 4.4.

[39] Ibid. s 3.2.

[40] Chairman of the Joint Chiefs of Staff Instruction (CJCSI) 5810.01D on the Implementation of the DoD Law of War Program (30 April 2010) ('Instruction on the Law of War Program') s 6(f)(4)(e)(1)–(2) http://www.dtic.mil/cjcs_directives/cdata/unlimit/5810_01.pdf. Accessed 22

A senior US military official stated in April 2003, when discussing US targeting practices in Iraq, that:

> [E]very time we have an incident [of civilian casualties], even if we don't think that we were involved, we go back with a detailed analysis to figure out what actually happened and figure out whether it was something that we did. Was there a mechanical failure? Did someone, a human being, make an error? And so we go to check the systems to, as quickly as possible, see if there is something systemic in our process that we can correct.[41]

According to this statement, a review procedure is carried out also in incidents that do not necessarily fall under the purview of a 'reportable incident' as it is not limited to those incidents which involve "[an] alleged violation of the law of war…". An investigation takes place following every incident of civilian casualties.

Similarly, the UK examines civilian casualties caused in the course of its military operations without limiting the review to cases of apparent criminal LOAC violations, and in fact the mere occurrence of civilian damage seems to trigger an investigation. UK officials insist that whenever British forces in Afghanistan and Iraq become aware of incidents in which they may have caused civilian casualties, they undertake an investigation.[42] According to operational orders, each and every civilian death is initially examined through a Shooting Incident Review (SIR) held by a Commanding Officer (CO). A SIR is to be completed within 48 h and will involve the collection of relevant documents and operational logs, as well as reports from those who were present during the incident.[43] While a SIR follows every case of civilian casualties, it is not required where the persons killed were enemy combatants.[44]

(Footnote 40 continued)
May 2013.; see also Manual for Courts-martial (2012) r 303 which allows commanders to hold a preliminary inquiry even in cases of a prima facie offence which falls within the jurisdiction of a court-martial.

41 DoD, 'Coalition Targeting Procedures' (Foreign Press Center Briefing, a brief by Major General Stanley A. McChrystal, 3 April 2003) <http://2002-2009-fpc.state.gov/19326.htm>. Accessed 22 May 2013.

42 MoD, 'Top British Commander in Afghanistan Speaks about Minimising Civilian Casualties' (20 August 2009) <http://www.mod.uk/DefenceInternet/DefenceNews/DefencePolicyAndBusiness/TopBritishCommanderInAfghanistanSpeaksAboutMinimisingCivilianCasualties.htm>; MoD, *Operations in Afghanistan* (November 2010) ('Operations in Afghanistan') para 19.2 http://www.publications.parliament.uk/pa/cm201011/cmselect/cmdfence/writev/afghanistan/opa7.htm. Operations. Accessed 22 May 2013; see also official statements in the British Parliament, for example, HC Deb 14 April 2003, vol 403, col 571 W; HL Deb 5 July 2007, vol 693, col WA183.

43 Operations in Afghanistan (n 42 above, Annex 2010) para 19.3; *Al-Skeini v UK* App no 55721/07 (ECHR, 7 July 2011) para 26.

44 Given there is no indication of a violation of the Rules of Engagement (ROE) or LOAC such as targeting combatants *hors de combat*, see Annex 2010 ('Battle-Group Operational Order'), paras 26–27; This document was created in the context of UK operations in Afghanistan however submitted to the Baha Mousa Inquiry and reflects also the applicable policy during its operations in Iraq.

The Code of Conduct for Canadian Forces Personnel states that it is essential that any alleged breaches of LOAC will be "investigated rapidly in as impartial a manner as possible".[45] The use of the term "a breach of LOAC" in the Code extends the reporting and investigation duties to cases which involve a suspected failure to take feasible precautions. Further, Canadian operational practice in Afghanistan indicates that every instance of death or injury caused by Canadian Forces (CF) is to be reported to the military police and subsequently investigated, usually by the CF National Investigation Service (CFNIS).[46]

A general requirement to investigate civilian casualties is noticeable also in the practice of NATO Members States in Afghanistan. For example, a *2008 Tactical Directive* instructed commanders "to acknowledge civilian casualties immediately and transparently investigate allegations rapidly".[47] In addition, the International Security Assistance Force (ISAF), led by NATO, has developed procedures for reporting and reviewing incidents that involve civilian casualties. The incident is to be reported, initially examined within 48 h, and it is possible to deploy a team to conduct fact-finding with the unit involved, preferably at the scene.[48] Notably, the UN Security Council has recognized the efforts taken by ISAF and other international forces to minimize the risk of civilian casualties in Afghanistan, and repeatedly noted the importance of, or called for, "the continuous review of tactics and procedures and *the conduct of after-action reviews and investigations* in cooperation with the Afghan Government in cases where civilian casualties have occurred [emphasis added]".[49]

Looking at Israeli practice, soon after the Second Intifada erupted in the occupied Palestinian territory (oPt) in September 2000, Israel began to use command investigations, a post-attack review usually carried out by the on-site commander as opposed to a criminal investigation by the military police, as the common procedure to examine Palestinian civilian casualties allegedly caused by Israeli personnel.[50] These command investigations (sometimes called 'operational debriefings') are taking place following every civilian death shortly after its occurrence and the findings are reported to the Israeli Military Advocate General (MAG).[51] Whilst each and every incident is reported and reviewed, a command

---

[45] Office of Judge Advocate General Canada 2001, para 3.

[46] Deputy Chief of the Defense Staff (DCDS) 2009, ch 7, s 4, para 709; Military Police Technical Directive (Op Archer) March 2006, paras 11, 14. Cited in Military Police Complaints Commission (MPCC) 23 April 2009, paras 80, 100.

[47] NATO 2009, p. 10.

[48] Operations in Afghanistan (n 42 above) para 19.5.

[49] UNSC Res 1776 (2007), 1833 (2008), 1890 (2009), 1917 (2010), 1943 (2010), 1974 (2011), 2011 (2011), 2041 (2012).

[50] HCJ 9594/03 *Btselem v Military Advocate General* (judgment of 21 August 2011) ('*Btselem* case') para 2.

[51] MAG, 'Submission to the Turkel Commission' (19 December 2010) ('MAG submission') pp. 12–13. <http://turkel-committee.gov.il/files/wordocs/niar_emda_eng.pdf>. Accessed 22 May 2013.

investigation is not required when it is clear that the person who was hurt was a civilian participating in the fighting.[52]

The Israeli High Court has reinforced this practice in the *Targeted Killings* case (2006). The Court opined that during armed conflict and following Israeli attacks on Palestinian militants, an independent post-attack examination is required "regarding the precision of the identification of the target and the circumstances of the attack", and in appropriate cases compensation shall be considered due to the harm caused to innocent civilians.[53] The holding essentially concerns a possible failure to take feasible precautions, including possible negligence in verifying the status and legitimacy of the target.[54] The duty to examine incidental civilian loss, albeit not necessarily through a criminal investigation, was affirmed in subsequent cases discussed by the Israeli Court.[55]

Given this accumulated state practice, the impression is that these investigation procedures are employed on a routine basis and cover cases of civilian casualties caused by erroneous attacks or by attacks that were directed at military targets and their collateral damage was considered by the responsible State to be proportionate. From the foregoing, it is clear and indeed supported by state practice that under LOAC and general international law, there is an obligation to investigate civilian casualties when credible information suggests a LOAC violation notwithstanding it does not amount to a war crime.

This applies also when a reliable complaint suggests that collateral damage was caused due to a failure to take feasible precautionary measures. Two remarks are however in order with respect to the substantive duty of precautions. First, while a

---

[52] IDF, 'Chief of General Staff Order: Procedure for Reporting Incidents Where Palestinian Civilians Were Hurt, 20 November 2005' (annexed to the Israeli government submission to the High Court of Justice in the *Btselem* case, 28 November 2005) (in Hebrew). According to this procedure, in case of doubt whether a victim "was involved" in the fighting, the incident shall be reported to the MAG and reviewed through a command investigation.

[53] HCJ 769/02 *Public Committee Against Torture v Government of Israel* (judgment of 14 December 2006) ('*Targeted Killings* case') para 40. Based on the plain text of the judgment, one may argue that a review procedure is required even when the only person who was hurt was a civilian taking a direct part in hostilities and thus in fact constituted a legitimate target. The High Court opined that since September 2000 an international armed conflict is taking place between Israel and Palestinian armed groups in Israel and the oPt, see paras 1, 16.

[54] AP I, Article 57(2).

[55] *Hess* case (n 12 above), paras 7, 9; *Btselem* case (n 50 above) para 11 ("Even when there is no ground for a criminal investigation, the authorities are not necessarily exempted from the need to consider other means, including those which concern lessons learned in relation to the activity of the armed forces during hostilities, and the need to compensate due to the damage caused to civilians"); HCJ 3292/07 *Adalah v Attorney General* (judgment of 8 December 2011) ('*Adalah* case') para 19 ("…during hostilities, and due to tactics used by terrorist organizations, innocent civilians might get hurt even when Israeli forces act lawfully. Dealing with these fatalities is not necessarily—and should not always be—in the form of criminal prosecution. We deem fit to emphasise again—and the Government did not dispute—when there is a risk of deviation from proper norms of behaviour, even if there is no ground for prosecution, the investigative bodies should hold an examination of the incident using the appropriate tools").

failure of precautions is related to problems such as the imprecise identification of the target, the wrongful use of specific munitions or tactics, insufficient or inaccurate intelligence and a failure to give an advance warning to civilians, in order to establish a prima facie violation in this context, it is insufficient that a certain attack caused civilian casualties or even that certain precautions were not taken. It is further required to show that the necessary precautions were also feasible or that alternatives were available to the commander and while they were less harmful to the civilian population, they enabled to gain a similar military advantage.[56] The ICRC Commentary refers to precautions which are "practically possible taking into account all circumstances ruling at the time, including humanitarian and military considerations".[57] The assessment is in the eyes of the reasonable commander based on the information reasonably available to him from all sources at the time of occurrence.[58]

Second, notice that under LOAC an investigation is not required when only combatants, including civilians taking a direct part in hostilities, were killed or injured. The obligation to take feasible precautions refers only to civilians and civilian objects, while those who fight are not protected from direct attacks.[59] This is on condition that there is a clear indication in relation to their actual participation in the fighting and to their status as military objectives (bearing in mind there is no absolute certainty in time of war). Otherwise, the identity of civilians that were deliberately attacked and their status as legitimate targets should be clarified, and such an examination might lead to a criminal investigation if a suspicion of a war crime comes to light.[60]

7.4 A Duty to Investigate All Cases of Civilian Casualties?

7.4.1 General

The next question to consider is whether under LOAC the duty to investigate is actually broader and covers each and every case of civilian casualties. There are indications in the state practice described earlier that this is the case. Indeed it has

---

[56] AP I, Article 57.

[57] Sandoz et al. 1987, p. 683.

[58] Rogers 2004, p. 111. A number of states have made such declarations when ratifying AP I.

[59] *Cf* the UK interpretation of the obligation to give an advance warning in attacks which may affect the civilian population (unless circumstances do not permit such a warning) embodied in AP I, Article 57(2)(c): "Obviously, the point does not arise as a matter of law if military operations are being conducted in an area where there is no civilian population or if the attack is not going to affect the civilian population at all", MoD 2004, para 5.32.8.

[60] *Cf* AP I, Article 50(1); While this initial investigation may require legal expertise and thus conducted by, or with the assistance of, legal advisers, at this stage it does not seem to be bound by criminal rules of evidence or to attribute criminal responsibility. Therefore a criminal investigation is not necessarily required.

been argued, especially by human rights activists, that even during armed conflict every incident of civilian casualties should be investigated, in the same manner fatalities caused by State-agents during law-enforcement operations are examined.[61]

This requirement however exceeds the obligations under *lex lata* LOAC and ignores the supremacy of LOAC during hostilities as the *lex specialis*.[62] Clearly, under LOAC not every case of civilian loss requires an investigation as the basic premise is that during armed conflict civilian casualties do not necessarily indicate criminal behavior or another unlawful activity, and as one leading commentator puts it "zero collateral damage to civilians (or civilian objects) is not a hard-headed scenario in war, and LOAC recognizes that naked truth".[63] Often, States choose to attack civilians who take a direct part in hostilities or other military objectives with the full knowledge in advance that innocent civilians, physically present in close proximity to these lawful targets, will be hurt. These attacks are lawful inasmuch as the expected collateral damage was not excessive and feasible precautionary measures were taken.[64] Indeed, civilian casualties may occur—and may even be foreseen—notwithstanding all feasible precautions had been adopted. Hence there is no legal ground to investigate civilian casualties when there was no violation of LOAC targeting rules, and similarly there is no point in investigating what is already known and executed lawfully as planned.[65] The Israeli High Court, recently scrutinizing the Israeli government's investigation policies, has expressed this properly:

[61] See Commission on Human Rights 2006, paras 36–37, 42; The Afghan Independent Human Rights Commission (AIHRC), for example, maintained that international and local forces in Afghanistan "should initiate prompt and thorough investigations in any incident of alleged civilian casualties and publicly release details of their findings" [emphasis added], AIHRC 2008, p. 3; In the Israeli context, see *Btselem* case (n 50 above) paras 3, 7; ACRI Submission 2011a, paras 11, 118; ACRI Testimony 2011b, pp. 5, 10, 15–16. It should be noted however that this argument, raised by Israeli human rights NGOs in the Israeli-Palestinian context, is possibly limited to the situation of active hostilities in occupied territory. For the legal 'trigger' under IHRL for the investigation of deaths caused as a result of the use of force by State-agents, see Basic Principles on the Use of Force and Firearms by Law Enforcement Officials (adopted by the Eighth UN Congress on the Prevention of Crime and the Treatment of Offenders, Havana, Cuba, September 1990) Articles 6, 22; *McKerr v UK* App no 28883/95 (ECHR, 4 May 2001) paras 110–115; Watkin 2004, pp. 1, 19.

[62] *Legality of the Threat or Use of Nuclear Weapons*, Advisory Opinion, ICJ Rep 1996, 226, 240, para 25.

[63] Dinstein 2011, pp. 483, 489.

[64] Under the Rome Statute, it is necessary to demonstrate that those involved in the attack knew or should have known that the expected collateral damage will be *clearly excessive* in relation to the overall expected military advantage, Rome Statute, Article 8(2)(b)(iv).

[65] Cf Boothby 2012, p. 543. Noting that where damage caused to civilians despite taking all feasible precautions and the appropriate degree of care due to, for example, a technical fault or a mistake, "there is no breach of the law of armed conflict on which to base a claim in compensation".

> Accepting [the possibility of] collateral damage derives from the understanding that a duty to completely avoid harm to civilians during hostilities will negate the ability to fight in the modern era. Such damage *does not* constitute a violation of the laws of war, even when expected, as long as it adheres to the principles of proportionality and distinction… It should be emphasised: the duty is not to investigate every death, but to investigate *every death in which there is a concern that it was caused by prohibited behaviour* [emphasis in original].[66]

The duty to investigate therefore arises only in response to a suspected violation of targeting rules, rather than in each and every case, and this notion reflects the balance States were seeking to construct between military necessity and humanitarian considerations. It is also supported by reasons of practicality as investigating every incident during armed conflict is simply impossible. In circumstances of intense fighting, of many civilian casualties, or where the responsible State does not have effective control where the attacks in question took place, it would be impossible not only to clarify the circumstances of every incident but even to confirm whether, and how many, fatalities have occurred in a specific incident.[67] Conducting an investigation in all cases would involve tremendous resources, and most importantly would disrupt ongoing operations. Thus imposing such a far-reaching requirement creates a risk that the military mission will be compromised in a manner that will distort the balance between military necessity and humanitarian considerations.

Indeed, there must be an additional element to the very occurrence of civilian casualties that would trigger the obligation to investigate. In this context, the Turkel Report, which has discussed the duty to investigate LOAC violations focusing on the Israeli experience, notes that in the absence of a reasonable suspicion that a war crime has been committed, "a fact-finding assessment" is still required when "there has been an exceptional event or incident such as unanticipated civilian casualties".[68] Although the Report does not explicitly mention a specific LOAC violation, it essentially refers to a suspected failure to take feasible precautions in the targeting process. In scenarios when an attack caused unexpected civilian casualties—including when innocent civilians were targeted by mistake, when the attacked military target was not hurt but only civilians were, when civilians were hurt however the military advantage is unclear, when reliable information suggests that a targeted civilian was not taking a direct part in hostilities and when the number of casualties is higher than initially estimated—there is an indication that something went wrong. This gives rise to a reasonable inference regarding insufficient precautionary measures such as insufficient

[66] *Btselem* case (n 50 above), paras 9–10; see also *Adalah* case (n 55 above) para 19 requiring "a risk of deviation from proper norms of behaviour" in order to hold "an examination of the incident using the appropriate tools".

[67] See, for example, Operations in Afghanistan (n 42 above) para 19.6; MAG submission (n 51 above) pp. 4–5.

[68] Turkel Commission 2013, p. 149. The Report also suggests that such an assessment is required when the information received, regarding a war crime, is only partial or circumstantial.

intelligence gathering, mistakes in planning and executing including in choosing the targets and appropriate munitions, and technical faults that might have been avoided.[69] Still, the analysis leaves a distinct group of fatalities that includes civilians who were taking a direct part in hostilities and the lawful and proportionate collateral damage which does not raise a problem of precautions. With respect to this group, an investigation is not required.

Certainly, and given that military operations and the related decision-making are not transparent for obvious reasons, there might be an expectation from the relevant State to come forward and explain why a specific attack should be regarded as lawful and why it does not merit an investigation. The State might choose—without launching an investigation—to provide details on the circumstances of the attack and its objectives, including the anticipated military advantage, the expected collateral damage and the precautionary measures that were adopted. Nonetheless, while this more transparent practice is desirable, it is not identical to a legal obligation to investigate all resultant civilian casualties when there is no indication that LOAC targeting rules were violated.

7.4.2 State Practice

It is true that the state practice described above seems to take a broader approach than the existing LOAC requirements and the impression is that investigations are initiated in response to each and every civilian death. However there are a number of caveats to consider when evaluating this state practice. First, the terms 'investigate' or 'investigation' used in some manifestations of state practice may be misleading as they do not necessarily suggest a formal investigation by the military police or by another professional investigative body. This terminology rather refers to a more flexible and informal procedure, namely one that is carried out by the chain of command, even by low level on-site commanders. Second, one should take caution when seeking to infer an emerging legal norm that requires to examine *all* cases of civilian deaths during armed conflict.

Indeed the state practice discussed above is not sufficiently general to establish a new norm of customary law[70] and there are additional difficulties which make the assertion of such a customary broad obligation quite uncertain. In some cases when investigations are initiated, the exact source in international law which requires an investigation is ambiguous. LOAC is the *lex specialis* during armed conflict and thus regulates the use of force as well as the duty to investigate in the

---

[69] On the planning process of targeting operations, see Boothby 2012, pp. 476–478.

[70] See ICJ Statute, Article 38(1)(b); Schmitt 2011, pp. 56–57 argues that the practice of some developed common-law States (the US, UK, Canada and Australia) reflects a high threshold of performance with respect to investigations which is based on their extensive experience and resources; however state practice that falls short of this high standard does not necessarily violate international law.

context of hostilities. But when civilian casualties have occurred, for example, during hostilities in occupied territory, in certain periods in Iraq or in the oPt, one may argue that the UK or Israel respectively were implementing their obligation to examine each and every case under the law of occupation and human rights law (IHRL).[71]

Another hurdle in referring to the reviewing procedures adopted in state practice in terms of an emerging new norm is the need to trace the dominant motivation behind a State's behavior, namely whether the investigation of every case derives from the State's conviction that there is a legal obligation to do so, or rather from other considerations such as policy decisions and various requirements in domestic law.[72] Investigating civilian casualties may be part of a State's effort to gain international and local legitimacy for its use of force. It seems particularly important in counter-insurgency operations, and indeed securing the support and cooperation of the local population is evidently a pivotal element of ISAF operations in Afghanistan where the issue of civilian casualties is a matter of ongoing tension between the multinational force and the Afghan government.[73]

Finally, given that investigation policies as well as the investigation findings in specific cases may involve sensitive issues of national security, information regarding this process is not commonly disclosed thus making the proper evaluation of state practice even harder. It is difficult to assess to what extent the formal procedures embodied in official statements and military regulations are implemented when it comes to action on the ground. This is important not only in order to verify whether various manifestations of state practice are consistent, but also in order to realize whether the policy stated and formalized in orders and regulations is sustainable in operational context.

The Canadian practice highlights this challenge. It was stated that every instance of civilian death or injury caused by CF is reviewed by the CFNIS. This practice however should be considered in light of the data reported in 2008 that only 10 Afghan civilians were killed by Canadian soldiers since Canadian involvement in Afghanistan began in 2001 (while 698 civilian deaths were

---

[71] The *Targeted Killings* case illustrates this normative ambiguity as the Israeli Court opined that attacks during armed conflict in the oPt which are governed by LOAC targeting rules are subject to additional requirements emanated from IHRL, see *Targeted Killings* case (n 53 above) para 40.

[72] *Cf* Dinstein 2009, pp. 43, 52. Discussing the Rules of Engagement (ROE) applicable to US soldiers in Afghanistan which are responsive to the concerns of the Afghan government and thus more restrictive than LOAC targeting rules. Moreover, an investigation may serve also operational purposes, for instance assessing the precision of weapon used rather than concerns over civilian casualties, see Ministry of Foreign Affairs, *Gaza Operation Investigations: an Update* (January 2010) ('Israel First Update') para 54 <http://www.mfa.gov.il/NR/rdonlyres/8E841A98-1755-413D-A1D2-8B30F64022BE/0/GazaOperationInvestigationsUpdate.pdf>. Accessed 22 May 2013.

[73] For example, ISAF 2009; Rajiv Chandrasekaran, 'NATO Orders Probe of Afghan Airstrike Alleged to Have Killed Many Civilians' *Washington Post* (5 September 2009).

recorded in Afghanistan in the first five months of 2008).[74] The Canadian policy of examining civilian casualties in Afghanistan, and in particular the use of a professional criminal investigations agency, therefore seemed possible only given the small number of civilian deaths attributed to Canada, a figure which appears to be exceptional in a large-scale combat.

In sum, while some States are reviewing each and every case of civilian damage, this 'extension' of the existing legal requirement—only to investigate credible information that LOAC targeting rules have been violated—is neither an evidence of the general state practice, nor sufficiently conclusive to denote a binding customary norm. While investigating each and every case during armed conflict is desirable whenever possible, it is questionable whether this practice could be maintained in a large-scale combat when a State has to deal with a significant number of civilian casualties. It is therefore important not to misrepresent the applicable LOAC requirements and to confuse policy choices with legal obligations. There is a risk of introducing expectations that States are unable to fulfil during armed conflict, and of incorrectly labeling States that do not adhere to these expectations as acting in violation of international law.

7.5 How to Investigate Once the Duty has Materialized

7.5.1 General

LOAC does not say much on the appropriate form of investigation once civilian casualties have occurred due to a prima facie violation of targeting rules: how to perform the investigation, whether it should conform to specific standards, and who in the responsible State is to undertake this task. A prominent question in this context is whether, and to what extent, the investigations of LOAC violations (criminal and non-criminal ones) should resemble IHRL-type investigations or whether a less formal procedure, such as a fact-finding procedure by on-site commanders, is allowed.

The ICRC Commentary provides some indication with regard to the powers of commanders in theatre to carry out a factual review as part of their duty to prevent and suppress breaches of the Geneva Conventions and AP I. Given their proximity to the events in time and place, commanders are responsible to inform superior officers of what is taking place in their sector, draw up a report following a LOAC breach, take disciplinary measures within their competence and remit the case to judicial authorities when necessary "with such factual evidence as it was possible to find".[75] In order to do so, "a commander of a unit would act like an

[74] Jeff Davis, 'Canada's Record and Compensation Policy for Afghan Civilian Casualties' *Embassy: Canada's Foreign Policy Newsweekly* (10 September 2008).

[75] Sandoz et al. 1987, p. 1023.

investigating magistrate" and assistance from the military police and legal advisers should be available at the appropriate levels "at the request of the commanders concerned".[76]

7.5.2 Criminal Investigation

States usually entrust their military justice systems with the task of investigating serious violations of LOAC allegedly committed by members of their armed forces.[77] As noted, civilian casualties caused by a prima facie war crime trigger individual criminal responsibility and thus compel the opening of a criminal investigation. Though LOAC formally grants commanders the power to investigate, it does not seem sensible for them to carry out criminal investigations. These investigations concern serious cases and their purpose is to find the perpetrators and gather evidence which will be used in potential judicial proceedings. They are therefore complex, must adhere to the rules of evidence and due process acceptable in a criminal trial and require certain expertise that commanders lack. Normally a professional investigative body, the military police or its equivalent—rather than the chain of command—will therefore be responsible for the investigation.[78]

The somewhat limited guidance in LOAC regarding how to investigate raises the possibility of filling the gap by referring to IHRL as it is widely accepted today that the latter continues to apply during armed conflict and that both bodies of international law may complement each other.[79] The question whether IHRL standards apply to the investigation of serious violations of LOAC is not without controversy.[80] Michael Schmitt, for instance, maintains that "it is inappropriate to refer to human rights law practice to fashion standards for investigations of war crimes occurring during hostilities" however at the same time he acknowledges that these investigations are subject to four "universal principles": independence,

---

[76] Ibid.

[77] UN Human Rights Council, *Report of the Committee of Independent Experts in International Humanitarian and Human Rights Laws to Monitor and Assess Any Domestic, Legal or Other Proceedings Undertaken by Both the Government of Israel and the Palestinian Side, in the Light of General Assembly Resolution 64/254, Including the Independence, Effectiveness, Genuineness of these Investigations and their Conformity with International Standards* 21 September 2010, para 34; Turkel Commission 2013, pp. 257–260; see also a discussion of the US and UK investigations practices, Garraway and Watts 2012.

[78] Turkel Commission 2013, pp. 259–260.

[79] *Legal Consequences of the Construction of a Wall in the Occupied Palestinian Territory*, Advisory Opinion, ICJ Rep 2004, 136, at 177–181, paras 105–106; Human Rights Committee General Comment No. 31 2004, para 11.

[80] Report of the Committee of Independent Experts (n 77 above), para 29.

effectiveness, promptness and impartiality.[81] Others, most notably the European Court of Human Rights (ECtHR), take the view that the same IHRL standards that apply to the investigation of deaths caused as a result of the use of force by State-agents in time of peace continue to apply "in difficult security conditions, including in a context of armed conflict".[82]

The gap between these views becomes narrower bearing in mind that even under IHRL, the quality of a criminal investigation is assessed, first and foremost, in light of the reasonable and available investigative means that were adopted by the investigators rather than by the results of their investigation.[83] Thus while IHRL standards generally apply to the investigation of LOAC criminal violations, these standards "must be applied realistically" and "take account of specific problems faced by investigators".[84] The ECtHR and others that have discussed the obligation to investigate civilian casualties during armed conflict have recognized that given the practical constraints inherent to the investigation of events that have occurred during armed conflict and/or when the investigation itself is taking place during on-going combat, some IHRL standards might be difficult to meet, and the relaxation of certain standards may become inevitable.[85]

Thus on a case-by-case basis, less effective investigative measures may be used or an investigation may be delayed when, for example, security problems do not enable the access of the military police to the combat zone. The *lex specialis* status of LOAC takes into account further operational considerations, such as the protection of intelligence and classified combat methods and technologies, as well as the difficulty to obtain access to enemy nationals that are present in an area controlled by the adversary or to obtain their cooperation once contacted.

---

[81] Schmitt 2011 p. 55.

[82] *Al-Skeini* (n 43 above), para 164 and the sources cited there. While under IHRL some of the obligations are subject to derogation in time of public emergency which threatens the life of the nation, it is recalled that the right to life is non-derogable, for example, International Covenant on Civil and Political Rights (1966) 999 UNTS 171, Article 4(2). Under the European Convention on Human Rights (ECHR) derogation from the right to life is possible "in respect of deaths resulting from lawful acts of war". This implies that, subject to derogation, deaths that are lawful under LOAC do not require an investigation which is normally necessary following a possible violation of Article 2 (Right to life) of the ECHR. This notion creates difficulty when suggesting that the applicability of LOAC in time of armed conflict depends upon an explicit derogation by the belligerent State. At any rate, it is recalled that when credible information suggests that the deaths in question have occurred in violation of LOAC, these deaths cannot be regarded as "lawful acts of war" and thus they do seem to trigger a duty to investigate under IHRL. Inconsistency between LOAC and IHRL however remains with respect to the review procedure of LOAC violations which do not trigger individual criminal responsibility as the investigation is commonly carried out by the chain of command and does not fully adhere to IHRL standards, see discussion below at 23 onwards.

[83] For example, *Mcshane v UK* App no 43290/98 (ECHR, 28 May 2002) para 96.

[84] *Al-Skeini* (n 43 above) para 168.

[85] Ibid, para 164; Commission on Human Rights 2006, para 36; Report of the Committee of Independent Experts (n 77) paras 32–33; Turkel Commission 2013, pp. 138, 149–150; Droege 2008, pp. 501, 542.

Therefore, the requirements of transparency and victim participation in the investigation proceedings may often be impossible to accommodate.

7.5.3 Post-attack Review

It is less clear whether investigations which are initiated to examine violations that do not amount to criminal wrongdoing under LOAC are subject, as a matter of law, to IHRL investigation standards. In case this procedure is *arguendo* to be carried out in the same manner that civilian deaths during law-enforcement operations are examined, and in accordance with the standards developed, for example, in the jurisprudence of the ECtHR, it should adhere to criminal rules of evidence and include, inter alia, questioning relevant eye-witnesses, collecting forensic evidence and where appropriate conducting an autopsy, involving the victim's next-of-kin in the investigation and securing sufficient public scrutiny of the investigation and its results.[86]

Clearly the investigation of LOAC non-criminal violations is not subject to a higher standard than the one applicable to the investigation of LOAC criminal violations, and which must be applied realistically given the armed conflict context. It is important to remember that the examined collateral damage suggests a less serious violation which in the present context concerns a suspected failure to take feasible precautions. In fact, there is no reason to impose on States the same heavy burden as in cases of prima facie war crimes, and to demand a formal criminal investigation by professional investigators. An investigation that will conform to IHRL standards also including in those cases that do not cross the threshold of criminality involves tremendous resources as well as possible disruption to ongoing operations. While IHRL favors a formal investigation by professional investigators *whenever* individuals have been killed as a result of the use of force, in the context of armed conflict this seems to be reserved only to serious cases that seem to involve criminal responsibility under LOAC. The Turkel Report also observed that in the absence of a credible suspicion of a war crime, other LOAC violations are subject to "an examination" or to "a fact-finding assessment", thus implying a lower standard of inspection than a criminal investigation.[87]

States are therefore required to initiate a *post-attack review*, a more flexible procedure that is not bound by a strict investigative protocol as the latter is applicable only in cases of criminal wrongdoing. A post-attack review may be carried out by commanders (command investigations), military legal advisers, civilian experts, members of the military police or others however it is neither

[86] See Commission on Human Rights 2006, paras 36–37, 42; *Isayeva v Russia* App no 57947/00 (ECHR, 24 February 2005) paras 211–213; *Al-Skeini* (n 43 above) paras 166–167.

[87] Turkel Commission 2013, pp. 149, 382–383.

bound by criminal rules of evidence and proof, nor aims to assign individual criminal responsibility. It varies in its level of thoroughness and the scope of investigative actions taken. For instance, unlike in the case of a suspected war crime, the obligation to investigate non-criminal violations may be discharged by an administrative investigation held for the purpose of paying compensation to innocent civilians who were hurt.[88] The issue of feasibility is highly relevant in this context. A post-attack review should include practically possible and reasonable actions bearing in mind the circumstances of armed conflict and that there is no prima facie criminal behavior involved in causing civilian casualties. Admittedly, practical constraints during large-scale operations which often involve a high toll of civilian casualties may entail only a minimal level of review by low-level commanders.[89] However when a post-attack review is taking place where the troops have already managed to establish effective control, when the level of violence decreased and/or where the civilian damage is severe, it is reasonable to expect a higher quality of review, for instance, one that is conducted by more senior commanders dedicating additional resources to the review process.

7.5.4 Implementation in State Practice

Against this background, it comes with little surprise that a post-attack review is normally conducted by on-site commanders. Indeed, the state practice scrutinized here indicates that States do not use criminal investigations to examine incidents of civilian casualties that do not suggest criminal wrongdoing. In these circumstances, the common mechanism in the US, the UK, Israel and also the relevant procedures employed by ISAF in Afghanistan, is a fact-finding procedure carried out by the chain of command which is not subject to the rules of evidence or to the standard of proof applicable in criminal proceedings.[90] These reviews are normally conducted by officers from the same unit whose members are involved in the incident in question, and they neither satisfy the IHRL standards of independence,

---

[88] See generally CIVIC 2010.

[89] Turkel Commission 2013, pp. 382–383, recommends that a special team, rather than on-site commanders, will carry out the "fact–finding assessment". The team "shall be comprised of experts in the theatre of military operations, international law, and investigations". Yet, it is unclear how this arrangement differs, on a substantive level, from sending professional investigators of the military police to the scene, and it is therefore questionable whether this recommendation would be practical during high-intensity hostilities.

[90] For the US practice, see AR 15-6 Investigations (n 37 above) ss 1-5, 2-1, 3-7, 3-10(b); For the UK practice, see Battle-Group Operational Order (n 44 above) paras 26–27; Operations in Afghanistan (n 42 above) paras 19.3–19.4. For Israeli practice, see IDF Supreme Command Order 2.0702, Article 8; HCJ 2366/05 *Al-Nabari v IDF Chief of General Staff* (judgment of 29 June 2008) ('*Al-Nabari* case') paras 10, 12. As for ISAF, it has no disciplinary powers, let alone criminal powers, over deployed troops, and soldiers are subject to their own State's national service laws, Operations in Afghanistan (n 42 above) para 19.5.

victim participation and transparency,[91] nor are they carried out by professional investigators with access to medical and forensic expertise.[92]

Interestingly in the Israeli context, it has been argued that the judgment in the *Targeted Killings* case supports the notion that the same *modus operandi* of investigating fatalities in law-enforcement operations which is governed by IHRL should apply to all civilian casualties during armed conflict notwithstanding that LOAC is the *lex specialis* and without distinguishing between criminal and non-criminal LOAC violations.[93] The Israeli High Court indeed opined in the *Targeted Killings* case that the targeting of Palestinian militants during the Second Intifada may be subject, in certain circumstances, to some IHRL-based limitations on the use of force, and indeed ruled, as noted earlier, that the attack and its collateral damage should be retroactively reviewed. Nonetheless, the Court did not refer to a criminal investigation but rather to an "examination". Moreover, in subsequent cases where Israeli attacks on military objectives caused civilian casualties, or when doubts arose in relation to the identity of targeted Palestinian civilians and to whether they were directly participating in the hostilities, the High Court refused to order the Israeli authorities to open a criminal investigation noting that these incidents were already reviewed through command investigations and no ground for a criminal investigation was found by the MAG.[94] In 2011, the Court formally upheld the MAG's general policy that during armed conflict, in the absence of credible indication of criminal wrongdoing, command investigations—rather than criminal investigations—are the appropriate mechanism to examine civilian casualties.[95]

In spite of the foregoing, Cohen and Shany identify an "increasing support in state practice for the need to ensure the independence of military investigations through removing investigative bodies from the chain of command" and "to prefer military police investigations to traditional investigations orchestrated by unit commanders on the ground".[96] They further conclude that the use of command

---

[91] In Israel, for example, in order to encourage the cooperation of soldiers and to enhance the investigation's effectiveness, the report of a command investigation generally cannot be disclosed or used as evidence in criminal proceedings and will not be shared with the military police should the MAG decides to open a criminal investigation based on an earlier command investigation, Military Justice Act [1955] Article 539A; *Al-Nabari* (n 90) paras 15, 18.

[92] For example, *Al-Skeini v Secretary of State for Defence* [2004] EWHC 2911 (Admin), [2004] 2 WLR 1401 [49]–[50].

[93] See *Btselem* case (n 50 above) paras 2, 5. Prior to the eruption of violence in September 2000, and during the Palestinian First Intifada (1987-1993), violent confrontations between Israel and Palestinians, mainly unarmed demonstrations in areas where Israel maintained effective control, were not classified as an armed conflict and dealt with by Israel using policing tools. Thus, every Palestinian death caused by Israeli security forces led to the opening of a criminal investigation, MAG Submission (n 51 above) pp. 9–10.

[94] *Hess* case (n 12 above); HCJ 474/02 *Tabet v Attorney General* (judgment of 30 January 2011).

[95] *Btselem* case (n 50) paras 12–13; *Adalah* case (n 55 above) para 13; HCJ 1901/08 *Dababse v Military Advocate General* (judgment of 15 July 2012).

[96] Cohen and Shany 2011, pp. 67, 70.

investigations in Israel appears to be "out of step with these developments in other States and in tension with the standards of independence and impartiality".[97]

This conclusion appears to be overstated. It is important to notice that this trend of referring incidents of civilian casualties to professional investigations outside the chain of command concerns only the investigation of LOAC violations that trigger individual criminal responsibility (grave breaches of the Geneva Conventions and AP I and other war crimes under the Rome Statute) and therefore a formal criminal investigation is already required under LOAC. Still, as evident from relevant state practice, this practice does not cover cases of civilian casualties where there is no prima facie criminality. Proportionate collateral damage following attacks on military objectives or civilian loss which is the outcome of erroneous attacks are routinely examined through command investigations. This state practice continues at present and seems to accurately reflect *lex lata* LOAC which does not require a formal criminal investigation in cases of non-criminal collateral damage.

Admittedly, in certain instances a suspected failure to take sufficient precautions is examined from the outset through a criminal investigation. In these cases, there are some aggravating circumstances that blur the line between a breach of the duty to take feasible precautions and a more serious violation which carries criminal implications, such as an indiscriminate attack or even a deliberate attack on civilians. Circumstances may suggest a reckless failure to mitigate civilian damage by not employing necessary precautions and consciously ignoring the possible fatal consequences of the attack. This may amount to the intent requirement in a criminal responsibility framework. Clearly, when credible information comes to light that criminal misconduct was involved in causing civilian casualties, LOAC requires more than an informal post-attack review. In borderline cases, a criminal investigation may be launched in order to ensure an investigative response that is consistent with LOAC obligations attached to suspected war crimes.

In other cases—especially when the resultant civilian damage is severe albeit in the absence of an apparent criminal misconduct—while only a post-attack review is required under LOAC, certain provisions in domestic law or policy considerations usually related to public opinion and international relations, lead to the opening of an investigation by the military police despite a questionable ground for a criminal investigation in international law. Indeed it was suggested earlier that extending the duty to investigate to each and every case of civilian casualties is probably motivated by policy decision-making rather than by a clear *opinio juris*. In a similar manner, policy considerations may play a role in the opening of criminal investigations when in fact only a post-attack review, a flexible procedure that is not concerned with criminal responsibility, is required.

In this context, civilian casualties attributed to Canadian forces are admittedly reported to and investigated by the CFNIS, a professional investigative body

[97] Ibid. p. 72.

separate from the ordinary chain of command. These cases are referred to the military police as a matter of course instead of being handled by commanders; however, this does not necessarily denote that the CFNIS will launch a criminal investigation automatically in each and every case. A preliminary assessment and a decision on a case-by-case basis will suffice. Further, the mandate of the CFNIS is to investigate "serious and sensitive matters" related to the CF,[98] thus implying that the CFNIS is called to examine civilian casualties due to their sensitivity and not necessarily due to a legal obligation.

7.6 Command Investigations

7.6.1 A Controversial Mechanism

Lex lata LOAC gives on-scene commanders a significant role in conducting initial investigations.[99] As evident from treaty-law and state practice, civilian casualties are commonly reviewed by unit commanders. Indeed, command investigations provide a prompt investigative response as they normally take place at the scene, have relatively easy access to evidence and are carried out by individuals who are familiar with the operational context and using available unit assets for the investigation with little disruption to the military mission. Hence a command investigation can be quite effective, and in fact in many cases this is the only feasible manner of review, especially when combat is ongoing and/or where the responsible State does not possess effective control in the area where civilian casualties have occurred.

While the use of command investigations usually satisfies the duty to investigate in cases of collateral damage which does not suggest prima facie criminal wrongdoing, it seems necessary to address the harsh criticism expressed in relation to command investigations, in particular with respect to their limited thoroughness and independence. It was mentioned that commanders are not professional investigators and do not have access to medical and ballistic tests. It was further argued that command investigations are usually limited to the soldiers' testimonies and may delay and thus hinder the effectiveness of a potential criminal investigation.[100] In addition, it has been highlighted that given that command investigations are carried out by commanders from the same unit whose soldiers are possibly implicated in the incident under review, commanders are in a conflict of

[98] CFNIS website, http://www.vcds.forces.gc.ca/cfpm-gpfc/cfp-ggp/nis-sne/index-eng.asp. Accessed 22 May 2013.

[99] Sandoz et al. 1987, pp. 1022–1023.

[100] For example, *Al-Skeini v Secretary of State for Defence* [2005] EWCA Civ 1609, [2007] QB 140 [27]; For complaints made in the Israeli context, see B'tselem 2010, pp. 43–45; Yesh Din 2011, pp. 35–36; ACRI Submission 2011a, para 84; Human Rights Watch 2005, pp. 41–43.

interest when required to investigate an attack in which they might have been involved, directly or indirectly, or may find it difficult to question soldiers of their own unit.[101] This is problematic especially in military justice systems where commanders have the power to decide whether, and at what stage, to engage the military police for a professional investigation, which might turn out to have adverse findings against them.[102]

These constraints are inherent to command investigations whenever and wherever used. For example, the flaws in command investigations employed by the UK to examine civilian casualties in Iraq were discussed in *Al-Skeini* and led the British Courts and the ECtHR to conclude that command investigations cannot be considered effective, nor independent, and that "if international standards are to be observed", the investigation of civilian casualties cannot be the responsibility of the chain of command but only of the Royal Military Police.[103]

The shortcomings of command investigations are admittedly troubling. Yet, the above critical observations are inconsistent with LOAC which empowers commanders to investigate possible violations of LOAC including those that resulted in civilian casualties. The legal authority of commanders clearly stems from the operational reality during combat. Further, when 'only' non-criminal violations seem to be involved, LOAC permits a post-attack review which does not amount to a formal criminal investigation subject to IHRL standards.

There is indeed tension between the need to ensure a prompt, potentially effective and—no less important—pragmatic investigative response to civilian casualties and the call for an independent, transparent and professional review process which is completely outside the chain of command. This tension was considered in the jurisprudence of the Israeli High Court which in contrast to the *Al-Skeini* holding has recognized the value of command investigations, and while

---

[101] Ibid. The investigations of wrongdoing by Canadian Forces during peacekeeping operations in Somalia (1992–1993) came under serious criticism on similar grounds which led to a comprehensive reform in Canada's military justice system, see Report of the Somalia Commission of Inquiry 1997.

[102] US commanders—whose unit is implicated in the incident in question—appoint Investigating Officers at their discretion, set the terms of reference for the investigation, and based on the investigation's findings decide how to proceed and whether to engage the Army Criminal Investigative Command (CID) for further investigation, AR 15-6 Investigations (n 37 above) ss 2-1, 2-3, 3-11, 3-20; Instruction on the Law of War Program (n 40 above) para 6.f.(4)(e)(2). The investigation findings and recommendations will be reviewed by the servicing Judge Advocate; however, the appointing commander is not bound by the legal advice given. UK commanders decide based on a Shooting Incident Review (SIR) "whether or not to instigate a subsequent Service Police investigation", Battle-Group Operational Order (n 44 above) paras 26–27; Operations in Afghanistan (n 42 above) paras 19.3–19.4. Presumably, this practice changed when the 2006 Armed Forces Act came into full effect (only in 2009); however, the Act does not impose a duty to report all civilian casualties to the Royal Military Police (RMP) but only when they constitute a prima facie grave breach of the Geneva Conventions or a war crime under the ICC Statute (a 'Schedule 2 Offence'), AFA 2006 s 113.

[103] *Al-Skeini v Secretary of State for Defence* [2005] EWCA Civ 1609 [140]; *Al-Skeini* (n 43 above) para 171.

noticing their limitations, endorsed them as an appropriate investigative mechanism to examine civilian casualties that do not suggest criminal wrongdoing:

> Indeed, there might be downsides to a command investigation as a tool which the MAG relies upon in his decision [whether civilian casualties require a criminal investigation], and biases such as those mentioned by the petitioners should be taken into account while examining command investigations in order to decide whether to open a criminal investigation. However, it is unavoidable to use this mechanism as it is the only mechanism for a prompt examination of the military unit conduct.[104]

7.6.2 Evaluating Command Investigations in Light of Their Function

These different views and discrepancies seem difficult to reconcile but the criticism of command investigations should be put into the proper context. The material question is the relevant function which a command investigation comes to fulfil: is there credible information that a war crime has been committed that needs to be addressed through a criminal investigation; does the examination of civilian casualties serve merely as a post-attack review or rather tend to replace or impede a criminal investigation when the latter is required under LOAC or based on other grounds.

It is important to notice that the civilian deaths discussed in *Al-Skeini* by the ECtHR have occurred between May and November 2003. The end of major combat operations in Iraq was already announced and the UK already became an occupying power in southeast Iraq. It was increasingly engaged in law-enforcement operations, and thus bound vis-à-vis the local population by obligations under the law of occupation and IHRL, including obligations under the European Convention on Human Rights which—according to the Court's judgment—applied extra-territorially to UK actions in Iraq at that period.[105] The ECtHR has clarified that these civilian casualties should have been investigated by the Royal Military Police according to the standards developed in the Court's jurisprudence. As the duty to investigate in these cases derives from the procedural obligation attached to a possible violation of Article 2 (right to life) of the European Convention, it clearly cannot be replaced by a command investigation as the latter does not meet the required standards.

Conversely, the Israeli High Court was preoccupied with a different normative framework. According to the Israeli government whose position was adopted by the Court, the level of violence during the Second Intifada in the oPt has justified the shift from a law-enforcement paradigm to an armed conflict paradigm and thus enabled the examination of civilian casualties through command investigations.

---

[104] Btselem case (n 50 above) para 12.

[105] *Al-Skeini* (n 43 above) paras 10, 149.

Even though this procedure does not meet the requirements of an IHRL investigation, given that LOAC is the *lex specialis*, a mere post-attack review would legally suffice to examine LOAC violations which do not trigger individual criminal responsibility.[106]

As an illustration, the analysis may provide an explanation to an apparent friction between members of the UN Fact-Finding Mission on the December 2008-January 2009 Gaza conflict following the publication of the 'Goldstone Report' and Israel's announcement that it had examined more than 150 incidents arising from the conflict, and opened more than 400 command investigations.[107] Justice Richard Goldstone, who chaired the Fact-Finding Mission, seemed to be satisfied with this mechanism, concluding that these investigations "indicate that civilians were not intentionally targeted as a matter of policy" and that the investigations also clarify the status of those killed, whether they were civilians or combatants.[108] Other members of the Fact-Finding Mission however continued to express discomfort with regard to the use of command investigations to review the incidents documented in the Goldstone Report. They pointed out that "[c]ommand investigations are operational, not legal, inquiries and are conducted by personnel from the same command structure as those under investigation". They highlighted additional problems such as insufficient transparency and lack of participation of victims in the process.[109]

It is recalled that the Goldstone Report detailed a number of incidents that indeed constituted prima facie war crimes and merited a criminal investigation under LOAC, for instance, allegations regarding the direct shooting at civilians

---

[106] Interestingly, in both *Al-Skeini* and *Btselem* the determination of the applicable paradigm—of law-enforcement or of armed conflict—did not always coincide with the factual circumstances on the ground. The ECtHR seemed to 'stretch' its law-enforcement characterization to periods in Iraq when, according to the Court's own description, "crime and violence were endemic" and the situation may amounted to an armed conflict. A similar 'normative stretch', albeit in the opposite direction, was taken by the Israeli Court. By the time the judgment was delivered (in 2011) the Court took for granted that LOAC remained applicable in the oPt continuously since violence broke out in September 2000. However it is highly dubious that an armed conflict was still taking place in the West Bank as the level of violence there had already decreased dramatically in recent years, see, MAG Testimony in front of the Turkel Commission (11 April 2011) pp. 10–11. http://turkel-committee.gov.il/files/wordocs/Chief_MAG_testimony_minutes.pdf, accessed 22 May 2013, noting that since the end of the year 2010 the main activity of Israel's security forces in the West Bank is law-enforcement-related and that "the factual change has to be projected onto the investigative policies".

[107] UN Human Rights Council 2009 ('Goldstone Report'); Israel First Update (n 72) para 8; UN Human Rights Council 2011, para 24. Israel also reported it opened more than 50 criminal investigations in this context.

[108] Richard Goldstone, 'Reconsidering the Goldstone Report on Israel and War Crimes' *Washington Post* (2 April 2011).

[109] Hina Jilani et al, 'Goldstone Report: Statement Issued by Members of UN Mission on Gaza War' *Guardian* (14 April 2011). These concerns referred also to criminal investigations by the Israeli Military Police.

holding white flags or the use of civilians as human shields.[110] Nonetheless, other incidents mentioned in the report, as well as the high toll of civilian fatalities during the Gaza conflict, do not necessarily suggest criminal behavior but rather, as the Fact-Finding Mission noted, "the reportedly exceedingly high percentage of civilians among those killed raises concerns about the precautions taken by Israel in launching attacks".[111] This second group of incidents was apparently reviewed in accordance with the common Israeli practice, through command investigations, a mechanism which fulfils the requirement of a post-attack review when civilian casualties do not suggest criminal wrongdoing. They rather focused on precautionary measures including the feasible steps taken by Israel to verify that the attacked targets were military objectives.

It is therefore possible to extract common lines from various observations made in relation to command investigations that seem contradictory at first glance. Command investigations do not fully comply with IHRL standards and thus cannot replace or frustrate a criminal investigation when the latter is required to examine civilian casualties. Therefore, a command investigation is inadequate when there is a ground for a criminal investigation under LOAC, and it is also inappropriate when fatalities have occurred during law-enforcement operations as these deaths ordinarily merit a criminal investigation. Similarly, when a command investigation reveals suspicions of criminal misconduct, it compels the opening of a criminal investigation without delay.

7.7 Conclusion

Military actions during armed conflict resulting in the loss of civilian life are not necessarily unlawful, let alone criminally unlawful. Still, under LOAC, credible information that targeting rules were possibly violated triggers a duty to investigate. When this information reasonably suggests that a war crime, such as an indiscriminate or disproportionate attack, has, or may have, been committed, it must lead to the opening of a criminal investigation. Further, when this information indicates that civilian casualties have occurred in violation of the duty of feasible precautions, the responsible State is required to look into the incident notwithstanding that it does not seem to involve criminal wrongdoing. The State must ascertain that everything feasible was done to verify that the attacked targets were military objectives and that practically possible measures were taken to avoid or minimize collateral damage. Where these measures were not adopted, those responsible should be held accountable and appropriate remedies for civilian

---

[110] UN Human Rights Council 2009, paras 55, 703, 1028; Fourth Geneva Convention, Article 146; Rome Statute, Article 8.

[111] UN Human Rights Council 2009, para 360.

victims should be considered. This may include disciplinary proceedings and civil remedies as well as the reviewing and reforming of orders and training programmes.

Nonetheless, various calls to investigate each and every incident of civilian casualties during armed conflict, and in particular the demand for an IHRL-type investigation in every case, ignore the supremacy of LOAC as the *lex specialis* and are largely detached from the operational reality on the ground. While prima facie war crimes are investigated through a criminal investigation, civilian casualties that were allegedly caused as a result of a non-criminal LOAC violation are usually reviewed by on-scene commanders in an informal and flexible manner. The scope of the review varies according to the circumstances such as: the seriousness of the civilian damage, the complexity of the matter and, importantly, the practical possibility to hold a review during combat and/or in areas where the responsible State does not have effective control. An investigation is not required when there are no civilian casualties, meaning when it is clear that only combatants, including civilians taking a direct part in hostilities, were hurt. At times, the question whether a targeted person was indeed a lawful target is to be clarified through an informal post-attack review which will allow an informed decision as to whether a criminal investigation is required.

Finally, as command investigations are commonly employed in state practice to examine civilian casualties, it is important to be aware of their limitations. The assessment whether a command investigation is adequate in a specific case depends upon the classification of the general context and of the legal framework applicable to the incident under consideration. In any event, a command investigation cannot replace or frustrate a criminal investigation when the latter is required under LOAC or another legal regime that governs the incident.

References

ACRI (Association for Civil Rights in Israel) (2011a) Submission to the Turkel Commission ('ACRI Submission'). http://www.turkel-committee.com/files/wordocs/ACLU_submissions.pdf. Accessed 22 May 2013.

ACRI (Association for Civil Rights in Israel) (2011b) Testimony in front of the Turkel Commission. <http://www.turkel-committee.com/files/wordocs/ACLU_protocol.pdf>. Accessed 21 May 2013.

AIHRC (2008) From Hope to Fear: An Afghan Perspective on Operations of Pro-Government Forces in Afghanistan.

Annex (2010) Annex to the Battle-Group Operational Order Based on Task Force Helmand (TFH) Policy (2010) (document MIV004963 annexed to witness statement by Deputy Assistant Chief of Staff Col Rufus McNeil in front of the Baha Mousa Inquiry) ('Battle-Group Operational Order'). http://www.bahamousainquiry.org/module_4/mod_4_witness_statem/exhibit_rm.htm. Accessed 22 May 2013.

Boothby W (2012) The Law of Targeting. Oxford University Press, Oxford.

B'tselem (2010) Void of Responsibility: Israel Military Policy Not to Investigate Killings of Palestinians by Soldiers. http://www.btselem.org/download/201009_void_of_responsibility_eng.pdf. Accessed 22 May 2013.

CIVIC (Campaign for innocent victims in conflict) (2010) Addressing Civilian Harm in Afghanistan: Policies and Practices of International Forces. http://www.civicworldwide.org/storage/documents/afgh%20white%20paper%20colo%20final.pdf. Accessed 22 May 2013.

Commission on Human Rights (2006) Extrajudicial, Summary or Arbitrary Executions: Report of the Special Rapporteur. (E/CN.4/2006/53, 8 March 2006) ('Report of the Special Rapporteur').

Cohen A, Shany S (2011) Beyond the Grave Breaches Regime: The Duty to Investigate Alleged Violations of International Law Governing Armed Conflicts. Yearbook of International Humanitarian Law 14:37–84.

Crawford J (2008) State Responsibility. In Wolfrum R (ed), Max Planck Encyclopaedia of Public International Law, Online ed, Oxford University Press.

Yesh Din (2011) Alleged Investigation: The Failure of Investigations into Offenses Committed by IDF Soldiers Against Palestinians. http://yesh-din.org/infoitem.asp?infocatid=165. Accessed 22 May 2013.

Deputy Chief of the Defence Staff (2009) Direction for International Operations (DDIO). http://www3.thestar.com/static/PDF/afghandocs/SCA%200810.pdf. Accessed 22 May 2013.

Dinstein Y (2009) Terrorism and Afghanistan. In: Schmitt M (ed) The War in Afghanistan: A Legal Analysis, International Law Studies Naval War College, Newport, 85:43–55.

Dinstein Y (2011) LOAC and Attempts to Abuse or Subvert It, International Law Studies 87:483–496.

DoD (Department of Defence) (2006) Directive 2311.01E Law of War Program. http://www.au.af.mil/au/awc/awcgate/dod/231101p.pdf. Accessed 22 May 2013.

Droege C (2008) Elective Affinities? Human Rights and Humanitarian Law. International Review of the Red Cross 90:501-548.

Garraway C and Watts S (2012) Accountability for Violations of the Laws of Armed Conflict: A Duty to Investigate and Prosecute? Chatham House, International Law Programme Meeting Summary. http://www.chathamhouse.org/sites/default/files/public/Research/International%20Law/050712summary.pdf. Accessed 22 May 2013.

Groeben C von der (2010) Criminal Responsibility of German Soldiers in Afghanistan: The Case of Colonel Klein, German Law Journal 11:469–492.

Henckaerts J, Doswald-Beck L (2005) Customary International Humanitarian Law vol. I ('ICRC Study'), Cambridge University Press, Cambridge.

Human Rights Watch (2003) Off Target: the Conduct of the War and Civilian Casualties in Iraq.

Human Rights Watch (2005) Promoting Impunity: Israel's Failure to Investigate Wrongdoing.

Human Rights Committee (2004) General Comment No. 31: Nature of the General Legal Obligation Imposed on States Parties to the Covenant.

International Law Commission (2001) Draft Articles on Responsibility of States for Internationally Wrongful Acts, with Commentaries. Yearbook of International Law Commission II(2):31–143.

ISAF (2009) ISAF Commander's Counterinsurgency Guidance http://www.nato.int/isaf/ docu/official_texts/counterinsurgency_guidance.pdf. Accessed 22 May 2013.

Judge Advocate General's Legal Center and School (2008) Forged in the Fire: Lessons Learned from Military Operations 1994-2008. US Army, Charlottesville Virginia.

Margalit A (2012) Did LOAC Take the Lead? Reassessing Israel's Targeted Killing of Salah Shehadeh and the Subsequent Calls for Criminal Accountability. Journal of Conflict & Security Law 17:147–173.

Military Police Technical Directive (Op Archer) (2006) cited in Military Police Complaints Commission (MPCC) (23 April 2009) Chairperson's Final Report Concerning the Afghan Detainees (MPCC 2007-003). http://www.mpcc-cppm.gc.ca/alt_format/300/3700/2007-003/2007-003-eng-rev.pdf. Accessed 22 May 2013.

MoD (Ministry of Defence UK) (2004) Joint Service Manual of the Law of Armed Conflict.

NATO (2009) Afghanistan Report http://www.isaf.nato.int/pdf/20090331_090331_afghanistan_report_2009.pdf. Accessed 22 May 2013.

Office of Judge Advocate General Canada (2001) Code of Conduct for CF Personnel http://www.forces.gc.ca/jag/publications/oplaw-loiop/cfcc-ccfc-eng.pdf. Accessed 22 May 2013.

Rogers A (2004) Law on the Battlefield. Juris Publishing, New York.

Report of the Somalia Commission of Inquiry 1997. http://www.dnd.ca/somalia/somaliae.htm. Accessed 22 May 2013.

Sandoz Y et al. (1987) Commentary on the Additional Protocols of 8 June 1977 to the Geneva Conventions of 12 August 1949. Martinus Nijhoff Publishers, Geneva.

Schmitt M (2011) Investigating Violations of International Law in Armed Conflict. Harvard National Security Journal 2:31–84.

Turkel Commission (2013) Turkel Commission: Public Commission to Examine the Maritime Incident of 31 May 2010 (2013) Second Report: Israel's Mechanisms for Examining and Investigating Complaints and Claims of Violations of the Laws of Armed Conflict According to International Law ('Turkel Report') http://www.turkelcommittee.gov.il/files/newDoc3/The%20Turkel%20Report%20for%20website.pdf. Accessed 22 May 2013.

Uhler O et al. (1958) Commentary on the Geneva Conventions of 12 August 1949 Volume IV. ICRC, Geneva.

UN Human Rights Council (2009) A/HRC/12/48 Report of the UN Fact-Finding Mission on the Gaza Conflict ('Goldstone Report') http://www2.ohchr.org/english/bodies/hrcouncil/docs/12session/A-HRC-12-48.pdf. Accessed 22 May 2013.

UN Human Rights Council (2010) A/HRC/15/50 Report of the Committee of Independent Experts http://www2.ohchr.org/english/bodies/hrcouncil/docs/15session/a.hrc.15.50_aev.pdf. Accessed 22 May 2013.

UN Human Rights Council (2011) A/HRC/16/24 Report of the Committee of Independent Experts in International Humanitarian and Human Rights Law Established Pursuant to Council Resolution 13/9. http://www2.ohchr.org/english/bodies/hrcouncil/docs/16session/A.HRC.16.24_AUV.pdf. Accessed 22 May 2013.

Watkin K (2004) Controlling the Use of Force: a Role for Human Rights Norms in Contemporary Armed Conflict. American Journal of International Law 98:1–34.

Chapter 8
Year in Review 2012

Christophe Paulussen and Jessica Dorsey

Contents

Dr. Christophe Paulussen, LL.M., M.Phil., is a senior researcher international humanitarian law/international criminal law at the T.M.C. Asser Instituut. Jessica Dorsey, J.D., LL.M. is a researcher in international humanitarian, human rights and criminal law at the T.M.C. Asser Instituut and is a Ph.D. candidate at the University of Amsterdam. The *Year in Review* is not meant to be a comprehensive summary of all events that occurred in 2012, but rather a sampling of events of note with particular relevance to international humanitarian law. We would like to thank our colleagues from the Asser Public International Law Cluster, in particular Nadia Melehi, LL.M. and Fenna van Kempen, LL.M., for their invaluable assistance in the preparation of this article.

C. Paulussen (✉) · J. Dorsey
T.M.C. Asser Instituut, The Hague, The Netherlands
e-mail: c.paulussen@asser.nl

J. Dorsey
e-mail: j.dorsey@asser.nl

T. D. Gill et al. (eds.), *Yearbook of International Humanitarian Law 2012*,
Yearbook of International Humanitarian Law 15, DOI: 10.1007/978-90-6704-924-5_8,

8.1 Situations and Phenomena

8.1.1 Afghanistan

The current conflict in Afghanistan has been in existence since October 2001, following the attacks on the United States (US) on 11 September 2001.[1] Due in part to the 2011 death of Osama bin Laden and the further dismantling of Al-Qaeda, on 21 May 2012 the leaders of the NATO-member countries met in Chicago and agreed upon an exit strategy.[2] The NATO-led ISAF Forces plan to give Afghan forces command of all combat missions by mid-2013, and move from combat roles to a role of supporting, advising, training and assisting the Afghan security forces.[3] The withdrawal of the remaining 130,000 foreign troops is set to occur by the end of 2014.

8.1.2 Colombia

The conflict in Colombia, categorized by most as a non-international armed conflict,[4] continued between government forces and FARC (*Fuerzas Armadas Revolucionarias de Colombia*) rebels, resulting in what Human Rights Watch (HRW) terms "serious abuses" by the rebel guerrilla groups and paramilitary organizations. As a result of this conflict, ongoing since 1964, figures cited by HRW show more than four million Colombians have been displaced and more

---

[1] *See* 'Afghanistan Profile', *BBC News* (31 March 2013) http://www.bbc.co.uk/news/world-south-asia-12024253 (accessed 27 May 2013).

[2] *See* the Chicago NATO Summit website http://www.chicagonato.org (accessed 27 May 2013).

[3] *See* 'Chicago Summit Declaration on Afghanistan', NATO Press Release (2012) 065 (21 May 2012) http://www.nato.int/cps/en/natolive/official_texts_87595.htm?mode=pressrelease (accessed 27 May 2013).

[4] *See* 'Colombia: the challenges of a continuing armed conflict', Interview with Christophe Beney, Head of the ICRC Delegation in Colombia (29 September 2011) http://www.icrc.org/eng/resources/documents/interview/2011/colombia-interview-2011-09-29.htm (accessed 30 May 2013). *See also* Sivakumar 2012, p. 230: "Despite their very real cross-border elements, the non-international character of the Colombia/FARC armed conflict…is not seriously challenged."

than 100,000 are displaced each year that the conflict continues.[5] In November, the first peace talks in approximately a decade between the FARC and Colombian government officials began in Norway.[6]

8.1.3 Cyber Warfare

2012, much like the previous years, saw an increased discussion on cyber crime, cyber attacks and cyber warfare.[7] In response to several years of development of cyber threats, a group of experts met at the NATO Cooperative Cyber Defence Centre of Excellence, in Tallinn, Estonia, to examine "how extant international law norms apply to this 'new' form of warfare."[8] The result of their three-year effort is the *Tallinn Manual on the International Law Applicable to Cyber Warfare*, which was published online in September 2012. It explores issues of *jus ad bellum*, *jus in bello*, as main focal areas and other related bodies of law, including the law of State responsibility and the law of the sea are covered within the context of these topics. For more on the Tallinn Manual and cyber warfare, see the various articles in this Yearbook of International Humanitarian Law.

8.1.4 Democratic Republic of the Congo

In 2012 in the Democratic Republic of the Congo (DRC), there were clashes between the various rebel factions and the Congolese government in North Kivu in a continuation of fighting since 2003, when the second Congo War formally ended. In April, a group of up to 700 ethnic former National Congress for the Defense of the People (CNDP) soldiers, with alleged ties to the government of Rwanda, had an uprising against the DRC government, which at the time was supported by the peacekeeping mission MONUSCO. This group of mutineers formed the March 23 Movement (M23). In November, M23 soldiers took control of Goma[9] and forced more than 140,000 residents to flee their homes. As a result of a peace deal

[5] *See* Human Rights Watch 2013, p. 214. Amnesty International said that figures were very difficult to verify, but at least tens of thousands of people per year are displaced due to the conflict, *see* Amnesty International 2013, p. 65.

[6] *See* 'Colombia's FARC peace talks resume in Cuba', *BBC News* (5 December 2012) http://www.bbc.co.uk/news/world-latin-america-20618131 (accessed 30 May 2013).

[7] *See* 'Study Says Cyber Crime Increases, Attacks More Malicious', *CBS News* (8 October 2012) http://sanfrancisco.cbslocal.com/2012/10/08/study-says-cyber-crime-increases-attacks-more-malicious (accessed 30 May 2013).

[8] NATO Cooperative Cyber Defence Centre of Excellence website: 'Tallinn Manual' http://www.ccdcoe.org/249.html (accessed 7 May 2013).

[9] *See* Pete Jones, 'DR Congo fighters jubilant after taking Goma', *Al Jazeera* (22 November 2012) http://www.aljazeera.com/indepth/features/2012/11/20121122135813464750.html (accessed 30 May 2013).

organized by Uganda, M23 rebels agreed to withdrawal on their own from Goma and they left the city in December.[10] HRW found several instances of war crimes and crimes against humanity had taken place as at least 36 women and girls were reported as being raped during the crisis, at least 24 allegations of summary executions were recorded, children were allegedly forcefully recruited and hundreds of homes, offices and vehicles were reportedly looted.[11]

8.1.5 Detainee Handling

Since 2007, two high-level international conferences and an expert seminar have taken place in Denmark on the issue of treatment of detainees. As a result of these meetings, the *Copenhagen Process on the Handling of Detainees in International Military Operations* emerged and were concluded in October 2012.[12] The initiative was launched by the Danish Government in 2007 to confront multiple practical and legal challenges that had arisen for States and organizations taking part in international military operations, in particular related to detention. This came as a response to a growing need to search for a multilateral and sustainable solution to the many legal questions surrounding the handling of detainees in international military operations. These guidelines contain a set of legally non-binding principles and guidelines on how to treat detainees in conflicts that can be classified as internationalized internal armed conflicts as well as in peace operations.

8.1.6 Israel/Palestine

2012 was another eventful year in the Israel/Palestine conflict. In March, there were clashes between Palestinian militants in the Gaza Strip and Israeli forces, with targeted killings being carried out by Israel against Palestinian militants. In return, the Palestinians armed factions fired rockets at southern Israel over the course of three days.

---

[10] *See* Nick Long, 'DRC Government Accuses M23 of Scores of Murders', *Voice of America News* (28 November 2012) http://www.voanews.com/content/m23-to-leave-goma-rebel-chief-says/1554337.html (accessed 30 May 2013).

[11] *See* Human Rights Watch, 'DR Congo: War Crimes by M23, Congolese Army' (5 February 2013) http://www.hrw.org/news/2013/02/05/dr-congo-war-crimes-m23-congolese-army (accessed 28 May 2013).

[12] *See* Copenhagen Process on the Handling of Detainees in International Military Operations, 2012 http://um.dk/en/~/media/UM/English-site/Documents/Politics-and-diplomacy/Copenhagen%20Process%20Principles%20and%20Guidelines.pdf (accessed 27 May 2013).

Hamas' military chief Ahmed Jabari was killed in a targeted strike by the IDF on 14 November 2012 in Operation Pillar of Defense.[13] As fighting escalated in response, three Israeli civilians were killed by a barrage of rocket attacks in southern Israel launched from the Gaza Strip.[14] Tel Aviv was also targeted by two rockets from the Gaza Strip on 15 November[15] and on 16 November, Palestinian militants fired a rocket aimed at Jerusalem.[16] During this conflict, HRW found that there were violations of international humanitarian law from both sides, including that both Israel and Palestine unlawfully targeted civilians and civilian objects.[17] Amnesty International summarized it similarly by stating: "In November, Israel launched an eight-day military campaign against Palestinian armed groups who fired rockets indiscriminately from Gaza into Israel; more than 160 Palestinians as well as six Israelis were killed, including many civilians. Both sides violated international humanitarian law in the conflict."[18] A ceasefire negotiated and announced by Egyptian Foreign Minister Kamel Amr and US Secretary of State Hillary Clinton occurred on 21 November.[19]

In other events of note, Palestine pushed for recognition in the General Assembly for upgraded status from observer to non-member observer State status and on 29 November 2012, this was granted by a vote of 139 in favor, nine against, and 41 abstaining in the General Assembly.[20]

---

[13] *See* Elior Levy and Yoav Zitun, 'IDF kills top Hamas Commander; prepares for ground offensive' *Ynet News* (14 November 2012) http://www.ynetnews.com/articles/0,7340,L-4305343,00.html (accessed 28 May 2013).

[14] *See* 'Three dead in rocket attack on Kiryat Malachi', *Times of Israel* (14 November 2012) http://www.timesofisrael.com/rockets-rain-down-on-south-after-israel-launches-operation-pillar-of-defense (accessed 30 May 2013).

[15] *See* Yaakov Lappin, 'Gaza terrorists fire two rockets at Tel Aviv', *Jerusalem Post* (16 November 2012) http://www.jpost.com/Defense/Gaza-terrorists-fire-two-rockets-at-Tel-Aviv (accessed 30 May 2013).

[16] *See* 'Hamas fires rocket at Jerusalem', *Belfast Telegraph* (16 November 2012) http://www.belfasttelegraph.co.uk/news/world-news/hamas-fires-rocket-at-jerusalem-28922929.html (accessed 30 May 2013).

[17] For violations by Israel, *see* Human Rights Watch, 'Israel/Gaza: Unlawful Israeli Attacks on Palestinian Media' (20 December 2012) http://www.hrw.org/news/2012/12/20/israelgaza-unlawful-israeli-attacks-palestinian-media (accessed 30 May 2013). For violations by Palestine, *see* Human Rights Watch, 'Gaza: Palestinian Rockets Unlawfully Targeted Israeli Civilians' (24 December 2012) http://www.hrw.org/news/2012/12/24/gaza-palestinian-rockets-unlawfully-targeted-israeli-civilians (accessed 30 May 2013).

[18] Amnesty International 2013, p. 133.

[19] *See* Peter Beaumont et al. 'Gaza ceasefire announced in Cairo', *The Guardian* (21 November 2012) http://www.guardian.co.uk/world/2012/nov/21/gaza-ceasefire-announced-cairo (accessed 30 May 2013).

[20] *See* UN General Assembly, 'General Assembly Votes Overwhelmingly to Accord Palestine 'Non-Member Observer State' Status in United Nations', Press Release (29 November 2012) http://www.un.org/News/Press/docs/2012/ga11317.doc.htm (accessed 30 May 2013).

8.1.7 Mali

Beginning in January 2012, several insurgent groups started a campaign for independence or autonomy for northern Mali in the Azawad area against the Malian government.[21] The National Movement for the Liberation of Azawad (MNLA), initially backed by the Ansar Dine Islamist group, led the campaign with the aim of creating an independent homeland for the Tuareg people. After the 22 March 2012 *coup d'état* of president Amadou Toumani Touré, the MLNA had taken complete control of the region and had claimed that the Azawad region would become an independent homeland for Tuareg people, even declaring it independent from Mali (a decision rejected by the African Union (AU) and the European Union).[22] This move was condemned by the UN Security Council.[23] After the Malian military left Azawad, Ansar Dine and other Islamist groups began a campaign to institute Sharia law. Given their differing visions of the future of the Tuareg state, the two factions clashed. By mid-July 2012, the MNLA had lost most of its control over Malian cities to Ansar Dine.[24] The conflict continued between the various factions through November 2012. The UN Security Council passed Resolution 2056 on 5 July 2012 calling for a roadmap and restoration of constitutional order in Mali due to the deteriorating security situation.[25] After several requests from the Malian government and ECOWAS, the UN Security Council passed Resolution 2071 unanimously on 12 October 2012 to assist the army in Mali with fighting the Islamists.[26] This particular resolution did not give authorization to use force, though it mandated that an actionable plan regarding military intervention should be made within the next 45 days by the AU and ECOWAS.[27] Subsequently, UN Security Council Resolution 2085, passed 20 December 2012,

---

[21] *See* Office of the Prosecutor of the International Criminal Court 2012, para 168: "Since 17 January 2012, there is an ongoing non-international armed conflict in the territory of Mali between the government forces and different organized armed groups particularly Mouvement National de Libération de l'Azawad (MNLA), Al-Qaeda in the Islamic Maghreb (AQIM), Ansar Dine and Mouvement pour l'Unicité et le Jihad en Afrique de l'Ouest (MUJAO) and 'Arab militias,' as well as between these armed groups without the involvement of government forces".

[22] *See* Bate Felix, 'AU, U.S. reject Mali's rebels independence declaration', *Reuters* (7 April 2012) http://uk.reuters.com/article/2012/04/06/uk-mali-idUKBRE83503Y20120406 (accessed 26 March 2013).

[23] *See* 'UN Security Council condemns Mali coup as World Bank cuts aid', *Deutsche Welle* (23 March 2012) http://www.dw.de/un-security-council-condemns-mali-coup-as-world-bank-cuts-aid/a-15826550 (accessed 7 May 2013).

[24] *See* Adam Nossiter, 'Jihadists' Fierce Justice Drives Thousands to Flee Mali', *New York Times* (17 July 2012) http://www.nytimes.com/2012/07/18/world/africa/jidhadists-fierce-justice-drives-thousands-to-flee-mali.html?pagewanted=all (accessed 6 May 2013).

[25] *See* UN Security Council Resolution 2056 (5 July 2012) http://www.un.org/ga/search/view_doc.asp?symbol=S/RES/2056(2012) (accessed 7 May 2013).

[26] *See* UN Security Council Resolution 2071 (12 October 2012) http://www.un.org/ga/search/view_doc.asp?symbol=S/RES/2071(2012) (accessed 6 May 2013).

[27] *See* ibid.

authorized an African-led International Support Mission in Mali (AFISMA), initially for a year to assist authorities to recover rebel-held regions in the north and to restore unity of the country.[28]

During the conflict, several human rights groups expressed concern about potential war crimes, such as shooting and raping civilians, indiscriminate attacks, the denial of food sources, the refusal of access to humanitarian aid, prevention of civilians from leaving conflict areas as well as the arbitrary arrest of civilians.[29] In May 2012, Amnesty International referred to it as "Mali's worst human rights situation in 50 years."[30] The International Criminal Court (ICC) received a letter from the Malian government to open an investigation into war crimes committed during the conflict, see also below under Sect. 8.2.1.4.[31]

8.1.8 Nigeria/Boko Haram

Boko Haram is a Salafi-Islamist group based in northern Nigeria that seeks to establish "pure" Sharia law in the country.[32] Boko Haram, which forbids Western influence including education, began in 2001 by Mohammed Yusuf and in its quest to implement Sharia law, schools, mosques, and churches as well as bars and beer gardens have been bombed or attacked. More than 1,000 civilians were killed in 2012 through various clashes with the group.[33]

In April 2012, President Goodluck Jonathan was elected, followed by violent attacks and rioting. After several bomb blasts in April, the Chief of Army Staff in Nigeria proclaimed that the Nigerian forces were in a non-international armed conflict with the group.[34] The fighting intensified throughout the remainder of

---

[28] *See* UN Security Council Resolution 2085 (20 December 2012) http://www.un.org/ga/search/view_doc.asp?symbol=S/RES/2085(2012) (accessed 6 May 2013).

[29] *See* Human Rights Watch, 'Mali: War Crimes by Northern Rebels' (30 April 2012) http://www.hrw.org/news/2012/04/30/mali-war-crimes-northern-rebels (accessed 6 May 2013).

[30] Amnesty International, 'Mali's Worst Human Rights Situation in 50 Years' (16 April 2012) http://www.amnesty.org/en/news/mali-s-worst-human-rights-situation-50-years-2012-05-15 (accessed 7 May 2013).

[31] *See* M. Coulibaly, 'Renvoi de la situation au Mali' (13 July 2012) http://www.icc-cpi.int/NR/rdonlyres/A245A47F-BFD1-45B6-891C-3BCB5B173F57/0/ReferralLetterMali130712.pdf (accessed 10 March 2013).

[32] *See* Walker 2012.

[33] *See* Amnesty International 2013, p. 196.

[34] *See* Luka Binniat, 'Nigeria: Fresh bomb attacks—we're at war with Boko Haram—Army Chief', *All Africa News* (11 April 2012) http://allafrica.com/stories/201204110031.html?cid=nlc-dailybrief-daily_news_brief-link16-20120411 (accessed 7 May 2013).

2012, with a December report lamenting the situation of embedded fighters in the city as it was "impossible to distinguish their fighters from civilians."[35]

HRW released a report in October 2012 documenting potential widespread and systematic murders, citing a figure of more than 1,200 civilian Christian and Muslims killed since 2009[36] and allegations of religious persecution as it is understood under international criminal law.[37] In both January and June of 2012, the High Commissioner for Human Rights, Navi Pillay, stated that there may be talk of a population "cleansing" based on religion or ethnicity.[38] Amnesty International also published a report in August of 2012 detailing unlawful killings, attacks on churches, journalists under attack, and schools that were burned down.[39] These various concerns voiced by the human rights groups were also found within the already-mentioned 'Report on Preliminary Examination Activities 2012', produced by the Office of the Prosecutor (OTP) of the International Criminal Court.[40] The Prosecutor's report also said the following regarding classification of

---

[35] Yvonne Ndege, 'Inside the lion's den of Nigeria's Boko Haram', *Al Jazeera* (4 December 2012) http://blogs.aljazeera.com/blog/africa/inside-lions-den-nigerias-boko-haram (accessed 7 May 2013).

[36] *See* Human Rights Watch, 'Spiraling Violence: Boko Haram Attacks and Security Force Abuses in Nigeria' (2012) http://www.hrw.org/sites/default/files/reports/nigeria1012webwcover_0.pdf (accessed 30 May 2013), p. 76.

[37] *See* ibid.

[38] *See* UN High Commissioner for Human Rights, 'Pillay urges concerted effort by Nigerian leaders to halt spiralling sectarian violence', Press Release (12 January 2012) http://www.ohchr.org/EN/NewsEvents/Pages/DisplayNews.aspx?NewsID=11756&LangID=E (accessed 7 May 2013). *See also* UN High Commissioner for Human Rights, 'Press briefing notes on new report on UN treaty bodies, Nigeria, Togo and Mexico', Press Statement (22 June 2012) http://www.ohchr.org/EN/NewsEvents/Pages/DisplayNews.aspx?NewsID=12272&LangID=E (accessed 7 May 2013).

[39] *See* Amnesty International, 'Nigeria: Trapped in The Cycle of Violence' (November 2012) http://www.amnesty.org/en/library/asset/AFR44/043/2012/en/04ab8b67-8969-4c86-bdea-0f82059dff28/afr440432012en.pdf (accessed 27 May 2013).

[40] *See* Office of the Prosecutor of the International Criminal Court 2012, pp. 20–21. The pertinent text states: "there is a reasonable basis to believe that since July 2009, Boko Haram has committed the following acts constituting crimes against humanity: (i) murder under article 7(1)(a) and (ii) persecution under article 7(1)(h) of the Statute. In particular, the information available provides a reasonable basis to believe that since July 2009 Boko Haram has launched a widespread and systematic attack that has resulted in the killing of more than 1,200 Christian and Muslims civilians in different locations throughout Nigeria…The consistent pattern of such incidents indicates that the group possesses the means to carry out a widespread and/or systematic attack, and displays internal coordination and organizational control required to that end. The attacks have been committed pursuant to the policy defined at the leadership level of Boko Haram, which aims at imposing an exclusive Islamic system of government in northern Nigeria at the expense of Christians specifically. Opponents to this goal have been targeted as well. Boko Haram leaders or spokesmen have issued public statements evincing the intention to attack civilians in furtherance of this policy, including a January 2012 ultimatum urging Christians to leave Northern Nigeria. The targeting of an identifiable group or collectivity on political, racial, national, ethnic, cultural, religious, gender or other ground is a constitutive element of the crime of persecution under article 7(1)."

the conflict: "there is currently no reason for [the OTP] to believe that the confrontations between the security forces and Boko Haram amount to an armed conflict. There is also currently no reasonable basis to believe that the confrontations between the security forces and Boko Haram amount to an armed conflict."[41]

8.1.9 Sudan and South Sudan

The current situation between Sudan and South Sudan can be traced back many years through two separate civil wars. Much of the current conflict stems from the disputed region of Abyei as well as the disagreement regarding the Greater Nile Oil Pipeline.[42] In January 2012, South Sudan shut production down at all oil fields due to a disagreement sparked by the transport fees Sudan was demanding.[43] In March of 2012, tensions flared once again about the control of the oil-rich Abyei region and escalated into a bombing campaign in the South Sudanese state of Unity in late March.[44] In early April, South Sudanese forces captured the Sudanese Heglig oilfield (referred to as Panthou by South Sudan). In mid-April, the Sudanese launched a counter-offensive in Heglig that continued through the end of May, when Sudan recaptured Heglig. Negotiations between the two parties reconvened in June 2012 under the envoy appointed by the AU, Thabo Mbeki.

Throughout the duration of the conflict, reports from organizations such as Amnesty International and HRW have detailed alleged crimes against humanity and war crimes that have been committed by both sides in the conflict. Amnesty International found violations such as shooting and raping of civilians by police forces, indiscriminate attacks and arbitrary arrests and HRW detailed indiscriminate bombing.[45]

---

41 Ibid., para 91.

42 *See* 'Sudan and South Sudan in fierce border clashes', *BBC News* (27 March 2012) http://www.bbc.co.uk/news/world-africa-17515209 (accessed 6 May 2013).

43 *See* ibid.

44 *See* ibid.

45 *See* Amnesty International, 'South Sudan army and police forces shooting and raping civilians' (3 October 2012) https://www.amnesty.org/en/news/south-sudan-army-and-police-forces-shooting-and-raping-civilians-jonglei-2012-10-03 (accessed 11 February 2013). *See also* Amnesty International, 'Sudan's civilians in crisis: Indiscriminate attacks and arbitrary arrests pervade Southern Kordofan', Public Statement (11 December 2012) http://www.amnesty.org/en/library/asset/AFR54/051/2012/en/d84e4390-2032-4def-b39e-b379cf247d08/afr540512012en.pdf (accessed 26 March 2013). Regarding indiscriminate bombing, *see* Human Rights Watch, 'Sudan Civilians Describe Toll of Attacks' (11 December 2012) http://www.hrw.org/news/2012/12/11/sudan-civilians-describe-toll-attacks (accessed 26 March 2013).

8.1.10 Syria

The conflict in Syria—which began as protests from those opposed to the Syrian's Ba'athist regime in response to the Syrian government's attempts to quell an uprising in 2010s Arab Spring and has now developed into an armed rebellion—has taken a massive civilian casualty toll. Since February 2012, the UN has been active in urging Syria to stop alleged crimes against humanity, with the General Assembly passing a resolution condemning the violence.[46] Despite an attempt at a ceasefire in April, fighting continued in June.[47] In July, the International Committee of the Red Cross (ICRC) declared that the situation in Syria amounted to an armed conflict, as opposed to various internal disturbances and tensions, such as riots and isolated and sporadic acts of violence, triggering the application of international humanitarian law.[48] Allegations against the Syrian government of using civilians as human shields as well as the commission of other war crimes surfaced from HRW[49] as did allegations of crimes against humanity, such as unlawful killings, torture and arbitrary detention, from Amnesty International.[50] Many attempts for peace talks, including a UN-appointed peace envoy, and the arranged exit of President Bashar Al-Assad, have not been successful and it remains to be seen at what point the conflict will come to its end.[51]

8.1.11 United States versus Al-Qaeda and Associated Forces

The US has continued to employ tactics of targeted killing, including deployment of unmanned aerial vehicles (UAVs or drones) to carry out targeted killings of suspected terrorists in its fight against Al-Qaeda and affiliated forces in Pakistan,

---

[46] *See* UN General Assembly Document of the 124th Plenary meeting A/66/PV.144 (3 August 2012) http://www.un.org/ga/search/view_doc.asp?symbol=A/66/PV.124 (accessed 26 March 2013).

[47] *See* 'Deadly violence flares in Syria as EU/Russia seek solutions', *Al Arabiya* (4 June 2012) http://english.alarabiya.net/articles/2012/06/04/218430.html (accessed 23 May 2013).

[48] *See* International Committee of the Red Cross, 'Syria: ICRC and Syrian Arab Red Crescent maintain aid effort amid increased fighting, operational update' (17 July 2012) http://www.icrc.org/eng/resources/documents/update/2012/syria-update-2012-07-17.htm (accessed 26 March 2013).

[49] *See* Human Rights Watch, 'Syria: Local Residents Used as Human Shields' (25 March 2012) http://www.hrw.org/news/2012/03/25/syria-local-residents-used-human-shields (accessed 26 March 2013).

[50] *See* Amnesty International, 'Syria: Fresh evidence of Syria's armed forces ongoing crimes against humanity' (13 June 2012) http://www.amnesty.org/en/news/syria-fresh-evidence-armed-forces-ongoing-crimes-against-humanity-2012-06-13 (accessed 31 March 2013).

[51] *See* 'Assad's safe exit 'could be arranged,' British PM Cameron tells Al-Arabiya', *Al-Arabiya* (6 November 2012) http://english.alarabiya.net/articles/2012/11/06/247989.html (accessed 13 May 2013).

Afghanistan, Somalia and Yemen.[52] In April 2012, several authorities in Pakistan demanded an end to the drone strikes within Pakistani borders, to which the US responded that the strikes would continue.[53] These and other drone strikes have caused concern at the international level, with UN High Commissioner for Human Rights, Navi Pillay, stating that the drone strikes "raise questions" about their legal justification after a fact-finding mission in Pakistan.[54] The UN Special Rapporteur on the promotion and protection of human rights and fundamental freedoms while countering terrorism, Ben Emmerson, announced in October 2012 his intent to open an investigation into the civilian impact on drone use for presentation to the General Assembly.[55] The investigation began in December 2012.

Despite these concerns, several US officials made speeches in 2012 in order to justify the employment of drones and targeted killings, especially with respect to the targeting and use of lethal force against American citizens.[56] These 2012 speeches have followed in line from previous speeches from other administration officials, namely that of then State Department Legal Advisor Harold Koh in 2010,[57] and then White-House chief counterterrorism adviser John Brennan in 2011.[58] This legal authority, according to the US officials, stretches to areas

---

[52] *See* Chris Woods, Jack Serle and Alice K. Ross, 'Emerging from the shadows: US covert drone strikes in 2012', *The Bureau of Investigative Journalism* (3 January 2013) http://www.thebureauinvestigates.com/2013/01/03/emerging-from-the-shadows-us-covert-drone-strikes-in-2012-2 (accessed 6 May 2013). *See also* International Human Rights and Conflict Resolution Clinic at Stanford Law School and Global Justice Clinic at NYU School of Law 2012.

[53] *See* Salman Masood, 'Pakistan gives U.S. a list of demands, including an end to C.I.A. drone strikes', *New York Times* (12 April 2012) http://www.nytimes.com/2012/04/13/world/asia/pakistan-demands-an-end-to-cia-drone-strikes.html?_r=0 (accessed 6 May 2013).

[54] *See* 'UN drone strikes 'raise questions'—UN's Navi Pillay', *BBC News* (8 June 2012) http://www.bbc.co.uk/news/world-asia-18363003 (accessed 6 May 2013).

[55] *See* Owen Bowcott, 'UN to investigate civilian deaths from US drone strikes', *The Guardian Online* (25 October 2012) http://www.guardian.co.uk/world/2012/oct/25/un-inquiry-us-drone-strikes (accessed 3 May 2013).

[56] *See* 'Attorney General Eric Holder Speaks at Northwestern University School of Law', United States Department of Justice (5 March 2012) http://www.justice.gov/iso/opa/ag/speeches/2012/ag-speech-1203051.html (accessed 27 May 2013); Jeh Charles Johnson, General Counsel of the US Department of Defense, 'The Conflict Against Al Qaeda and its Affiliates: How Will It End?', Oxford Union, Oxford University (30 November 2012) http://www.lawfareblog.com/2012/11/jeh-johnson-speech-at-the-oxford-union (accessed 6 May 2013). 'Remarks of CIA General Counsel Stephen W. Preston at Harvard Law School' (10 April 2012) https://www.cia.gov/news-information/speeches-testimony/2012-speeches-testimony/cia-general-counsel-harvard.html (accessed 27 May 2013).

[57] *See* Harold Hongju Koh, Legal Adviser, US Department of State, 'The Obama Administration and International Law' (25 March 2010) http://www.state.gov/s/l/releases/remarks/139119.htm (accessed 27 May 2013).

[58] *See* 'Remarks of John. O. Brennan, "Strengthening our Security by Adhering to our Values and Laws"' (16 September 2011) http://www.whitehouse.gov/the-press-office/2011/09/16/remarks-john-o-brennan-strengthening-our-security-adhering-our-values-an (accessed 6 May 2013).

beyond the "hot battlefield" of Afghanistan, potentially opening the door to the use of lethal force on a global scale.[59] This particular focus on justification of the US position was made in response to the September 2011 killing of dual Yemeni-American citizen Anwar Al-Awlaki.[60] Questions still remain regarding the appropriate legal framework to be applied to these particular counterterrorism situations, though the US continues to state that they are carried out under the laws of self-defense and the strikes comport with all principles of the laws of armed conflict.[61]

8.2 Tribunals and Courts

8.2.1 International

8.2.1.1 International Court of Justice

At the International Court of Justice (ICJ), an important decision was issued in the efforts to bring Hissène Habré to justice. Habré was President of Chad from 7 June 1982 to 1 December 1990. During that time, large-scale violations of human rights were allegedly committed. After his overthrow in 1990 and a brief stay in Cameroon, Habré requested and was granted political asylum from the Senegalese Government.[62] Following a failed attempt in 2000 to bring Habré to justice in Senegal,[63] a Belgian national of Chadian origin filed a complaint against Habré with a Belgian investigating judge for, among other things, serious violations of international humanitarian law, torture and genocide. Other complaints in Belgium followed.[64] On 19 September 2005, the Belgian investigating judge issued an international warrant *in absentia* for the arrest of Habré, indicted as the perpetrator or co-perpetrator, among other things, of serious violations of international humanitarian law, torture, genocide, crimes against humanity and war crimes. Belgium also transmitted the warrant to Senegal, requesting Habré's extradition.[65] On 25 November 2005, the *Chambre d'accusation* of the Dakar Court of Appeal

---

[59] *See* Laurie Blank, 'Where is the battlefield in the war on terror?' *Jurist* (1 December 2010) http://jurist.org/forum/2010/12/where-is-the-battlefield-in-the-war-on-terror-the-need-for-a-workable-framework.php (accessed 6 May 2013).

[60] *See* Van Schaack 2011, pp. 255–325.

[61] For a more in-depth analysis of relevant issues, *see* Dorsey and Paulussen 2013.

[62] *See* ICJ, *Questions Relating to the Obligation to Prosecute or Extradite (Belgium v. Senegal)*, 'Judgment' (20 July 2012) http://www.icj-cij.org/docket/files/144/17064.pdf (accessed 20 May 2013), para 16.

[63] *See* ibid., paras 17–18.

[64] *See* ibid., para 19.

[65] *See* ibid., para 21.

held in part that it could "not extend its jurisdiction to matters relating to the investigation or prosecution of a Head of State for acts allegedly committed in the exercise of his functions"[66] and that it therefore could not adjudicate the lawfulness of the proceedings and the validity of the warrant.[67] The day after, Senegal referred the matter to the AU.[68] When Belgium was informed about the referral of the 'Habré case' to thc AU, it stated that it interpreted the (*aut dedere aut judicare* obligation of Article 7 of the) Convention against Torture as imposing obligations on a *state*, and that Senegal had to notify Belgium of its final decision to either grant or refuse the extradition request.[69] Senegal, conversely, argued that it had already responded to the request and that by referring the case to the AU, it had acted in accordance with the spirit of the *aut dedere aut punire* principle.[70] Many other developments followed since, such as legislative reforms in Senegal,[71] the remark of Senegal that financial problems hindered the opening of the trial,[72] a decision by the ECOWAS Court of Justice in November 2010 that Senegal's legislative reforms might not be in compliance with the principle of non-retroactivity of criminal laws and that the trial against Habré should take place in the framework of special *ad hoc* international proceedings[73] and new requests for extradition by Belgium.[74] On 19 February 2009, Belgium filed an application instituting proceedings against Senegal with the Registry of the ICJ, basing its claims on both the Convention against Torture and customary international law.

On 20 July 2012, the ICJ found, among other things, that it had jurisdiction to entertain the dispute concerning the interpretation and application of certain provisions of the Convention against Torture, but that it could not look at the alleged violations by Senegal of its obligations under customary international law.[75] It found, by fourteen votes to two, "that the Republic of Senegal, by failing to make immediately a preliminary inquiry into the facts relating to the crimes allegedly committed by Mr. Hissène Habré, ha[d] breached its obligation under Article 6, paragraph 2, of the [Convention against Torture]"[76] and "that the Republic of Senegal, by failing to submit the case of Mr. Hissène Habré to its competent authorities for the purpose of prosecution, ha[d] breached its obligation under Article 7, paragraph 1, of the [Convention against Torture]".[77] In this

66 Ibid., para 22.

67 *See* ibid.

68 *See* ibid., para 23.

69 *See* ibid., para 25.

70 *See* ibid., para 26.

71 *See* ibid., para 28.

72 *See* ibid., para 33.

73 *See* ibid., para 35.

74 *See* ibid., paras 37–38 and 40.

75 *See* ibid., para 122.

76 Ibid.

77 Ibid.

context, it considered that Senegal's duty to comply with its obligations could not be affected by the 2010 ECOWAS Court of Justice decision,[78] that the financial difficulties raised by Senegal could not constitute a justification for not starting proceedings against Habré[79] and that the referral to the AU could not justify Senegal's delays in complying with its obligations under the Convention against Torture.[80] Finally, it concluded, unanimously, "that the Republic of Senegal must, without further delay, submit the case of Mr. Hissène Habré to its competent authorities for the purpose of prosecution, if it does not extradite him."[81]

In another case from 2012, the ICJ decided that the Italian Republic had violated its obligation to respect the immunity which the Federal Republic of Germany enjoys under international law, among others, by allowing civil claims to be brought against on it based on violations of international humanitarian law committed by the German Reich between 1943 and 1945 and by declaring enforceable in Italy decisions of Greek courts based on violations of international humanitarian law committed in Greece by the German Reich.[82]

8.2.1.2 International Criminal Tribunal for the Former Yugoslavia

At the International Criminal Tribunal for the former Yugoslavia (ICTY), a number of interesting developments transpired in 2012. One of those was the acquittal, on 16 November 2012, of Ante Gotovina and Mladen Markač.[83] The Appeals Chamber, with Judges Agius and Pocar dissenting, decided to reverse the 2011 convictions of the two Croat generals, who were sentenced to 24 and 18 years' imprisonment respectively, for crimes against humanity and war crimes committed during Operation Storm in 1995.[84] The Appeals Chamber opined in part that there had not been a joint criminal enterprise (JCE) to permanently remove the Serb civilian population from the Krajina region by force or threat of

[78] *See* ibid., para 111.

[79] *See* ibid., para 112.

[80] *See* ibid.

[81] Ibid., para 122.

[82] *See* ICJ, *Jurisdictional Immunities of the State (Germany v. Italy: Greece Intervening)*, 'Judgment' (3 February 2012) http://www.icj-cij.org/docket/files/143/16883.pdf (accessed 20 May 2013).

[83] *See* ICTY, Appeals Chamber, *Prosecutor v. Ante Gotovina and Mladen Markač*, 'Judgement', Case No. IT-06-90-A (16 November 2012) http://www.icty.org/x/cases/gotovina/acjug/en/121116_judgement.pdf (accessed 22 April 2013).

[84] *See* ICTY, Trial Chamber I, *Prosecutor v. Ante Gotovina, Ivan Čermak and Mladen Markač*, 'Judgement (Public)', Case No. IT-06-90-T (15 April 2011) http://www.icty.org/x/cases/gotovina/tjug/en/110415_judgement_vol1.pdf (vol. 1) (accessed 22 April 2013) and http://www.icty.org/x/cases/gotovina/tjug/en/110415_judgement_vol.2.pdf (vol. 2) (accessed 22 April 2013).

force.[85] The decision led to strong reactions from all sides. Croatia saw the ruling as a justification for its war of independence, whereas Serbia denounced it as a sign of the ICTY's bias. The dissenting judges also used strong words, with Judge Pocar concluding that the judgment "contradicts any sense of justice".[86]

Two weeks later, another acquittal made the headlines, this time in the case against Ramush Haradinaj, former prime minister of Kosovo and commander of the Kosovo Liberation Army (KLA) in the Dukagjin area in Western Kosovo, Idriz Balaj, former member of the KLA and commander of a special unit known as the Black Eagles and Lahi Brahimaj, another KLA member who worked closely with Haradinaj. The three men were alleged to have been co-perpetrators in a JCE, the purpose of which was to consolidate the total control of the KLA over the Dukagjin area by the unlawful removal and mistreatment of civilians who were, or were perceived to have been, collaborating with Serbian forces or otherwise not supporting the KLA. According to the indictment, the KLA also established a KLA headquarters and detention facility in Jablanica in Western Kosovo, where detainees were mistreated and killed. On 3 April 2008, Trial Chamber I acquitted Haradinaj and Balaj of all charges, found Brahimaj guilty of two counts, sentenced him to six years' imprisonment for cruel treatment and torture (violations of the laws or customs of war), and acquitted him of all other charges. On 21 July 2010, the Appeals Chamber quashed the Trial Chamber's decisions to acquit the accused of certain counts in the indictment in relation to crimes allegedly committed at the KLA headquarters and the prison in Jablanica and ordered a partial re-trial. On 29 November 2012, Trial Chamber II acquitted the three accused of all charges.[87]

Other noticeable developments at the ICTY were the start, on 16 May 2012, of the trial against Ratko Mladić, Commander of the Main Staff of the Bosnian Serb Army, who was charged with genocide, crimes against humanity and war crimes; the oral decision, on 28 June 2012, of Trial Chamber III dismissing the motion of Radovan Karadžić, former President of the Republika Srpska, head of the Serb Democratic Party and Supreme Commander of the Bosnian Serb Army, for a judgment of acquittal on ten counts in the indictment (but granting his motion in relation to count one of the indictment, in which he was charged with genocide in relation to the crimes allegedly committed between 31 March and 31 December 1992 in several municipalities of Bosnia and Herzegovina) pursuant to Rule 98*bis* of the ICTY Rules of Procedure and Evidence; the start of the final trial at the ICTY, on 16 October 2012, against Goran Hadžić, the former President of the Government of the self-proclaimed Serbian Autonomous District Slavonia, Baranja and Western Srem and the former President of the Republic of Serbian

[85] *See* ICTY, Appeals Chamber, *Prosecutor v. Ante Gotovina and Mladen Markač*, 'Judgement', Case No. IT-06-90-A (16 November 2012) http://www.icty.org/x/cases/gotovina/acjug/en/121116_judgement.pdf (accessed 22 April 2013), para 98.

[86] Ibid., 'Dissenting Opinion of Judge Fausto Pocar', para 39.

[87] *See* ICTY, Trial Chamber II, *Prosecutor v. Ramush Haradinaj, Idriz Balaj and Lahi Brahimaj*, 'Public Judgement with Confidential Annex', Case No. IT-04-84*bis*-T (29 November 2012) http://www.icty.org/x/cases/haradinaj/tjug/en/121129_judgement_en.pdf (accessed 28 April 2013).

Krajina who allegedly participated in a JCE to permanently and forcibly remove a majority of the Croat and other non-Serb population from a large part of the Republic of Croatia in order to make it part of a new Serb-dominated state; and finally the judgment of the Appeals Chamber in the case against Milan Lukić and Sredoje Lukić on 4 December 2012.[88] The chamber affirmed the earlier Trial Chamber's sentence of life imprisonment for Milan Lukić and reduced Sredoje Lukić's sentence of 30 years' to 27 years' imprisonment. Milan Lukić was the leader of the 'White Eagles' or 'Avengers', a group of local Bosnian Serb paramilitaries in Višegrad (Bosnia and Herzegovina), which, with others, inflicted a reign of terror upon the local Muslim population. Among other things, he was found guilty of murdering 53 Bosnian Muslim women, children and elderly men in a house on Pionirska Street in Višegrad by barricading the victims in the house, setting the house on fire and then shooting at those who tried to escape through the windows (the Pionirska Street incident) and of murdering at least 60 Bosnian Muslim women, children and elderly men in a house in the village of Bikavac, by forcing the victims in the house, barricading all exits and throwing in several explosive devices (the Bikavac incident). His cousin Sredoje was also member of the 'White Eagles'/'Avengers' and was found guilty of, among other things, substantially contributing to the Pionirska Street incident.

8.2.1.3 International Criminal Tribunal for Rwanda

At the International Criminal Tribunal for Rwanda (ICTR), the Appeals Chamber delivered its judgment, on 8 May 2012, in three cases: the Ntabakuze, Hategekimana and Kanyarukiga cases.

In the case of Ntabakuze, the commander of the Para-Commando Battalion of the Rwandan Army at Camp Kanombe, Kigali, who was found guilty by Trial Chamber I on 18 December 2008 of genocide, crimes against humanity and serious violations of Article 3 Common to the Geneva Conventions and of Additional Protocol II, the Appeals Chamber reduced his life sentence to 35 years' imprisonment.[89] The Appeals Chamber affirmed Ntabakuze's convictions as a superior for genocide, extermination and persecution as crimes against humanity, and violence to life as a serious violation of Article 3 Common to the Geneva Conventions and of Additional Protocol II based on the participation of members of the Para-Commando Battalion in the killings of Tutsi civilians perpetrated at Nyanza hill on 11 April 1994 and at the *Institut african et mauricien de statistiques et d'économie* in the Remera area of Kigali around 15 April 1994. However, it

---

[88] *See* ICTY, Appeals Chamber, *Prosecutor v. Milan Lukić and Sredoje Lukić*, 'Judgement (*Public*)', Case No. IT-98-32/1-A (4 December 2012) http://www.icty.org/x/cases/milan_lukic_sredoje_lukic/acjug/en/121204_judgement.pdf (accessed 28 April 2013).

[89] *See* ICTR, Appeals Chamber, *Aloys Ntabakuze v. The Prosecutor*, 'Judgement', Case No. ICTR-98-41A-A (8 May 2012) http://www.unictr.org/Portals/0/Case/English/Ntabakuze/Judgement/120508.pdf (accessed 28 April 2013).

reversed Ntabakuze's convictions as a superior for preventing the refugees killed at Nyanza hill from seeking sanctuary on 11 April 1994 and for the killings of Tutsi civilians perpetrated in the Kabeze area of Kigali on 7 and 8 April 1994. It also found that Trial Chamber I was wrong in holding Ntabakuze responsible as a superior for the commission of crimes by militiamen. Finally, the Appeals Chamber reversed Ntabakuze's convictions for murder as a crime against humanity.

In the case of Hategekimana, the commander of the Ngoma Military Camp in Butare Prefecture, the Appeals Chamber affirmed the life sentence[90] to which he was convicted by Trial Chamber II on 6 December 2010, which found him guilty of genocide for, among other things, the killing of approximately 500 mostly Tutsi refugees at the Ngoma Parish, of murder as a crime against humanity and, as a superior, of rape as a crime against humanity.

In the case of Kanyarukiga, a former businessman from the Kivumu Commune, the Appeals Chamber affirmed the sentence of 30 years' imprisonment[91] to which Trial Chamber II had convicted him on 1 November 2010 for planning with others the destruction of the Nyange Church, located in the Kivumu Commune, which resulted in the death of approximately 2,000 Tutsi civilians who were barricaded in the church (genocide and extermination as a crime against humanity).

Furthermore, on 20 December 2012, Trial Chamber II convicted former minister Ngirabatware of genocide, direct and public incitement to commit genocide and rape as a crime against humanity and sentenced him to 35 years' imprisonment.[92] The judges found that Ngirabatware committed direct and public incitement to commit genocide with his speech to a crowd gathered at the Cyanika-Gisa roadblock in February 1994. They further found that on 7 April 1994, Ngirabatware instigated and aided and abetted genocide through his words and actions in distributing weapons at two roadblocks in Nyamyumba Commune. The Trial Chamber also found Ngirabatware guilty of participating in a JCE, whose purpose was to destroy, in whole or in part, the Tutsi ethnic group as such, and exterminate the Tutsi civilian population in Nyamyumba Commune. The Trial Chamber finally found Ngirabatware guilty for committing rape as crime against humanity, through the extended form of JCE liability. The judgment was historic in that it marked the completion of the trial phase of the ICTR's mandate.

---

[90] *See* ICTR, Appeals Chamber, *Ildephonse Hategekimana v. The Prosecutor,* 'Judgement', Case No. ICTR-00-55B-A (8 May 2012) http://www.unictr.org/Portals/0/Case/English/Hategekimana/judgement/120508.pdf (accessed 29 April 2013).

[91] *See* ICTR, Appeals Chamber, *Gaspard Kanyarukiga v. The Prosecutor,* 'Judgement', Case No. ICTR-02-78-A (8 May 2012) http://www.unictr.org/Portals/0/Case/English/Kanyarukiga/judgement/120508.pdf (accessed 29 April 2013).

[92] *See* ICTR, Trial Chamber II, *The Prosecutor v. Augustin Ngirabatware,* 'Judgement and Sentence', Case No. ICTR-99-54-T (20 December 2012) http://www.unictr.org/Portals/0/Case/English/Ngirabatware/Judgement%20and%20Sentence/Ngirabatware%20121220.pdf (accessed 29 April 2013).

Another momentous occasion for the ICTR (and the ICTY) in 2012 was the launch of the Arusha Branch of the Mechanism for International Criminal Tribunals (MICT) on 1 July 2012. The MICT was established in the context of the Completion Strategies of the *ad hoc* tribunals and is mandated to continue a number of functions from the ICTY and ICTR after they have completed their mandate and to preserve their legacy. On 5 October 2012, the Arusha Branch of the MICT also issued its first appeal decision, upholding a decision of the ICTR to transfer the case of Phénéas Munyarugarama to Rwanda.[93]

8.2.1.4 International Criminal Court

2012 was a historic year for the International Criminal Court (ICC), and not just because of its 10th anniversary. Arguably the most important developments in this festive year stemmed from the situation in the DRC, in particular in the case against Thomas Lubanga Dyilo. On 14 March 2012, the ICC issued its very first verdict. Trial Chamber I decided unanimously that Thomas Lubanga Dyilo was guilty, as a co-perpetrator, of the war crimes as described in Article 8, para 2 (e) (vii) of the ICC Statute of conscripting and enlisting children under the age of 15 and using them to participate actively in hostilities from 1 September 2002 to 13 August 2003.[94] These crimes were committed in the context of a non-international armed conflict between the UPC (*Union des Patriotes Congolais*)/ FPLC (*Force Patriotique pour la Libération du Congo*) and other armed groups, such as the *Armée Populaire Congolaise* and the *Force de Résistance Patriotique en Ituri* in Ituri (the DRC).[95] According to the Trial Chamber, Thomas Lubanga Dyilo "and his co-perpetrators agreed to, and participated in, a common plan to build an army for the purpose of establishing and maintaining political and military control over Ituri. This resulted, in the ordinary course of events, in the conscription and enlistment of boys and girls under the age of 15, and their use to participate actively in hostilities."[96] The judges opined that Thomas Lubanga Dyilo, President of UPC/FPLC and Commander-in-Chief and political leader of the army, exercised an overall coordinating role over the activities of the UPC/ FPLC, actively supported recruitment initiatives and personally used children below the age of 15 amongst his bodyguards, among other things.[97]

---

[93] *See* MICT, Appeals Chamber, *Phénéas Munyarugarama v. Prosecutor*, 'Decision on Appeal Against the Referral of Phénéas Munyarugarama's Case to Rwanda and Prosecution Motion to Strike', Case No. MICT-12-09-AR14 (5 October 2012) http://unmict.org/files/cases/munyarugarama/acdec/en/121005.pdf (accessed 29 April 2013).

[94] *See* ICC, Trial Chamber I, *Situation in the Democratic Republic of the Congo, In the Case of The Prosecutor v. Thomas Lubanga Dyilo*, 'Judgment pursuant to Article 74 of the Statute (Public)', ICC-01/04-01/06 (14 March 2012) http://www.icc-cpi.int/iccdocs/doc/doc1379838.pdf (accessed 9 March 2013).

[95] *See* ibid., para 567.

[96] Ibid., para 1351.

[97] *See* ibid., para 1356.

Four months later, another historic decision was issued, namely the ICC's very first sentencing. On 10 July 2012, the same Trial Chamber I, considering "the widespread recruitment and the significant use of child soldiers during the timeframe of the charges; the position of authority held by Mr. Lubanga within the UPC/FPLC and his essential contribution to the common plan that resulted, in the ordinary course of events, in these crimes against children; the lack of any aggravating circumstances; and the mitigation provided by his consistent cooperation with the Court during the entirety of these proceedings, in circumstances when he was put under considerable unwarranted pressure by the conduct of the prosecution during the trial",[98] sentenced Thomas Lubanga Dyilo to 14 years' imprisonment.[99]

The next interesting development followed one month later, when the ICC issued its first decision on reparations for victims, one of the unique features of the ICC Statute. On 7 August 2012, Trial Chamber I decided on the principles and procedures to be applied to reparations for victims in the context of the case against Thomas Lubanga Dyilo.[100] The Trial Chamber, "accept[ing] that the right to reparations is a well-established and basic human right",[101] and noting that victims of crimes, together with their families and communities, should be able to participate throughout the reparations process,[102] opined, among other things, that the Trust Fund For Victims should determine the appropriate forms of reparations

---

[98] ICC, Trial Chamber I, *Situation in the Democratic Republic of the Congo, In the Case of The Prosecutor v. Thomas Lubanga Dyilo*, 'Decision on Sentence pursuant to Article 76 of the Statute (Public)', ICC-01/04-01/06 (10 July 2012) http://www.icc-cpi.int/iccdocs/doc/doc1438370.pdf (accessed 9 March 2013), para 97.

[99] On 3 December 2012, Thomas Lubanga Dyilo filed his appellate briefs against the verdict of 14 March 2012 and against the sentence of 10 July 2012, *see* CPI, La Chambre d'Appel, *Situation en République Démocratique du Congo, Affaire Le Procureur c/Thomas Lubanga Dyilo*, 'Mémoire de la Défense de M. Thomas Lubanga relative à l'appel à l'encontre du « *Jugement rendu en application de l'Article 74 du Statut* » rendu le 14 mars 2012 (Version Publique Expurgée, Annexes 1 et 2 publiques et Annexe 3 version publique expurgée)', ICC-01/04-01/06 (3 décembre 2012) http://www.icc-cpi.int/iccdocs/doc/doc1529983.pdf (accessed 9 March 2013), and ICC, The Appeals Chamber, *Situation in the Democratic Republic of the Congo, In the Case of The Prosecutor v. Thomas Lubanga Dyilo*, 'Mr. Thomas Lubanga's appellate brief against Trial Chamber I's 10 July 2012 *Decision on Sentence pursuant to Article 76 of the Statute* (Public Document)', ICC-01/04-01/06 (3 December 2012) http://www.icc-cpi.int/iccdocs/doc/doc1519202.pdf (accessed 9 March 2013).

[100] *See* ICC, Trial Chamber I, *Situation in the Democratic Republic of the Congo, In the Case of The Prosecutor v. Thomas Lubanga Dyilo*, 'Decision establishing the principles and procedures to be applied to reparations (Public)', ICC-01/04-01/06 (7 August 2012) http://www.icc-cpi.int/iccdocs/doc/doc1447971.pdf (accessed 9 March 2013). Note that the Trial Chamber stressed that these principles and procedures "are limited to the circumstances of the present case. This decision is not intended to affect the rights of victims to reparations in other cases, whether before the ICC or national, regional or other international bodies." (Ibid., para 181.).

[101] Ibid., para 185.

[102] *See* ibid., para 203.

and implement them.[103] As to the forms of reparations, the Trial Chamber opined that these could include restitution, compensation, rehabilitation (the ones explicitly mentioned in Article 75 of the ICC Statute), but that the Court is also "entitled to institute other forms of reparation, such as establishing or assisting campaigns that are designed to improve the position of victims; by issuing certificates that are designed to improve the position of victims; by issuing certificates that acknowledge the harm particular individuals experienced; setting up outreach and promotional programmes that inform victims as to the outcome of the trial; and educational campaigns that aim at reducing the stigmatisation and marginalisation of the victims of the present crimes."[104]

In the context of the situation in the DRC, another important decision was issued. On 21 November 2012, Trial Chamber II notified the parties and participants in the case of *The Prosecutor v. Germain Katanga and Mathieu Ngudjolo Chui* that the mode of liability under which Germain Katanga stood charged was subject to legal re-characterization and consequently decided to sever the charges against his co-accused Mathieu Ngudjolo Chui.[105] Shortly after, on 18 December 2012, in what had become the case *The Prosecutor v. Mathieu Ngudjolo Chui*, the ICC issued its very first acquittal.[106] The judges were of the opinion that the Prosecution had not proven beyond a reasonable doubt that Chui was the commander of the Lendu combatants from Bedu-Ezekere during the attack against the Bogoro village on 24 February 2003 and that he was thus not responsible, pursuant to Article 25, para 3 (a) of the ICC Statute, for the three counts of crimes against humanity and seven counts of war crimes charged against him.

Finally, and again in the situation in the DRC, an arrest warrant was requested—and issued—for Sylvestre Mudacumura, the Supreme Commander of the *Forces Démocratiques pour la Libération du Rwanda*. Mudacumura was charged with nine counts of war crimes allegedly perpetrated from 20 January 2009 to the end of September 2010, in the context of the conflict in the Kivus.[107]

Several other individuals found themselves subject to the Prosecutor's scrutiny in 2012: on 29 February 2012, an arrest warrant was issued under seal against

---

[103] *See* ibid., para 266.

[104] Ibid., para 239.

[105] *See* ICC, Trial Chamber II, *Situation in the Democratic Republic of the Congo, In the Case of The Prosecutor v. Germain Katanga and Mathieu Ngudjolo Chui*, 'Decision on the implementation of regulation 55 of the Regulations of the Court and severing the charges against the accused persons (Public document)', ICC-01/04-01/07 (21 November 2012) http://www.icc-cpi.int/iccdocs/doc/doc1529337.pdf (accessed 9 March 2013).

[106] *See* CPI, La Chambre de Première Instance II, *Situation en République Démocratique du Congo, Affaire Le Procureur c. Mathieu Ngudjolo*, 'Jugement rendu en application de l'article 74 du Statut (Public)', ICC-01/04-02/12 (18 décembre 2012) http://www.icc-cpi.int/iccdocs/doc/doc1529535.pdf (accessed 9 March 2013).

[107] *See* ICC, Pre-Trial Chamber II, *Situation in the Democratic Republic of the Congo, In the Case of The Prosecutor v. Sylvestre Mudacumura*, 'Decision on the Prosecutor's Application under Article 58 (Public redacted version)', ICC-01/04-01/12 (13 July 2012) http://www.icc-cpi.int/iccdocs/doc/doc1441410.pdf (accessed 9 March 2013).

Simone Gbagbo, the wife of Laurent Gbagbo, the former President of Côte d'Ivoire who was already in ICC custody. Simone Gbagbo is the first woman against whom the ICC has issued an arrest warrant. According to the judges of Pre-Trial Chamber III, there were reasonable grounds to believe that Simone Gbagbo bore individual criminal responsibility as an indirect co-perpetrator for four counts of crimes against humanity committed in the territory of Côte d'Ivoire between 16 December 2010 and 12 April 2011.[108]

The next day, the ICC issued another arrest warrant, now in the context of the situation in Darfur, Sudan.[109] Abdel Raheem Muhammad Hussein, Minister of National Defense, former Minister of the Interior and former Sudanese President's Special Representative in Darfur, was charged, as an indirect co-perpetrator, with 41 counts of crimes against humanity and war crimes.

As regards the situation in the Republic of Kenya, on 23 January 2012, Pre-Trial Chamber II issued its decision in the context of two cases. Case 1, *The Prosecutor v. William Samoei Ruto, Henry Kiprono Kosgey and Joshua Arap Sang*, involved crimes against humanity of murder, deportation or forcible transfer of population and persecution. Whereas Ruto and Kosgey were charged as indirect co-perpetrators, Sang was charged as having contributed to these crimes. The Pre-Trial Chamber declined to confirm the charges against Kosgey, but did confirm the charges against Ruto and Sang.[110] Case 2, *The Prosecutor v. Francis Kirimi Muthaura, Uhuru Muigai Kenyatta and Mohammed Hussein Ali*, involved crimes against humanity of murder, deportation or forcible transfer of population, rape and other forms of sexual violence, other inhumane acts and persecution. Muthaura and Kenyatta were charged as indirect co-perpetrators, whereas Ali allegedly contributed to these crimes. In this case, the Pre-Trial Chamber declined to confirm the charges against the latter suspect, but did confirm the charges against Muthaura and Kenyatta (except for the charge of other forms of sexual violence) and committed them to trial on the charges as confirmed.[111]

---

[108] *See* ICC, Pre-Trial Chamber III, *Situation in the Republic of Côte d'Ivoire, In the Case of The Prosecutor v. Simone Gbagbo*, 'Warrant of Arrest for Simone Gbagbo (Under Seal, *Ex parte* Prosecution and Registry only)', ICC-02/11-01/12 (29 February 2012) http://www.icc-cpi.int/iccdocs/doc/doc1344439.pdf (accessed 9 March 2013). (This decision was reclassified as public on 22 November 2012.).

[109] *See* ICC, Pre-Trial Chamber I, *The Situation in Darfur, The Sudan, In the Case of The Prosecutor v. Abdel Raheem Muhammad Hussein*, 'Warrant of Arrest for Abdel Raheem Muhammad Hussein (Public Document)', ICC-02/05-01/12 (1 March 2012) http://www.icc-cpi.int/iccdocs/doc/doc1344965.pdf (accessed 9 March 2013).

[110] *See* ICC, Pre-Trial Chamber II, *Situation in the Republic of Kenya, In the Case of The Prosecutor v. William Samoei Ruto, Henry Kiprono Kosgey and Joshua Arap Sang*, 'Decision on the Confirmation of Charges Pursuant to Article 61(7)(a) and (b) of the Rome Statute (Public Document)', ICC-01/09-01/11 (23 January 2012) http://www.icc-cpi.int/iccdocs/doc/doc1314535.pdf (accessed 12 May 2013).

[111] *See* ICC, Pre-Trial Chamber II, *Situation in the Republic of Kenya, In the Case of The Prosecutor v. Francis Kirimi Muthaura, Uhuru Muigai Kenyatta and Mohammed Hussein Ali*, 'Decision on the Confirmation of Charges Pursuant to Article 61(7)(a) and (b) of the Rome

In the situation of Libya, on 17 March 2012, Mauritania announced that it had arrested former head of the Libyan Military Intelligence Abdullah Al-Senussi, against whom the ICC had issued an arrest warrant on 27 June 2011 for crimes against humanity allegedly committed throughout Libya from 15 February 2011 until at least 28 February 2011.[112] On 5 September 2012, Mauritania extradited Al-Senussi to Libya, whose Government had challenged, on 1 May 2012, the admissibility of the case related to Al-Senussi and Muammar Gaddafi's son Saif Al-Islam,[113] against whom the ICC had also issued an arrest warrant on 27 June 2011 for crimes against humanity.[114] In its admissibility challenge, Libya submitted, "[i]n accordance with the principle of complementarity (...)[,] that this case is inadmissible on the grounds that its national judicial system is actively investigating Mr. Gaddafi and Mr. Al-Senussi for their alleged criminal responsibility for multiple acts of murder and persecution, committed pursuant to or in furtherance of State policy, amounting to crimes against humanity."[115] According to news reports, whereas Al-Senussi is now in the custody of the Libyan national authorities in Tripoli,[116] the same cannot be said of Saif Al-Islam, who continues to be detained by the Zintan Brigade that captured him on 19 November 2011.[117] On 7 June 2012, when visiting Saif Al-Islam in Zintan, four ICC staff members from the Office of Public Counsel for the Defence were detained for allegedly breaching Libya's national security.[118] According to the ICC, the visit of the staff

(Footnote 111 continued)
Statute (Public Redacted Version)', ICC-01/09-02/11 (23 January 2012) http://www.icc-cpi.int/iccdocs/doc/doc1314543.pdf (accessed 12 May 2013).

[112] *See* ICC, Pre-Trial Chamber I, *Situation in the Libyan Arab Jamahiriya,* 'Warrant of Arrest for Abdullah Al-Senussi (Public)', ICC 01/11 (27 June 2011) http://www.icc-cpi.int/iccdocs/doc/doc1099332.pdf (accessed 11 March 2013).

[113] *See* ICC, Pre-Trial Chamber I, *Situation in Libya, In the Case of The Prosecutor v. Saif Al-Islam Gaddafi and Abdullah Al-Senussi,* 'Application on behalf of the Government of Libya pursuant to Article 19 of the ICC Statute (*Public & Redacted, with 6 Public and 5 Confidential Annexes*)', ICC-01/11-01/11 (1 May 2012) http://www.icc-cpi.int/iccdocs/doc/doc1405819.pdf (accessed 11 March 2013).

[114] *See* ICC, Pre-Trial Chamber I, *Situation in the Libyan Arab Jamahiriya,* 'Warrant of Arrest for Saif Al-Islam Gaddafi (Public)', ICC-01/11 (27 June 2011) http://www.icc-cpi.int/iccdocs/doc/doc1099329.pdf (accessed 11 March 2013).

[115] ICC, Pre-Trial Chamber I, *Situation in Libya, In the Case of The Prosecutor v. Saif Al-Islam Gaddafi and Abdullah Al-Senussi,* 'Application on behalf of the Government of Libya pursuant to Article 19 of the ICC Statute (*Public & Redacted, with 6 Public and 5 Confidential Annexes*)', ICC-01/11-01/11 (1 May 2012) http://www.icc-cpi.int/iccdocs/doc/doc1405819.pdf (accessed 11 March 2013), para 1.

[116] *See* R. Jawad, 'Fair trial urged as spy boss Senussi deported to Libya', *BBC News* (5 September 2012) http://www.bbc.co.uk/news/world-africa-19496096 (accessed 12 March 2013).

[117] *See* M.-L. Gumuchian, 'Prisoner of Zintan: Gaddafi son in Libyan limbo', *Reuters* (24 February 2012) http://www.reuters.nl/article/2012/02/24/us-libya-saif-idUSTRE81N11J20120224 (accessed 12 March 2013).

[118] *See* 'ICC staff 'in jail' in Libya after Saif Gaddafi visit', *BBC News* (11 June 2012) http://www.bbc.co.uk/news/world-africa-18394191 (accessed 12 March 2013).

members to Saif Al-Islam, "authorised by the ICC's judges, had the purpose of preserving the rights of the defence in the case against him before the ICC."[119] On 2 July 2012, the four staff members were released.[120]

Another remarkable moment in the context of the ICC occurred on 3 April 2012, when the ICC's OTP issued its document 'Situation in Palestine'. In this document, the OTP assessed that it is not for the OTP, but "for the relevant bodies at the United Nations or the Assembly of States Parties to make the legal determination whether Palestine qualifies as a State for the purpose of acceding to the Rome Statute and thereby enabling the exercise of jurisdiction by the Court under article 12(1)".[121] (As mentioned in Sect. 8.1.6, on 29 November 2012, Palestine was granted non-member observer State status in the UN General Assembly.)

2012 was also characterized by the arrival of the new Prosecutor Fatou Bensouda, who took over from Luis Moreno-Ocampo on 15 June 2012.[122] Moreover, in the same year, repeated calls were made on the UN Security Council to refer the situation in Syria to the ICC.[123] Finally, and as already mentioned in Sect. 8.1.7, in July 2012, the Government of Mali referred "the situation in Mali since January 2012" to the ICC.[124]

8.2.2 Hybrid

8.2.2.1 EULEX Kosovo

The District Court of Priština, in a trial panel composed of one local and two EULEX (European Union Rule of Law Mission of Kosovo) judges, handed down its judgment on 2 May 2012 in the case against Naser Krasniqi, Nexhimi Krasniqi, Fatmir Limaj and Naser Shala. The men were charged with war crimes perpetrated against Serbian prisoners of war and (Kosovo) Albanian civilians in or near Klecka

---

[119] ICC Press Release, 'The four ICC staff members released in Libya' (2 July 2012) ICC-CPI-20120702-PR820 http://www.icc-cpi.int/en_menus/icc/press%20and%20media/press%20releases/news%20and%20highlights/Pages/pr820.aspx (accessed 19 March 2013).

[120] *See* ibid.

[121] ICC, The Office of the Prosecutor, 'Situation in Palestine' (3 April 2012) http://www.icc-cpi.int/NR/rdonlyres/9B651B80-EC43-4945-BF5A-FAFF5F334B92/284387/SituationinPalestine030412ENG.pdf (accessed 10 March 2013), para 6.

[122] *See* ICC Press Release, 'Ceremony for the solemn undertaking of the ICC Prosecutor, Fatou Bensouda' (15 June 2012) ICC-CPI-20120615-PR811 http://www.icc-cpi.int/en_menus/icc/press%20and%20media/press%20releases/Pages/pr811.aspx (accessed 10 March 2013).

[123] *See, e.g.*, 'UN human rights chief renews call on Security Council to refer Syria to ICC', *UN News Centre* (2 July 2012) http://www.un.org/apps/news/story.asp?NewsID=42377 (accessed 19 March 2013).

[124] *See* M. Coulibaly, 'Renvoi de la situation au Mali' (13 July 2012) http://www.icc-cpi.int/NR/rdonlyres/A245A47F-BFD1-45B6-891C-3BCB5B173F57/0/ReferralLetterMali130712.pdf (accessed 10 March 2013).

(Kosovo) in 1999. All men, among whom well-known Kosovo politician Fatmir Limaj, who had earlier been acquitted by the ICTY in 2005 (Trial Chamber) and 2007 (Appeals Chamber), were found not guilty.[125] The Prosecution's case relied heavily on the declarations of a former member of the KLA (Agim Zogaj, also known as 'Witness X'), who committed suicide on 28 September 2011 and who could not testify at trial. However, on 20 November, the Kosovo Supreme Court, in a panel consisting of two local judges and three EULEX judges (one EULEX judge presiding), ordered a re-trial, ruling that the evidence of Agim Zogaj was admissible.[126] As a result, four days later, EULEX arrested Limaj and the other suspects for a re-trial.[127]

On 11 May 2012, the District Court of Priština, in a trial panel composed of one local and two EULEX judges, found Zoran Kolic guilty of committing war crimes against prisoners in the Lipjan prison in May 1999. The judges sentenced him to 14 years' imprisonment.[128]

And one month later, on 13 June 2012, EULEX formally started an investigation into the war crimes committed in the village of Mala Krusa on 25 and 26 March 1999, "allegedly one of the largest mass killings that took place during the 1999 conflict in Kosovo".[129]

An acquittal was issued on 23 November 2012 by the District Court of Priština. The judges were of the opinion that Aleksandar Bulatovic, who was charged with a war crime, namely in 1999 to have violated the bodily integrity and health of a Kosovo Albanian civilian named Xhaladin Idrizi, was not guilty of the charges.[130]

8.2.2.2 Extraordinary Chambers in the Courts of Cambodia

In the context of the Extraordinary Chambers in the Courts of Cambodia (ECCC), two interesting moments in 2012 should be addressed.

---

[125] The decision is available at: http://www.eulex-kosovo.eu/docs/justice/judgments/criminal-proceedings/DCPrishtina/2013-01-21%20DC%20Pristina%206%20Accused/2013-01-21%20DC%20Pristina%204%20Accused/Klecka%20Judgment%204%20Accused_02%2005%2012_FINAL%20-REDACTED.pdf (accessed 27 May 2013).

[126] *See* 'Supreme Court orders retrial against Limaj for war crimes', EULEX Press Release (20 November 2012) http://www.eulex-kosovo.eu/en/pressreleases/0375.php (accessed 27 May 2013).

[127] *See* Jerry Votava, 'EU Kosovo authorities arrest former commander for war crimes' *Jurist* (25 November 2012) http://jurist.org/paperchase/2012/11/eu-kosovo-authorities-arrest-former-commander-for-war-crimes.php (accessed 27 May 2013).

[128] The decision is available at: http://www.eulex-kosovo.eu/docs/justice/judgments/criminal-proceedings/DCPrishtina/408-11/img-5111111-0001.pdf (accessed 27 May 2013).

[129] 'EULEX investigates Krusha e Vogel/Mala Krusa massacre', EULEX Press Release (13 June 2012) http://www.eulex-kosovo.eu/en/pressreleases/0299-1.php (accessed 27 May 2013).

[130] *See* 'Bulatovic acquitted for war crimes', EULEX Press Release (23 November 2012) http://www.eulex-kosovo.eu/en/pressreleases/0377.php (accessed 27 May 2013).

The first one occurred on 3 February 2012, when the Supreme Court Chamber of the ECCC sentenced its very first accused to life imprisonment, for crimes against humanity and grave breaches of the 1949 Geneva Conventions.[131] Guek Eav Kaing, alias Duch, was arrested and detained by the Cambodian Military Court on 10 May 1999 for various charges under Cambodian law.[132] On 10 August 2001, the 'Law on the Establishment of the Extraordinary Chambers in the Courts of Cambodia' entered into force,[133] but according to the co-investigating judges of the ECCC, it was not until 22 June 2007, the date the Internal Rules of the ECCC entered into force, that the ECCC became operational.[134] On 31 July 2007, two co-investigating judges of the ECCC ordered that Duch be placed in the provisional detention of the ECCC and on 8 August 2008, they issued a Closing Order indicting Duch.[135] According to the co-investigating judges, there was sufficient evidence that Duch, "through his acts or omissions in Phnom Penh and within the territory of Cambodia, between 17 April 1975 and 6 January 1979, as Deputy Secretary or Secretary of [Security Prison] S21, planned, instigated, ordered, committed, or aided and abetted, or is responsible by virtue of superior responsibility"[136] for crimes against humanity and grave breaches of the 1949 Geneva Conventions. On 5 December 2008, the Pre-Trial Chamber confirmed and partially amended the indictment against Duch.[137] The Trial Chamber issued its verdict on 26 July 2010, finding Duch guilty of crimes against humanity and grave breaches of the 1949 Geneva Conventions and sentencing him to 35 years'

[131] *See* ECCC, Supreme Court Chamber, 'Appeal Judgement', Case File 001/18-07-2007-ECCC/SC (3 February 2012) http://www.eccc.gov.kh/sites/default/files/documents/courtdoc/Case%20001AppealJudgementEn.pdf (accessed 4 May 2013).

[132] *See* ECCC, Trial Chamber, 'Decision on Request for Release (Public)', Case File 001/18-07-2007/ECCC/TC (15 June 2009) http://www.eccc.gov.kh/sites/default/files/documents/courtdoc/E39_5_EN.pdf (accessed 4 May 2013), para 2.

[133] *See* ibid.

[134] *See* ECCC, Office of the Co-Investigating Judges, 'Order of Provisional Detention', Criminal Case File 002/14-08-2006, Investigation No. 001/18-07-2007 (31 July 2007) http://www.eccc.gov.kh/sites/default/files/documents/courtdoc/Order_of_Provisional_Detention-DUCH-EN.pdf (accessed 4 May 2013), para 20.

[135] *See* ECCC, Office of the Co-Investigating Judges, 'Closing Order Indicting Kaing Guek Eav alias Duch (Public Redacted Version)', Criminal Case File 002/14-08-2006, Investigation No. 001/18-07-2007-ECCC-OCIJ (8 August 2008) http://www.eccc.gov.kh/sites/default/files/documents/courtdoc/Closing_order_indicting_Kaing_Guek_Eav_ENG_0.pdf (accessed 4 May 2013).

[136] Ibid., p. 44.

[137] *See* ECCC, Pre-Trial Chamber, 'Decision on Appeal against Closing Order Indicting KAING Guek Eav Alias "Duch" (Public)', Case File 001/18-07-2007-ECCC/OCIJ (PTC 02) (5 December 2008) http://www.eccc.gov.kh/sites/default/files/documents/courtdoc/D99_3_42_EN_0_1.pdf (accessed 4 May 2013). The judges found that the domestic crimes of torture and premeditated murder as defined by the 1956 Penal Code of Cambodia had to be added to the Closing Order.

imprisonment.[138] On the one hand, the Trial Chamber noted the seriousness of the crimes, but on the other, it concluded that there were "significant mitigating factors which mandate the imposition of a finite term of imprisonment rather than a life sentence",[139] such as Duch's "cooperation with the Chamber, admission of responsibility, expressions of remorse (although undermined by his request for acquittal during closing statements), the coercive environment in DK [Democratic Kampuchea] in which he operated, and his potential for rehabilitation."[140] The judges were also of the opinion that Duch had been illegally detained by the Cambodian Military Court between 10 May 1999 and 30 July 2007 and should as a consequence receive a reduction of five years.[141]

On 3 February 2012, the Supreme Court Chamber of the ECCC issued its decision. It also found Duch guilty of crimes against humanity and grave breaches of the 1949 Geneva Conventions (although it quashed the Trial Chamber's decision to subsume under the crime against humanity of persecution the other crimes against humanity for which it found Duch responsible—and thus also convicted Duch for the crimes against humanity of extermination (encompassing murder), enslavement, imprisonment, torture, and other inhumane acts),[142] but it sentenced Duch to life imprisonment. The judges held that "the Trial Chamber attached undue weight to mitigating circumstances and insufficient weight to the gravity of the crimes and aggravating circumstances in this case."[143] In this context, the Chamber noted that Duch held a central leadership role at the Security Center S-21,[144] which was "the factory of death".[145] Indeed, "[h]e mercilessly terminated the lives of at least 12,272 individuals, including women and children."[146] This, the judges opined, "along with the extended period of time over which the crimes were committed (more than three years), undoubtedly place this case among the gravest before international criminal tribunals."[147] Furthermore, a majority of the judges did not agree with the Trial Chamber's reduction of Duch's sentence with five years for his illegal detention.[148] Finally, it is important to mention that the Supreme Court Chamber concluded that, in addition to those Civil Parties already

[138] *See* ECCC, Trial Chamber, 'Judgement (Public)', Case File 001/18-07-2007-ECCC/TC (26 July 2010) http://www.eccc.gov.kh/sites/default/files/documents/courtdoc/20100726_Judgement_Case_001_ENG_PUBLIC.pdf (accessed 11 May 2013).

[139] Ibid., para 629.

[140] Ibid.

[141] *See* ibid., para 632.

[142] *See* ECCC, Supreme Court Chamber, 'Appeal Judgement', Case File 001/18-07-2007-ECCC/SC (3 February 2012) http://www.eccc.gov.kh/sites/default/files/documents/courtdoc/Case%20001AppealJudgementEn.pdf (accessed 4 May 2013), p. 320.

[143] Ibid., para 373.

[144] *See* ibid., para 377.

[145] Ibid., para 380.

[146] Ibid.

[147] Ibid., para 376.

[148] *See* ibid., para 399.

admitted by the Trial Chamber in 2010, an additional 10 Civil Party appellants had demonstrated that they had suffered harm as a direct consequences of the crimes for which Duch was convicted.[149]

The second event in 2012 at the ECCC worth mentioning here concerned Thirith Ieng, the Minister of Social Affairs of the Democratic Kampuchea regime.[150] On 14 November 2007, Thirith Ieng (and her husband Sary Ieng) was detained by order of the co-investigating judges and transferred to the ECCC.[151] On 14 January 2010, the co-investigating judges concluded the judicial investigations[152] and on 15 September 2010, Thirith, her husband Sary, Chea Nuon and Samphan Khieu were indicted. According to the co-investigating judges, Thirith Ieng, together with the others, participated in a JCE,[153] which resulted in/involved the commission of crimes against humanity, grave breaches of the 1949 Geneva Conventions and genocide.[154] In addition, she was also indicted for having planned,[155] instigated,[156] and aided and abetted[157] genocide, grave breaches of the 1949 Geneva Conventions and crimes against humanity. Moreover, she gave orders to her subordinates in the Ministry of Social Action (another name for the Ministry of Social Affairs), which contributed to the commission of crimes against humanity.[158] Alternatively, it was asserted that there was sufficient evidence that she was responsible in her capacity as a superior because of the effective control she exercised over her subordinates at the Ministry who committed these crimes against humanity.[159] Finally, all the accused, including Thirith Ieng, were committed to trial for charges of murder, torture and religious persecution, as defined under the 1956 Penal Code of Cambodia.[160]

However, on 17 November 2011, the Trial Chamber of the ECCC found Thirith Ieng unfit to stand trial and ordered her unconditional release.[161] This decision was set aside by the Supreme Court Chamber on 13 December 2011, directing the Trial Chamber to request additional treatment and to order that Thirith Ieng undergo a

---

[149] *See* ibid., p. 321.

[150] *See* ECCC, Office of the Co-Investigating Judges, 'Closing Order', Case File 002/19-09-2007-ECCC-OCIJ (15 September 2010) http://www.eccc.gov.kh/sites/default/files/documents/courtdoc/D427Eng.pdf (accessed 12 May 2013), para 63.

[151] *See* ibid., para 8.

[152] *See* ibid., para 13.

[153] *See* ibid., paras 1529 and 1538–1540.

[154] *See* ibid., para 1525.

[155] *See* ibid., para 1546.

[156] *See* ibid., para 1549.

[157] *See* ibid., para 1552.

[158] *See* ibid., para 1555.

[159] *See* ibid., paras 1561–1562.

[160] *See* ibid., para 1576.

[161] *See* ECCC, Trial Chamber, 'Decision on IENG Thirith's Fitness to Stand Trial', Case File 002/19-09-2007-ECCC-TC (17 November 2011) http://www.eccc.gov.kh/sites/default/files/documents/courtdoc/E138_EN.PDF (accessed 20 May 2013).

new examination to see whether she is fit to stand trial.[162] On 13 September 2012, the Trial Chamber concluded that she remains unfit to stand trial and ordered again her unconditional release.[163] The day after, the co-prosecutors appealed this decision because they were of the opinion that her release should not have been ordered unconditionally. On 16 September 2012, the President of the Supreme Court Chamber ruled as a provisional measure that Thirith Ieng be released conditionally, pending the decision of the Supreme Court Chamber on the merits of the appeal by the co-prosecutors.[164] Finally, on 14 December 2012, the Supreme Court Chamber of the ECCC set aside the Trial Chamber's decision of 13 September 2012, ordering a regime of judicial supervision pursuant to which Thirith Ieng is obliged, among others, to undergo six-monthly medical examinations and to make herself available for security checks by the judicial police once a month.[165]

8.2.2.3 Special Court for Sierra Leone

2012 was also an important year for the Special Court for Sierra Leone (SCSL), established to prosecute persons who bear the greatest responsibility for serious violations of international humanitarian law and Sierra Leonean law committed in the territory of Sierra Leone since 30 November 1996.

On 26 April 2012, the judges of Trial Chamber II delivered their long-awaited verdict in the case against former Liberian President Charles Taylor. On 7 March 2003, Taylor, at that time still head of state of Liberia, was indicted (under seal) on 17 counts of crimes against humanity, violations of Article 3 Common to the Geneva Conventions and of Additional Protocol II and other serious violations of international humanitarian law. On 4 June 2003, the indictment and arrest warrant (also issued on 7 March 2003) against Taylor were disclosed to the public at a press conference in Freetown by the then Prosecutor, David Crane, and on

---

[162] *See* ECCC, Supreme Court Chamber, 'Decision on Immediate Appeal against the Trial Chamber's Order to Release the Accused IENG Thirith', Case File 002/19-09-2007-ECCC-TC/SC(09) (13 December 2011) http://www.eccc.gov.kh/sites/default/files/documents/courtdoc/E138_1_7_EN-1.PDF (accessed 20 May 2013).

[163] *See* ECCC, Trial Chamber, 'Decision on Reassessment of Accused IENG Thirith's Fitness to Stand Trial Following Supreme Court Chamber Decision of 13 December 2011', Case File 002/19-09-2007-ECCC-TC (13 September 2012) http://www.eccc.gov.kh/sites/default/files/documents/courtdoc/E138_1_10_EN.pdf (accessed 20 May 2013).

[164] *See* ECCC, Supreme Court Chamber, 'Decision on Co-Prosecutors' Request for Stay of Release Order of IENG Thirith', Case File 002/19-09-2007-ECCC-TC/SC(16) (16 September 2012) http://www.eccc.gov.kh/sites/default/files/documents/courtdoc/E138_1_10_1_2_1_EN.pdf (accessed 12 May 2013).

[165] *See* ECCC, Supreme Court Chamber, 'Decision on Immediate Appeal against the Trial Chamber's Order to Unconditionally Release the Accused IENG Thirith', Case File 002/19-09-2007-ECCC-TC/SC(16) (14 December 2012) http://203.176.141.125/sites/default/files/documents/courtdoc/2013-01-04%2010:44/E138_1_10_1_5_7_EN.PDF (accessed 12 May 2013).

11 August 2003, Taylor resigned as President of Liberia. He then went into exile in Nigeria, where he was arrested on 29 March 2006. On 3 April 2006, Taylor appeared for the first time before the SCSL in Freetown, pleading not guilty to all the charges brought against him. For security reasons, Taylor's trial was transferred to The Hague.

The (second) amended indictment, the one used in the proceedings that led to the verdict on 26 April 2012, charged Taylor with 11 counts, namely five counts of crimes against humanity (murder, rape, sexual slavery, other inhumane acts and enslavement), five counts of violations of Article 3 Common to the Geneva Conventions and of Additional Protocol II (acts of terrorism, violence to life, health and physical or mental well-being of persons, in particular murder, outrages upon personal dignity, violence to life, health and physical or mental well-being of persons, in particular cruel treatment, and pillage) and finally one other serious violation of international humanitarian law, namely conscripting or enlisting children under the age of 15 years into armed forces or groups, or using them to participate actively in hostilities.[166] According to the indictment, Taylor, by his acts or omissions, is individually criminally responsible pursuant to Article 6, para 1 of the SCSL Statute for these crimes, which he planned, instigated, ordered, committed, or in whose planning, preparation or execution he otherwise aided and abetted, or which crimes amounted to or were involved within a common plan, design or purpose in which he participated, or were a reasonably foreseeable consequence of such common plan, design or purpose.[167] In addition, or alternatively, pursuant to Article 6, para 3 of the SCSL Statute, the indictment asserted that Taylor, "while holding positions of superior responsibility and exercising command and control over subordinate members of the RUF [Revolutionary United Front], AFRC [Armed Forces Revolutionary Council], AFRC/RUF Junta or alliance, and/or Liberian fighters, is individually criminally responsible"[168] for these crimes. Taylor, the indictment continued, "is responsible for the criminal acts of his subordinates in that he knew or had reason to know that the subordinate was about to commit such acts or had done so"[169] and Taylor "failed to take the necessary and reasonable measures to prevent such acts or to punish the perpetrators thereof."[170] All these crimes allegedly took place from 30 November 1996 to 18 January 2002, in several locations within six districts of Sierra Leone.

On 26 April 2012, the judges of Trial Chamber II unanimously found Taylor guilty of aiding and abetting the crimes as mentioned in counts one to 11 of the indictment pursuant to Article 6, para 1 of the SCSL Statute during the indictment

---

166 *See* SCSL, Office of the Prosecutor, *The Prosecutor Against Charles Taylor*, 'Prosecution's Second Amended Indictment (Public)', Case No. SCSL-03-01-PT (29 May 2007) http://www.sc-sl.org/LinkClick.aspx?fileticket=lrn0bAAMvYM%3d&tabid=107 (accessed 1 May 2013).

167 *See* ibid., para 33.

168 Ibid., para 34.

169 Ibid.

170 Ibid.

period.[171] The Trial Chamber also held that Taylor, together with former RUF leader Sam Bockarie, planned the commission of the crimes set forth in counts one to 11 pursuant to Article 6, para 1 of the SCSL Statute "in the attacks on Kono and Makeni in December 1998, and in the invasion of and retreat from Freetown, between December 1998 and February 1999".[172] However, it rejected the Prosecution's submission that Taylor participated in a JCE, which amounted to or involved the commission of a crime within the jurisdiction of the SCSL.[173] The Trial Chamber, having already found that Taylor was criminally responsible for aiding and abetting the charged crimes, did not find that he also instigated those crimes.[174] Finally, it concluded that Taylor could not be held responsible for ordering the commission of crimes.[175] As to the allegations on the basis of Article 6, para 3 of the SCSL Statute (superior responsibility), the judges opined that Taylor had substantial influence over the leadership of the RUF, and to a lesser extent that of the AFRC, but that substantial influence over the conduct of others falls short of effective control over subordinates (the material ability to prevent or punish the commission of the offence), which is needed to establish criminal liability under Article 6, para 3 of the SCSL Statute.[176] On 30 May 2012, the same Trial Chamber sentenced Taylor to 50 years' imprisonment.[177]

This case is special in that Taylor is the first former head of state to be judged by an international criminal tribunal since Karl Dönitz, who briefly led Nazi Germany following Adolf Hitler's suicide, was convicted by the International Military Tribunal of Nuremberg on 1 October 1946.[178]

On 1 October 2012, the Prosecution and the Defence filed their appeals against both the Judgment and the Sentencing Judgment.

---

[171] *See* SCSL, Trial Chamber II, *Prosecutor v. Charles Ghankay Taylor*, 'Judgement', Case No. SCSL-03-01-T (18 May 2012) http://www.sc-sl.org/LinkClick.aspx?fileticket=k%2b03KREEPCQ%3d&tabid=107 (accessed 29 April 2013), para 6994. Note that on 26 April 2012, the judges rendered their judgment in summary form, whereas the judgment was filed on 18 May 2012.

[172] Ibid.

[173] *See* ibid., para 6900.

[174] *See* ibid., para 6972.

[175] *See* ibid., para 6973.

[176] *See* ibid., paras 6978-6979 and 6986.

[177] *See* SCSL, Trial Chamber II, *Prosecutor v. Charles Ghankay Taylor*, 'Sentencing Judgement', Case No. SCSL-03-01-T (30 May 2012) http://www.sc-sl.org/LinkClick.aspx?fileticket=U6xCITNg4tY%3d&tabid=107 (accessed 2 May 2013).

[178] Note that former Yugoslav President Slobodan Milošević died before the ICTY could issue a judgment.

8.2.2.4 Special Tribunal for Lebanon

Another important development could be identified in 2012, at the Special Tribunal for Lebanon (STL). In its decision of 1 February 2012, the Trial Chamber decided to proceed to try four accused, namely Salim Jamil Ayyash, Mustafa Amine Badreddine, Hussein Hassan Oneissi and Assad Hassan Sabra, *in absentia*. In contrast to other modern[179] international criminal tribunals, trials *in absentia* can take place before the STL pursuant to Article 22 of its Statute, which stipulates, in part, that "[t]he Special Tribunal shall conduct trial proceedings in the absence of the accused, if he or she: (...) (c) Has absconded or otherwise cannot be found and all reasonable steps have been taken to secure his or her appearance before the Tribunal and to inform him or her of the charges confirmed by the Pre-Trial Judge." The Trial Chamber concluded that "[a]ll attempts by the Lebanese authorities to date to apprehend them have failed",[180] that "massive if not blanket coverage was given in the Lebanese media both to the indictment itself and to connecting Mr. Ayyash, Mr. Badreddine, Mr. Oneissi and Mr. Sabra with the indictment"[181] and that "it is inconceivable that they could be unaware that they have been indicted".[182] The Trial Chamber moreover found that the four men "have also each been notified according to Lebanese criminal procedural law of the indictment and of various Tribunal documents informing them of their rights to participate in the trial without being physically present in the court room."[183] As a result, the Trial Chamber concluded that the four men had absconded, that all reasonable steps had been taken to inform them of the charges and to secure their appearance before the STL and hence that they may be tried *in absentia*.[184]

Defense counsel for Badreddine and Oneissi subsequently asked the Trial Chamber to reconsider its decision, whereas counsel for Ayyash and Sabra asked the Trial Chamber to stay the decision or, failing that, to clarify several aspects of it. Counsel argued, among other things, that the men had not absconded, had not properly been notified of the charges and—more generally—that trials *in absentia* are a violation of human rights. However, the Trial Chamber concluded, on 11 July

[179] Note that Martin Bormann was tried, and sentenced to death, *in absentia* on 1 October 1946 by the International Military Tribunal of Nuremberg, whose Charter states in Article 12: "The Tribunal shall have the right to take proceedings against a person charged with crimes set out in Article 6 of this Charter in his absence, if he has not been found or if the Tribunal, for any reason, finds it necessary, in the interests of justice, to conduct the hearing in his absence."

[180] STL, Trial Chamber, *The Prosecutor v. Salim Jamil Ayyash, Mustafa Amine Badreddine, Hussein Hassan Oneissi & Assad Hassan Sabra*, 'Decision to Hold Trial *In Absentia*', Case No. STL-11-01/I/TC (1 February 2012) http://www.stl-tsl.org/index.php?option=com_k2&view=item&task=download&id=1037_f8b251460940c8fc6b7cc815f9ca294b (accessed 2 May 2013), para 105.

[181] Ibid., para 106.

[182] Ibid.

[183] Ibid.

[184] *See* ibid., paras 107 (Ayyash), 108 (Badreddine), 109 (Oneissi) and 110 (Sabra).

2012, that it "cannot find any new facts, or new arguments showing an error of legal reasoning necessitating a reconsideration of its Decision of 1 February 2012 to avoid an injustice to any of the four Accused."[185]

This decision was appealed, but on 1 November 2012, the Appeals Chamber of the STL unanimously dismissed the challenges, concluding, among other things, that "the Trial Chamber applied the highest evidentiary standards in establishing that the Accused were informed of the charges against them, of their right to participate in the proceedings and of the consequences if they did not appear. These standards are also reflected in the Trial Chamber's findings, which leave no doubt as to the Trial Chamber's satisfaction that the Accused were properly notified in the specific circumstances of this case."[186]

Another fundamental decision of the STL involved the same case. On 4 May (Ayyash), 9 May (Sabra) and 10 May 2012 (Oneissi and Bedreddine), counsel for the four accused filed motions challenging the legality and jurisdiction of the STL, reminiscent of the famous *Tadić* judgment before the ICTY. It was argued, among other things, that the STL was unlawfully established by (the) UN Security Council (Resolution 1757 of 30 May 2007), that its establishment violated the sovereignty of Lebanon and that its establishment and selective jurisdiction violated fundamental human rights and principles of fairness and equality.

On 27 July 2012, the Trial Chamber dismissed all the motions of the Defense counsel in their entirety, holding, among other things, that the STL was established by a body having the power to establish a criminal tribunal, that the Trial Chamber cannot judicially review the UN Security Council's actions in establishing the STL, that the Trial Chamber was unable to find that the STL's existence violated Lebanon's sovereignty and finally that the STL's Statute and Rules of Procedure and Evidence guarantee to the four men all fundamental human rights.[187]

---

[185] STL, Trial Chamber, *The Prosecutor v. Salim Jamil Ayyash, Mustafa Amine Badreddine, Hussein Hassan Oneissi & Assad Hassan Sabra*, 'Decision on Reconsideration of the Trial *In Absentia* Decision', Case No. STL-11-01/PT/TC (11 July 2012) http://www.stl-tsl.org/index.php?option=com_k2&view=item&task=download&id=1515_40169873b0e324d4117ab15433824676 (accessed 3 May 2013), para 12.

[186] STL, Appeals Chamber, *The Prosecutor v. Salim Jamil Ayyash, Mustafa Amine Badreddine, Hussein Hassan Oneissi and Assad Hassan Sabra*, 'Decision on Defence Appeals against Trial Chamber's Decision on Reconsideration of the Trial *In Absentia* Decision', Case No. STL-11-01/PT/AC/AR126.1 (1 November 2012) http://www.stl-tsl.org/index.php?option=com_k2&view=item&task=download&id=1923_7b2280191963a8fdb82312ac3964ea15 (accessed 3 May 2013), para 46.

[187] *See* STL, Trial Chamber, *The Prosecutor v. Salim Jamil Ayyash, Mustafa Amine Badreddine, Hussein Hassan Oneissi & Assad Hassan Sabra*, 'Decision on the Defence Challenges to the Jurisdiction and Legality of the Tribunal', Case No. STL-11-01/PT/TC (27 July 2012) http://www.stl-tsl.org/index.php?option=com_k2&view=item&task=download&id=1591_90fc237485b3e4c79636bd0da425e46e (accessed 3 May 2013), para 2.

Counsel for Ayyash, Badreddine and Oneissi appealed the decision, basically arguing that the STL was established illegally and that it had no authority to try the accused. On 24 October 2012, the Appeals Chamber issued its decision.[188] It unanimously determined that the appeals had to be dismissed.[189] It affirmed the Trial Chamber's decision that the STL was legally established by UN Security Council Resolution 1757 of 30 May 2007 and four of the five judges agreed with the Trial Chamber that it could not judicially review the UN Security Council's actions.[190] The majority noted that "once the Security Council has established the existence of a threat to international peace and security under Article 39 of the United Nations Charter, it retains the sole and exclusive prerogative to determine which measures under Articles 41 and 42 of the Charter are required to maintain or to restore international peace and security."[191] Hence, the provisions of the UN Charter "provide the Security Council with broad discretion as to which measures appropriately "give effect to its decisions." [original footnote omitted]"[192] And this may include the establishment of an international criminal tribunal (cf. the ICTY and ICTR). The four judges stressed that "[w]hat is important is that this decision is essentially political in nature, and as such not amenable to judicial review."[193] The fifth judge, STL President Baragwanath, disagreed on this last point and opined that "Security Council Resolution 1757 is not beyond review by the Tribunal".[194] He argued that "[t]o assert that there is no judicial review of a decision-maker's decisions is to give it plenary authority."[195] Nevertheless, he admitted that "the difficulty and complexity of the Council's task, the extent of its resources and experience, and the scope of what is a matter of pure judgment must narrowly limit the scope of such review. (...) [A] judicial tribunal must withhold interference unless breach of the bounds of the Council's authority is clearly shown."[196] And this was not the case, as he concluded that Defense counsel failed to establish that the UN Security Council had acted beyond its authority in passing Resolution 1757.[197]

---

188 *See* STL, Appeals Chamber, *The Prosecutor v. Salim Jamil Ayyash, Mustafa Amine Badreddine, Hussein Hassan Oneissi and Assad Hassan Sabra*, 'Decision on the Defence Appeals against the Trial Chamber's "Decision on the Defence Challenges to the Jurisdiction and Legality of the Tribunal"', Case No. STL-11-01/PT/AC/AR90.1 (24 October 2012) http://www.stl-tsl.org/index.php?option=com_k2&view=item&task=download&id=1896_c560779c8576c735c89c37b12f3e3704 (accessed 3 May 2013).

189 *See* ibid., para 2.

190 *See* ibid.

191 Ibid., para 52.

192 Ibid.

193 Ibid.

194 Ibid., 'Separate and Partially Dissenting Opinion of Judge Baragwanath', para 82.

195 Ibid., para 71.

196 Ibid., para 82.

197 *See* ibid., para 91.

8.2.3 *Domestic*

8.2.3.1 Bangladesh

In Dhaka, Bangladesh, the International Crimes Tribunal (ICT) continued its work investigating and prosecuting suspects of international crimes committed during the 1971 Bangladesh Liberation War. The oft-criticized[198] ICT is trying persons who allegedly collaborated with Pakistani forces who tried to prevent Bangladesh (then East Pakistan) from becoming an independent state. Many suspects are linked to the opposition party Jamaat-e-Islami (JI), which opposed the independence of Bangladesh from Pakistan. After the establishment of Tribunal 1 on 25 March 2010, a second tribunal was established on 22 March 2012.

Various other developments occurred at the ICT in 2012: on 3 April 2012, an arrest warrant was issued by the ICT against Moulana Abul Kalam Azad, a former leader of JI. Azad absconded however. Therefore, the ICT decided, on 7 October 2012, to hold his trial *in absentia* and on 4 November 2012, Justice Fazle Kabir read out the indictment against Azad, charging him with genocide and crimes against humanity (murder, rape, abduction, confinement and torture).[199]

On 4 April 2012, Bangladesh Nationalist Party (BNP) leader Salahuddin Qader Chowdhury was indicted for 23 counts of genocide and crimes against humanity.[200]

Another indictment was confirmed on 13 May 2012 against former JI leader Golam Azam for, among other things, crimes against humanity[201] and on 5 June 2012, Azam's trial started.

Two other indictments were confirmed on 28 May 2012, one against JI leader Motiur Rahman Nizami, charged with, among other things, genocide and crimes against humanity,[202] and one against Abdul Quader Molla, a deputy of Nizami, charged with crimes against humanity.[203] Their trials commenced on 16 July 2012 and 20 June 2012, respectively.

---

[198] *See, e.g.*, Katherine Iliopoulos, 'Bangladesh: A Free and Fair War Crimes Tribunal?', *Crimes of War* (26 August 2010) http://www.crimesofwar.org/commentary/bangladesh-a-free-and-fair-war-crimes-tribunal (accessed 25 May 2013).

[199] The charge framing order is available at: http://bangladeshwarcrimes.blogspot.nl/2013/01/4-nov-2012-azad-charge-framing.html (accessed 25 May 2013).

[200] The charge framing order is available at: http://bangladeshtrialobserver.files.wordpress.com/2012/12/charge-framing-order.pdf (accessed 25 May 2013).

[201] The charge framing order is available at: http://bangladeshtrialobserver.files.wordpress.com/2012/12/ga-charge-framing-order-no-25-part-1.pdf and http://bangladeshtrialobserver.files.wordpress.com/2012/12/ga-cuarge-framing-order-no-25-part-2.pdf (accessed 25 May 2013).

[202] The charge framing order is available at: http://bangladeshtrialobserver.files.wordpress.com/2012/12/nizami-charge-framing-order.pdf (accessed 25 May 2013).

[203] The charge framing order is available at: http://bangladeshtrialobserver.files.wordpress.com/2012/12/qader-mollah-charge-framing-order.pdf (accessed 25 May 2013).

Also the assistant secretary-general of JI, Muhammad Kamaruzzaman, was indicted on 4 June 2012 with seven counts of crimes against humanity[204] and his trial commenced on 2 July 2012.

The indictment of BNP leader Md. Abdul Alim, charging him with genocide and crimes against humanity, was read out on 11 June 2012[205] and his trial started on 9 July 2012.

Finally, on 21 June 2012, the ICT indicted Ali Ahsan Muhammad Mujahid, JI's secretary general, for charges of crimes against humanity and genocide.[206]

8.2.3.2 Bosnia and Herzegovina

The War Crimes Section of the Court of Bosnia and Herzegovina was very active in 2012, issuing many decisions. However, only a small selection of developments can be highlighted here.

The first interesting event occurred on 21 January 2012, when Radovan Stanković was arrested. Stanković had already been found guilty of crimes against humanity and was sentenced on 28 March 2007 to 20 years' imprisonment by the Appellate Panel of Section I for War Crimes of the Court of Bosnia and Herzegovina, but he escaped in May 2007 from a prison in Foča. Stanković was also the first ICTY indictee whose case was transferred from the ICTY to a national court (in September 2005) pursuant to Rule 11 *bis* of the ICTY Rules of Procedure and Evidence and as part of the ICTY's completion strategy.[207]

Four days later, on 25 January 2012, the Appellate Panel of Section I for War Crimes found Radomir Vuković guilty of aiding in genocide and sentenced him to 31 years' imprisonment. According to the judges, Vuković participated in the execution of more than 1,000 Bosniak males after the fall of Srebrenica in July 1995. The appeal of his co-accused, Zoran Tomić, was granted however. The Panel acquitted him for lack of evidence.[208]

On 19 April 2012, the trial against eight Bosnian Muslims, who allegedly abused and tortured Serbian civilians in detention camps in the Sarajevo suburb of Hadžići during the siege of Sarajevo, commenced before Section I for War

---

204 The charge framing order is available at: http://bangladeshtrialobserver.files.wordpress.com/2012/12/kamaruzzaman-charge-framing-order-04-06-2012.pdf (accessed 25 May 2013).

205 The charge framing order is available at: http://bangladeshtrialobserver.files.wordpress.com/2012/12/alim-charge-framing-order-11-06-12.pdf (accessed 25 May 2013).

206 The charge framing order is available at: http://bangladeshtrialobserver.files.wordpress.com/2012/12/mujahid-charge-framing-order1.pdf (accessed 26 May 2013).

207 More information on the case is available at: http://www.sudbih.gov.ba/index.php?opcija=predmeti&id=20&jezik=e (accessed 26 May 2013).

208 More information on the case is available at: http://www.sudbih.gov.ba/index.php?opcija=predmeti&id=157&jezik=e (accessed 26 May 2013).

Crimes.[209] The case, Mustafa Đelilović et al. is special in that it is one of the few brought *against* Bosnian Muslims.[210] (However, on 22 June 2012, the Court also sentenced two Bosnian Muslim brothers, Šaban and Elvir Đelilbašić, each to six years' imprisonment on the basis of a guilty plea agreement for murdering two Serbian civilians in Turbe (war crimes against civilians) after the two brothers had found out that another brother had been killed at the front-line in the combat against the Army of the Republika Srpska.)[211]

In April 2012, the Court, upon consideration and acceptance of a plea agreement, found Rasema Handanović guilty of war crimes against civilians and against prisoners of war and imposed a sentence of five years and six months.[212] Handanović, who participated in the execution-style killing of several prisoners of war and civilians in the context of an attack on the village of Trusina, was the first woman convicted of war crimes by the Court of Bosnia and Herzegovina.[213]

On 25 May 2012, the Trial Panel of Section I for War Crimes found Duško Jević and Mendeljev Đurić guilty of genocide and sentenced them to 35 and 30 years' imprisonment, respectively. At the same time, the two co-accused, Neđo Ikonić and Goran Marković, were acquitted of the genocide charge. According to the judges, Jević and Đurić took part in the forcible removal and killing of Muslims during the 1995 Srebrenica massacre.[214]

Another conviction related to the Srebrenica killings was handed down on 15 June 2012, when the Trial Panel of Section I for War Crimes found Franc Kos, Stanko Kojić, Vlastimir Golijan and Zoran Goronja guilty of crimes against humanity (persecution). The four former Bosnian Serb soldiers were sentenced to imprisonment of 40, 43, 19 and 40 years, respectively. The judges stated that they, together with others, summarily executed around 800 captured Bosniak men from Srebrenica, among other things.[215]

On 28 June 2012, the Trial Panel of Section I for War Crimes found Saša Zečević, Radoslav Knežević and Marinko Ljepoja guilty of crimes against humanity and sentenced them each to 23 years' imprisonment. The co-accused

---

[209] More information on the case is available at: http://www.sudbih.gov.ba/index.php?opcija=predmeti&id=683&jezik=e (accessed 26 May 2013).

[210] *See* Matthew Pomy, 'Bosnian Muslims on trial for war crimes against Serbs', *Jurist* (20 April 2012) http://jurist.org/paperchase/2012/04/bosnian-muslims-on-trial-for-war-crimes-against-serbs.php (accessed 26 May 2013).

[211] More information on the case is available at: http://www.sudbih.gov.ba/index.php?opcija=predmeti&id=668&jezik=e (accessed 26 May 2013).

[212] More information on the case is available at: http://www.sudbih.gov.ba/index.php?opcija=predmeti&id=699&jezik=e (accessed 26 May 2013).

[213] *See* Maja Zuvela, 'Bosnian war crimes court jails first woman', *Reuters* (30 April 2012) http://www.reuters.com/article/2012/04/30/us-bosnia-warcrimes-idUSBRE83T0KK20120430 (accessed 26 May 2013).

[214] More information on the case is available at: http://www.sudbih.gov.ba/index.php?opcija=predmeti&id=266&jezik=e (accessed 26 May 2013).

[215] More information on the case is available at: http://www.sudbih.gov.ba/index.php?opcija=predmeti&id=316&jezik=e (accessed 26 May 2013).

Petar Čivčić and Branko Topola were acquitted of the crimes against humanity charges. According to the judges, the accused persecuted the Bosniak population of Prijedor municipality on ethnic and religious grounds, among other things through murders.[216]

However, acquittals were also issued. For instance, on 3 October 2012, thc Trial Panel of Section I for War Crimes acquitted Dragan Nešković and Zoran Ilić, who were charged with crimes against humanity (persecution), also in relation to the Srebrenica massacre.[217]

On 9 November 2012, the Trial Panel of Section I for War Crimes found Jasko Gazdić guilty of crimes against humanity for his role in the widespread and systematic attack against the Bosniak civilians of the Foča municipality. Among other things, he had raped female civilians and had enabled others to rape women. As a result of this, he was sentenced to 17 years' imprisonment.[218]

Finally, on 15 November 2012, the Trial Panel of Section I for War Crimes issued its verdict in the Eso Macić case, finding the accused guilty of war crimes against civilians and imposing a sentence of 15 years of imprisonment. It was held that Macić had acted contrary to international humanitarian law by participating in the inhumane treatment of the prisoners of the Čelebići camp. For instance, together with other guards, Macić beat up an elderly Serb civilian, and he also shot one Serb civilian in the chest and head, killing him on the spot.[219]

8.2.3.3 Brazil

On 13 March 2012, Brazilian prosecutors announced that they would bring charges against Colonel (ret.) Sebastião Curió Rodrigues de Moura for his alleged role in five enforced disappearances in 1974.[220] It was the first time that Brazil prosecuted human rights violations that occurred during the country's military dictatorship, from 1964 to 1985.[221] The five people who disappeared—Maria Célia Corrêa, Hélio Luiz Navarro de Magalhães, Daniel Ribeiro Callado, Antônio de Pádua

---

[216] More information on the case is available at: http://www.sudbih.gov.ba/index.php?opcija=predmeti&id=218&jezik=e (accessed 26 May 2013).

[217] More information on the case is available at: http://www.sudbih.gov.ba/?id=2587&jezik=e (accessed 26 May 2013).

[218] More information on the case is available at: http://www.sudbih.gov.ba/index.php?opcija=predmeti&id=496&jezik=e (accessed 26 May 2013).

[219] More information on the case is available at: http://www.sudbih.gov.ba/index.php?opcija=predmeti&id=333&jezik=e (accessed 26 May 2013).

[220] The original accusation (in Portuguese) is available at: http://www.prpa.mpf.gov.br/news/2012/Denuncia_Guerrilha_Araguaia_versao_divulgacao.PDF%20-%20Adobe%20Acrob.pdf (accessed 28 May 2013).

[221] *See* Rupert Colville, 'Briefing note on Brazil', Office of the UN High Commissioner for Human Rights http://www.ohchr.org/EN/NewsEvents/Pages/DisplayNews.aspx?NewsID=11970&LangID=E (accessed 28 May 2013).

Costa and Telma Regina Cordeiro Corrêa—were part of an insurgency group opposing the military regime ('Guerrilha do Araguaia') and were detained during military operation Marajoara. Although on 28 August 1979, Brazil adopted Law No. 6683/79 granting amnesty to the military (among others), the Inter-American Court of Human Rights, in the *Gomes-Lund et al. ("Guerrilha do Araguaia") v. Brazil* case,[222] ruled that "[t]he provisions of the Brazilian Amnesty Law that prevent the investigation and punishment of serious human rights violations are not compatible with the American Convention, lack legal effect, and cannot continue as obstacles for the investigation of the facts of the present case, neither for the identification and punishment of those responsible, nor can they have equal or similar impact regarding other serious violations of human rights enshrined in the American Convention which occurred in Brazil."[223] In this case, the Court also made reference to, among others, the five individuals mentioned above.[224] The prosecutors also argued that the disappearances were not covered by the amnesty law as the crimes are essentially still ongoing in view of the fact that the victims' bodies have not been found yet.[225] In connection to this case, HRW stated that "[u]nder international humanitarian law, enforced disappearances are absolutely prohibited and can never be justified".[226]

Reportedly, the accusation was rejected on 16 March 2012 by judge João Cesar Otoni de Matos, who criticized the prosecutors for circumventing the already-discussed amnesty law,[227] but in appeal (on 29 August 2012), judge Nair Pimenta de Castro accepted the accusation.[228] Sebastião Curió Rodrigues de Moura subsequently filed a writ of habeas corpus and on 3 December 2012, judge Olindo

---

[222] *See* Inter-American Court of Human Rights, *Gomes-Lund et al. ("Guerrilha do Araguaia") v. Brazil*, 'Judgment (Preliminary Objections, Merits, Reparations, and Costs)' (24 November 2010) http://corteidh.or.cr/docs/casos/articulos/seriec_219_ing.pdf (accessed 28 May 2013).

[223] Ibid., para 325.

[224] *See* especially ibid., paras 125 and 251.

[225] *See* Rupert Colville, 'Briefing note on Brazil', Office of the UN High Commissioner for Human Rights http://www.ohchr.org/EN/NewsEvents/Pages/DisplayNews.aspx?NewsID=11970&LangID=E (accessed 28 May 2013).

[226] Human Rights Watch, 'Brazil: Human Rights Prosecution a Landmark Step' (13 March 2012) http://www.hrw.org/news/2012/03/13/brazil-human-rights-prosecution-landmark-step (accessed 28 May 2013). *See also* Henckaerts and Doswald-Beck 2009, p. 343: "[A]ny enforced disappearance is a violation of international humanitarian law and human rights law."

[227] *See* D. Zampier, 'Juiz federal nega denúncia contra major Curió e critica Ministério Público por tentar driblar Lei de Anistia', *Agência Brasil—EBC* (17 March 2012) http://amazonia.org.br/2012/03/juiz-federal-nega-den%c3%bancia-contra-major-curi%c3%b3-e-critica-minist%c3%a9-rio-p%c3%bablico-por-tentar-driblar-lei-de-anistia (accessed 28 May 2013).

[228] *See* D. Jinkings, 'Justiça processa coronel Sebastião Curió por crimes na Guerrilha do Araguaia', *Agência Brasil – EBC* (31 August 2012) http://amazonia.org.br/2012/08/em-uma-decis%c3%a3o-in%c3%a9dita-a-justi%c3%a7a-federal-em-marab%c3%a1-no-par%c3%a1-decidiu-processar-o-coronel-da-reserva-do-ex%c3%a9rcito-sebasti%c3%a3o-curi%c3%b3-rodrigues-de-moura-e-o-major-da (accessed 28 May 2013).

Herculano de Menezes suspended the case.[229] Finally, on 17 December 2012, the prosecutors issued an opinion recommending the court to deny the writ.[230]

8.2.3.4 Denmark

On 26 April 2012, the Danish Supreme Court issued an interesting order in the case against T., a school inspector and teacher who allegedly acted as the head of a death squad during the Rwandan genocide. T. fled to Denmark, where he was arrested in December 2010. The Prosecution's primary charge concerned genocide. T. argued that Danish law does not allow for the prosecution of a person for genocide committed in another country by foreign nationals in 1994 and both the Court of Roskilde (on 31 May 2011) and the 6th Division of the Eastern High Court (on 26 October 2011) agreed, holding that Denmark lacked jurisdiction to try T. for genocide. However, on 26 April 2012, the Danish Supreme Court held that the 1955 Danish Genocide Act has universal scope.[231] It noted that "[t]he legislative history of the Genocide Act, including the comments on the obligation to prosecute genocide under Article VI of the [Genocide] Convention, does not provide any basis for finding that the intention of the Act was to limit the scope of the criminality of genocide to the territory of Denmark."[232] As a consequence, the primary charge of genocide was upheld.

8.2.3.5 Guatemala

2012 was an important year for Guatemala, as the immunity of General Efraín Ríos Montt, the country's former head of state (between March 1982 and August 1983), was lifted when his term in Congress ended on 14 January 2012. Twelve days later, Ríos Montt was formally accused by judge Flores Polanco of genocide and crimes against humanity, joining a case with three other retired generals, namely Jose Mauricio Rodríguez Sánchez, Héctor Mario López Fuentes and Oscar Humberto Mejía Victores. (The charges of the latter were suspended because of

---

[229] *See* 'Suspensa ação contra Curió', *Correio Braziliense* (4 December 2012) http://amazonia.org.br/2012/12/suspensa-a%c3%a7%c3%a3o-contra-curi%c3%b3 (accessed 28 May 2013).

[230] The original opinion (in Portuguese) is available at: http://www.prpa.mpf.gov.br/news/2012/arquivos/HC%20692%20PA%20-%20trancamento%20acao%20penal%20-%20crimes%20contra%20a%20liberda.pdf (accessed 28 May 2013).

[231] Information taken from the case overview of the T.M.C. Asser Instituut's DomCLIC database http://www.asser.nl/default.aspx?site_id=36&level1=15248&level2=&level3=&textid=40366 (accessed 29 May 2013).

[232] The English translation of this order is available at: http://www.asser.nl/upload/documents/20120614T104012-120426%20Danish%20Supreme%20Court%20on%20%20application%20of%20the%20Danish%20Act%20on%20Genocide%20EN.pdf (accessed 29 May 2013).

his poor state of health.) On 1 March 2012, Ríos Montt's claim that he enjoyed amnesty was rejected, paving the way for a trial. On 17 March 2012, the Prosecution presented a formal indictment against Ríos Montt and Rodríguez Sánchez for the massacre of 1,771 Mayan Ixils, the forcible displacement of 29,000 people, sexual violence against at least eight women and torture of at least 14 people in the Quiche region. On 21 May 2012, new charges against Ríos Montt for genocide and crimes against humanity were accepted by judge Flores Polanco, now in connection with the deaths of 201 people in Dos Erres (Petén) in December 1982.[233]

8.2.3.6 Senegal

As already mentioned under Sect. 8.2.1.1, in the *Habré* case, the ECOWAS Court of Justice decided in November 2010 that the trial against Habré should take place in the framework of special *ad hoc* international proceedings. Four days after the ICJ issued its judgment, in which it considered that Senegal's duty to comply with its obligations could not be affected by the 2010 ECOWAS Court of Justice decision, Senegal and the AU reached a preliminary agreement on how to try Habré and on 22 August 2012, the agreement was signed. According to HRW, which has closely followed the developments in the *Habré* case, "[t]he new agreement calls for "Extraordinary African Chambers" to be created inside the existing Senegalese court structure in Dakar. The chambers' mandate will be to prosecute the person or persons most responsible for atrocity crimes committed in Chad between 1982 and 1990. The chambers will have sections to handle investigations, trials, and appeals, and will consist of Senegalese and other African judges."[234] On 19 December 2012, the Senegalese National Assembly adopted laws establishing the extraordinary chambers, hence opening the way for a trial against Habré in Senegal.

8.2.3.7 Serbia

On 16 March 2012, the High Court in Belgrade (War Crimes Department), in the retrial of the *Lički Oski* case, confirmed the sentences of 12 years' imprisonment against Čedo Budisavljević and Mirko Malinović and reduced the sentences of 12 years to ten years for Milan Bogunović and Bogdan Gruičić. The four were found guilty of a war crime against the civilian population, namely the killing of the Rakić family.[235]

---

[233] For more information on this case, see the case overview of the T.M.C. Asser Instituut's DomCLIC database, available at: http://www.asser.nl/default.aspx?site_id=36&level1=15248&level2=&level3=&textid=40058 (accessed 27 May 2013).

[234] *See* Human Rights Watch, 'Senegal: New Court to Try Chad Ex-Dictator in Senegal' (22 August 2012) http://www.hrw.org/news/2012/08/22/senegal-new-court-try-chad-ex-dictator-senegal (accessed 28 May 2013).

[235] For more information on this case, *see* Humanitarian Law Center 2013, pp. 42–45.

In the *Bytyqi Brothers* case, the High Court in Belgrade, on 9 May 2012, cleared the defendants Sreten Popović and Miloš Stojanović of charges related to a war crime in Petrovo Selo in 1999, by which three prisoners of war, the brothers Illy, Agron and Mehmet Bytyqi, were murdered.[236]

On 4 June 2012, the High Court in Belgrade issued its judgment in the *Bijeljina (Jović et al.)* case. It found Dragan Jović, Zoran Đurđević and Alen Ristić guilty of a war crime against the civilian population, which took place in Bijeljina in 1992 and sentenced them to 15, 13 and 12 years' imprisonment, respectively. According to the court, the men were involved in a campaign of terror when they raped, insulted and committed other acts of inhumane treatment upon civilians. Jović was also found guilty of killing a Bosnian civilian named Ramo Abdić.[237]

In the *Vukšić et al.* case, the High Court in Belgrade, on 19 June 2012, found Zoran Vukšić, Slobodan Strigić, Branko Hrnjak and Velimir Bertić guilty of a war crime against the civilian population committed in Beli Manastir (Croatia) in 1991. They were sentenced to 20, 10, five and one year and a half years' imprisonment, respectively.[238]

One week later, on 26 June 2012, the High Court issued its verdict in a case involving 14 defendants, according to the Office of the War Crimes Prosecutor "one of the most complex and complicated war crimes cases handled by this Office and by Serbia's judicial authorities in general."[239] The Court found the defendants, members of the Yugoslav Army and paramilitaries, guilty of war crimes committed against dozens of Croat civilians in Lovas (Croatia) in 1991 and sentenced them to a total of 128 years in prison, with the primary accused, Ljuban Devetak, receiving a sentence of 20 years. It was established, among other things, that civilians were forced to walk through mine fields in order to demine them.[240]

In another case involving several defendants (the *Gnjilane Group* case), the High Court convicted 11 Albanians, former members of the KLA, of war crimes in Kosovo in 1999, but acquitted six. In this retrial, the convicted men were sentenced to between five (Shefqet Musliu) and 15 (Samet Hajdari) years' imprisonment for torturing, beating and raping two Kosovo Serb women.[241]

Finally, on 19 November 2012, the High Court sentenced Marko Kashnjeti to two years' imprisonment for a war crime (unlawfully detaining and beating civilians) in Prizren, Kosovo.[242]

---

[236] For more information on this case, *see* ibid., pp, 50–52.

[237] For more information on this case, *see* ibid., pp. 38–42.

[238] For more information on this case, *see* ibid., pp. 67–70.

[239] Republic of Serbia, Office of the War Crimes Prosecutor, Public Relations Service, 'For A War Crime Against Croat Civilians in Lovas, Defendants get 128 Years in Prison', Press Release (26 June 2012) http://www.tuzilastvorz.org.rs/html_trz/VESTI_SAOPSTENJA_2012/VS_2012_06_26_ENG.pdf (accessed 26 May 2013).

[240] For more information on this case, *see* Humanitarian Law Center 2013, pp. 53–61.

[241] For more information on this case, *see* ibid., pp. 61–67.

[242] For more information on this case, *see* ibid., pp. 45–50.

In 2012, the Belgrade Court of Appeals (War Crimes Department) issued four judgments on appeals against decisions of the High Court in Belgrade. On 5 March 2012, it confirmed the judgment of the High Court in the *Rastovac* case from 23 September 2011 against Veljko Marić,[243] on 4 October 2012, it affirmed the judgment of the High Court in the *Zvornik III/IV* case from 16 December 2011, but modified the sentence of Goran Savić (from 18 months to three years) and Darko Janković (from 15 to 20 years),[244] on 26 October 2012, it reversed in part a second-instance judgment in the *Medak* case of the same Court of Appeal handed down on 11 January 2012 and acquitted Perica Đaković[245] and on 30 November 2012, it acquitted another person, Duško Kesar, of charges of a war crime against the civilian population in the *Prijedor* case.[246]

Also one Serbian court of general jurisdiction handed down a verdict in 2012 in a war crimes case, the High Court in Niš. On 3 August 2012, its judges found Zlatan Mančić, Rade Radojević, Danilo Tešić and Mišel Seregi guilty of a war crime against the civilian population and sentenced them to 14, nine, seven and five years' imprisonment, respectively.[247]

8.2.3.8 Sri Lanka

On 16 December 2011, the Government of Sri Lanka released the final report of the Commission of Inquiry on Lessons Learnt and Reconciliation (LLRC), a commission of inquiry established after the yearlong civil war in the country.[248] However, the report was quickly criticized for failing to adequately address alleged violations of international humanitarian law and international human rights law committed by both the government forces and the opposing Liberation Tigers of Tamil Eelam (LTTE) group in the final months of their armed conflict.[249] On 2 January 2012, it was reported that a five-member Court of Inquiry was appointed by the Sri Lankan Army Commander Jagath Jayasuriya to further delve into the observations of the LLRC report, but in its annual report over 2012, HRW noted that "[t]here has been no information regarding actions of the special army courts of inquiry, supposedly established in 2012 to look into allegations of war crimes."[250]

---

[243] For more information on this case, *see* ibid., pp. 72–73.

[244] For more information on this case, *see* ibid., pp 76–77.

[245] For more information on this case, *see* ibid., pp. 77–82.

[246] For more information on this case, *see* ibid., pp. 74–75.

[247] For more information on this case, *see* ibid., pp. 70–72.

[248] The report, dated 15 November 2011, is available at: http://www.slembassyusa.org/downloads/LLRC-REPORT.pdf (accessed 29 May 2013).

[249] *See, e.g.*, Amnesty International, 'Sri Lanka Report Falls Short', Press Release (16 December 2011) http://www.amnesty.org/en/for-media/press-releases/sri-lanka-report-falls-short-2011-12-16 (accessed 29 May 2013).

[250] Human Rights Watch 2013, p. 369.

8.2.3.9 The Netherlands

On 14 November 2012, the Court of Appeal in The Hague annulled the District Court in The Hague's earlier decision on the sum to be paid by Frans van Anraat to the State of the Netherlands for illegally obtained profits. Van Anraat was a Dutch businessman who was an important supplier of chemicals to the regime of Saddam Hussein in the 1980 s. On 9 May 2007, the judges of the Court of Appeal concluded: "During a number of years the defendant supplied raw material to the Iraqi regime for the production of chemical weapons. From 1985 until early 1988, in a total of twenty shipments he supplied at least more than 1,100 tons of Thiodiglycol (TDG) on the basis of three Letters of Credit. That substance was used for the production of mustard gas that was deployed during the war in Iran as well as in Iraq. By doing so during a number of years, the defendant has consciously made a substantial contribution to the continuing violation of the laws and customs of war committed by the Iraqi regime."[251] On 16 December 2010, the District Court in The Hague ruled that Van Anraat had to pay a sum of €3,493 for illegally obtained profits,[252] but on 14 November 2012, the Court of Appeal in The Hague ruled that Van Anraat was to pay a sum of €545,370.[253]

Also, on 22 October 2012, the case against Yvonne Basebya started before the District Court in The Hague. Basebya was born in Rwanda and came to the Netherlands in 1998, where she obtained the Dutch nationality in 2004. On 21 June 2010, she was arrested by the Dutch authorities and charged with genocide, attempted genocide, murder, conspiracy to commit genocide, incitement to genocide and war crimes in her area of residence in Rwanda from 1990 to 1994.[254]

Finally, there was also a development in the case of the *Mothers of Srebrenica v. the Netherlands and the UN*. On 4 June 2007, ten women from Bosnia and Herzegovina and the 'Mothers of Srebrenica Association' started a civil procedure against the UN and the State of the Netherlands before the District Court in The Hague. As summarized by the Supreme Court of the Netherlands in its judgment

---

[251] Court of Appeal in The Hague, 'Judgment', LJN: BA4676, 2200050906—2, 9 May 2007 http://www.asser.nl/upload/documents/DomCLIC/Docs/NLP/Netherlands/vanAnraat_Appeal_Judgment_09-05-2007_EN.pdf (accessed 27 May 2013), para 16. On 30 June 2009, the Supreme Court of the Netherlands issued its judgment in this case, upholding the 2007 conviction, but reducing the sentence (of 17 years) by six months. For more information on this case and particular decision, see the case overview of the T.M.C. Asser Instituut's DomCLIC database, available at: http://www.asser.nl/default.aspx?site_id=36&level1=15248&level2=&level3=&textid=40025 (accessed 27 May 2013).

[252] An English translation of the decision is available at: http://www.asser.nl/upload/documents/DomCLIC/Docs/Court%20Documents/Van%20Anraat%20English.pdf (accessed 27 May 2013).

[253] The decision is available at: http://www.asser.nl/upload/documents/20121129T050644-Van%20Anraat%2014%20november%202012%20Court%20of%20Appeals%20Judgment.pdf (accessed 27 May 2013).

[254] For more information on this case, see the case overview of the T.M.C. Asser Instituut's DomCLIC database, available at: http://www.asser.nl/default.aspx?site_id=36&level1=15248&level2=&level3=&textid=40631 (accessed 27 May 2013).

of 13 April 2012: "They held the State (and Dutchbat, the Dutch unit under UN command) and the UN partly responsible for the fall in 1995 of the Srebrenica enclave in Eastern Bosnia, where Dutchbat was based and which had been designated a 'Safe Area' under the protection of the UN peacekeeping force UNPROFOR by Security Council resolutions, and for the consequences of its fall, in particular the genocide committed subsequently which cost the lives of at least 8,000 people, including relatives of [the ten women]. They sought, in brief, a declaratory judgment to the effect that the State and the UN acted wrongfully in failing to fulfil undertakings they had given before the fall of the enclave and other obligations, including treaty obligations, to which they were subject, in addition to (advances on) payments in compensation, to be determined by the court in follow-up proceedings."[255] On 10 July 2008, the District Court in The Hague ruled that it had no jurisdiction to hear the case brought against the UN, citing the immunity of the UN enshrined in Article 105 of the UN Charter. On 30 March 2010, the Court of Appeal in The Hague upheld the decision. The Mothers of Srebrenica subsequently went to the Supreme Court of the Netherlands. On 13 April 2012, the Court, referring among other things to the 3 February 2012 judgment of the ICJ in the case '*Jurisdictional Immunities of the State (Germany vs. Italy: Greece intervening)*' (see Sect. 8.2.1.1), rejected the appeal and decided that the UN's immunity is absolute.[256]

8.3 Arms Control and Disarmament

8.3.1 Conventional Weapons

8.3.1.1 Arms Trade Treaty Conference

At the end of 2009, the General Assembly decided to bring together representatives for a Conference on the Arms Trade Treaty (ATT) in 2012 "to elaborate a legally binding instrument on the highest possible common international standards for the transfer of conventional arms."[257] The Conference was preceded by four Preparatory Committee sessions.[258] The United Nations Conference on the ATT

---

[255] Supreme Court of the Netherlands, 'Judgment', 10/04437 EV/AS, 13 April 2012, available at: http://www.asser.nl/upload/documents/20120905T111510-Supreme%20Court%20Decision%20English%2013%20April%202012.pdf (accessed 28 May 2013), para 3.2.1.

[256] For more information on this case, see the case overview of the T.M.C. Asser Instituut's DomCLIC database, available at: http://www.asser.nl/default.aspx?site_id=36&level1=15248&level2=&level3=&textid=39956 (accessed 28 May 2013).

[257] United Nations Office for Disarmament Affairs, 'Frequently Asked Questions' http://www.un.org/disarmament/ATT/media/presskit/2013_FAQ.pdf (accessed 30 May 2013).

[258] For more information about the Preparatory Committee, *see* http://ww.un.org/disarmament/ATT (accessed 28 May 2013).

took place in New York City at the UN Headquarters from 2-27 July 2012. After four weeks of negotiations, the Conference ended without an agreement on a treaty text as reported in the *New York Times* because "major weapons exporting nations, including the United States, [Russia and China] said more time was needed to finalize an agreement."[259] Member States did in fact come near to finalizing a treaty text and hoped to come together again in the near future to work toward negotiating an agreement soon. The follow-up negotiations conference, aiming to build on work done at the 2012 conference and deemed the "Final United Nations Conference on the Arms Trade Treaty", will take place at the New York UN Headquarters from 18-28 March 2013.[260]

8.3.1.2 Landmines

In January, Finland[261] and in December, Poland[262] ratified the Mine Ban Treaty. With these two signatures, all European Union countries and all NATO countries, except for the US, are signatories of the instrument, bringing the total to 160 countries throughout the world that have ratified the ban.[263] At the end of the 12th Annual Mine Ban Treaty meeting on 7 December, the US said it would make a decision "soon" as to whether to ratify the treaty or not.[264] Of the 35 countries that have yet to ratify the treaty, HRW reported that over "the past couple of years, antipersonnel landmines have been used by Syria, Burma, Israel, and Libya…" and that "[i]n 2012, there have been serious allegations of antipersonnel mine use by the armed forces of Sudan and Yemen, both Mine Ban Treaty states parties, though neither government appears to have initiated an investigation into the allegations. A small number of rebel groups also continue to use antipersonnel mines."[265]

---

259 Rick Gladstone, 'UN Misses Its Deadline for Final Approval', *New York Times* (27 June 2012) http://www.nytimes.com/2012/07/28/world/proponents-of-arms-trade-treaty-urge-final-approval.html?_r=0 (accessed 30 May 2013).

260 For more information on the 2013 UN Conference on the Arms Trade Treaty, *see* United Nations Office for Disarmament Affairs, 'Frequently Asked Questions' http://www.un.org/disarmament/ATT/media/presskit/2013_FAQ.pdf (accessed 30 May 2013).

261 *See* Human Rights Watch, 'Finland Joins Landmine Ban Treaty' (11 January 2012) http://www.hrw.org/news/2012/01/11/finland-joins-landmine-ban-treaty (accessed 29 May 2013).

262 *See* International Campaign To Ban Landmines, 'Poland Ratifies the Mine Ban Treaty' (27 December 2012) http://www.icbl.org/index.php/icbl/Library/News/Universal/poland-ratification (accessed 30 May 2013).

263 *See* ibid.

264 *See* Human Rights Watch, 'Landmine Ban: Poland Final EU Member to Join' (7 December 2012) http://www.hrw.org/news/2012/12/07/landmine-ban-poland-final-eu-member-join (accessed 30 May 2013).

265 Ibid.

8.3.1.3 Small Arms and Light Weapons

From 27 August to 7 September 2012, the second UN conference to review the 2001 Programme of Action on trafficking in small arms and light weapons met and ultimately "adopted a consensus outcome document that highlighted the international community's renewed commitment to preventing, combating and eradicating the illicit trade."[266] This renewed commitment had implementation elements at the national, regional and international level and was an agreement to take place between 2012 and 2018 to: "address the close links between the illicit trade in small arms and light weapons and armed violence, conflict, terrorism, crime, including transnational organized crime, and trafficking in humans, drugs and certain natural resources, and resolve to strengthen national, regional and international efforts aimed at combating this trade."[267] Additionally, there was a commitment "to mobilizing the necessary political will and resources to implement the Programme of Action and the International Tracing Instrument. Taking into account national and regional circumstances, [countries] aim to achieve clear and tangible results over the next six years that will improve the security, safety and livelihoods of our people by undertaking the measures in the accompanying implementation plans."[268]

8.3.2 Nuclear Weapons

8.3.2.1 March 2012 Seoul Nuclear Summit

On 26 and 27 March 2012, the 2012 Nuclear Security Summit was held in Seoul, South Korea. It was the second conference after the 2010 Summit in Washington, D.C. Three main issues were discussed at the Summit: cooperative measures to combat the threat of nuclear terrorism, protection of nuclear materials and related facilities and prevention of illicit trafficking of nuclear materials. 58 world leaders from 53 states and four international organizations, including the UN, the International Atomic Energy Agency, the European Union and INTERPOL, participated in the Summit.[269] The next Nuclear Summit will be held in 2014 in The Hague, the Netherlands.[270]

---

[266] UN General Assembly 'Review Conference Adopts Text Renewing Commitment to Prevent, Combat, Eradicate Illicit Trade in Small Arms, Light Weapons', Press Release (7 September 2012) http://www.un.org/News/Press/docs/2012/dc3389.doc.htm (accessed 29 May 2013).

[267] UN Report 2012, para 17.

[268] Ibid., para 18.

[269] *See* US Department of State, 'Key Facts on the 2012 Seoul Nuclear Security Summit' (28 March 2010) http://www.state.gov/t/isn/rls/fs/187208.htm (accessed 30 May 2013).

[270] *See* Nuclear Security Summit, 2014, The Hague. Website found at: http://www.nss2014.com (accessed 30 May 2013).

8.3.2.2 Non-Proliferation and the International Atomic Energy Agency

Democratic People's Republic of Korea

On 13 April, the Democratic People's Republic of Korca (DPRK) launched a rocket to celebrate the 100th birthday of the country's founder, a launch many criticized as a disguised test of long-range missile technology banned by the UN.[271] Meeting on 16 April, in the wake of that satellite launch, the Security Council issued a statement strongly condemning the event and deploring the grave security concerns it posed in the region. According to the press release, "[i]t underscored that the satellite launch, as well as any launch using ballistic missile technology, 'even if characterized as a satellite launch or space vehicle', was a serious violation of resolutions 1718 (2006) and 1874 (2009)." Two months later, on 12 June, the Security Council extended the mandate of the expert panel charged with monitoring compliance with the sanctions imposed on DPRK.[272]

Additionally the International Atomic Energy Agency (IAEA)'s board found that "[t]he nuclear programme of the DPRK is a matter of serious concern and statements by the DPRK about uranium enrichment activities and the construction of an LWR [light water reactor] in the DPRK continue to be deeply troubling."[273] The IAEA is continuing to monitor the situation in verifying DPRK's nuclear program.

Iran

Four of the Security Council's meetings on nuclear non-proliferation in 2012 concerned Iran. On 21 March, the Chair of its committee monitoring sanctions imposed in 2006 over that country's nuclear programme briefed on alleged violations as members warned that Iran's stonewalling of the IAEA on the true nature of its nuclear activities had created an "unsustainable and dangerous status quo."[274] On 7 June, the Security Council extended the monitoring Committee's expert panel by unanimously adopting resolution 2049 (2012) and asking it to report regularly on compliance. On 12 June, the Committee presented the panel's report for 2012, noting that, while the sanctions had been effective, the "cost of

[271] 'North Korea Rocket Launch Fails', *BBC News* (13 April 2012) http://www.bbc.co.uk/news/world-asia-17698438 (accessed 30 May 2013).

[272] UN Security Council, 'New Crises Seize Security Council's Attention in 2012 As Continuing Change Around Arab World Sparks Second Year of Tumultuous Transitions' (14 January 2012) http://www.un.org/News/Press/docs/2013/sc10881.doc.htm (accessed 31 May 2013).

[273] International Atomic Energy Agency DPRK 2012, para 14.

[274] UN Security Council, 'Chair of Security Council Committee Monitoring Sanctions Against Iran, Imposed over Nuclear Programme in Resolution 1737(2006), Briefs on Alleged Violations', Press Release (21 March 2012) http://www.un.org/News/Press/docs/2012/sc10584.doc.htm (accessed 30 May 2013).

acquisition" had not yet forced Iran to reach a compromise solution. A final briefing by the Committee, on 13 December, highlighted ballistic missile tests by Iran as some Council members called for an investigation of reported Iranian arms flows to conflict areas in the region.[275]

In the IAEA's last Board of Governors meeting of 2012, grave concern was expressed. The conclusion of the Director General's report was, in part, that "[w]hile the Agency continues to verify the non-diversion of declared nuclear material at the nuclear facilities and LOFs [location outside facilities] declared by Iran under its Safeguards Agreement, as Iran is not providing the necessary cooperation, including by not implementing its Additional Protocol, the Agency is unable to provide credible assurance about the absence of undeclared nuclear material and activities in Iran, and therefore to conclude that all nuclear material in Iran is in peaceful activities"[276] and urged Iran to engage with the IAEA and comply with the safety obligations it has with respect to nuclear non-proliferation.[277]

8.3.2.3 Russia's Non-Renewal of CRT Program

On 10 October, Russia's government announced that it would not renew the Cooperative Threat Reduction (CTR) program (also known as the Nunn-Lugar program) when it expires in early 2013. The program, under which Russia and the US safeguard and dismantle nuclear and chemical weapons in former Soviet countries such as Belarus, Ukraine and Kazakhstan, has been running since 1992.[278]

8.3.2.4 The Conference on Disarmament and UN General Assembly Resolution 67/39

The Conference on Disarmament is a forum that the international community established, now with 65 member states, with the purpose of negotiating arms control and disarmament agreements, including the Biological Weapons Convention and the Chemical Weapons Convention.[279] It often reports its annual

---

275 *See* UN Security Council, 'Non-Proliferation Committee, Briefing Security Council, Highlights Ballistic Missile Tests by Iran, Possible Arms Transfers to States in Region', Press Release (13 December 2012) http://www.un.org/News/Press/docs/2012/sc10856.doc.htm (accessed 30 May 2013).

276 International Atomic Energy Agency Iran 2012, para 53.

277 *See* ibid., para 57.

278 *See* David Herszenhorn, 'Russia Won't Renew Pact with US on Weapons', *New York Times* (10 October 2012) http://www.nytimes.com/2012/10/11/world/europe/russia-wont-renew-pact-with-us-on-weapons.html?_r=1& (accessed 29 May 2013).

279 For more information about the Conference on Disarmament, *see* http://www.unog.ch/80256EE600585943/(httpPages)/6286395D9F8DABA380256EF70073A846?OpenDocument (accessed 29 May 2013).

findings to the UN General Assembly. In December 2012, the General Assembly adopted Resolution 67/39 based upon the Conference on Disarmament's annual report, in which it decided to convene a high-level meeting of the General Assembly on nuclear disarmament, to be held in September 2013, "to contribute to achieving the goal of nuclear disarmament."[280]

8.4 Miscellaneous

After a meeting of AU Government Experts (7–11 May 2012) and of AU Ministers of Justice/Attorneys General (14–15 May 2012) in Addis Ababa (Ethiopia), the latter group considered and adopted the Draft Protocol on Amendments to the Protocol on the Statute of the African Court of Justice and Human Rights.[281] The protocol provides, among other things, for the expansion of the jurisdiction of the African Court on Human and Peoples' Rights/the African Court of Justice and Human Rights[282] to also cover international crimes such as genocide, crimes against humanity and war crimes. The Draft Protocol was discussed during the AU Assembly, held in Addis Ababa on 15–16 July 2012. The Assembly "request[ed] the [AU] Commission in collaboration with the African Court on Human and Peoples' Rights to prepare a study on the financial and structural implications resulting from the expansion of the jurisdiction of the African Court on Human and Peoples' Rights and submit the study along with the Draft Protocol on Amendments to the Protocol to the Statute of the African Court of Justice and Human Rights for consideration by the policy organs at the next summit slated for January 2013".[283]

---

[280] UN General Assembly Resolution A/Res/67/39 (4 January 2013) http://www.un.org/ga/search/view_doc.asp?symbol=A/RES/67/39 (accessed 30 May 2013).

[281] The Draft Protocol is available at: http://africlaw.files.wordpress.com/2012/05/au-final-court-protocol-as-adopted-by-the-ministers-17-may.pdf (accessed 29 May 2013).

[282] Note that the Draft Protocol refers to the 'African Court of Justice and Human Rights', a new court, merging two existing institutions, namely the African Court on Human and Peoples' Rights and the Court of Justice of the AU. Nevertheless, the 'African Court of Justice and Human Rights' has not been established yet, as there are not yet fifteen ratifications of the 2008 'Protocol to the Statute of the African Court of Justice and Human Rights', the required number of ratifications before the Protocol can enter into force. M. Du Plessis explained in this context: "On paper Africa's principal judicial organ is the African Court of Justice and Human Rights. In practice, however, this task remains the responsibility of the African Court on Human and Peoples' Rights," (Du Plessis 2012, p. 3).

[283] Assembly/AU/Dec.427(XIX), 'Decision on the Protocol on Amendments to the Protocol on the Statute of the African Court of Justice and Human Rights', Doc. Assembly/AU/13(XIX)a http://www.au.int/en/sites/default/files/Assembly%20AU%20Dec%20416-449%20(XIX)%20_E_Final.pdf (accessed 29 May 2013).

References

Amnesty International (2013) Report 2013: The State of The World's Human Rights http://files.amnesty.org/air13/AmnestyInternational_AnnualReport2013_complete_en.pdf (accessed 28 May 2013).
Dorsey and Paulussen (2013) The Boundaries of the Battlefield: A Critical Look at the Legal Paradigms and Rules in Countering Terrorism. ICCT Research Paper http://papers.ssrn.com/sol3/papers.cfm?abstract_id=2251866 (accessed 3 May 2013).
Du Plessis (2012) Implications of the AU decision to give the African Court jurisdiction over international crimes. Institute for Security Studies, Paper No. 235 http://www.issafrica.org/uploads/Paper235-AfricaCourt.pdf (accessed on 29 May 2013).
Henckaerts and Doswald-Beck (2009) Customary International Humanitarian Law, Volume I: Rules. Cambridge University Press, Cambridge http://www.icrc.org/eng/assets/files/other/customary-international-humanitarian-law-i-icrc-eng.pdf (accessed 28 May 2013).
Humanitarian Law Center (2013) Report on war crimes trials in Serbia in 2012, Belgrade http://www.hlc-rdc.org/wp-content/uploads/2013/02/Report-on-war-crimes-trials-in-Serbia-in-2012-ENG-FF.pdf (accessed 26 May 2013).
Human Rights Watch (2013) World Report 2013 – Events of 2012 https://www.hrw.org/sites/default/files/wr2013_web.pdf (accessed 29 May 2013).
International Atomic Energy Agency DPRK (2012) Application of Safeguards in the Democratic People's Republic of Korea http://www.iaea.org/About/Policy/GC/GC56/GC56Documents/English/gc56-11_en.pdf (accessed 31 May 2013).
International Atomic Energy Agency Iran (2012) Implementation of the NPT Safeguards Agreement and Relevant Provisions of Security Council Resolutions in the Islamic Republic of Iran http://www.iaea.org/Publications/Documents/Board/2012/gov2012-55.pdf (accessed 30 May 2013).
International Human Rights and Conflict Resolution Clinic at Stanford Law School and Global Justice Clinic at NYU School of Law (2012) Living Under Drones: Death, Injury, and Trauma to Civilians From US Drone Practices in Pakistan. http://livingunderdrones.org/wp-content/uploads/2012/10/Stanford-NYU-LIVING-UNDER-DRONES.pdf (accessed 21 May 2013).
Office of the Prosecutor of the International Criminal Court (2012) Report on Preliminary Examination Activities 2012 http://www.icc-cpi.int/NR/rdonlyres/C433C462-7C4E–4358-8A72 8D99FD00E8CD/285209/OTP2012ReportonPreliminaryExaminations22Nov2012.pdf (accessed 26 March 2013).
Sivakumar (2012) Law of Non-International Armed Conflict. Oxford University Press, Oxford.
UN Report (2012) Report of the United Nations Conference to Review Progress Made in the Implementation of the Programme of Action to Prevent, Combat and Eradicate the Illicit Trade in Small Arms and Light Weapons in All Its Aspects http://www.poa-iss.org/RevCon2/Documents/RevCon-DOC/Outcome/PoA-RevCon2-Outcome-E.pdf (accessed 30 May 2013).
Van Schaack (2011) The Killing of Osama Bin Laden and Anwar Al-Aulaqi: Uncharted Legal Territory. Yearbook of International Humanitarian Law, Vol. 14, T.M.C. Asser Press, The Hague.
Walker (2012) Special Report: What is Boko Haram? United States Institute of Peace http://www.usip.org/files/resources/SR308.pdf (accessed 7 May 2013).

Table of Cases[1]

International

[1] The table of cases was compiled by Mrs C.C. Diepeveen, Middelburg, The Netherlands, cdiep@zeelandnet.nl.

T. D. Gill et al. (eds.), *Yearbook of International Humanitarian Law 2012*,
Yearbook of International Humanitarian Law 15, DOI: 10.1007/978-90-6704-924-5,

International Criminal Court

International Criminal Tribunal for the Former Yugoslavia

International Criminal Tribunal for Rwanda

Mechanism for International Crimial Tribunals, Arusha Branch

Nuremberg International Military Tribunal

Permanent Court of International Justice

National

Index[2]

[2] The Index was compiled by Mrs C.C. Diepeveen, Middelburg, The Netherlands, cdiep@zeelandnet.nl.b

T. D. Gill et al. (eds.), *Yearbook of International Humanitarian Law 2012*,
Yearbook of International Humanitarian Law 15, DOI: 10.1007/978-90-6704-924-5,

D

I

T

Printed by Printforce, the Netherlands